MAN'S PAST:
MAN'S FUTURE

Stephen Raushenbush

MAN'S PAST: MAN'S FUTURE

A HUMANISTIC HISTORY FOR TOMORROW

DELACORTE PRESS
NEW YORK, N.Y.

This book is dedicated to my children
Stephanie, Burns, Roger, and Carl
and to their exciting generation

ACKNOWLEDGMENTS

It is impossible to thank all of the two hundred or more students of history whose books have been pondered during ten years in preparation of this particular one. But I wish to express sincere appreciation to several friends who have given me valuable comments on individual chapters. These include Professor Walter R. Agard, Mr. John Fishburn, Professor Edward W. Fox, my brother Paul A. Raushenbush and the late Mrs. Emma Woytinsky. I owe a special debt of gratitude to Mr. Ludwell Denny for encouragement and criticism over a prolonged period. The completion of the research and writing would never have been possible without the loyal, painstaking and scholarly assistance throughout long years of Joan Burns Raushenbush, my wife. Here my obligation is unlimited. I appreciate also the thoughtful editorial advice of Mr. Richard Kennedy, senior editor of the Delacorte Press. The responsibility for any shortcomings of the book cannot, of course, be shared.

S. R.

Contents

MAN'S PAST:
MAN'S FUTURE

Choices and Failures—
Theirs and Ours

The future is everybody's child. At present it is difficult to be sure which parents will influence its development the most. The huge muscular structure of the two superpowers will impress it profoundly, yet may be found to be inadequate to its human needs. It may indeed be bewildered and confused by the fateful way in which individuals within those two areas become increasingly helpless as their societies accumulate machinery, weapons, and power. It may even carry over from the present a traumatic revulsion at their common readiness to set themselves up as sole judges of what is right and wrong in their dealings with other nation-states.

Possibly the foresighted Scandinavians, or the war-punished peoples of Western Europe—the English, French, Italians, and Germans—may be the ones to give the future a brighter view of what life at its best can become than the two supergreats can. Or such a magnetizing insight may in time be offered by the people of Japan, or those of China—which is still regarded as the Athens of the East by many Asians—or by some men in Latin America. They may break away from their current adolescent convulsions more rapidly than their neighbors now expect. They may then give the first evidence of having learned the moral to be drawn from the choice between death and a community of men working for one another's good that the physical scientists have now given the world. It is a choice that the ruins of great past civilizations and power centers have already spelled out for each living society. Today's physical scientists have simply increased the scale to encompass all societies.

Each one of these smoldering, sparkthrowing centers of human hope and frustration has some potential for altering the course of a world which has rather suddenly been instructed to discard rapidly many of its most cherished beliefs and habits of behavior. Yet in the competition for the formation of the future character of this imperiled world the people of the United States are, at the very least, among the potentially most influential parents. Their peculiar admixture of hopeful striving, freedom, violence, wealth, and personal and social distress makes them the observed of all observers, their progress through history too large and spectacular a galaxy of mingled challenge, triumph, and danger to be ignored. Not all other peoples, now dragging their institutions, habits, and beliefs into the modern industrial world, will necessarily copy the American form or style. But American triumph or disaster will profoundly influence the world's future. The hopes of peoples everywhere are still centered around the concepts of personal freedom and equal opportunity, and the outcome of the American efforts to retain the one and expand the other can create progress or cause despair in distant lands. On the American success in achieving a mutually satisfying way of living, an agreement for common progress with its own minority, which is both underprivileged and racially different, may also depend some of the world's future chances of avoiding centuries of malevolent and violent conflict between the world's dominant white minority and its overwhelming majority of yellow, brown, and black men who are both underprivileged and exasperated.

Because of these several factors attention is focused first on the challenges facing the people of the United States in the years just ahead. They will test the capacity of man everywhere to construct a future free of the built-in readiness for obsolescence and ruin that has marked so many of his efforts from the days of ancient Greek glory into the present.

Nobody can any longer be sure of what American civilization will be like even fifty years from now; how its inheritors will describe it; whether they will cheer or mourn it. Too many of the same kinds of convulsions are brewing which brought other ambitious societies down to their knees to allow much confidence. Miracles of wisdom and good fortune are possible, yet failure and even disaster cannot be excluded.

In the early twentieth century the United States was still the great and envied hope of the world. By the 1960s it had become the most watched, most criticized and occasionally most feared world power. By then it had begun to show several of these signs of outward arrogance and unbearable inner stress which marked the disintegration of other major cultures in the past. These warning signals flared at the very moment when it eclipsed all the potentials of other historic societies: no other culture ever had its capacity to enrich or, alternatively, to destroy life and hope throughout the whole world; no other ever had so many billions of people ultimately dependent, in one way or another, on its wisdom, its decisions, its example.

In which of these two opposing ways American power is used will probably be determined long before the twentieth century has staggered to its close. To obtain a reasonable chance of enduring success, the people of the United States will first have to traverse four major problem areas. All of these four are heavily mined and widely booby-trapped. A remarkable combination of courage, will and wisdom will be required to move through and beyond them unwounded and un-defeated.

This need can be asserted with some confidence, for several of the same challenging difficulties, singly or together, have already caused a number of historic tragedies. Nine of the major ones are described in the following chapters. A few characteristics common to them are worth noting, a few elements of failure worth identifying. One is the rapidity with which disaster can follow the making of only a few shortsighted decisions. These little choices froze the ambitious societies into major commitments, hard or impossible to alter. Within a hundred years—a short time in the life of a nation or culture—these small human errors determined that inventive Greece would no longer be able to demon-strate democracy to the world, that mighty Rome would not be able to keep its republic. No longer period was required to transform the early Christian Church from a voluntary brotherhood of merciful, humble and indignant people into an imperial agency determined to destroy other dissenters. After the nostalgic decisions in the age of the great church councils of the fifteenth century, even less time intervened before the separate nationalisms felt free to identify the will of God with their own will, and before the enduring schism marked by the Protestant Revolution took place. Spain required less than ten decades to drop from domination of Europe to the position of conspicuous political inferiority which it has held ever since.

Drastic although lesser alterations in the human landscape have been accomplished in fewer years. The early successes of the revolutions which changed the face of France and Russia, after a few royal blunders, astonished even those who led them. From the founding of the United States, when the decision was made which ignored established slavery, to the American Civil War, only eighty years intervened. Only seven decades separated the odd decisions of the courts in the 1890s which permitted segregation by race in public facilities and intimidation at the polls, from the Negro revolution of the 1960s. The elapsed time from the American decision not to offset the dropout of Russia from the alliance of Western powers by joining them, to the Nazi conquest of Germany and Europe and the Second World War, was less than three decades. Time is the most perishable of all commodities. It can sometimes be gained, but only when men utilize the gain. It can readily be wasted.

Another common characteristic of most of these nine major failures of the past is that they were preceded by decisions to monopolize freedom and opportunity, to dominate and exclude groups of people who wished to become participating members of society. The wisdom of the ancient Greeks and early Christians about the requirements for a satisfying personal life and an excellent society were ignored, even by the discoverers themselves. Practically every culture which confused success and superiority with rights and righteousness encountered heavy penalties for its arrogance, its reluctance to adapt old institutions to new needs, its inability to disenthrall itself.

The people of the United States can expect to confront an interacting group of four major problems before the end of the twentieth century. While each might be solved separately—to the extent social problems are ever solved—their combination makes the task exceedingly difficult. A failure in any one of them would magnify the chances of defeat in the others.

The first of these is by all odds the hardest to handle. It derives from the depersonalizing impact of rapid technological change, crowding mass society and occasionally brutal competition for employment, affluence and status. The mechanics of mass aggregation and technological momentum are crushing some of the vital sparks of individual independence, idealism and conscience. Increasing numbers of apathetic or rebellious people are already surfacing, becoming visible, as the older forms of American community life shrink into the anonymity of large cities. Many people no longer feel needed by a society of fellow inhabitants who are no longer neighbors, whom they hardly know and see no reason to respect. Such alienation was already known in ancient Greece. It appeared after the Greeks had been worn raw by the inadequacy of their institutions. Rome, as we also see later, in its final moments of agony swarmed with multitudes aware of their own helplessness, resentful of the purposelessness of their existence. That great mass society in its worst moments also had a full quota of juvenile delinquents, soaring crime rates and civic irresponsibility. It even produced men who cheered its dissolution as a relief from insufferable obligations, who bartered their diminished freedom for safety. The ideal of a noble, disciplined life built around a community which constantly nourished it had been lost earlier in the competitive struggles for power and survival. But the people of these two great civilizations had been treated to more savage disillusionments than ours have ever known, so the cases are not comparable, or at least not yet.

The quality of humanity visibly disintegrates in some minds under the pressures of modern industrial and urban society, when old ties to a small community are broken, a sense of helplessness develops, or one of hostility toward the unknown others who may wish to injure or exploit. Difficult to explain in any other way is the behavior of the famous forty neighbors in New York, who refused to concern themselves in any way with the slow murder of a woman which was going on under their eyes, or the famous twenty bus passengers in Washington who refused to become witnesses against the juvenile delinquents who assaulted and robbed their driver. They hardly had the excuse of the Communist subofficials who killed men whom they knew to be innocent in the party purges of the 1930s or of the Nazi bureaucrats who took part in the largest planned mass murder of all history, that a fanatical nationalism or ideology forced their abdication of personal responsibility and conscience by the threat of death. They abdicated theirs without any such excuse and did not stand alone in doing so.

In addition to the apathetic are other alienated people, in more or less open rebellion against the wide gap between the ideals they have learned in schools and churches and the by-product brutalities of modern warfare, ethnic discrimination or public indifference to want. History gives us a long procession of their predecessors, including those monks and mystics who resented the power-hungry management of the Church in the days when that institution colored all European life. Their mood of protest must be distinguished from the savage resentment of those neighbors who have been taught that the villain behind all the changes in modern industrial society which annoy them is the government, and that their comfort and salvation depends on limiting its activities.

Such lost or revolted people are still in a small minority, but it is one expected to increase over the next few decades unless the society surrounding them improves. Such human beings are not exactly industrial by-product waste to be exuded into our social lakes and forgotten there until the pollution offends our esthetic sense. At the very least, they constitute warning signals along the American way of life. Their appearance on the scene evidences a problem of values and goals, one which cannot be fed into a computer for answers. It is close to the heart of many assumptions on which our affluent but also acquisitive and depersonalizing society has been built. At some time Americans may even find it necessary and desirable to turn seriously to the past and discover for themselves what alternative ways of living together might be possible if the Athenian and early Christian requirements for a good life were combined.

The second of these interlinked problems, more obvious, more immediately disruptive than the first, is the conflict between men—particularly black and white men—about the meaning and limits of freedom in the great republic. This is one of those clashes which can lead to complete frustration, endless recriminations and violence, extremism on both sides, much as its counterpart did over a century earlier. Awareness of the background of desperation in the pre-Civil War days, and again in Reconstruction days, is necessary if deep new wounds are to be avoided. In those days, too, men battled about freedom and status, human and property rights, and feared for the fate of the nation. Then, too, men were reluctant to pay the social costs of avoiding disunion and finally surrendered the Negroes to generations of poverty, submission and inequality. In our day that minority is not only raising the old questions which troubled Lincoln, but new ones. Negroes are seeking release from those conditions which make it impossible for them to attain the respect of their fellow citizens and even to retain their own self-respect.

Tragically, they bring with them the evidence of a century of neglect. Many show the slovenly, rough and reckless customs which are part of the process of living in poverty without hope of escape. Large numbers of them seek to enter the modern, intensely competitive society with a heritage of semi-illiteracy, with school-retarded children, with a minority of their minority reacting against unequal employment through crimes against property and persons. Some pent-up hatred at the callous treatment given them by the world's most affluent society accompanies them on their quest.

Many of their more fortunate fellow citizens see this evidence of neglect and mistake the whole inheritance of squalor for the Negro people themselves. They watch the burning of Watts and Washington, the riot scenes in a score of cities, the twisted face of violence. They fear that an influx of angry, handicapped people will lower the sales value of their homes, endanger their status, limit the opportunities of their children to enter college, trouble their pleasant neighborhoods with turmoil and crime. They move toward creating the equivalent of the Know-Nothing party of the 1850s, one directed against an earlier influx of unkempt neighbors and competitors, at that time the Irish immigrants. Once again, advocates of historic American ideals of freedom and equality of opportunity are discovering the difficulties which beset their cause whenever extremists on both sides manage to increase public fears and revive old prejudices.

A hard look at the operations of similar simple-solution extremists on both sides in the pre- and post-Civil War days shows a wreckage of high hopes. Those in the South called the abolitionists Communists, as their modern counterparts are labeled today. By the excesses of their insistence on expanding slavery into new states and their demands for immediate secession, they lost the very institution they most wished to retain. In the North some of their counterparts lauded murder in a good cause, later ignored the needs of both defeated whites and liberated Negroes for a Marshall Plan type of help in rebuilding, in creating opportunity, and played the divisive games of punishment and revenge instead, a cheap alternative.

Nor can any look at the American future be complete without noting the potentially revolutionary function of a status-threatened middle class, demonstrated for us by the French at one time and by the Germans in more recent days. Throughout the human past such groups of people have played the role of Lady Macbeth, who saw only immediate gain for herself and no consequences in retribution or degeneration. So she had the ignorant audacity which allowed her to bully the more farsighted Macbeth into murder. Her followers have been among those present at the downfall of almost every society which sought some greater glory than survival.

An alert awareness of the cumulative price of neglect and indifference, not only in our own past but throughout other civilizations, brought to this second problem area, may help to avoid a repetition of disaster.

Both the normal antifeudal revolts and the hunger revolutions in tomorrow's least favored lands will apparently demarcate a third major problem area for the people of the United States. The several billion people crowding the impoverished lands can be expected, in their century-long process of modernizing their systems of production and distribution, to vent their disappointments in a series of civil conflicts. A widely held and reasonable view is that the prevailing malnutrition among them will develop into mass starvation for great multitudes. The timetable of early death is apparently this: parts of Asia in the 1970s, Latin America in the 1980s, North Africa in the 1990s, give or take a few years. What is usually not mentioned is the high degree of probability that not all candidates for early death will accept their fate quietly. Consequently, hunger revolts and revolutions will be added to the normal antifeudal disturbances. The potential victims may have become convinced that the world now has the capacity to feed all its inhabitants and lacks only the conscience and will to do so.

The United States, the world's greatest food producer and largest arms depot, will surely be called upon to intervene in any such hardship and hunger revolutions. The revolutionaries may ask only for food; the endangered parts of the local power structure, for protection as well. Reports of Communist activity will give urgency to the invitations, even though Russia and China may themselves continue their policy of avoiding direct confrontation with the United States. Any number of treaties and promises of support against Communist advance obligate the United States. It is caught up in the credibility trap, as old as the Roman Empire. Unless it meets every threat, fulfills every promise, danger may be multiplied. At the same time the United States is moved by the idealistic hope that if nations are only allowed to remain independent, they will find their way to personal liberty for their people in due time, and even to peace, that they will somehow escape the punishment of enduring a brutal and primitive collectivism.

Not the probability of a series of Vietnam-type interventions but their outcome is unpredictable. Not even the most powerful nation in the world can expect to win every time. Not even imperial Rome at the height of its rule could do so, not even ideologically united and dominant Spain in its glamorous sixteenth century. Surely some of the classic errors of the past, such as attempting to support a counterrevolution without outmatching the revolutionaries' promises, will be repeated. Some frustrations, some losses can be expected. Only a few of these are required to make our new Greeks, who see in every defeat only evidence of treason, more embittered, more eager for extreme measures, for supplanting a civilian government with a military one, or for retreating to a barracks state.

Meanwhile, most of the surplus which might have been used to eliminate some of the causes of continuing poverty will have been diverted to the interventions, as indeed it already was in the late 1960s. The nation's piled-up needs—for the eradication of poverty, for educational and health facilities—and those of the big cities for homes and transportation will be ignored. With such continued neglect, the frustration which threatens to become an inherent part of the second problem area can be prolonged and magnified.

After some decades of such interventions and frustrations, what the world and the United States will look like at the end of the century is anybody's guess. A remarkable effort to hold a psychologically divided nation together—one even greater than that achieved at the time of the nation's founding by its heroic and skilled builders—will clearly have to be made before that time. At some moment during the intervening period a military and political genius may be able to prove to a still rational people that the vast costs of eliminating the various causes for Communist success in the world are nevertheless likely to be less than the costs of killing most of the people abroad who become Communists because those causes have not been eliminated. But then again, some other man may even before that moment have rediscovered the German route of the 1920s and 1930s—destroy a faltering democracy by insisting on his superior hatred of all opponents of American hopes—and may have found an already irrationalized people eager to give him the free hand he desires.

When historians look back at this American problem from the vantage point of another hundred years, say in 2070, they may possibly see behind all these chances for frustration and defeat one of those occasional great opportunities to enrich the character of life everywhere in the world which have so often been ignored on a smaller scale in the past. If there are any historians then.

The fourth problem is as old as the close of the Golden Age of the Greeks. Since nations supplanted the once universal church as the bearers of the only true ideology, it has become more complicated. It has been made more immediately perilous by the invention and proliferation of nuclear, chemical and bacteriological weapons. A future competition in interventions throughout the hardship areas of the world may increase that danger even more.

Now it is the problem of how, and how soon, two or three large political units and a number of smaller ones can prevent themselves and their neighbors from destroying a large part of the earth's population in the belief that this is necessary for their national safety. That the victims—both direct and indirect—might include vast numbers of innocent people who had no such weapons and were in no way responsible for the conflict is considered an important element only in determining which will be the most hated nations in what survives of the earth.

The new look of the innovations does not change the question over which civilization has often stumbled: How can people with diverse, sometimes conflicting interests, different customs and languages, set some common boundaries to their several capacities to destroy life? Neither the fact that nuclear weapons are more productively horrible than any known in past history, nor the fact that the thirty-minute flight time of a ballistic missile has supplanted the thirty years of warfare which disillusioned the Greeks with life, alters the question.

The key element in the present deadlock is fear of being left defenseless, of being tricked. The two nations which could end it approach negotiations trailing their own bitter memories. One of them goes back to the Western intervention in Russia after the Communist seizure of power. It includes a bad moment when Western powers in Europe seemed willing to let Nazi Germany have whatever it wanted as long as it was headed eastward against Russia. It continues with the Chinese claims that their new empire is encircled and openly threatened with devastation. That souring recollection is matched by another one, which includes the Communist takeover of Eastern Europe after the Second World War, an attempt to starve Berlin into submission, episodes of subversion and espionage, the bloody repression of the East German and Hungarian revolts for freedom, the placing of nuclear missiles in Cuba, and the Soviet invasion of Czechoslovakia, in 1968.

The resulting suspicions are coupled with the intense conviction that each nation in the world has a God-given right to do whatever it wants in the name of national defense, even in these days when nuclear war takes the meaning out of the victory by inflicting death on half or more of each nation's people, not to mention the millions of by-product deaths among innocent bystanders in other areas. Here, as dramatically as at any time in its past, is civilization bound in the chains of its past, almost helplessly waiting its extinction. The irony of its imprisonment is that civilization is almost at the point of being physically able to move all humanity above the flood levels of poverty, illness and ignorance, and is not too far from achieving the sense of an obligation to do so.

A point of no return to the solving of this particular problem of living together in a common nuclear atmosphere has even been conjectured. In the mid-1960s such respected and thoughtful individuals as Kenneth Boulding and Jerome Wiesner, both American scholars, separately warned the world that unless there was a complete change in people's thinking within twenty-five years—by about 1990—the disaster of a nuclear war could hardly be averted. Neither expressed much optimism about the possibility of reeducating people in all the key nations to the advantages of sharing with others their supposedly God-given privilege to do as they pleased regardless of consequences, and instead share some sovereignty with the rest of humanity soon enough to prevent such a catastrophe.

These four seem to be the most important problem areas which the people of the United States will have to cross successfully before they can take a deep breath and begin thinking of transforming their cultural system into a truly memorable one, enriching life, and recreating freedom and hope in the world. They may even find that their success in overcoming such a fearful combination of difficulties has made them the great nation they have hoped to be.

Looking from these four explosive problems ahead of the United States in the coming decades to the misadventures of other men and societies faced with somewhat similar ones, it is pertinent to note that, while history never repeats itself exactly, the human problems do so. Examination of lost opportunities and tragic moments in the life of past great societies should not create any belief that the Americans will not do better. On the contrary, they may do much better.

These earlier moments of decision and agony open opportunities for contrast and comparison. From them observers may note that disasters are usually avoidable up to some moment in time, and learn the peril of letting key moments pass without a positive choice. They can rediscover the fact that costs of prevention are usually much smaller than the burdens of neglect. They can watch weakness as well as power corrupt men, and look at the fate of great institutions which refused to adapt themselves to changing needs. In one or another of these accounts they can see the best and the worst of men trying to work their will, can mark the urge to crusade and the disillusion of crusading, the tendency of men to set traps for their successors, the frustrations involved in oversimplifying complex problems, the time limits on self-delusion. They can become aware of the ways in which excessive conservatism can breed radicalism and the reverse, as well as the brutal end results to which logic can push originally noble ideas of nationalism or salvation, the limitations on the effectiveness of military triumphs, and the endless skill of violent extremists in exploiting the natural resources of fear and gullibility.

Some urgency justifies this proposed reexamination of the causes for the major human failures of the past. It is not unimportant to the future of democracy to know which errors were unwittingly repeated at the time of the Vietnam war. It is not unimportant that the hard-earned American moral leadership of the world was lost, through those mistakes, even in the minds of the very people who suffered most from the Munich that American leaders saw themselves preventing in Asia. They stopped respecting the United States and began to fear it. It may not be an entirely casual coincidence that Athens, at the very height of its power and glory, lost the respect of its friends rather suddenly and was at that moment unknowingly far along the road to its own self-destruction.

In this particular demonstration of the difficulty in upholding an outworn social structure with superbly mechanized weapons of destruction, the means used tended to vitiate even the best of the intentions proclaimed. So much harm has been inflicted so often in the same way that Walter Lippmann at one time sought to have all the universities teach the nation's future rulers Plato's royal science for distilling the essence of wisdom, the capacity to judge. The heart of this science, as he saw it, was the presentation of history and the practice of judging it rightly in a choice of means and ends. That surely deserves consideration, but not all causes are lost because the means employed defeat the objectives. Many others have been lost for lack of simple humaneness, lack of awareness that the desired social harmony of the nation would be forwarded by ending exclusion, lack of foresight and willingness to sacrifice in order to achieve a long-term rather than a short-term goal.

In a world of accumulated neglect at home and abroad, in an era of intensified alienation and resentment, it may yet become a capital crime for the nation's leaders to ignore the accessible warnings of the past. Not the wealth but the character of the nation, the chances of freedom among masses of people throughout the world are involved in every such act of neglect. It is not only probable that the American philosopher George Santayana was correct in predicting that those who ignored history were doomed to repeat it. It is also probable that he understated the consequences of such a practice. Since he made his comment, warfare has become more obliterating, more suicidal to civilization than it was in his day. More devastating disasters than past history ever saw in all its many eras of blood and pain have now become possible, thanks to our scientifically minded friends. There is surely no obligation to clutter our brightly dangerous future with the defaults which led to tragedy in the past.

CHAPTER 2

The Great and Vulnerable Greeks

Devoted admirers of the ancient Greek civilization cannot be charged with perpetrating a fraud on a credulous public. Magnificence, excellence, patriotism, nobility and social cohesion did exist for a while in their best century. Any seeker for a great society, be he president or student, will find himself drawn toward the ancient Greeks by those magnets. He may, indeed, be at a loss for a better place to search.

Everyone who looks closely at the Hellenic adventure will grow in capacity to measure the processes, values and effects of modern societies. He may absorb some of the excitement of the Greeks' early quest for knowledge. He may share some of their deeply tragic sense of human life, lived without a hell to punish or a heaven to reward. These may be valuable to him at some time in his life. However, something else needs to be recalled. It is that the ancient Hellenes gave their brilliant civilization and one another a brutal, ultimately fatal treatment. They wrote a cultural tragedy which moved across the ranges of reason and emotion and through the full gamut of physical violence. When it was completed, the blazing light of their freedom no longer clarified the world. The human cause suffered from their failure to conserve what they had achieved, to advance beyond it. Not until after very dark centuries did their art, literature and thought again awaken the world.

Why was this to be their fate? The actions, ideas and decisions which marked their golden century with so much suffering and frustration suggest a number of explanations.

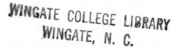

The Greeks were sufficiently modern to be useful to us in many ways. Anyone who enjoys the freedom to think can find his way about among them without too much difficulty. As in our societies, a large number of their people sought to live nobly, had a strong sense of responsibility, a very real patriotism. As in ours, many of them found that a democratic government, in spite of all its faults, was the most effective guarantor of personal freedom. They, too, had a burst of intellectual discovery and advance, but like ours it was not particularly helpful in solving the major problems of their society. Unity of a large number of separate patriotisms was also exceedingly difficult for them to achieve, because two of them were far more powerful than any of the others. These two, a somewhat communistically organized power center (Sparta) and a somewhat democratically organized one (Athens), were in almost constant conflict. Extremists found in the combined nationalistic and ideological conflicts their best opportunities to disrupt democracies and prevent peace. Even great danger and loss of life did not create effective international institutions to maintain peace and order. No sense of an inevitable, continuing progress prevailed. Men were most uncertain about the future. The inadequacy of older institutions to protect against danger, to meet personal needs finally led many of them to a peculiar combination of disengaged individualism and indifferent acceptance of their fate.

One Greek discovery might be used constructively in an area where our own society is showing weakness, the place where individual character and pride in community are both being atomized by mass pressure. The ancient Hellenes were able to enter their golden century (500–400 B.C.) only after they had made this discovery. They found the necessary ways to tie the needs and purposes of their individual citizens together by creating an excellent, satisfying community life. That fulfilling community life is the characteristic of earlier American society most endangered by recent changes.

People are being pushed together as never before. By 1990 certainly three quarters of the inhabitants of the United States will be living in very large cities, and 150 million of them in huge metropolitan aggregations. Those moving into them will have broken their ties to the rural or small-town communities and will not readily form new ones. A depersonalizing process and an estrangement have already produced "lonely crowds." These may become frightened and frightening crowds. Mental illness and the crime rate, both indices of social and personal maladjustment, have already risen in these huge areas, along with a breakdown of parental authority and with increased juvenile delinquency. The mass movement of relatively unschooled Negroes from the South has complicated the situation, emphasizing the need of all people for status, respect. Poverty in inner cities faces luxury in the suburbs, while violence on the streets grows. Clearly the task of holding the loyalty of people living in such conditions of individual separateness and mass crowding to the nation's older ideals of freedom and democracy can become an enormously difficult one. The uprooted people are already emotionally torn between their need to receive increased aid from society in adjusting to their new conditions, and their equation of government help with loss of freedom. The political system can expect to suffer recurrent shocks in the Roman fashion when the forcedly unemployed of all Italy poured into that city.

The Greeks did not have to deal with such a sudden or large mass migration into their cities, although Athens had some experience with it. They suffered their downfall in quite different ways than Rome did. However, before they were able to achieve the great society of their Golden Age, they created communities in which people could live close together and feel that they were living well. This particular accomplishment is the one which may turn out to be most useful to us whenever the future of the new American communities is in doubt.

The Greek discovery was that three elements were necessary for a good life and that they had to be linked together to produce a satisfying personal or community life. The first was that the individual was part of the community in which he lived. His life was enriched when he acted for others as well as for himself. It was narrowed when he acted only for himself. He could not escape the community, and it could not ignore him. They were permanent parts of one another. The second element was that a man needed respect as an individual, a person, not because he was a human being, but because he earned that respect. The respect was given only to the extent it was earned. When his courage, wisdom or justice were useful to the community, he was to be honored for those qualities. When he failed to demonstrate those qualities, he was not to be honored or respected. No matter how rich or powerful the man became he would not be respected in the absence of evident community service. The third element in the combination was personal freedom. For respect to prevail, men had to see one another as full and politically equal members of the community. By tying these three elements together, the Greeks met most of the human and community needs at the same time. They proclaimed that enduring happiness could be achieved only in a happy and healthy community. Men felt that they were contributing to their own personal lives when they added to the glory and strength of their home cities.

The remarkable individual life and responsible patriotism which this Greek combination of personal and community needs achieved have raised questions about modern civilization with which men can expect to live for a long time: Can any truly great society be shaped in any other way? Is the Greek way still useful for meeting the problems of huge metropolitan areas? Can it ever serve societies which have already linked respect to wealth and power instead of to other qualities and values?

The Greek tragedy consisted in the destruction of the remarkable combination of elements which had raised men and cities to greatness together. It took place because their city-state integration of personal and social life was not expanded beyond its original narrow limits. The small units of concentrated loyalty ultimately tore one another apart and made the national survival of Greece impossible. A series of decisions—choices between short-term and long-term alternatives—determined that this would be the fate of the Hellenes. In this narrative those crucial moments of decision are marked out, with the obvious advantage of hindsight. The Greeks could not know at the time they made their choices that their consequences would be disastrous. They were in almost the same category as the authors of the Constitution of the United States, who could not guess the consequences of their decision to avoid a relatively small conflict and omit a terminal date for slavery from that document. But there was a difference. The Greeks had no history of free people to guide them. We had the experience of both the Greeks and the Romans with slavery to guide us.

In this tragedy the main characters were the two leading city-states of mainland Greece. One was restless, expansionist, intellectually proud Athens, on the east coast with easy access to the Aegean Sea. The other was inland Sparta, master of the southern half of the mainland, the Peloponnese. As a powerful soldiers' state, its ideals were physical courage, discipline, conformity. Each of these rivals was at one time a conqueror, at another time a victim. Their conflicts and ambitions demoralized many more than their own citizens, and destroyed the possibility that Greek culture would humanize the ancient world.

These competing champions were surrounded by supporters, frightened observers and enemies from the rest of Greece. Corinth, an important business rival of Athens on the strip connecting the Peloponnese with the northern mainland, was one of Sparta's strong supporters. Thebes, another adherent of Sparta, slunk on to the stage ashamed of its role in aiding Persia, Greece's enemy, against the other Hellenes. An important part in the drama was enacted by the pro-Athenian Ionian city-states on the Aegean islands between Greece and Asia. They lived on the dangerous frontier of the mighty empire of the Medes and Persians. Those islands and coastal cities of Greece in Asia had been the center of the earlier Greek intellectual explosion. They were a catalyst for Athenian ambitions and finally an inducement to Spartan venality.

Other Greek city-states, such as Syracuse in Sicily, also had significant secondary roles. Not unlike individuals in any modern family drama, this Hellenic cast was torn in purpose and loyalty. In those city-states managed by the old aristocracy and called "oligarchies," a cult of democratic Athens could be found; while in the democratic cities, a cult of Sparta could be discovered.

Audacious tourists in the land of our intellectual ancestors, we mount the steps of the shining, still unruined Acropolis in Athens and take our stand beside Pericles, the man who has directed the democracy of that city-state for most of thirty years. He is about to make the first decision of four which we know, with the advantage of hindsight, will determine that Greek civilization will be deprived of the force and faith necessary for its political survival. The time is the year 432 B.C.

A message has come from the rough Spartans in their valley home among the mountains of the Peloponnese to the southwest. It says: "Liberate Greece and we will call off our attack." Those are stinging words for the leader of the one city-state which, above all others, boasts of the personal freedom of its citizens. Pericles is aware of the irony in the fact that the words come from the one city-state, among all others, which most despises democracy.

Pericles, from all reports, is a great man. Tall, bearded, always helmeted in public because of the awkward onion shape of his head, this is the thinker in arms, the patron of the arts, the educated and charismatic leader who has been elected chief general and administrator of his city-state again and again. This ancient prototype of Bismarck, Roosevelt, Churchill and de Gaulle comes from one of the old families, the "well-fathered" group. He is getting old now, at 59, and has less than four years to live and lead. He has raised no man able to succeed himself, starting an unfortunate tradition among great men in democratic nations. At this moment he is under attack from that odd alliance of forces which appears again and again in history, the older privileged and the new underprivileged, with no common aim except the destruction of the moderate man. They have not dared to go at him directly as yet, although they will. But his close friends are being accused of impiety—the equivalent of treason. One has been ostracized; another, who was head of his brain-trust, has fled; a third, the sculptor Phidias, will soon be jailed.

What is in his mind as he ponders his reply and the decision he will ask the Assembly (*ecclesia*) of Athens, the ancient town meeting, to accept? As we look out with him through the clear, bracing air to surrounding Attica, the countryside belonging to Athens, all seems quiet and under control. To the east is a break through the hills where the

Long Walls begin which protect Athens' access to its harbor at Piraeus and its hundreds of naval vessels. They insure Athens' mastery over the Aegean Sea, its control of the essential sea route to the wheat of the Bosporus.

Pericles must be pondering the old, unhappy and now inexorable choice before him. He can no longer escape the consequences of fifty acquisitive and frequently brutal years of empire building. His choices lie between admitting error and losing honor thereby, or risking severe battles to hold what has been obtained, or losing the whole empire.

There is much to lose. What there is to gain by admitting error—a new chance to build a united Greece on some other basis than one city's empire—seems vague, uncertain. At this moment Athens has arrived at one of the high summits of life. It is at the top of the civilized world, the culture center of the whole Mediterranean. This is one of the very first democracies, the first imperial one, a major maritime empire. Compared to Athens, Persia is asleep, Macedon hardly born. Remarkable events may perhaps be taking place in remote China, far to the east, but they will not touch Western life for a few centuries. Toward the west, the young Romans are not yet quite sure of their ability to protect their rude huts on their seven hills against neighboring tribes. Here in Athens however, centuries in which chaos was converted into order give an illusion of enduring grandeur.

This architect of Athenian progress for three decades may well be asking himself how much strain his Athenian society can stand. He clearly believes that it can stand stress well, for he has in mind a war plan which few other societies have been able to apply. It is to allow the enemy—Sparta, the greatest military power, and all its allies—to bring their troops right up to the walls of Athens, destroying every living thing in Attica, to do so for at least two years, during which Athens is to win no major battles at all. It is a strategy of exhaustion, of war without victory, with an incomplete Athenian naval blockade to strangle the enemy's food supply and trade. A wearied foe would then stop fighting. The fact that Pericles would even consider such a strategy indicated his faith in Athenian society, in himself.

Was Athens really invulnerable to shock? Surely other Greek city-states had an almost equal supply of valor, skill, leadership, luck and arrogance. Athens had a silver mine, which helped. Its earlier leaders had brought in craftsmen from all over to make it a great industrial and commercial center. It had allies throughout the Aegean, onetime members of the old free League of Delos. That league had been founded on the basis of one vote for each member state, like the General Assembly of the United Nations in the twentieth century, but had been taken over by its largest and strongest member, Athens, and converted into an empire. The allied or satellite members still paid contributions to Athens in return for protection against Persia and pirates. These achievements had given the city some dynamism, some function for all citizens. There was even, reportedly (this is hard to believe), an equality of pay, so that the stone mason working on the Acropolis received no less than Phidias, the famous sculptor. On every level recognition was awarded for achievement and public service. This whole Athenian amalgam had been brought about in the hard way. Kings had become despots and were followed by oligarchies of the old nobility, who had also ruled brutally. These, in turn were succeeded by tyrants, men who came to power illegally, representing the protest of the masses against the nobles, and they too ruled unjustly. The nobility's bitter experience with exile and loss of property under the tyrants, and the commoners' disillusionment with the nobles brought both groups to accept democracy as an alternative superior to endless rounds of violent civic conflict.

Anyone curious about the possibility of establishing a similar great society in a modern industrial city may remind himself that the philosopher Aristotle, a century later, was to say that a city of 100,000 people was too large to achieve any such objective. Athens, with surrounding Attica, had about 425,000 inhabitants in 432 B.C. About the same proportion of its people had voting rights as in the England of 1832. Perhaps 200,000 were members of citizen families (with 40,000 male voters), 60,000 were foreign-born craftsmen and 165,000 were slaves. The right to become a citizen was taken away, in 451, from all men who could not prove that both of their parents had been of Athenian birth. This law, which Pericles sponsored, has occasionally been described as the watershed of the Athenian empire. It not only took 5,000 men off the voting rolls of Athens, it marked off a status of inferiority for all the people in the city-states which were members of the Athenian empire. No common citizenship would bind them together, as it later did in Rome.

Several peculiarities mark Athens off from a modern democracy, in addition to the preference of the people for the esteem of their fellows over wealth and power. They lived modestly. They were not consumption mad. The first duty of the citizen was not that of buying things. Also, no one questioned the morality of slavery. Further, they avoided political faction and so made things a little easier for themselves, by allowing any 6,000 of the 40,000 voting male citizens to ostracize (send into exile for some years) any political leader whom they considered dangerous. They were able to take care of occasional unemployment by sending out colonists to the member states of their empire, particularly to those whom they were punishing for some offense. While they had opened up their assembly, courts and juries to the poor, their civil-rights legislation turned out to be ineffective in times of stress. For a while, at least, they had on the books a law allowing every citizen to go to court on behalf of anyone else to whom an injustice had been done by his neighbors or by the city, but actually this proved to be of little protection during wars. It was not any shining, dreamlike Camelot of an ideal city. The poor were not content with their lot, and the rich were not sure of their continued fortune. Superstition and fear gave every virtue a stiff competition.

What has brought Greece to this crisis of conscience, ideology and power in 432 B.C.? It is one which, as time will tell, will not be resolved by warfare, and one which they will not solve at all, but which will invite Philip of Macedon and his brilliant son Alexander to put an end to all Greek independence a century later.

The military weakness of maritime and imperial Athens at this moment lies in its lack of friends and allies on the mainland of Greece and its own relatively small land forces. Two decades earlier it had tried to remedy this vulnerability to attack by conquests on the mainland. These alarmed Sparta, the lion protector of the southern half of Greece, the Peloponnese, and Athens was forced to yield back everything it had gained by force on the mainland. Athens was left with only its maritime empire, more than 200 little city-states on the Ionian isles and around the Aegean Sea. A thirty-year peace with Sparta, dating from 446 B.C., supposedly governs the relationship of the two major powers in Greece. But recently Athens has raised the terrifying threat of starvation against all the members of the Peloponnesian League. It has made an alliance with the people of Corcyra (modern Corfu), which lies only a little to the north of the trade routes used by those mainland cities to get grain from Sicily. Corcyra has the second largest Greek fleet. Together with the imperial Athenian fleet it will be able to stop the grain import from the west and starve the southern city-states. Athens already has control of the route to the grain of the Black Sea. Once the route to the wheat of Sicily is closed, there remains only Egypt as a supply source, and that is an ally of hostile Persia. Pericles has lost a whole fleet trying to wrest Egypt from Persian control.

The new threat not only alarms the members of the Sparta-dominated Peloponnesian League, but also involves directly one of Sparta's major allies, the rich commercial city of Corinth. A Corinthian fleet has found Athenian ships supporting Corcyra, its own former colony, in a war Corinth is waging with the people of that island. In addition, Athens is besieging Potidaea, a city in northern Greece founded by and linked to the same Corinth. (Socrates is in the ranks of the besieging army.) Even more alarming, Athens is apparently violating the thirty-year peace treaty by taking away home rule from the city-state of Aegina, on an island some twenty-odd miles south of Piraeus, which is the Athenian naval base and harbor. That peace with Sparta had left Aegina a member of the Athenian empire (the converted League of Delos) but had assured its right to self-government. Aegina is now appealing to the conscience of all Hellenes against Athens' effort to take away that allowed degree of independence. Even more threatening evidence of the ultimate intent of Athens to become the harsh master of all Greece is seen in the recently announced punishment to which it has exposed the little city of Megara. That city-state, only twenty miles away on the isthmus connecting the Peloponnese with the rest of the Greek mainland, is strategically important because it flanks the route of march of the Spartan army northeastward toward Athens. Years earlier, Megara had killed an Athenian garrison on duty there. More recently, it has been guilty of harboring slaves escaped from Athens. Athens has pronounced the equivalent of a death sentence: Megara will not be allowed to trade with any of the several hundred city-states within the Athenian empire. Without trade, Megara will starve.

With these acts and threats against its neighbors, Athens has become as morally vulnerable as it is militarily vulnerable. Those deeds seem to Athens' competitors evidence of arrogance and brutality, exactly the sins which the gods most deplore and are most wont to punish. They give Sparta, the dominant military power of the Peloponnese, the opportunity to take away from Athens the moral leadership of Greek society, to proclaim that it will lead all others in a war to liberate the Hellenes from the tyrant state of Athens.

What has happened to the conscience of Athens? How has a city-state which nourished respect for citizens at home become a despotic empire in Greece, without respect for the rights or aspirations of the other Hellenes? Three circumstances may account for the disparity between Athens' behavior at home and abroad. First, Athenian luck and success had been so great and prolonged, so free of danger to the city-state itself, that Athenians had rarely been forced to question the political or moral bases on which their empire was founded. Second, they lived at a time when only a major threat of foreign invasion from a barbaric (non-Hellenic) foe could produce a brief union of all or most of Hellenic society. That had taken place at the time of the Persian invasion of 480–479 B.C. The many little local patriotisms of Greece had frozen centuries earlier and had numbed minds, loyalties and morality beyond the point of flexibility. Even after the whole Hellenic civilization has started to unravel, most of their great thinkers will fail to recognize that these little city-states were becoming an anachronism and that large kingdoms, national republics and empires would soon take over their function in history. Finally, the Athenians were probably being pushed from one position to the next, into ever greater danger, by the simple mechanism of their own dynamism. Given certain basic assumptions, one act logically calls for the next, programs get underway and cannot be stopped unless equally practical alternatives have been readied to take their place. This seems to have been the experience of the European nations in 1914 when their separate mobilization plans, once in motion, nudged one nation after another on past the point of no return into the First World War. It also seems to have permitted the disastrous invasion of Cuba in 1961, with its two imitations of Spartan error, and later the escalation of small promises into very large commitments in a war in Vietnam, in the mid 1960s.

But what can Pericles say to the Athenian assembly about the peculiar fate which the leading democracy of the golden century of Hellas has brought upon itself, this taunt that its rivals now need to free Hellas from its tyranny? Perhaps he thinks that the Spartans, who have little democracy, are too vulnerable themselves to be effective advocates for freedom for any other city-states. In modern terms, are not Soviet Russia and China so undemocratic at home that they will have no influence on the uncommitted nations of the world when they talk about freedom from the influence and power of the West? Pericles tells the Assembly that it will be fighting for the liberty of its citizens. As far as the empire, the display case of Athens' moral limitations, is concerned, he says frankly that it is indeed a tyranny, which Athens may have been wrong to establish, but it is something which Athens can now not afford to lose. In his later, famous funeral oration over the dead of the first war years he can find little to add to that justification of the Athenian cause. His decision is to accept the war, and the Assembly agrees to do so.

So the first of the four fateful decisions has been made. In 432 probably Athens could make no other choice. In 436 B.C. the war might have been avoided, but in 432 it cannot be. The Athenian moves have been too provocative, the reaction of the Spartan allies too loud to allow any retreat. Once positions have been taken publicly, honor ritually demands the ordeal by battle. Pericles has suggested arbitration under the treaty of 446, but no court has been established to arbitrate anything or to impose any international law on the groupings of city-states. His offer was ignored. Perhaps if Athens would offer Sparta an alliance at that moment, open to all other city-states, the war could be avoided. But that would mean ending the Athenian empire and beginning a Greek Nation. Athens has not been prepared for any such break with its past, any such cooperation with an old, distrusted, oligarchic enemy.

Eleven years of savagery, death, plague, defeats and victories are to follow before such an alternative will be available to Greece. There was such an opening long before, in 479, during the great unifying exhilaration of triumph over the Persian invaders. At that moment the two great powers, Sparta and Athens, most of the medium-sized cities and hundreds of small ones were all in an Hellenic League. The two great ones could have been checked and balanced by the others. Their glory could have been found in a competition to serve Greece best. A functioning union might have been established, not only to ward off any renewed Persian thrust and to clear the seas of pirates, but to prevent any wars among the city-states or revolutions organized by exiles. The bad luck of Sparta in furnishing the joint fleet with an egoistical ass as commander, the converse luck of Athens in being chosen to replace Sparta as leader, the sulking withdrawal of Sparta and the supine willingness of the maritime city-states to allow Athens to abolish their participation in control, to change them from allies to satellites and to take their joint treasury to Athens for its own use, all ended the possibility for creating an inclusive union—one in which the two great powers were sufficiently balanced by all others to allow the peoples of their many small Rhode Islands to remain as free as those in their larger Virginias and New Yorks. The ideologies of democracy and oligarchy, with all their intermediate variations, could probably have remained in competition within each city-state without causing interstate wars. Surely this would have been a difficult task, but not so impossible as that of keeping the peace between two large power blocs when one insisted on expanding.

So, the decision to fight is made and war begins, because a unique opportunity was neglected long ago. With it the sense of unity which war usually induces starts to evaporate into thin air. The armies of Sparta march into Attica unopposed. The livestock of Athens' surrounding countryside has been moved safely to offshore islands. But the rural population crowds in to hide behind the city walls. There they stand and watch with dismay while every living thing on their farms is destroyed. The crops and homes are burned, the grapevines and olive trees are cut down. Superstitious, uneducated, culturally alien to the city folk, these rural people almost outnumber the city people of Athens. With their sudden intrusion into the city, several of the basic requirements for an excellent community are broken.

The curses laid on the big cities of the twentieth century begin to operate. Too many people crowd one another physically. They do not know one another well enough to pay or receive respect. They force two widely separated levels of culture into conflict. The newcomers are susceptible to a demagoguery against which the city dwellers have developed some immunity. They demand victory at once, and a return to their fields—or victims. In addition, the brutality which the citizen-soldiers have to exercise on the battlefield, now that prisoners are killed rather than ransomed, seeps back into the city as the men return from their campaigns. Soon the "well-fathered," who have in the past shown some friendliness toward individual Spartans, will become suspect of being pro-Spartan, of wishing defeat for Athens. There will be massacres and countermassacres. Something equivalent to a psychological plague has been let loose in the beleaguered city.

Now comes the other plague, that which kills the bodies of men, women and children. A form of typhus, it is brought in by Athenian sailors returning from duty on the Asian coast. The doctors know no cure, can find none. The one possible remedy, dispersal, is prevented by the enemy troops standing outside the walls. People die by the thousands, tens of thousands. The gods are angry. They must be appeased. Someone must be sacrificed. People turn against Pericles, accuse him of embezzlement, of impiety. He is voted out of office as the chief of the ten elected generals. No one else can be trusted to take his place. The supposed embezzlement turns out to have been a secret bribe years earlier to a Spartan king, to stop his advancing army from attacking Athens at a time when it was suffering from heavy losses on the mainland and might have been forced to surrender. Pericles is voted back into office. In the midst of all this turmoil, he delivers the well-known funeral oration, rephrased by the historian Thuycidides, in which he lauds the democratic ideal and announces that Athens is the school of Hellas, of all Greek society. This is already a more frightening suggestion than he intended, for his school has already, unwittingly, written textbooks of disruption. He dies in 429, and for the first time the leadership of the city-state is not voted to a member of the old families, but is given to a leader of the commercial group, Cleon. He is spokesman for both the masses and those who have gained much from Athenian imperialism, head of a war party which prefers complete victory to peace.

The calculations have gone somewhat awry. Sparta and its allies are not being exhausted rapidly by the naval blockade. Year after year they move north into Attica and redestroy it. Athens has few important victories to console its people or give them hope. The plague strikes again. Altogether 80,000 out of the 300,000 within the walls die. Athens, under Cleon's leadership, turns savage. In 427 one of the member states of its empire, Mytilene, on the distant island of Lesbos, revolts, wants out of the empire. Athens conquers it. The Assembly of Athens, at Cleon's urging, votes death to all the males in the rebel city-state, slavery for all the women and children. A ship sails to take the barbarous news to the Athenian troops on Lesbos. Another Assembly meeting is called for the next day. No appeal to the conscience of the Athenians is made, simply an argument that such a death sentence for all males is counter productive. It will function like an unconditional-surrender demand, informing all future rebels that they might as well fight to the death because they will all be killed anyhow if they lose. The argument is persuasive. With oarsmen pulling madly, a second ship overtakes the first. Only a few of the men of Mytilene are killed. Shrewdness, not conscience, governs when nonmembers of the city are involved.

Has Sparta, the legendary land of military heroes, the victor during the first years of war, been underrated by the Athenians? Did the Athenians forget that this barracks state, with its semicommunistic ownership of land and slaves, kept the peace for a long time in the southern half of Greece by sheer force, that it was sufficiently fore-sighted to prevent Athens from gaining strong points on the mainland in the 450s? Possibly it is simply an underdeveloped nation which lacks only a little capital before it, too, will use its remarkably disciplined people to start on an imperial conquest of its own.

A temptation to underrate the endurance of Sparta, which is later to become the successive idol of many military élites, is hard for Athenians to resist. Long before this golden century of Hellas, Sparta has wounded itself grievously. Invaders from the north, the Spartiates had enslaved, under state ownership, one half of the people whose territory they took (helots) and had turned the other half ("dwellers about") into second-class inhabitants. With those acts Sparta converted itself into a perma-nent police state, an armed camp busy with preventing revolution at home. Boys left home for the camps at the age of ten and stayed there until they were in their forties. Throughout later time many societies will become prisoners of their ideologies, but Sparta remains the classic example of a society imprisoned by its own prisoners. In addition, Sparta forbade labor and commerce to its citizens as undignified. Burdened by these two restrictions, Sparta became and remained technologically and materially poor, and rationalized the virtues of austerity. On top of this, the Spartans refused full citizenship to the sons of any family whose state-granted farm and helots could not send enough figs, barley and grapes to the army clubs to sustain the young soldiers. These boys were forced to drop out, become "lesser men," and usually left Sparta to seek work, function and respect elsewhere in Greece. This was a process that bled even their great army thin in the course of time.

More, instead of cherishing the family as a source of national strength as the Romans later did, the Spartans forced the men in camp to meet their wives surreptitiously. More significantly, they purposely isolated themselves from the new ideas moving through the rest of Greece, which they considered radical and upsetting. They jeered alike at the debates about democracy, the meaning of life and the cult of science in Thebes and Athens, and at the rich merchants of their ally, Corinth.

Doubt about the Spartan devotion to freedom could be justified, for the Lacedemonians had not shared the experience of most of the rest of Hellas with the popular tyrant. This person, seizing power illegally, was usually supported by the least favored citizens and served to prove to one and all that rule by an oligarchy of nobles was neither god-given nor necessary for the welfare of the community. The doubt about Sparta's identification with the rest of Hellas in this matter of personal freedom was very similar to the later twentieth century doubt about Germany, which had also skipped a step in its evolution which the surrounding nations had experienced. Germany moved from an old feudal rule based on agriculture to a new feudal rule based on industry, without the intermediate stage of a liberating revolution or any other evidence of passionate devotion to a charter of civil rights. Like Sparta, it seemed to bear the tradition of a strong military and feudal caste and a subservient, silenced and authority-oriented citizenry.

These peculiarities limited the Spartan capacity for intellectual and moral leadership in Greece much as their poverty limited their capacity to undertake the long and distant military campaigns that the expansion of power required. Twenty years after our meeting with Pericles on the Acropolis, these people were to follow three Athenian mistakes with one characteristically their own, and this was to be the culminating one in the Greek disaster. It was to mark the Greek point of no return.

Although Sparta and Athens had different forms of government, there was no crusading ideological rivalry between them, comparable to the modern dispute between Communism and what the Communists call Capitalism. Even during the wars which began in 431 the differences were at first keyed low. Spartan success in battle was usually accompanied by a local triumph of the oligarchs in any conquered city, Athenian success by a local triumph of the democrats. Some horrible massacres, particularly one in Corcyra in 427, accompanied these changes of political control. Only later, after the hardships and defeats of war had amoralized life, did ideological differences become sharp weapons. It was in the fourth century, after the glory had gone, that a group of oligarchs vowed to one another, "I will be hostile to the people and will plan whatever evil I can against them."[1]

Anyone interested in the sharp differences between the depersonalized warfare of the late twentieth century and the way of life among the

Greeks before war had completely degraded their values, will find them illustrated in the Spartans' sudden offer to stop the war in 424, after seven years of successful struggle against Athens. They respected the efforts of their citizens to fight in their behalf. Wars were still personal conflicts fought by all citizens of military age, known to all. No mass bombings or burnings of soldiers or civilians had dulled their sense of individual loss or the respect due to their own men in the field or their value to the community. The only clever general the Athenians had managed to produce (Demosthenes) lured some Spartan troops onto a small peninsula south of Sparta, starved them with a blockade, burned out their protective covering and overcame their superiority at infighting by reviving the use of arrows. Some 240 men, including some Spartiate nobles, did what no Spartans had done for centuries—surrendered instead of dying on the field of battle. This was news which shocked Sparta and astonished the world of that day. The offer to make a peace in order to get its citizen-soldiers back alive, as well as the nearby Athenian strongpoint, was not peculiarly Spartan. Some decades earlier Athens had given up some of its mainland conquests because several hundred of its citizen-soldiers had surrendered and their lives had to be saved.

Here certainly, in 424 B.C., was a chance to stop the hemorrhage which was draining Greece, to allow Athens to reconsider its aggressive imperialism, to permit men to live again as they wanted to do. Sparta was not defeated. It was still busily engaged in liberating members of the Athenian empire in northern Greece, allowing them to choose their own form of government, if only they stopped aiding Athens. The Spartans were slowly moving toward the Bosporus, the crucial wheat source. Yet this small victory sent Athens into a delirium of triumph and confidence. Moderation and perspective were lost. Much later, according to Edmund Burke, a single British victory on Long Island over the colonists in North America in the late eighteenth century was to do the same for opinion in England. He wrote that after this one victory "the frenzy of the American war broke in upon us like a deluge. . . . We lost all measures between end and means; and our headlong desires became our politics and our morals. All men who wished for peace, or retained any sentiments of moderation, were overborne or silenced."[2] Cleon's war party ended the chance for peace by demanding the impossible: All of the mainland conquests of Athens lost more than two decades earlier were to be restored by Sparta to Athens. Sparta had no power to send other city-states into the pens of the Athenian empire, and Cleon surely knew this. That outrageous demand was simply one way of prolonging the war. Several others, such as unconditional sur-render and refusal to deal directly with revolutionaries during a military intervention, have been devised since then. In Greece the war went on, but with one important difference. The surrendered Spartans were made hostages against any new invasions of Attica.

Finally, in 420 B.C., there arrived the only promising opportunity for a union as well as for peace in all Greece since 479. A peace had been patched up a year or two earlier. It provided that each side should renounce its wartime conquests. But no agency existed or was set up to enforce that agreement. The captive Spartiates were returned to their homes instead of being held hostages for its enforcement. Hot recriminations were expressed. On top of them, a renewed commercial rivalry between Athens and Corinth, Sparta's main ally, caused fresh trouble. The Greeks, long immersed in the task of warfare, had not figured out how to make peace function. But the great moment came a year later. Sparta, probably harried by fear of a helot revolt, offered a defensive alliance to Athens, which that city-state accepted.

Here was a remarkable reward for eleven years of sacrifice and suffering. A union of the two great powers might well have kept all Hellas free from any more wars and might have provided the basis for a federation of all the city-states, great and small, with votes based on the size of their contributions to the common military forces and common welfare. But certain events had to take place first, to overcome the humiliation for Sparta incurred by its offer of alliance. More, that proud city-state needed psychological compensation and material aid to compensate for the loss and dispersal of its age-old Peloponnesian League. It needed some facsimile of laurels. It could have been given the first presidency of the alliance. Religious festivals and games in honor of Sparta as the great peacemaker could have been held throughout Greece to sanctify the achievement. Sparta could have received a share of the contributions paid into Athens by its old allies and satellites, members of the former League of Delos. Ways for bringing Sparta's allies and the neutrals into the alliance, among them the important cities of Thebes, Argos and Corinth, had to be worked out. Here was a moment which cried out for a super-Solon, a super-Pericles, and found only small men tired out by incessant war and by the endless suspicions of one another which war produces.

At this most crucial moment, creative social engineering and ingenuity were neglected by the Greeks as thoroughly as they were to be by the victors of the First World War twenty-four centuries later. The war party in Athens, not unlike its successor in France, stressing only enmity, rancor and revenge, had done its work too well. In that vacuum of inactivity the old allies of Sparta felt deserted and rushed off to make alliances with others to ward off the threat of a combined Athenian-Spartan dominance of the area. This anxiety of these former close allies of Sparta in 420 B.C. was not unlike the fear within Germany in the late 1960s that the United States and Soviet Russia would make a pact at German expense. This failure to welcome Sparta into major partnership in the Athenian empire, or alternatively into a national republic of all Greece—this willingness to remain negative when positive actions were required—can be attributed only to Athens. In effect, this negativeness constituted a decision to risk again its own peace and that of its empire and all Greece on Athens' own, limited strength, which was in naval rather than in land forces. This was the second of the four decisions which determined that the end of Greek independence and personal opportunity to enjoy freedom would come soon.

Athens was not to be the last great power to expose itself to the danger of allowing its people to believe in their own omnipotence, their capacity to win everywhere, every time, against all odds, to be able to threaten, kill and subjugate with complete impunity. Rome, Spain, France and Germany were all to experience the same heady hallucination. The Athenian awakening from their peculiarly self-righteous drugging was simply a little more ironic than that of the others.

Once the misery of others had shaken the people of Athens. Ages earlier, in 494, they had failed in an effort to save people of their own stock, Ionians, in the city of Miletus on the coast of Asia Minor. A dramatist had presented the tragedy of their death, the people of Athens had wept for the slaughter of the men, the slavery of women and children accomplished by the great King of Kings, the ruler of Persia. The dramatist was fined. Since that day they had learned to face the suffering of others dry-eyed. They had turned allies into subjects, had taken land away from those who wanted to leave the League of Delos, had excluded all their allies from Athenian citizenship, had used the funds those allies contributed for defense to build the Parthenon, in spite of protests from their own fellow citizens that Athens was making itself the whore of the Mediterranean, decking itself with other men's money. Conscience still flickered among some of the citizens, although more and more rarely. Each act of brutal disregard for the rights and needs of others seemed to justify the next. By 416 B.C. they had dropped below the twentieth-century level of killing civilians in a belligerent nation or in a nonbelligerent revolutionary nation by killing all the males and selling into slavery all the women and children on the island of Melos, which had been neutral in the war. Perhaps at this time Athens even probed the still uncertain twenty-first-century apogee at which the refusal of neutrals to enter the ideological or power disputes of that day would carry no protection against deadly nuclear fallout for more hundreds of millions than would be directly engaged in war. In

416, the rulers of this neutral city-state were simply told that might made right, that Athens would conquer Melos and kill its men because it wanted to and had the power. Here Athens met a people who preferred certain death to the loss of independence. They knew in advance that their efforts were hopeless. They foresaw their fate and accepted it with a courage rarely equaled.

From this accomplishment, the Athenians stepped directly into their audacious enterprise to conquer Syracuse in far-off Sicily, an expedition which superstition and patriotism bewitched from the very start. There was no major quarrel between the two city-states. The Athenians made no bones about the purpose of their attack. The young aristocrat Alcibiades, who initiated it, told the Assembly what that intent was. After Athens had conquered this rich western part of Magna Graecia (southern Italy) and obtained control over the food supply of much of southern Greece, which came from Sicily, Athens would have enough force to become master of all mainland Greece. That word sped quickly to Sparta and all its former allies, who saw themselves as the designated slaves of the new master to be. A respected but bumbling and elderly Athenian general, the man who held the lucrative contract for slave labor in the silver mine, by name Nicias, was so opposed to this wild expedition into glory that he thought to kill it by proposing a force so large, so ostentatiously costly that rational Athens would, he was sure, turn down the whole idea. His gamble lost, the Assembly voted the huge force and made Nicias one of three generals to conduct a campaign of which he disapproved. Alcibiades, ablest of the three, was charged by the pure patriots with impiety, which, as noted earlier, meant treason, a day after he and his supporters had sailed for Syracuse. He escaped from the police force sent after him and offered himself as adviser to the Spartans, justifying this course by his love for a city-state which had obviously gone mad and needed to be redeemed. He found the Spartans willing to believe him.

While charges of impiety at home removed the one decisive man from the conduct of this bold expedition of conquest, fear of possible offense against piety, coupled with inexcusable ignorance, managed to ruin Athens completely on the battlefield at Syracuse. Nicias had not caught up with the scientific discovery which Thales of Miletus had made in 585, some 170 years earlier, that an eclipse of the moon was predictable, a natural event, not a token of divine wrath. Pericles, during an eclipse of the sun, had demonstrated this simple fact to his frightened soldiers with the use of two shields and a torch. In Syracuse the outcome of the Athenian operations, due to the dawdling and uncertainty of Nicias, was in extreme doubt. The one clever general of the Athenians, Demosthenes, who had been sent later to advise, ordered a night attack at once, to be followed by immediate withdrawal of all forces from Sicily in case it failed. This, incidentally, was a remarkable moment in history. A man emerged who had the military reputation which allowed him to propose that, when there was no outcome to war except defeat, immediate withdrawal was the best alternative. He saw that the disgrace of a withdrawal was not so punishing as the cost of defeat. The night attack failed, withdrawal began, but then came an eclipse of the moon. Nicias ordered a ritual, a twenty-seven-day stop to all operations out of respect for the gods who had caused the eclipse. This was the irony of Athens' defeat, that the most educated people in the Western world would fall victims to an uneducated superstition on the part of one of their own leaders. During that suicidal delay, the Syracusans bottled up the whole Athenian fleet in the harbor, put sharp iron prows on their own ships, destroyed the Athenian vessels and massacred the troops on board. The troops on land tried to escape into the hills, but were cut down by cavalry. The generals were captured and killed. Seven thousand Athenians were enslaved for life in the limestone quarries. Athens' loss is sometimes put at 40,000 men and 200 triremes. The third crucial Greek decision, to extend Athens' mastery by conquering a distant land and controlling a major source of food for Greece, ended in catastrophe.

Even worse, the Athenians found that they had stepped into a new and different war, which they had not directly asked for. The process was similar to the one in Korea. The original war had been one in which the South Koreans and the United Nations were joined to push back an invasion from North Korea in the early 1950s. When their combined troops reached the old boundary line, that war was over. But when their troops crossed into North Korea and began to push northward, the Chinese came in, and it was suddenly a different war entirely. The Spartans had aided the people of Syracuse with military advisers. From there it was only a step toward exploiting the Athenian defeat. With that step, it became a new war. From that moment on until 404 B.C. war raged again almost incessantly in Greece.

The opportunity for a Spartan empire opened with this crucial Athenian disaster. The Spartans had received ample warning of the continuing Athenian purpose of becoming sole masters of all Greece. By the tests of modern sociologists, they may have been a retarded society, but they were not stupid. They knew that this was their moment to act. They also knew that they were too poor and weak in resources to master Greece without outside aid. They still lived in fear of a helot revolt. They fell heir to the old historical principle which Lord Acton later forgot to state, that weakness corrupts and absolute weakness corrupts absolutely. The Spartans went to the old enemy, Persia, for gold. Their part of the bargain was later to be the surrender to the Persians of the Greek city-states and islands along the Asian coast, objectionable show-cases of democracy. The Persians gained much more than that before the Spartan empire, in turn, crashed in two battles. This corruption of a major Greek city-state by the old enemy of Hellas marked a major change among all the Greek city-states. It was comparable to the introduction of poison gas or nuclear weapons against adversaries lack-ing means of defense or retaliation. The Persians had bought a satisfac-tory chaos in all Greece.

The Spartans first had to finish off declining Athens. This took some time. Athens could take defeat after defeat and still build a new fleet and sail it into battle, even refuse new peace offers. Meanwhile, however, its people were demonstrating that the irresponsibility of victories could be matched by the demoralization of defeats. The 20,000 slaves in Athens' silver mine were freed by the Spartans and fled. The cities of the empire were falling away. An oligarchic group seized power. In the year 411 they set up a Council of 400 to govern, and killed, exiled, or imprisoned, and also expropriated the leaders of the democratic group. Assassination almost became standard operating pro-cedure. The men in the fleet of Athens, harbored on Samos across the Aegean to protect the islands off the Asian coast, would not accept this oligarchy. They elected as general Alcibiades, who had fled from Sparta, and under him won some naval battles.

A seesaw of power at home and abroad went on. Athens won some conspicuous naval battles, but now the Spartans had the funds to build ships of their own to offset their losses. They were becoming a com-bined land and naval power for the first time. Their fleet threatened the grain supply from the Bosporus, finally caught the Athenian fleet drawn up near shore at that vital point and crashed the last ships which Athens possessed. This took place at Aegospotami in 405. On the night that the news finally reached Athens no one slept. All their other nearby sources of food supplies had been taken over by the Spartans. This was the last. They haggled a while about keeping their walls to Piraeus, but yielded, starved, surrendering their empire and destroying the walls. Sparta refused a demand from Corinth to level Athens to the ground. They explained this decision by the respect due to the leading part Athens had taken in defeating the Persians at the early part of the century. A Spartan garrison moved in to support a new reign, that of the Thirty Tyrants. Theirs was a rule of terror.

Even while Sparta was both supporting the horror and proclaiming that finally all Hellas was free, a group of Athenian democrats was gathering outside Athens to bring down the Thirty. Thebes, which had suddenly wakened to the fact that a Greece under complete Spartan domination was little better than a Greece under an Athenian empire, helped to arm and feed this group. These democrats balked attack on their strongpoint from the oligarchs in Athens and, during a brief truce for the burial of the dead, shouted to the Athenians that the Thirty had killed more Athenian men for the sake of their private gain than the Peloponnesians had killed in ten years of war. Gradually support for the Thirty weakened in Athens. The Spartans, finally appalled by the terror of the Thirty, refused their further calls for help. A remarkable truce was then patched up. An amnesty included all except the Thirty and a few of their most conspicuous murdering supporters. Athens thereby saved itself from a final bloody civil war. The spirit of tolerance reappeared briefly after almost thirty years of war. But now Athens, only twenty-eight years after it had invited the great conflict, was only one weakened nation among many, no longer ruler over any others, briefly content to be able to rule itself. Sparta was now the predominant power, although only by grace of Persian gold.

Several great nations have in recent times tasted, in various ways, the fruits of confusion and disappointment which can accompany the idea of freedom and which made the Spartan effort to establish an empire a bitter banquet. The United States, along with Western Europe, talked about a "free world" as its goal in the mid-twentieth century. That particular world was cluttered with personal dictatorships and even a few racially oriented minority governments, inviting charges of hypocrisy. The goal could have been described more accurately as one of a world of sovereign nations which were not controlled in either their foreign relations or their domestic arrangements by any power such as Soviet Russia or China, not even theoretically favoring personal freedom for citizens.

Greece had long suffered from the same confusion between freedom in the sense of national independence and freedom in the sense of personal liberty for citizens. Sparta, in 432, could claim to be liberating Hellas from Athens at the very time that Athens was boasting that it had brought freedom to Hellas. In 404 Sparta could again boast that it was freeing the Greek world at the very moment that its troops were supporting the bloody terror of the Thirty Tyrants in Athens and their violation of personal freedom. The Spartan policy changed after the fall of Athens. During the 420s the Spartan statesman-general Brasidas had weaned northern city-states away from the Athenian empire with the promise that they could keep their democratic rule and any existing or future personal freedom. But the Spartan leader who had conquered Athens, Lysander, found it easier and safer to encourage oligarchies in the old member states of the Athenian empire which he busied himself to acquire. However, the task of returning oligarchies or dictatorships to power after people have experienced or even learned a little about democracy is a bloody business, an invitation to revolt, and a source of new appeals for arms to support the unpopular rulers. Not only personal freedom but national sovereignty are likely to disappear in the process. With that disappearance all talk of freedom becomes evident fraud.

Since two of the errors which that strong military power made were to be repeated by counterrevolutionary nations, even as late as the 1960s, they can be considered classic errors, deserving some mention. The first mistake was to escort the old, exiled leaders of the oligarchy, with all their hates and feuds undiminished, back to the very nations where people had gained something concrete and valuable by eliminating those men. The second was to use Spartan soldiers rather than local leaders to institute a pro-Spartan government. The Spartans thereby diverted to themselves most of the local blame for the acts of oppression and failure of the oligarchs. Hatred of reaction became hatred of Sparta, almost automatically. The native oligarchs, in turn, became visible puppets of a foreign power, put into office and held there by foreign soldiers. This was not a skillful act of counterrevolution in areas which had known some degree of democracy. The monarchists of Europe intervening in France in the late eighteenth century, the French and English intervening actively, the Americans less resolutely in Russia in the early 1920s, the émigré intervention in Cuba in the 1960s which had United States support are among the many occasions on which these two classic errors have been imitated.

An empire of subservient oligarchies might have been built by Sparta, nevertheless, if it had not, some years earlier, inaugurated the process of accepting Persian pay. Once this corruption by a foreign power had been begun, it spread. As Spartan power grew, the Persian king and his satraps on the Asian coast had second thoughts about the value of destroying Athenian power simply to replace it by Spartan power. So Athens, Thebes and other cities began to receive Persian funds to wage war against Sparta. It was a Persian fleet, commanded by an Athenian general, which ended Sparta's sea power at Cnidus in 394.

No record exists of a Greek rebellion of conscience at accepting Persian funds for self-defense against Sparta. Envoys from the other Greek city-states went to Persia begging for those funds. Probably as little protest was expressed as in the United States in the 1940s when the mass bombing of civilians during World War II became standard operating procedure, and the Secretary of War, Henry Stimson, asked Robert Oppenheimer, the atomic physicist, what kind of a country this was which expressed so little indignation at the murderous fire-bombing of Japanese cities. Old and modern history both indicate that normal revulsions can be overcome whenever a claim of danger to life or power can be made. In modern times the process of governments outdoing their competitors in brutality has become part of the depersonalizing process of life. Individuals find that decisions are constantly being made which affect them profoundly sooner or later but which they have become less and less able to control in any way.

The Spartan effort to unite Greece under its own rule failed as the city-states formed regional confederations to protect themselves against the new great power. Sparta could no longer claim any great moral cause. Its obligation to Persia had to be paid off by giving Persia mastery of the Greek city-states on the Asian coast and the islands near it. Persia got more than the destruction of Athens out of its subsidies and more than the removal of these showcases of democracy from its neighborhoods. It obtained a completely and permanently divided Greece. In 386 the Great King was able to tell Sparta and Athens to stop fighting or he would come over and wage war himself. He could impose a peace which forbade all regional confederations and all alliances between city-states. Each city-state was to stand absolutely alone. A permanently atomized Greece was no menace to any foreign power, no protection to Greek civilization. The end of the Spartan effort to hold on to power came in 371, when at Leuctra it was defeated by Thebes in a land battle. After this, it too became a second-rate city-state. For Greece the irony lay in the fact that the Persians, without moving a man into Greece, had won the objective of their costly war a century earlier. For Persia the irony came fifty years later, when that kingdom needed a united Greece to withstand Alexander of Macedon's attack. Then, due in large part to its own intervention, there was no united Greece, there were instead only obedient Greek soldiers swept up by Alexander to win his battles in Persia.

Three lives illuminate the period of Greek disintegration as no chronology can do.

Two of the three were touched by the misfortune that the Greeks, who had discovered the genetic mating qualities of personal freedom and an aristocratic way of life, had also found, under stress, that they could destroy both qualities by calling in their fear of the jealous gods. Enough people eager to assume the role of defenders of the gods against any possible slight were always available to wreak this destruction. They believed that they had learned one truth which others neglected. It was that the gods, rather than men, determined the outcome of battles and wars, and that the gods functioned on a *quid pro quo* basis: whichever side paid them the most rigorous respect, won. Lack of respect for the gods was impiety and, since it served to defeat the national purpose, was treason. These were the people who worried profoundly about the growing rationalism of Greece, a school of thought which sought to tie up cause and effect as natural processes, not subject to any Olympian interventions. They had forced some of Pericles' close friends into exile, had put the famous sculptor Phidias into jail, where he died before his trial. They had deprived Athens of the leadership of Alcibiades at Syracuse by bringing charges of impiety against him, a process which doubtless frightened Nicias so thoroughly that he took his fateful decision to stop fighting and to honor the gods for twenty-seven days, and with that lost Athens' huge army and fleet. They seem to have been obsessed with the idea that complete conformity to their criteria of respect assured complete victory.

One unfortunate victim of these self-righteous people was the youngest son of Pericles. Elected one of the ten generals of Athens, he would normally have been granted a measure of glory for helping to win the greatest naval battle in Greek history, an action against the Spartans in 406 at Arginusae. So successful were the Athenians that the Spartans promptly offered peace. But Athens was again as irrational and absolutist in its hopes for regaining its old dominance in Greece as it had been in 420. Again its leaders, unable to imagine that they were only two years away from complete defeat, refused the peace offer. This great victory simply proved to them again that the gods were with Athens if only Athens continued to stamp out all lack of respect for them. It was this conditional clause which was to bring to young Pericles the command to drink the hemlock.

The six generals of Athens had indeed triumphed magnificently in that naval battle, and they had fought it in a choppy sea, in the face of a coming storm. Some Athenian ships had sailed away from the scene in pursuit of the fleeing Spartans, others had sought a safe harbor from the blow. As a result, the final funeral rites for the men lost in the battle at sea had not been observed. This was impiety. Possibly some survivors might have been found. This endangered the outcome of later battles. All six generals were ordered to report to Athens for trial. Two had observed the bloodthirsty impiety hunters in action and declined to return. Their failure to do so cast a presumption of guilt on the four who still trusted their community to do justice. Socrates, presiding over the Assembly that day, refused to put the motion for a death verdict to a vote, stating that the case should be tried before a court, not before the Assembly. He was overridden, the men were sentenced to death. Twenty-four years after Pericles had proclaimed that Athens was the school of Hellas, the last of his two sons died at the hands of a frightened, distrustful and divided people. His first had died during the plague.

In the same year, 406, that Athens was compounding its folly, another Greek in another place was rising to power by his ability to create internal distrust. This man, Dionysius, not an aristocrat but a clerk, had fought in the ranks of Syracuse in a skirmish against invading troops from Carthage. The Syracusans lost that small battle. Dionysius then rose in the *agora*, the marketplace, to charge the elected generals, members of the aristocracy of the city, with lack of a will to win. In modern terms, the accusation would be that of possessing a "no win" policy. He caused a profound sensation. He rose the next day and charged the city's generals with treason. No evidence except the loss of a battle was presented, but Dionysius offered himself as an eyewitness, one who knew more than any others.

An astonished people, unaccustomed to complete personal irresponsibility, became a madly frightened one. If they could not trust the supposedly patriotic members of their aristocracy, whom could they trust? Dionysius then demanded the dismissal of the generals without a trial. Why without a trial? Because the whole government was packed with fellow traitors. He alone was the true patriot, the one whom they could trust, the one man who could distinguish between loyalty and treason. He was chosen a general, but he refused to associate with the other generals. In a moment of governmental weakness they were dismissed, an act which strengthened the popular belief that his original charges had been correct. He announced the discovery of a plot against his life, further evidence of prevailing treason, and was given the bodyguard he demanded. He doubled it in size and ordered the army out beyond the city walls. Then he took absolute power for himself from the democracy of Hellenic Syracuse. Dionysius I ruled Syracuse and most of Sicily as tyrant from 406 to 467, one of the earliest known discoverers of the rich natural resources of public gullibility and of the means by which a democracy can be frightened into destroying itself. Hitler, 2,300 years later, merely imitated.

The third person was Socrates, the most famous teacher in Athens during his lifetime. He was probably the first Western man to posit the existence of a soul. In 399 B.C., five years after Athens had lost its empire, he was charged with impiety and the corruption of youth. He stated that he believed in God and that there was no evidence at all that he had ever corrupted any youth. None was offered. He also stated that he did not teach, he was not wise enough to do so. He only asked questions. His relentless question and answer process forced men to reexamine the basic assumptions from which they reached their conclusions about life, action and morals. False assumptions always led to false conclusions. The first intellectual problem men had to meet was that of choosing the right question to ask themselves.

No historian of the period has given us a full and adequate picture of the nature of the animus against Socrates. We know that two of his close friends and admirers had antagonized large sections of opinion. One was Alcibiades, who had so resented the charges of impiety brought against him after his own supporters had sailed off to war, that he became an adviser to the Spartans, later was elected general by the Athenian sailors at Samos, and won victories for Athens. Another friend was Critias, one of the hated Thirty Tyrants. We know also that Socrates had questioned the premises of both democracy and oligarchy. Yet we do not know whether he was popularly identified with the anti-war group in Athens or the pro-Sparta group, or even whether they were identical at this time. What seems most likely is that the extreme pietists were frightened of his rationalism, his belief that knowledge by itself might lead to a virtuous and possibly even a happy life. They may have been joined by others on the jury of 501 who felt obliged to seek someone other than themselves who could be held responsible for the disintegration which Athens was suffering at the time.

His direct accusers were apparently more interested in getting him out of Athens than in taking his life. A promise to be silent, an acceptance of an open opportunity to escape and exile himself would probably have ended the matter. But Socrates had only a small remaining part of his life to lose and tried to prevent Athens from degrading itself and from proving itself guilty of violating its traditional esteem for wisdom and justice. The Athens of 399, however, was no longer interested in such an appeal to its former ideals. The democracy of Pericles, built on freedom, was no longer concerned with the freedom to think and speak. Socrates was ordered to drink the hemlock. He did so with the grace and confidence of a man who has retained his integrity completely.

The four errors named as those which brought the institutions and achievements of Greek civilization down in ruins may seem, at first glance, to be minor misjudgments, the consequences of other and more important conceptions. The first, it will be recalled, was the decision of Pericles and Athens to leave unchecked the momentum of their escalating imperial brutality against neighboring city-states and to accept helplessly the war which it had induced. A second was the Athenian refusal to use Sparta's later peace offer and then Sparta's offer of alliance as magnificent opportunities to create together the needed federation and conditions for pan-Hellenic peace which the Athenian empire had demonstrably failed to do alone. The third was the blunder of undertaking a power-directed war of conquest in far-off Syracuse, handicapping it with fateful superstition and giving Sparta a new chance to win. The fourth was Sparta's combined error of importing Persian gold and control into Greece and at the same time arousing the antagonism of every defeated city-state by identifying itself with the oppressive oligarchs whom it restored to power. Behind these four mistakes were layers of accumulating overparochial patriotism, ages of legend about Olympian interventions in wars, and generations of unexamined credulity about the omnipotence and invincibility of the two leading city-states. Coupled with the Greek tragic sense of life, these various beliefs prevented them from seeing that war itself was becoming an institution, that as such it demanded reexamination by the mentally aware, and that, prolonged beyond a certain time or point of destruction, it could ruin both victors and defeated and all the values both once treasured. The basic attitudes led to the mistakes, and the mistakes were then cumulative in their effect. The whole world lost when the Greeks stumbled and fell.

The people of Greece began to desert their society in the fourth century, to leave behind them both physically and spiritually the *polis*, the community which had failed to protect their lives and personal freedom and had destroyed their joy in living and their pride in living nobly. As the institution of the city-state turned out to be too small to prevent war and defeat, the inner community which had nourished it broke apart. The loyalty of men was withdrawn. Many migrated. Some women stopped having children. Unemployed young men by the tens of thousands became mercenaries for others, even fought against their home cities. Citizens began refusing the century-old obligation of military service and declined to be elected general officers. Paid soldiers and professional officers took their places. Wealthy men for the first time began going to court to prove that the contributions they were called upon to make were too great, that certain others could pay more than themselves. In Athens, citizens refused to attend the Assembly and had to be paid to participate. In the general hardship of the period, conflicts between rich and poor accentuated the old quarrels between the political groups.

Hope was placed for a while in the idea of regional confederations. These developed some aspects of federalism and means to offset the hegemony of one great power within that group. Some of the federations appeared intermittently for centuries in spite of the edicts of the Great King of Persia and later of Alexander against them. Several fought the Romans much later in the name of freedom. They were studied carefully by the founding fathers of the federal United States in the late eighteenth century. Like the idea expressed by Greek thinkers after the fall of Athens and Sparta, that only a government of all Greece which gave absolutely equal respect to all Hellenes could survive, the confederations came too late, and none had the power or will to create such a universal society.

Without hope or promising programs to absorb their energies many

Greeks became utterly cynical, sure that all others acted only from the most ignoble motives and consequently deserved no respect for anything they did or proposed. Before the conquest of Greece by Macedon, made complete by the battle of Chaeronea in 338, the Athenian statesman Demosthenes demanded a last great effort by all Greece against Macedon. He was suspected of receiving Persian gold for his attempts. His opponents, notably Isocrates, who urged obtaining the aid of Macedon for a unifying war against Persia, were suspected of receiving gold from Macedon. It was in this period that the Cynic philosopher Diogenes could take a lantern and claim to be searching for a single honest man. It was a time when only a very few of the city-states of the Hellenes would find it worthy of their heritage and in their interest to fight against Philip of Macedon in 338. Subsequently, Greece was to experience almost 2,000 years of rule by foreign monarchs.

But men deprived of the values and institutions of the past apparently need more than cynicism to enable them to stay alive and justify their survival to themselves. The Greeks began to turn to those philosophers of the day who were able to clothe the long generations of personal withdrawal with adequate intellectual garments to cover the new nakedness of the Hellenes. Some of them were imported from Asia. With their help, individualism stripped of social obligation but covered with a depersonalized *Weltanschauung* was let loose on the world, to run its course through time up to the psychiatrists and seekers for the return to a golden age in the late twentieth century.

This Greek development has been described by the perceptive English historian of the classical period, M. I. Finley, in these words:

> The dominant trend became a flight, whether to self-indulgence or to a blinkered concentration on the small details of daily living, to contemplation, indifferent to the goods or ills alike of the physical world.[3]

> Henceforth the search for wisdom and moral existence concentrated on the individual soul so completely that society could be rejected as a secondary and accidental factor.[4]

The failure of the Greeks to widen the boundaries of their world of morality indirectly cursed their successors in other lands. The conquering Alexander the Great talked nobly about an empire built on human brotherhood, knowing no boundaries of culture, nation or race, but he could borrow no blueprints from his vanquished Greeks with which to build it. He left a subdued Asia in which a veneer of Greek customs and language covered a mass of superstition and submission to rulers who called themselves divine, as he did himself. In due time, the Romans found ready to hand the Greek philosophy of spiritual isolationism waiting for them in the wreckage of their own community, the contribution of their Hellenic tutor-slaves. Roman culture, some centuries after the Greek personal withdrawal from the community, followed the Hellenes into Epicureanism and Stoicism. Those were rationalizations for taking pleasure or enduring life instead of mastering it, for suffering gallantly instead of eliminating the causes of the suffering. About these two ways of viewing life Arnold Toynbee wrote:

> In attempting the *tour de force* of making themselves superhuman the Stoics and Epicureans made themselves inhuman. They could not make themselves invulnerable except at the cost of casting out love and pity for their fellow human beings, as well as patriotism and public spirit. And this studied callousness made it impossible for them to save either their neighbors or themselves.[5]

The story of Greece stays alive. Neither our problem area of alienation and depersonalization nor that involving class and racial harmony can be traversed successfully without full consideration of the Greek discovery of the human need for esteem and self-respect and their incorporation of that discovery into their social system. Instead of becoming wealth-oriented and status-motivated as we are, they became proud and respected members of the communities to which all contributed. The alienation of the Greeks, we will also remember, came after their prolonged wars, after their cherished institutions had failed to protect them from the results built into the inadequacy of their many small city-states. So also our other two problem areas cannot be crossed successfully without recalling the early demonstration given by the Greeks of three still modern defaults in the world's international arrangements. One was that too many small and frozen local patriotisms prevented a needed unification. The second was that a duopoly of power, their Sparta and Athens, our United States and Russia, was no guarantee of peace and survival. The third was that a dynamic, expanding power such as Athens or the United States runs the risk of neglecting and humiliating all its actual and potential allies, acquires a material and intellectual arrogance, and overestimates its own strength and appeal. The experience of the United States with its control of the North Atlantic Treaty Organization and its venture in Southeast Asia underline the comparison.

To those curious about the process by which a civilization moves from institutional inadequacy to a destruction of its inner social architecture, and from there to helplessness, and who wish to avoid it, Greece supplies one of several types of raw material for examination. The Greek adventure was replaced, as we know, after an interval of several centuries by the Roman concept, swinging almost monolithic power behind the courage, skill, ambition and discipline of its people to create a Roman peace throughout the Western world. That culture, which is closer to the aspirations, contradictions and revolutions of the twentieth century than the Greek one was, provides also a more varied dramatic development of an alliance between material success and disintegration.

CHAPTER 3

Rome: Republic and Empire

The Classic Invitation to Dictatorship

Along the thousand-year highway of Rome we can recognize friends, neighbors and opponents from various corners of today's world. Pouring in from the fields of Italy are hordes of the same farm people who now surround the cities of Latin America in tight and menacing slum belts and throng the cities of the United States in search for work, lost dignity and excitement. On another stretch of road are young people disillusioned by the life of their parents, some engaging in wild personal adventures and conspicuous exhibitionism, others being tempted to become radicals or Christians or both. Here are throngs gambling their small earnings on the altar of the only goddess they worship, Fortuna. In the shadows, those who have long been treated as inferiors are brooding about their exclusion from society, meditating personal revenge and civil revolt. In the open sunlight are wealthy, nostalgic worshipers of the old ways who are unwittingly becoming the most radical transformers of society in all Rome. At one crossroads stand the rising men who believe they have discovered that Roman life is a racket, with rewards reserved exclusively for the most brutal, the least scrupulous. At another are the sometimes hated heretics, the Christians, praying that God will either convert or destroy the whole wickedness that is Rome.

In the forum we hear an orator who will become known to millions of later school children, Cicero. He is explaining that the chief reason for founding government is the protection of private property. Cynically listening are clusters of young centurions who know that in the end only might makes right, preparing to take and then sell control of the state to the highest bidder. Near them are the toga-clad patricians who have lost faith in the capacity of a republic to govern itself, readying themselves for the delights of collusion, prepared to welcome to their company military rulers or other despots, anybody except their despised fellow citizens. Bustling about are men of the business class, with a sharp eye for the benefits of tax farming and moneylending, ready to turn every imperial accession into gold and to grasp the reins of power as they fall from the enfeebled hands of the older aristocracy. Here, too, are the wily tricksters who will see to it that the wrong type of citizen does not have an opportunity to vote. Here are Stoics, who withdraw in sadness even before defeat, vowing their sense of a brotherhood of men in misery, yet unwilling to live for it. But here also are the honored mothers of Rome, who raise their children to practice the virtues and respect the gods, to learn the difference between a man and a person, to serve the public cause, the *res publica*, and to die heroically for their convictions and nation in the great tradition. Scattered along the illustrious trail through the centuries are finally some of their sons who have now and again put up a fight for justice and freedom for their deprived fellow citizens.

Among them all are famous men who seemed fated to destroy their own cause, one of them the old censor Porcius Cato, who strove harder than all others to keep Rome free from the amoralization creeping in from the east, but who, more than all others, insisted on a final destruction of Carthage. With that one act and its immediate consequences he unwittingly did more to prepare the demoralization of his beloved Rome than any other Roman. Among those sons of honored mothers are also the tyrannicides whose daggers bloodied their cherished city with one more evidence of civic unreadiness and with one more civil war than the nation could endure and remain a self-governing republic.

The internal hemorrhage from which the Roman republic was slowly bleeding to death had begun when Rome's old nobility and its business groups underwent the shock of becoming exceedingly wealthy from foreign conquests. Originally the Romans had fought against attack. Highly disciplined by the process and confident that important gods protected them, they first widened their rule to include most of Italy. In this period they were a nation in arms. Their stories told of elected leaders who gave their lives, even slew their own sons and daughters for the safety and honor of the city. Their elected governments showed energy, their citizens patriotism, their patricians determination and the capacity to sacrifice themselves and their property for the common good. The Romans moved from mastery of the western Mediterranean, after long and almost fatal wars with their rival, Carthage, to control of the eastern areas of that inland sea, then far into Asia. The wealth and loot from conquest and the wealth and labor of war prisoners sold as slaves poured in on them. The third and final war with Carthage, which Romans, including the older Cato, had instigated out of fear, ended in 146 B.C. Most of the half million people in that North African city died of starvation during the siege, but the Romans took the 50,000 survivors as slaves, and the ownership of Spain as booty.

It turned out to be too much of a good thing. With this last accretion of slaves and wealth, life in the Roman countryside and then in all of Italy began to change. It was the critical mass necessary to trigger the explosion. At first, farm laborers lost their jobs and drifted, embittered, to the city. Then wealthy men found that with slaves they were able to operate very large plantations. They could wait—something farmers without capital could not do—while olive or citrus trees or vines grew old enough to bear or herds accumulated. They managed to take over large shares of the public commons, the pastureland historically shared by farmers' animals, also the common source of fuel. All this was economically efficient but socially counter productive, and in the end disastrously so. On top of this, grain for the pasta of the Roman people was brought in more cheaply by ship from conquered lands than from the Italian countryside. Suffering from this double competition, many free farmers gave up or sold out to wealthier men and joined their former farm laborers in Rome. They hated the men who had altered their lives, cut short their opportunities, diminished their sense of mastery over their own lives.

With this cityward movement the peculiar patron-client relationship which was to mark so much of later Italian life, with its combination of client sycophancy and mixed patronal contempt and fear, began to take root. One of its later flowerings was to be called "feudalism." The dispossessed multitudes from the land accepted food and the circuses of violence from their patrons as a poor substitute for independence and opportunity and later took their oblique revenge for the uneven exchange. The state's decision to provide food relief for them or low-cost food, later characterized as "pauperization," was intended to help these people stay out of the complete vassalage to their patrons which would have taken place if they had become entirely dependent on them for their food.

Nor was this the end of the dislocation. Slave revolts began, and all Rome had to be mobilized to subdue them. In Sicily the slaves fought for four years (135–131 B.C.) and defeated a Roman army of 20,000 before they were conquered. Two more revolts followed thirty years apart. After another in Sicily (104–100 B.C.), slaves taken to the imperial city as prisoners proudly killed themselves rather than entertain Roman mobs by fighting wild beasts in the arena. Still another revolt (73–71 B.C.) assembled 90,000 men, including free but dispossessed Italian and Latin farm people. With this adherence of freemen to a slave revolt, the disunifying forces became more formidable and obvious.

The erosion of the community could have been stopped. An opportunity to halt the process by which freemen were turned into rebellious dependents in the slums and slave revolts were injuring the nation was presented to the Roman leaders. But they were shrewd men who knew a good thing when they had it and would not let go. Their intellectual descendents later helped make possible the Communist takeovers in Russia and China and seem determined to do the same in Asia and much of Latin America. The moment for remedial action came with the first slave revolt in Sicily. While a huge Roman army was being defeated there, the people elected as their tribune and protector a young hero of the war against Carthage, a member of the reforming sector of the aristocracy. This was Tiberius Gracchus, who proposed to get back most of the land taken improperly from the public commons and give it to small farmers. The large landowners, operating through the Senate (a self-perpetuating body, not an elected one) found themselves unable to stop the passage of his law. But that meant almost nothing, since the Senate supervised the administration of the nation and could kill the law by fond neglect. The tribune foresaw this fate. He believed that it was necessary for him to be elected to a second one-year term to have the law put into effect. He thought that it would function successfully, because a legacy from a grateful Asian monarchy could be used to supply the small farmers with seeds, tools and work animals. The Senate chose to decide that no tribune of the people could hold office for more than one term in succession. A riot was created, Tiberius Gracchus was killed, along with three hundred of his followers, and their bodies thrown into the Tiber. His homesteading law died from intentional nonenforcement as a number of land-reform measures in recent decades have died in Latin America.

A second opportunity for remedial social therapy came with the election as tribune of his younger and shrewder brother, Gaius Gracchus, in 122 B.C. He managed to buy the support of the rising business class, the *equites*, by giving them tax-farming privileges in Asia and by allowing them to sit on those juries which judged the behavior of Roman officials abroad. These were the very officers who were supposed to prevent undue exploitation of conquered people by the business group. With that expensively purchased support, he was able to reenact his brother's agrarian legislation and also to found colonies for displaced farmers in

Italy and abroad. He also managed to reorganize the voting system to diminish the patrician group's control of the nation-empire.

But he took on a little too much at once. He had enough foresight to know that the Italian cities of the peninsula (originally less close allies of the Romans than those older friends called the Latin cities), smarting under a system of taxation and conscription without representation, might revolt. He suggested that these cities be given the franchise. However, their votes were a threat to the Senate's control. When he presented himself for reelection as tribune with a program of two colonies abroad for the dispossessed Roman farm people, his opponents put up a rival who promised not two but twelve such colonies, and all with rent-free trimmings. While many forms of demagoguery are known, this particular technique of outbidding the moderate in order to divide his support was one which became a favorite of Communist labor leaders in the United States in the 1920s and 1930s. In Rome a divided and confused people defeated Gaius Gracchus. Shortly thereafter he was murdered by persons perhaps unknown but certainly unpunished. Within eleven years (by 111 B.C.) all his land legislation was annulled, and all the remaining public land went under large private ownership. Nothing came of the proposal for twelve colonies, which had served its purpose.

The perverse character of this action by the Senate on behalf of the large landowners and slaveholders was that the withdrawal of the common lands from public use destroyed the customary method of paying pensions to the soldiers. A piece of public land was their pension. In making itself the anti-pension group, the Senate automatically made itself the target for attack by the soldiery. Their riotous generals could thereafter only get the soldiers' pensions by expropriating the private estates of Senators and *equites* who were hostile to them. These important groups consequently had a strong interest in muting their opposition to any general who sought control of the state. The old Roman system was struck two blows by the same stone, cast by its nominal supporters.

While the establishment won against the reformers for the moment, it soon found that it had created such a groundswell of resentment that it could no longer lead the nation. Under the pressure of a few military defeats tainted by corruption, it would yield civilian Rome to military rule. With yet another political assassination, it would provoke a war for civil rights within Italy. Within a few decades its patricians and businessmen would be slaughtered by the thousands. This was not, of course, the first or last time that the limited moral conscience of a group in search of increased power or wealth destroyed the hopeful strivings of a people toward a combination of personal freedom with law and order.

But it was one of the tragic occasions, since Rome held elements of greatness, and the effects of its turn toward despotism stretched out through ages.

Soon Rome was moving toward Caesarism with irresistible strides. The future *imperator*, Julius Caesar, was born a little before the last century of the pre-Christian calendar. More importantly, it was only a few years after the last of the public lands had been pillaged, and only a very few years after the consuls chosen by the Senate as generals began to lose battles, one after another, in North Africa and then in Gaul. Just before his birth another slave revolt began, and the people of Rome were again called on to pay in blood for the opportunity of the slaveholders to maximize their profits. He was twelve at the time of the Italian war for civil rights (90 B.C.).

While the Greeks, as we have noticed, saw treason as the most probable explanation for defeat of their armed forces, the Romans saw treason in such radicalism as land reform and civil-rights efforts. What they saw in defeat was not treason but corruption. Possibly they had some justification. The key incident occurred in an otherwise inconsequential little war in what is now Tunisia. The local king, Jugurtha, had apparently observed with some acuteness that the Romans liked to make money out of wars. With the hope of being left unharassed, he evidently scattered a considerable amount of gold where he thought it might do the most good. Roman officers seemed unable to catch or defeat him. This persistent coincidence attracted unfavorable attention in Rome. Charges of bribery were made. The Senate felt called upon to disprove those charges by winning the war. At this point the second in command, Gaius Marius, sailed back home and announced brashly that he could win the war. In that particular atmosphere, alive with frustration and suspicion, this was a challenge which the Senate felt unable to ignore. Marius was elected consul and told to go ahead and win the war. However, money was a consideration, and Marius was not given all the troops he wanted. He took advantage of the public climate and the fear in the suspect Senate to call for volunteers.

This was the moment to reaffirm civilian control over military affairs. Marius had been given no unlimited authority to call for volunteers and in that way to obligate the nation. He had been elected consul, not dictator. The tradition of civilian control over the armed forces was an old and important one. But the Senate seemed to think that nothing was more important than to prevent prolonged discussion of its suspected corruption and implications of treason. It failed to challenge Marius.

What happened then astonished everyone. The propertyless people, who had for some time not been allowed to carry arms for the city, suddenly saw job and even pension opportunities for themselves; they flooded the training camps. Marius had the army he wanted—Rome's army only in name. Marius won in North Africa by bribing a friend of the rebellious king to turn him over to the Romans. When the consul returned to Rome, he could not be called to account because the Senate's hand-picked generals in Gaul had started losing one battle after another. Marius was sent against the Gauls and, taking his time, defeated them. After that he was "the savior of society"; it was too late to restrain such a hero. Before he retired he had sent 100,000 Germans to the slave pens and had been elected consul for at least six terms. All the ambitious young centurions in the armies watched this new road to power with sharp eyes. They were interested particularly in the way the ties that bound the legions to the civil authorities had been severed.

Some of the more frustrated and bitter members of the discredited establishment managed, through another political assassination, to bring on a civil war. For years allied Latin and Italian cities had furnished troops for Rome. These Italians wanted full citizenship as Romans, but this was refused. Rome was not merely capital of the republican empire; it was both the republic and the empire, and a minority of its citizens managed the affairs of both. Toward 91 B.C. a tribune (Drusus) began negotiating quietly with the Latins and the Italians regarding citizenship, a most important matter of status to them. The Senate saw that an influx of new citizens would make its control more difficult, or even impossible. It looked on these potential new citizens with all the absence of enthusiasm that later animated some Southern senators in the United States at the prospect of new free states entering the Union in the 1850s. The tribune who sought to bring these Italians into the Roman community was called a traitor. His opponents and adherents armed for civil war. Then he was murdered by persons who remained unprosecuted. Inside Rome there was no civil war, but it broke out all over the peninsula.

That murder, following the earlier one of Gaius Gracchus, who had also championed their cause, convinced the people of the Italian communities that they would always be rejected by Rome, always remain subordinates. It was the old Athenian mistake of exclusion, dramatically repeated. Modern times saw a rough parallel to this outburst of resentment and violence when Jorgé Gaitan of Colombia was murdered in 1948, and the many people who had placed their hopes for a better life in him were convinced that it had been done by the power structure which he opposed. Killing, looting, brigandage and civil insurrection stretched out from Bogotá over 300 miles of mountains and valleys and fifteen years in time.

The subsequent conflict in Italy over civil rights (90–89 B.C.) has inadequately been named the Social War, because it was against the *socii*, or allies of Rome. The rebellious cities set up a new capital (Italica) and a new constitution. At times they seemed on the point of winning. After a fashion they did win, for Rome decided (dividing to conquer) to give citizenship to some of the cities, and then to all. However, after the war was over the Senate had a last word, somewhat lacking in honor and generosity. It put the new citizens into a few rural tribes that could easily be outvoted by many smaller tribes controlled by Roman patricians and businessmen. This not only perpetuated but accentuated the basically nondemocratic character of the political structure. Since all voting was done in Rome, the rural people had to come to the city to cast a ballot. This was easy for the few financed by large landowners, but difficult for others. If too many others came to vote, the complaisant augurs always could divine from the sacrificial fowl that the moment was inauspicious for public business, and key votes could be postponed until the enraged country folk had gone home. The result was that the *plebs*, always a majority, rarely were in control. Later, in the United States, politicians using similar techniques to retain their power, would call the process "gerrymandering."

The Establishment's policies in regard to slaves, wars of conquest, land, foreign grain, and colonial settlements had created the Roman mob. By preventing the *plebs* from sharing responsibilities of citizenship on some basis of equality, the ruling class turned the mob into a permanent threat. As Frank Burr Marsh puts it, "Owing to the system of group voting, the city mob was never able to dominate the republic, and the wealthy minority was always able to outvote the poor in the assembly if that minority was united."[1] This seems to have created cynicism and hatred, qualities often reciprocated in kind.

After the war for civil rights within Italy, there was a major economic crisis throughout the area. The conflict had drained the treasury and ruined many. Also, it had produced an ambitious new military leader.

As if all the internal hardship were not enough, the crisis was intensified by maneuvers of Mithradates VI of Parthia, a kingdom of western Asia. Not unlike the Romans themselves, he had harnessed financial advantage to his political purposes, but with a difference. To a debtor who would kill his creditor, the king offered a cancellation of half the debt. This royal populism worked after a fashion—for the creditors of the Parthians were the Roman businessmen abroad. It was to these intrusive foreigners the Parthians owed money. As a result of this get-rich-quick suggestion, several thousand Romans were murdered. Rome had to make war on Mithradates.

In this situation, another postponed problem was flaring back to accentuate other problems and failures. Too little had been done to move the conquered areas toward membership in the Roman republican and imperial enterprise. They had been allowed to keep their old kings, their old forms of government and oppression. To their old taxes were now added foreign tax collectors, bankers and businessmen. Romans paid no taxes and lived off the conquered peoples. In Randall's phrase, Rome's aim was "to convert real or theoretical sovereignty into hard cash."[2] Not until the time of Augustus were colonies considered something other than open gold mines.

The legend goes that Mithradates poured molten gold down the throat of a captured Roman officer to symbolize for his people the insatiable greed of the Romans. That greed was personified in the publicans, those businessmen who had bid highest on contracts for tax collections and were free to make as much out of these contracts as they could. They were hated everywhere, not only in Judea, where a famous statement combined sinners and publicans. They took over the local banking business in the colonies, where profits were very high. In the imperial interest the Roman governors sometimes tried to check them, but this had been made exceedingly difficult. The business group (*equites*) had been given the right to sit on Roman juries which audited the accounts of governors. So military governors, who were unpaid and dependent on income obtained at their posts, usually left the business group alone.

A natural result was that the military leaders participated in creating a climate of hatred and revolt in the conquered lands. Some years later the essayist-politician-philosopher Marcus Tullius Cicero, himself a member of the business order, was to write: "It is impossible to find words to express the hatred with which we are regarded by foreign peoples, because of the greed and violence of those who in recent years have been sent by us to command armies among them."[3]

When Mithradates VI revolted in Asia and slaughtered Roman businessmen there, the Senate named Sulla, who had been successful in the civil-rights war, to command the forces in Asia. He was an able cavalry general, chosen by the antireform majority in the Senate. It feared that its unpopular political decisions might be reversed once Sulla had left the country. So instead of sailing to subdue Asia and then returning to obtain power in Rome, as Marius had done after his victories in Gaul, Sulla reversed the procedure. He turned first against Rome, seized power, and only later went to Asia. He dispensed with the earlier formality of putting Rome into his debt before calling the loan with troops.

When Sulla entered Rome at the head of his legions, he sponsored measures shoring up the Senate's power. Before he left for Asia (87

B.C.), most politicians had learned to look to the armed forces rather than to the people. In Sulla's absence, however, reform measures were introduced to make effective political rights supposedly granted to the people of the Latin and Italian cities. One consul opposed them. He used force against eager new voters trying to register. The reform consul (Cinna) fled—to the loyal legions still in Italy. With those legions, and with supporting troops from the Latin and Italian cities, Cinna and the old war hero Marius returned. Their task of conquering Rome had been made easy by the Establishment's earlier policy decisions which put Roman farmers off the land in order to let in slaves and cheap grain from conquests abroad. That foreign grain had to move through Rome's one port, at Ostia; the city had made itself exceedingly vulnerable. The legions of Marius and Cinna simply blockaded Ostia and shut off the food. Rome had to submit. The year was 86 B.C.

This was the third military seizure of power in twenty-four years. This time the consequences were made plain to everyone. Marius instigated a frightful massacre of those in the Senate and elsewhere who had aided Sulla to build up the Senate at the expense of the rest of the community. Marius not only killed many leaders, he confiscated their property. All this was done in the name of the reformist party, the Populares. That violence promptly exposed the new regime to retaliatory action by any antireformist military leader, such as Sulla. A sense of doom prevailed. No one seems to have been able to organize out of all Italy a group strong enough to hold the nation in unity and in arms against Sulla's avenging return.

Retribution came. Sulla had been outlawed by the Senate when it was under the control of Marius and Cinna. But he had paid no more attention to that action than many later kings were to pay to papal excommunications. He returned from Asia in 83 with 40,000 troops. All of them knew that their pensions would be granted only if Sulla took power. In a way, this was part of the terrible revenge of the farmers who had been deprived of land and livelihood by a shortsighted Senate. Serving as troops and using both reformist and nonreformist generals as their instruments, they buffeted that institution as it had never been hammered before. Without too much trouble, Sulla routed or took over three opposing Roman armies. Then he entered Rome. He instituted a ferocious massacre by Roman soldiers against Roman citizens. It was directed against all of Sulla's enemies, all would-be reformers. He restored the old establishment. He persecuted children as well as adults. With little public land left for his soldiers' pensions, Sulla confiscated his opponents' private land and turned it over to his troops.

The moment of death was drawing closer. Sulla's massacres and proscriptions, coming on top of those by Marius, had disorganized life and destroyed hope. The whole peninsula was poverty-stricken and bleeding from what was to be an almost unending legacy of terror and hatred.

The problems could not be met by killing and confiscation, or by reinforcing powers of the Senate at the expense of the tribunes and the assembly of the tribes. The two thousand democratically inclined businessmen and Senators whom Sulla had killed could not be replaced overnight, or indeed within decades. Veterans placed on confiscated private lands or on the few strips of remaining commons refused to stay. Many sold out. This increased the number of *latifundia* (large landholdings), whose continued existence was to be a factor in Mussolini's rise in the 1920s. Many tracts wasted and eroded away. Brigandage increased. Sulla outraged the outlying areas by cheating them of their hard-won civic rights, abolishing the office of censor, the only official empowered to register new voters. In the city, people were harassed by Sulla's police force of about 8,000, much as the helots of Sparta had been attacked four centuries earlier. These measures could not, of course, restore the nation.

Lack of foresight and action to meet the slave-and-grain problem—which became the land-unemployment-instability problem, which became the unity problem, which became the authority problem, which became the military-control problem—resulted in a series of major failures and catastrophes. The enduring problem of a free and orderly society was posed again in 73 B.C. by another slave revolt.

This revolt was led by Europeans, including the gladiator Spartacus. It was joined by destitute Italian farm people. Armies of 90,000 came together and defeated both Roman consuls. Authority seemed to be collapsing. Armed forces of the republic had attacked a consul who wanted to reestablish the political position of the tribes. A rebellious (pro-Marius) governor in Spain was creating an independent army. In Asia, Mithradates was planning a new war against Rome. Roman general officers abroad were doing whatever they pleased. Without authority, one raided Pontus (modern northern Turkey) and sold so many into bondage that the international market price for slaves dropped to the equivalent of a few dollars. Another used a Roman army to devastate parts of Sicily for his own gain. Pirates burned the small Roman fleet off Ostia, a few miles from Rome itself. Everything was getting out of control.

Faced with the immediate threat at their gates, factions of the nation-empire came together. The last of the slave revolts was put down after three strenuous years. Five thousand were crucified along the Appian Way. Then the victorious generals returned to exact their reward in the form of power. One of them was the wealthy Crassus. Another was Pompey, who had managed to have the rebellious governor in Spain assassinated. They joined and sat outside the walls of Rome with their troops. Neither was eligible for the office, yet both were elected consuls. The Senate was troubled with new colonial scandals; its moral prestige was again low. In the process by which the military took over control from the civil authorities there seems to have been none of the later-day German and French romanticism about the superior patriotism of men who wore a uniform. The officers were able to take power because they had the military force, after civilian agencies had destroyed the moral authority of representative government.

The way was now almost open for Julius Caesar, who had been moving up the required ladder of elective office, a conspicuous and calculating member of the patrician group committed to social reform. It took only one more abdication of Senate power—that of giving Pompey a blank check to war against pirates wherever and however he saw fit—a financial panic, and a combination of debt-canceling reformers and Roman underworld brought together by Caesar's friend Cataline, to move power from the Senate and the people into the hands of a triumvirate. Caesar became its third member, in 59 B.C. With some technical respect for legal and republican forms, these men, Pompey, Crassus and Caesar, ruled in an almost monarchical manner. Rome had not experienced anything like it for centuries. Thirteen years later, after his military success in Gaul, Caesar took the rule of Rome for himself alone.

The disintegration of civil power was accompanied by a degeneration of faith, duty and hope. The longtime rulers of Rome were discovering slowly that, when they had cut their fellow citizens off from opportunity, they had also limited their own ability to master their lives and control the city and empire. They, too, were on their way to become dependents of others. The old Roman spirit of obligation had been fading. The glorious tradition of a united nation of free men driving persistent Carthaginians from their soil, of refusal to surrender when all seemed lost, of wealthy patriots donating a fleet to a bankrupt nation, was only a dim memory provoking pessimistic contrast. Rome still professed that it was bringing law, order and a higher civilization to the world, but the conquered peoples tended to look cynically at the golden threads of exploitation.

Extreme individualism without the discipline of social responsibility became the characteristic trait of these last republican days. As described by Charles N. Cochrane:

> The last shreds of traditional restraint had been contemptuously flung aside, and the dominant note was one of individual freedom and self-assertion. Inflamed by an insatiable thirst for novel forms of ex-

perience, members of the aristocracy let themselves go in a protracted orgy of extravagance and debauchery. . . . Nor was the epidemic confined to the more exalted circles of imperial society. Among the masses, bread and circuses on a rapidly expanding scale afforded a counterpart to the Lucullan banquets of the rich. . . . High and low alike, without distinction of age, rank or sex, the Romans indulged in a riot of sensationalism and emotionalism which, while it promoted social disintegration, at the same time stimulated that fierce competition for *dominationes* and *potentiae* which laid the political fabric in ruins.[4]

This was not only one lost generation but a procession of them. Perhaps the much discussed delinquent juveniles of that day had put their greedy, invertebrate and affluence-oriented fathers under close observation—a practice which may again be taking place—and were therewith demoralized.

Many Romans now turned to current Grecian philosophies of escapism, as they were to turn again in greater numbers under the emperors. Christianity with its ideals of love and responsibility was still to come, but other Eastern mystery religions, promising a happier after-life, became more popular. The Stoic virtue of endless endurance and inactive civic courage appealed to some, but that was hardly a stimulant for regeneration of Roman society. Others sought relief in the Epicurean idea that pleasure was the ultimate goal and salvation was to be achieved only through enlightenment—a cult with an individual sedative rather than a prod to common action.

All of this was nourishment for Caesarism. When the *imperator* crossed the Rubicon of illegality in 48 B.C., by refusing to obey a Senate decree withdrawing his command, he had a twenty-nine-year record as a reformer in addition to his spectacular conquests in Gaul. His share from the sale of 100,000 captured warriors had made him wealthy. Now he had only a few legions. But they were, in Mommsen's words,

> young men from the villages and towns of Northern Italy, who still felt freshly and purely the invigorating influence of the thought of civic freedom, who were still capable of fighting and dying for ideals; who had themselves received for their country in a revolutionary way from Caesar the citizenship which the Roman government had refused; whom Caesar's fall would leave at the mercy of the *fasces*.[5]

Opposing Caesar were the government and the armies led by Pompey, an able general but one preferring a three-to-one superiority before attacking. The government controlled the navy, ports, most of the overseas possessions, the grain supply, some of the treasure, and all the symbols of authority. It was supported by those who still believed in the republican ideal, including the younger Cato. Nevertheless, the government had a long record of greed and failure, of satiated self-interest, of inability to adjust and invent.

In a few astonishingly swift moves with his small force, Caesar pressed south toward Rome. The government and its armies fled by ship to the safety of Greece. There they seem to have been as rabid and vindictive as the later émigrés of the first French revolution in Koblenz, across the Rhine. They were humiliated by loss of homes and properties, critical of Pompey, bitter over their lot, the fate of Rome, the unkindness of the gods. They talked incessantly of a purge, "a reign of terror from which Marius and Sulla would themselves have recoiled in horror."[6] Their threats got back to Italy rapidly. Those who had been forced to accept Caesar's conquest as he swept south were now forced to think twice about turning against Caesar later on. The absent government's only program for Italy seemed to be more death, but of that men had had almost enough.

Caesar and his forces won. The people were exhausted after the three years of fighting in Greece, Egypt and North Africa (48–46 B.C.)—tired but still republican at heart. The popular hero of the wars was not victorious Caesar, but the younger Cato, who fell on his sword in Utica after the last defeat. Caesar began his rule in a hostile atmosphere.

This man, it will be recalled, entered the triumphant and anguish-marked Roman society after an early failure of conscience had broken the ancient authority. A little before he made his appearance on the scene, republican Rome had stopped facing up to its major crises of social decency and institutions and was suffering from the consequences of its default. An aristocrat from the top drawer of Roman society, claiming family descent from nobody less than the goddess Venus herself, he had early joined the sometimes rowdy camp of the reformers. Yet as a general officer and expert subduer of rebellions he himself later contributed heavily to the very chaos he sought to reform. This was a strange, exceedingly able man. One may smile at his insistence on covering his baldness with his laurel wreath, but at little else.

The new *imperator* was realistic and intelligent, whatever else he was. He knew that the nation needed quiet, rest and recuperation. He inaugurated no massacres or proscriptions. He kept his troops from looting. He scotched hopes of the anarchic fringe of the Populares party that he would cancel debts and hound the aristocrats. Caesar spoke well of Pompey, killed by his own officers in Egypt. Demolished statues of Sulla and Pompey were reerected. He restored membership in the Senate and civil rights to victims of past proscriptions. He gave high positions to Pompey's former officers, including that of *praetor* (prefect and chief judge of the city of Rome) to Marcus Junius Brutus, heir of a legendary family, who was soon to plot his death. He tried to heal some of the wounds.

Caesar in his short two years tried to revive rather than reform Roman society. To relieve unemployment and congestion in Rome, he restored and settled some decaying Italian cities and founded some colonies abroad. He reduced the number of recipients of low-priced or free grain from 320,000 to 150,000. He enfranchised some Gauls who had been promised the vote twenty years earlier. He let some provinces collect their own revenues without the dubious help of Roman tax farmers. He forbade the rich to display their wealth ostentatiously. He abolished political clubs that had furnished mercenary gang fighters for his own and other parties.

This was not a reconstruction such as Augustus achieved some years later, but it was a beginning on several fronts. Romans, finally alerted to their danger, were more republican in spirit than they had been for years. They had paid for disunity repeatedly and knew at least part of its price. A basis for common action might have been developed during some years of civic quiet, particularly as Caesar was planning to leave the city to lead the legions against the Parthians, who had killed his friend Crassus in battle. However, instead of attempting to consolidate the old and new groups in a common and renewed front of that once impressive secular system called *Romanitas* that even Caesar could not break—and which he might not want to break—his opponents conspired against his life. They confused the symbols with the basis of power.

No Sicilian-type vendetta of revenge caused so many daggers to be thrust into Caesar's body on the Ides of March in the year 44 B.C. That plethora of dagger blows was a carefully devised form of self-insurance. No one man of the conspirators could later be charged with sole guilt for the killing or receive the sole credit. It was a way of making sure that all of them would suffer or go to glory together. They were quite unsure of which fate awaited them and were equally unprepared for either. What they had accomplished was to add to the misery of the Roman people the one additional civil war and massive retribution which those people could no longer endure while retaining any faith in self-government. This was close to the type of civil war which raged in Spain from 1937 through 1939 and which left all survivors too exhausted even to think of regaining their liberties for decades on end.

Only a few cheered the news of the assassination, Cicero among them. Mostly there was silence and waiting. Would a well-organized group, with funds, men, leaders, plans, take power as expected? There was no such group. Caesar had considered for five years how to take over power. His assassins had not planned for one day. Yet mere republicanism, like simple murder, clearly was not enough to save the republic. To the horror and surprise of all, the power of the imperial Roman Republic had been thrown into the streets to be fought over in still another hemorrhage of the remaining thin stream of blood. The conspirators were true Romans of the time in their fine neglect of consequences, their resort to easy expedients while evading all of Rome's basic problems.

Following the murder, Mark Antony apparently made no rousing speech to friends, Romans and countrymen. He had not yet decided which way the wind would blow. While the other consul had come out for the conspirators, Antony had been busy calling Caesarian veterans and friends into Rome. Though undecided what to do,[7] he did raise one short, explosive question in the Senate:

And then all of Caesar's acts will be void?

It was the most effectively disruptive speech he could have made. The Senate had been discussing whether or not to reward the conspirators as liberators. This naturally led to the question whether Caesar had been a tyrant. If so, his body would be thrown into the Tiber, his killers would be acclaimed and, as Mark Antony's question suggested, all his official acts would be voided. But then many appointments to the Senate and to administrative positions would lapse. The gift of a large estate to Brutus's mother would be lost. The *tabula rasa* would go back to the bloody and uncertain end of Pompey's day. Some rights granted to previously disfranchised citizens would be revoked, and the angry countrymen pouring into Rome would be confirmed in their old suspicions of the Senate. Civil war would start at once.

On the other hand, if Caesar was not declared to have been a tyrant, just where did that leave the conspirators? In this dilemma the always willing Cicero helped out. He wrote what he called an "amnesty," leaving in effect all of Caesar's acts and properly signed but still unknown decrees, but deploring the fate of Rome under Caesar. So once the import of Antony's question was understood, Caesar's body, instead of being thrown into the Tiber, would have a state funeral and pyre; and his will, leaving considerable sums to all the citizens of Rome, would become known to them all. So a peaceful acceptance of the act of the conspirators would not take place. So a civil war might start. Either way, that would be the result of the assassination. It might have been foreseen.

Faced with mobs eager to burn their homes and do worse, the conspirators slipped out of Rome. The civil war came promptly. Octavian, who was named Caesar's main heir, with Mark Antony, Caesar's old lieutenant, and another Caesarian leader, Lepidus, inaugurated proscriptions and killings on a scale unknown since Sulla's day. More than 2,500 patricians and businessmen apparently were killed, first victims of the conspirators' unpreparedness. Cicero, one of many old opponents left untouched by Caesar, was among the dead. The Caesarians accumulated funds by expropriation and fought against the conspirators. Civil war lasted almost three years. When it ended (42 B.C.), the nation had little strength or desire left to fight for the republican ideal.

Even that was not quite the end. The Caesarians fell out. After ten years of occasionally riotous peace, Mark Antony joined the Queen of Egypt, Cleopatra, mother of Caesar's son, to fight Octavian. The third civil war within seventeen years had begun. Octavian, using modern propaganda devices, demoralized Antony's troops with tales that he and his Egyptian siren would turn Rome into an Asian despotism, lower its moral and cultural standards, and undermine all that was noble in the Roman character. In a decisive naval battle, Cleopatra's ships were suddenly and strangely withdrawn from the line. After this action at Actium (31 B.C.), Octavian was free to rule Rome. He established himself as *princeps* (first citizen) and as *augustus* (revered one). The Romans seem to have accepted this submissively. They were no longer free to rule themselves, but some of them were still alive and hoped to stay so.

Augustus Caesar began his principate by teaching the patricians that their function was not to command but to serve. The lesson, spiced with more open contempt, continued under his successors. All the separated elements gradually were reminded of the old Roman concept of a *res publica* more important than individual or group interests. The principate and then the empire extended legal protection and civic rights to members of the commonwealth; while this did not involve much self-rule in many parts of the empire, it was considered an achievement for that age. The long-dishonored tradition of a Roman community revived briefly but without the right of self-government. Such an achievement would have depended on recreating the mutual trust of men of all classes, which they had destroyed by greed and violent partisanship. Until then, Romans would go on being governed instead of governing themselves. In setting up a dynasty to succeed himself after his long reign, Augustus opened no new doors to that missing element. Romans were aware of Aristotle's observation that only as an active and responsible member of a city or society could man develop his full potential, but having lost their best opportunity for such free individual development, they were unable to regain it under Augustus or succeeding emperors.

Augustus stopped the ruinous sequence of conquest, slaves and unemployment. He refused to start the war against Parthia (Persia) which Julius Caesar had planned. Doors of the temple of Janus swung shut, signifying peace in the realm. With peace came prosperity. Capture of Egyptian treasure after the war against Antony had reduced interest rates from twelve to four percent. As the empire became less parasitic and tyrannical, there were fewer colonial revolts. He forced the old patrician group into the service of the state and created a civil service out of the business class which had provided the tax collectors, lenders and speculators. They lost even the desire to resist. They accepted the respect which the *princeps* seemed to pay to the forms of the republic, after the reality of self-rule and popular participation had been drained out of those forms.

Augustus Caesar gave survivors of the republic a lesson in preventing further military seizures of civilian power. He broke the ties between soldiers, centurions and generals, and moved junior officers around so none depended for promotion on loyalty to any one general. He cut the money nexus between generals and soldiers by setting up a national fund to buy land for veterans' pensions; after contributing initially a large share from his own resources, he established a tax for it. He fixed sixteen years of active military service as the time required to earn a pension. He also set up the Praetorian Guard to protect the city government itself from direct attack—a more questionable policy. With these decisions carried out, he could then safely reduce the legions to about 150,000 men. He boasted that he had settled over 300,000 veterans on land at home and abroad. However, by taking over from the Senate the payment of the armies, he transferred their loyalty to the *princeps*.

What Augustus Caesar may be said to have proved at the time of his death in 14 A.D. was that, given a period of peace, order, able leadership and limitation on greed, many of the Roman difficulties could be resolved. If the republic had been able to achieve these conditions and thereby to have avoided the long civil wars, it also could have obtained similar results. What Augustus did not prove was that a monarchy was more effective than a republic in the long run. For the dynasty he bequeathed to Rome, within forty years, produced a Nero. In time that dynasty was to reproduce in detail all the corruption of spirit and intellect, all the intrigues and royal-family homicides previously more familiar to Asia than to Rome.

Once the Roman people had sacrificed their republic, and with it their power to shape their own destinies, their future was at the mercy of troops installing their own emperors and of other troops advancing rivals. Political power gravitated to those men who had the physical power to obtain it, who then paid themselves in money and honors for their success. The contests helped drain and ruin the Roman Empire. But it was the expansion of that empire in the face of successive population wanderings from the east and north which led to the cruel and authoritarian character of its latter centuries and its final disintegration. It encountered the credibility syndrome. Roman leaders felt that, if they did not defend at every corner of their widespread rule, their enemies would feel free to attack everywhere. Rome and its rule were dissipated in the effort to hold more than the empire's resources permitted.

This was no sudden process. Time moved more slowly in those days. Decay was at first hardly noticed as it grew. Some golden moments occasionally promised that all would turn for the better. Now and again something was done to make life tolerable for the subject people. Under the Emperor Hadrian (117–138), for example, municipal life flourished, local magnates contributed large sums to beautification, land banks advanced low-cost funds to farmers, banking profits were used to feed and school some children. Slave owners were no longer allowed to kill their slaves, indeed, the owner's ancient right to put all his household slaves to death if one of them committed a murder was revoked. Under Hadrian's successor a moment came when an owner who misused a slave was deprived of him, an ethical level not always reached by early nineteenth-century slavery in the United States. Hadrian even saw that Rome had to be strengthened internally rather than expanded further, and gave back some conquests in Asia to the native rulers. It was during his rule that the Roman legions, like modern American troops, were baffled by guerrilla warfare. The revolt of the Jews in 132 took that form. Before it was over, 580,000 deaths were counted, and the destruction of a thousand villages. The Jewish nation was dispersed. Yet in spite of such internal revolts, Rome was considered to have had a fairly stable rule in Hadrian's day over 60 million people and 1,600,000 square miles, enforced by an army of 300,000 men.

Plague and invasions came with the rule of his successor, Marcus Aurelius (161–180). Germanic tribes defeated an army of 20,000 and poured into northern Italy. The emperor took slaves into the army in desperation. Another northern tribe broke into Greece in 170. Rome managed to survive, but it was on the defensive. In the 50 years from 235–285 practically all of its rulers were chosen by one or another of its border armies, and twenty-five out of twenty-six died violent deaths. Those were days when rebel bands and brigands pillaged and terrorized the countryside, and the famous Roman peace fell apart at home. By 211 all the Italians in the Praetorian Guard, which had become a collection agency levying fees on incoming emperors, had been replaced by men from the rest of the empire. Generals began setting up reigns of their own, twice in England and Palmyra, once in Gaul. Pay to keep soldiers quiet became the first charge on the treasury. Even that did not insure their loyalty. They found a simple way to prevent themselves from being defeated when they were called upon to fight for an incumbent emperor. They assassinated him before any battle began. This happened twice. All this was dangerous sport, for frequently the borders were left unguarded.

People no longer could call a halt to their rulers. The Roman

Empire's final centuries reveal a great culture suffering from intolerable self-imposed pressures. Men were fleeing as best they could from the burdens which a beleaguered state imposed on them, and from the crimes of violence which the state could no longer prevent. Some joined the Germanic and Gothic groups within the Empire's borders, who offered them a less burdened and less perilous existence. Others fled to big estates where powerful men could give them protection in return for a surrender of civil rights. They were locked onto the land. Feudalism was to be the next historical step in the West. Men no longer sought to protect themselves against their neighbors by organizing into a state; they bought individual protection by their serfdom.

From the close of the third century under the imperial drill master Diocletian (284–305) onward, the vicious circle caused by depleted land and manpower grew tighter in the West. The eastern part of the Empire, by now under a separate Augustus, had no similar shortage of manpower reserves, but the fact that it did have a different government, plus the probable reluctance of the Eastern people to accept living conditions in the cold and sometimes treacherous climate of the west, and their strong sense of cultural superiority to the people of the west, may account for the disparity between the manpower shortage in the west and its absence in the east. The eastern part of the Empire was to endure long centuries beyond that of the west. In the eastern sector authoritarianism was also far more customary and acceptable to the people than it was in the west. That swallowing up of all parts of society by the state was not due to any authoritarian philosophy held by the later emperors or anyone else. It was a desperate last resort to squeeze the final drop of effort out of the people, to obtain and supply the troops needed to defend the borders and to maintain the tax collectors and administrators who followed each saved coin to its hiding place and each draft evader to his refuge. In addition the troops had to put down the normal quota of civil disorders and the new ones caused by persecution of Christians, who dissented from the orthodox theology of their own leaders.

When the Emperor Julian, the last anti-Christian ruler, was defeated and died in Persia in 363, the northern people saw their great chance. Picts and Scots fought Romans in Britain, the Alamanni crossed the Rhine, while the Goths, pressed by Huns in retreat from Asia, moved down the Danube. A fighting emperor, Valentinian (364–375) managed to restore the frontiers, but Rome remained in a state of desperate siege. The Goths destroyed a major Roman army at Adrianople in 378 and in 410 were able to sack Rome.

Strict measures imposed under Diocletian in the third century were tightened in the fourth. Soldiers' sons were required to become soldiers.

Able-bodied monks, who had once been exempted, were forced to serve in the army. Persons mutilating themselves to escape military service, instead of being consigned to dirty work with the troops, were now ordered burned alive. Landlords whose serfs mutilated themselves to escape service were to be punished. The lower classes, if found guilty of harboring a deserter, were sentenced to the mines, the upper classes to loss of half their property.

State control was fastened on workers' associations and on professional groups alike. Doctors, for example, were required to care for the poor who could not pay, and received state reimbursement. The teaching profession became a state-controlled caste. Heavy obligations were attached to all property and to all holders of public honors. The motto was "From each according to his capacity to pay." Then restrictions were placed on the transfer of property. Growing danger brought even harsher laws. By 380 liberty was promised to slaves for informing on deserters. Recruits were branded like convicts so that they could be found easily if they deserted. By 398 the branding had been extended to workers producing weapons. Heavy fines were also imposed for hiding tax delinquents. Meanwhile, an imperial edict forbade all discussion of the merits of anyone chosen by the emperor for his service. About such laws Charles Norris Cochrane remarked:

> It is a grim comment upon the process of *Romanitas* that the state which, according to Cicero, had originated for the protection of property rights, should finally have transformed it into the basis of a system of servitudes unparalleled in the annals of civilized man.[8]

But not even all these exactions levied against the population enabled the empire to provide adequate protection to its citizens from foreign or domestic foes. With the victory of the Goths in 378, the occupation of Gaul by Vandals and Alans in 406 and the sack of Rome in 410, the border controls were broken for quite a while, although efforts were still to be made to enforce them. The default of internal policing power by the state was recognized before the end of the fourth century by an authorization to all individuals to do the policing job themselves, to exterminate brigands wherever they could be found. As J. B. Bury has remarked, there was no fall of the Roman Empire in the west in 476, for no Empire was then left there to fall.

Possibly men wanted and needed more than Rome, with all its power, pomp and grandeur, could offer to them. The American historian Chester Starr expressed this belief when he wrote:

> The ideal of the world-state, the physical rewards it offered, and the extension of Graeco-Roman civilization based on its prosperity were inadequate for the great bulk of mankind. . . . The goals which that

state offered to its subjects were inadequate, and in that fact lay the turning point of ancient civilization.[9]

In the world of the late twentieth century, when the United States appeared to be moving toward the Roman role of world policeman, this suggestion that neither world organization nor material prosperity for the Roman people turned out to be adequate life-giving ideals for a *Pax Romana*, raises a question about the adequacy of American ideals for any similar task. The latter are different and higher. Awareness of the enriching force of personal liberty touches them; they contain a non-Roman sense of compassion; they incorporate self-rule as a means of protecting personal freedom. Yet these, too, may be inadequate for men. They do not yet include the concept of racially equal societies, nor that of societies in which men have some nobler function than the self-centered one of wealth accumulation. They have not adjusted themselves to a generally accepted level of antipathy toward the mechanical and depersonalized barbarity of modern warfare. The world view of them on a hundred thousand flickering screens throughout the crowded cities of the earth is that of an almost unbelievable display of luxury and license in the face of the grinding poverty which the viewers see around them, an absorption with sex and violence which sometimes speaks louder than declarations of faith and intent.

The Romans contributed one of the world's first lessons about the subversive influence of concentrated wealth. They also contributed one of the first about the effect of a calculated policy of exclusion on the fate of a great republic. They gave an early demonstration of the disaster it inflicted on the men who engineered it. They gave all the later world a reading in the irrevocability of a loss of self-government, in the fantastic and miserable consequences of one-man rule, and then dependence on rival army commanders for the choice of an executive. They taught the world about the dangers of overexpansion, the regimentation which is inflicted on a population when its rulers feel that they have to be ready to defend on every frontier in order to prove to threatening invaders that they will defend on each frontier which is menaced. This was their credibility gap and the nation, even enslaved, was not strong enough to support it. The old claim to be the guarantor of world peace was finally surrendered. Rome's pretensions to greatness had become absurd.

As Rome entered its days of disintegration, a number of Romans started to turn away from the ancient classical culture. They were seeking the joy and salvation which Christianity promised. The Christian Church was beginning to form a society which was to be in competition for men's loyalty with Rome, and with later kingdoms and empires.

CHAPTER 4

The Church's Great Temptation

 One of the most ignored turning points of history fell on that day in the early part of the fourth century when the operational research group of the early Christian Church approached the Roman Emperor Constantine with its report.

Its findings impressed him. The figures showed, through an accounting of all the hardships and defeats the Roman Empire was suffering, that the pagan religion was apparently a nonsuccess creed for Rome. On the scorecard, the Olympian gods, even rebaptized with Roman names, were indifferent, or absent on personal affairs, or willing to see Rome go under. The report showed that many more emperors who had persecuted Christians had lost battles, or died young, or had succumbed to disgusting illnesses than those farsighted emperors who had refused to persecute the Christians. God was evidently displeased with the pagan persecutors and was showing his resentment. Christianity might be more of a success religion for Rome than the old classical worship was. The emperor was, in effect, invited to give the Christian creed a pragmatic test. Either it would work for him and Rome, or it would not.

Constantine, a remarkably able but thoroughly un-Christlike person, was willing to test this hypothesis. Along his embattled road to power he ordered his soldiers to mark their shields with a Christian symbol (something like the "xp" which were the first letters of Christ's name in Greek). The next day his legions won a battle against great odds at the

65

Milvian Bridge in Rome (312). While this success was persuasive, it was not conclusive. However, by accident, one of his opponents, the persecuting Caesar of the eastern part of the Empire, Maximin Daia, was soon to test the hypothesis. His pagan priests, after ritual examination of chicken entrails, assured him of a victory against one of Constantine's supporters, in 313. This was not an unreasonable assurance, since he had 70,000 troops against his opponent's 30,000. However, Maximin Daia saw his troops melt away, and lost the battle. He expressed his wrath against the priests and the pagan gods in ringing language. He died in the same year of a miserable disease, a fact which rapidly became further proof of the validity of the data and conclusion presented to Constantine. Here were three accidents in a row. Either battle might have gone the other way and Daia might have survived. Then the Roman Empire in the west might have staggered from authoritarian oppression into feudalism without influencing the Christian Church profoundly. Constantine might have stopped with the toleration of the new religion which was decreed in 313, and the Church might then have never been tempted to take on the characteristics of an empire.

Constantine apparently saw the primitive Christian Church, with its high sense of morality, its austerity, its elaborate organization of welfare activity throughout the Empire, as a source of strength and faith to the state. He went far beyond toleration of the new religion toward making it the state's favorite church. He heaped the Christian clergy with privileges and tax exemptions. He gave them dignities and free transportation to their church conferences, then called "synods." As a matter of course, since everything in the Empire had been made a part of the state organism, he took control of the appointment of bishops and, to some extent, of the formulation of Church doctrine. No one blocked his way. The Christian leaders very naturally hailed the end of the persecutions and became less critical of the Empire.

While Constantine's act was a radical one, since the classical culture had never favored any state church before, or any divinity similar to Christ, the acceptance of their altered status by the bishops of the day and their congregations was also a radical choice among alternative courses. The Christian Gospels had reported that Jesus had been led up to a high mountain by the tempter, been shown and offered worldly power, and had refused it. The Church leaders of the early fourth century did not refuse it. In the east they were grateful for the ending of the persecutions. Surely they foresaw a magnificent opportunity to further the Gospel from their new vantage point.

It was not long, however, before some of them became aware of the danger of having the Emperor mix into Church administration and doctrine. They asked loudly what the Emperor had to do with the

Church, and the Church with the Emperor. This grumbling rose to the point of armed opposition when those Church leaders who were close to the court made the decision, or acquiesced in it, to have the Roman legions punish and kill those people who had slightly different ideas from their own about Church doctrine. They agreed with Lactantius, "In freedom alone religion has its fortress." Faith could not be imposed by force.

This particular decision to accept the use of the armies to destroy the believers who held dissenting views was historic. It marked off the days of individual persuasion and conversion from the centuries of coercion of belief to the new faith which lay ahead. It is only by looking backward across time from the vantage point of our era when this practice had become unacceptable and nonproductive that men can see any comparison with the year 33 A.D. Once an earlier church hierarchy had accused a young man of preaching a new religious belief differing from the old one and had asked the Roman officials to kill him as an enemy of the state. This was done and became known as the crucifixion of Christ. Now the process was not only being repeated, but was becoming regularized, a standard operating procedure to be used against all nonconforming Christians.

This decision was strange because Constantine himself was aware of the troubles to the Empire which could be expected to result. While he had been Caesar and then Emperor in the western part of the Empire, he had tried using troops against Christian dissenters simply to maintain order. During an earlier persecution, some of the Christian clergy had obeyed the Roman command to turn over their religious books to the Roman officials. Later, Bishop Donatus in Egypt led a group which refused to allow these weak-kneed brethren to resume their Church offices. The legions Constantine sent in to punish the Donatists met with the fury of the Bishop's Egyptian supporters, including monks who rushed into battle with their stout staffs, praising the Lord. In 320, Constantine had second thoughts about punishing religious dissent by using the imperial troops. He granted the Donatists liberty of conscience. He declared that their differences with other Christians should be left to decision later by God. This wisdom, briefly achieved, was soon forgotten. Much of his later reign as emperor was devoted to the use of imperial force against dissenting Christian groups.

The vice of such a practice for the Empire soon became clear. Any rebels against the momentarily dominant Church group, either in doctrine or administration, automatically became rebels against the Empire, which supported that group. In turn, any political rebels against the Empire found themselves forced to become enemies of the Church, which supported that Empire.

Upon Constantine's death even the dominant Church group, which formulated and secured the approval of the Nicaean Creed in 325, was to experience persecution at the hands of the Empire. The Christian doctrine had been somewhat reformulated in the centuries intervening after the death of Christ, to meet the needs of Greek logic. The Nicaean Creed formalized the concept of a Trinity of Father, Son and Holy Spirit, which had not been mentioned by Christ or St. Paul, but which seemed to meet the new requirements. This was not accepted without hesitation and conflict. A certain Bishop Arius insisted on stressing the human character of Christ quite as much as, or even more than, the divine character. His leaning was toward monotheism pure and simple. His supporters, called "Arians," were persecuted by Constantine, although the Emperor later received his deathbed baptism from an Arian bishop. The legions were called upon to break up the Arian congregations, which were strong in the east. When one of the old Emperor's sons, Constantius, took his place, he turned the tables on the dominant orthodox Church leaders. He supported the Arians and banished the chief advocate of the Nicaean Creed, Athanasius. Not only did Constantius show that persecutions could be turned against the holy as well as the unholy, but he made it quite clear to all the Church leaders that the Emperor was in control of everything the Church did or thought. His statement in writing to one Church synod was "My will must be considered binding."

So the Church leaders had before them a fairly clear picture of what imperial control of their Church meant by the time the last pagan emperor, Julian, came to power in 361. He decreed toleration, but it was coupled with an active attempt to create what had never existed before, a pagan church to offset the Christian Church. This was marked by a close supervision of teaching in the schools and by propaganda defaming the Christians. However, the Christian Church leaders were no longer content with toleration. They had experienced power and privileges, one of them the right to run tax-exempt businesses, another the exemption of clergy from military duty. As soon as Julian died, in a losing battle in Asia in 363, they rushed back to participation in the affairs of state. Julian's pagan interlude had even brought their factions a little closer together. His defeat and early death were further proof of the success of the Christian religion, or at least of the nonsuccess of its opponents. The dual regime of Valentinian and Valens (364–378) saw a heroic effort to defend the invaded empire, but also an imperial awareness that Constantine's dream of a newly invigorated Roman rule had not become a reality. A brief return to a policy of toleration took place. Some of the special benefits of clergy were withdrawn.

The Empire in the west was still further along the road of losing control when Theodosius became emperor in 379, and sole ruler of both parts in 392. A military disaster at Adrianopolis had just taken place (378). Everyone was suffering new and heavy burdens. Men were being nailed to their habitations and tasks. Troops were being branded to prevent desertion. Yet this emperor chose this moment to enunciate new privileges for the Christian clergy and to give them immunity from trial in the ordinary courts. Riotous anticlerical protests were suppressed. More significantly, as early as 380 he declared that all people within the Empire must accept Catholicism as the state religion,

> adjudging all others madmen and ordering them to be designated as heretics . . . condemned as such, in the first instance, to suffer dire punishment, and therewith, the vengeance of that power which we, by celestial authority, have assumed.[1]

Just how he had acquired this celestial authority was not stated, but with this proclamation the wheel had turned full circle and a little farther. Nero had assumed that Christians had no right to live. A little more than 300 years later, Theodosius asserted that only Christians had a right to live, and only those among them who adhered to the dominant dogma. But something far more important was incorporated in his decree of 380. The old reason for the existence of the Empire was disappearing. It could obviously no longer protect life or property, maintain law or keep order. It needed a new justification for its existence. Theodosius thought that he might find one in the protection of the Christian Church. It was not adequate. The people did not rally to it. Nothing could have saved the Empire at that time. However, it provided the adolescent clerical institution with a heady, exciting concept of itself and of the state as its devoted servant, owing obedience to the Church. Bishop Ambrose of Milan even forced this Emperor to do public penance for the slaughter of people who had risen in revolt. That acceptance of superiority to the secular powers of the world survived the disappearance of Rome by many centuries.

Where would this early experience of the Church with the state lead? What would mastery by the Church of the state or its submission to the state do to alter the ideology which gave the Church its justification for existence? That originally magnificent creed of mercy and brotherly love, incorporated into an institution, was to affect life more profoundly than any other force for more than a thousand years. Even today, in the late twentieth century, we are all inheritors of the amazing and frustrating experiments of the church in exercising moral and political power, and in confusing the two. The moral Munich of the Christian churches in the late 1930s and early 1940s within and outside of Germany was only one part of that long legacy. We are members of states which, a long time ago, escaped the necessity for submitting their acts to the judgment of a universal religious ethic. We are subject to a competition among them in which each state makes its own moral code, and almost everyone considers this to be the normal situation. The crusading days of the Church in the medieval centuries moved us all a little farther along toward that anarchic result.

The fatal susceptibility of holy crusades to the bacteria of perversity and perversion has been duly noted by historians, and that bit of knowledge may be one of the rare tranquilizers of modern times. The tendency of crusades to be corrupted by the means utilized in search of a noble end and to disintegrate into disillusion because of the conflicting interests of participants, are key elements in this susceptibility.

The crusades to the Holy Land in the eleventh and twelfth centuries offer some wisdom to twentieth-century societies—wisdom that may be useful to Presidential advisers who turn over the use of American troops to distant allies who do not share the same interests or have the same confidence in democracy. The crusades may interest those who are troubled by the moral choice between eliminating and coexisting with men of conflicting ideological beliefs. They may even concern those who have watched the efforts of the Israelis to follow the crusaders in establishing a Western beachhead on the eastern shores of the Mediterranean. It may dismay those who heard an Irish-American Cardinal attempt to turn the Vietnam war into a crusade and then recall how the crusades to the Holy Land degenerated into holy wars against other Christian sects and finally against good, conforming Catholics, whose interests happened to diverge from those of the managers of those crusades.

The neglect of President Woodrow Wilson of the United States (1913–1921) to obtain in advance of American entry into the First World War an agreement from his prospective allies on the purposes of that war and the nature of the peace, and his subsequent neglect to obtain advance agreement of key Senate Republicans to his own peace proposals, led to disillusion and isolationism in the United States. Worse, it was partly responsible for disaster in Europe, fascism and an even greater world war. The pattern he followed was laid out in detail before the crusades to the Holy Land began, which also ended in a major Western defeat and disappointment.

Pope Urban II had four main purposes in mind when he summoned the nobility of France to liberate the Holy Lands from Moslem invaders, in 1095. That area in Syria was to be recovered from the Moslems, but was then to be placed under the rule of the Church in Rome. In return for military support given to the Emperor in Constantinople, the Greek Orthodox Church in the Eastern Empire was to return to the fold of Rome. The march of Islam was to be halted. The threat that the Normans in Sicily would encroach on the Church's principalities in central Italy was to be diverted.

Conspicuously missing here was an agreement, sworn, sealed and signed by all the major participants in the proposed effort. The restless and land-hungry nobility of Europe, including the Normans, were to be the agents of conquest. Would they be satisfied with the Pope's purposes, or would they demand dukedoms and principalities after their victories? And would the ruler of the Eastern Empire (also called the Byzantine or Greek Empire) grant these, or refuse them? And if he refused, what then? And what approval by the Patriarch and other leaders of the Greek Orthodox Church had been obtained to insure that that separate body would now become obedient to Rome? Only forty-one years before, in 1054, the two sects had interchanged the most scarifying anathemas. And who would arbitrate differences? Indeed, who would insure that the Church in Rome would actually obtain secular rule over Jerusalem for itself, a desired demonstration of the superiority of the Church over secular kings? So much was left unsettled that an unusual amount of divine favor had to be assumed.

Not much excuse can be found for the Pope's failure to make sure in advance that the Church's objectives were shared, first by the European nobility, and second by the Greek Emperor, and third by the Patriarch of the Greek Orthodox Church. Only eleven years earlier one of the greatest popes, Hildebrandt, who had taken the title Gregory VII, had received a punishing lesson in the harm which could be done to the Church by allies who had somewhat different purposes from his own. The episode, which should have been a traumatic one, arose out of the famous humiliation of Henry IV, ruler of the Holy Roman Empire, at Canossa in 1076. To avenge that disgrace, the Emperor rushed into Rome eight years later, in 1084, captured most of the city and tried to impose a pope of his own choosing. Gregory VII, besieged in the Castel' Angelo, called on the Normans in southern Italy to save him. In their own fashion they did, but they ruined him in the process. They took the city, but they brought with them an overstarved desire for loot. They gave Rome a thorough sacking, outdoing the Goths and the Vandals. The end product of their help to Gregory VII was that every man and woman still alive in Rome hated the pope who had called in the Normans. He could no longer live or rule there. He had to flee with the overeager helpers to the south, and died in Salerno a year later. He had made no advance agreement with them about what they were to do and what they had better leave undone. Pope Urban II, only eleven years later, failed to remember this event.

The first conflict of interest in the crusades came promptly, when the Emperor Alexius I, heir to the surviving remnant of the ancient Roman Empire, found 30,000 armed Franks in Constantinople, demanding a *quid pro quo* for services about to be rendered. They not only wanted him to make good his vague promises of troops, guides, money and food, they wanted the right to keep any lands they conquered from Turks or Arabs. Alexius hesitated. Many of the crusading nobles who faced him were rapacious, land-eating Normans who had taken England and Sicily in that century, and had even been fighting his own troops and ships in the Aegean, close to his home. He demanded that they swear feudal fealty to him, holding conquered lands only under his superior rule. In turn, the crusaders hesitated, faced with an awkward choice between refusing to do God's will at all, or getting inadequate payment for it. They finally swore the oath, but with tongue in cheek, intending to hold the Emperor to every single promise of aid and to use any default to justify their later disobedience. The oath endured three hundred miles.

Probably Jerusalem could have been captured by the crusaders very quickly. An unusually propitious situation existed. The ruler of Damascus and the ruler of Egypt were at odds and would not join to defend the Holy Land. But the crusade, after capturing Turk-held Nicaea, where the Christian creed had been drafted in the fourth century, moved on toward Antioch, grumbling because the Emperor had spared the inhabitants of Nicaea and had taken possession in his own name. Only a little plunder had been available. The crusade halted at Antioch, and its leaders decided that the Emperor had defaulted on his pledges and that the land was theirs for the taking. Almost two years passed before they felt obliged to move on toward Jerusalem. They settled down to besiege Antioch, and some of the more ambitious of them took their followings to other parts of Syria and the east to carve out principalities for themselves. Europe, where each fertile acre was held by other good Christian nobles, offered no equal opportunity for fame, prestige and power.

Lack of agreement, even among this one sector of the allies, prolonged the siege of Antioch for more than a year. Bohemund, the tall, powerfully built Norman leader, had made a secret arrangement with one of the Moslem leaders in the city to surrender several towers of the walled town to him. But Bohemund needed an agreement from the other leaders from different parts of France that he, not they, was to control Antioch after it was captured. They refused. They wanted their measure of honor and wealth from their exertions, too. Only when a Turkish army appeared on the horizon were the towers surrendered and the city taken. Then the victors were besieged and began to starve and fall ill. Fortunately for them, they believed in miracles. An astute cleric in the train of the Provençal Raymond of Toulouse was granted a vision. He dreamed that the holy lance, which had been thrust into Christ's side while he was on the cross, was located right there in Antioch, in a crypt. Frantic digging did not find it, but the young cleric jumped into the pit and came up with the lance head. Blessed by that evidence of divine favor, the crusaders charged out from the walls, seeing holy horsemen in the skies cheering them on, and defeated the surprised Turkish besiegers. It was a great victory, a vast turnabout of fortune, and Raymond immediately laid claims to some rights in Antioch, since one of his men had found the holy lance head. But while everybody was willing to believe in miracles, they were not all willing to believe in all miracles. The Normans cynically demanded that the cleric's truth be tested by the customary means, which was ordeal by fire. Unfortunately for Raymond, the young cleric died from burning, and the suspicion of fraud was hard to dispel. Antioch had now demonstrated a breaking of the feudal oath, dealing with infidels and skepticism, none of which was approved Christian practice in that day.

Only 13,000 men appeared before Jerusalem in 1099, out of the 30,000 who had mustered at Constantinople. The capture of that city by the Westerners was a bloody occasion on which a great number of civilian inhabitants were killed after the fighting was over. The crusaders thanked their God after killing the civilians for His help in allowing them to do this good deed. The event of the capture was great news to the Western world. Bells pealed in triumph all over Europe. It had been proved, as a thousand pulpits proclaimed, that God's Christian Church knew and expressed God's will.

The day was, however, also important in a reverse sense to the people of those two religions whose members were slaughtered so abundantly after the capture. The Moslems had experienced a few atrocities by some of their own leaders, but not as a matter of course or of principle, and only after a prolonged siege. They had developed a practice of allowing even captured warriors to ransom themselves or be sold into slavery. To Christians and Jews they usually gave three choices: conversion to Islam, death or taxes. They preferred to have them make the third choice. They did not expect the indiscriminate slaughter of men and women by the Christians, were horrified, and remembered it years later when a *jihad*, a holy war of sorts, was preached before Saladin recaptured the city in 1187. The crusaders and priests did not draw any distinction between Jews and Moslems. They slaughtered them alike, as infidels.

In the Middle Ages war was not total, but quite personal and usually hand-to-hand. Nationalism was not yet a religion. The treatment accorded to civilians in a captured city portrayed the character of the capturers, mirrored their culture and invited comparisons. For men who intended to stay in the conquered area, this effect was important. The massacre in Jerusalem, although equaled in other years by some of the more barbarous Moslem officers, affected the capacity of the Westerners to gain the loyalty of the conquered people. The crusaders were not yet aware that they were bringing a combatative ideology into an area where the ideological fervor of Islam had long since died out. In that situation the crusaders' governments might have been judged to be acceptable by a showing of good character and deeds, including tolerance, while their religious differences could have been ignored as an excusable eccentricity of strangers.

The explosive problem of coexisting with men of different beliefs, raised by the massacre of civilians at Jerusalem, has never been solved to everyone's complete satisfaction. The difficulties of sharing a life on earth with men of opposite values are considerable, even in modern days. In Western Europe in medieval years, the minds of the crusaders had been filled to the brim with antagonism for infidels who thwarted God's will and deserved extermination as a consequence. But after they arrived in Syria and took up landholdings, they found that they had to deal and live with those very infidels. They needed the local Moslem peasants for labor. They needed the neighboring Moslem emirs, viziers and governors as allies against more aggressive infidel rulers. Understandings and alliances developed. Certain virtues were found in the Arabic way of life, its chivalry and grace. Their physicians were so superior to those of the Franks that a badly wounded crusader knew that capture gave him his only chance for survival. The settled Franks moved into Moorish homes, wore flowing silk robes, decorated their women in Oriental fashions, joined the noble Arabs on hunting expeditions. While all this seemed natural and even excellent to them, it aroused the suspicions of new crusaders coming in from Europe. They found that the Franks of Syria were coexisting instead of slaughtering the infidels as crusaders were supposed to do. The newcomers considered the early comers to be soft on Islam, in the modern idiom, and were bewildered and frustrated by their discovery.

Dissension on the subject came to a head at the time of the Second Crusade (1147-1149). This had been called to revenge the Turkish capture of one of the crusaders' eastern outposts, Edessa, in 1144. Great kings joined it, Louis VII of France and Conrad II of the Germanies, while some towns in France were emptied of all able-bodied men, in order to avenge the reported slaughter of many Christians. On their way the two kings, joined by Baldwin III, then King of Jerusalem, yielded to the seductive notion of capturing the city of Damascus. This was an important Turkish governmental center, about 135 miles to the northeast of Jerusalem. A capture of this ancient and famous place would mark the royal leaders with infinite glory. They arrived safely at the walls of the city and sat down to besiege it. A number of important old Syria settlers, who had by this time been in the area for over a generation, had advised against the attack. Indeed the story was current among the troops that Louis VII had insisted on it only because he resented the conspicuous friendship of his wife, Eleanor of Aquitaine, and her uncle, one of the local Franks who had strongly opposed the Damascus adventure. In addition, the local barons wanted one of their number to become Lord of Damascus, if it were captured, while the two kings had chosen an outsider, the Count of Flanders. Why should the local Franks fight to help an outsider? At Damascus the Moslem emir and still other Franks persuaded the leaders of this Second Crusade that this siege was a very bad idea indeed. Horrified at such local opposition to their royal wills and such friendly dealings with some of the infidel enemy, the two kings broke off the siege after four days, and returned to Europe in disgust, without glory. An unhappy feeling that a cause was being betrayed by its own advocates was carried back to the West with them. After this, crusades would be harder than ever to organize.

The local Franks had used a strong argument. It was that the success of the First Crusade, while, of course, an act of God, also had a certain fortuitous character. It came at a time when the two great Moslem rulers in the area, one in Damascus, one in Egypt, had been at odds. They had not united to prevent the capture of Jerusalem. They hated one another more than they hated the invaders. That separation between the two neighboring Moslem rulers had to be maintained if any Christian-held Syria was to survive. A successful attack on Damascus would eliminate its ruler as a pacifying force. The new leader of Egypt, Nureddin (the Light of the Faith), would be able to replace the ruler of Damascus, and the Frankish holdings throughout Syria would be lost. Strategy and ideology had come into conflict and strategy had won. Then Nureddin did capture Damascus from his rival in 1154 and the fear was proved valid.

Jerusalem was recaptured by Islam in 1187. Saladin marked its siege by a vow to do unto others as they had done to his people, to massacre the Christians of the city as they had killed the Moslems when they took it. This met a counter threat by its defenders that they would kill all women and children (including the Christians among them) and all five thousand coexisting Moslems in the city, to destroy all wealth and booty, and to come out fighting to the death. A ransoming procedure was adopted as a compromise, and only some 10,000 or so poor people were sold into slavery. Those enslaved were annoyed that the Patriarch had decided to take the Holy Sepulcher funds to Europe with him instead of using them for ransoming money. He was surely under instruction not to give away the property of God, but he may have lost many thousands of souls to Islam by his act.

The effort to recover Jerusalem in the Third Crusade was taken over from the Church by the rulers of France, Germany and England. A "Saladin tax" was levied, perhaps the first nationwide form of levy in medieval Europe. Propaganda paintings showed infidel horses desecrating the Holy Sepulcher. The Christian clergy of Europe, somewhat overcome by the disaster of Jerusalem's fall, which seemed to cast doubt upon their direct communication with the divine will, turned to the practice of their Hebrew predecessors in times of adversity. They proclaimed that Jerusalem had been lost because the people were sinful and God was angry with them; spiritual reform was required.

The search for a whipping boy to be punished for the failure of all the crusades subsequent to the First and most successful one, began promptly with the Second, continued during and after the Third, and burst out into a furious attack on Constantinople in the Fourth. Some villainy had to be discovered, because God had been made the champion of the crusades, and the apparent withdrawal of His support could have unfavorable repercussions on all involved. The villain chosen for punishment was the Greek Empire.

An attempt was even made to blame the surrender of Jerusalem on that Empire. This was unjustified. No treason had helped Saladin conquer it. The guardians of the city had allowed themselves to be trapped into a long march in heavy armor through the desert in the day's heat before they came back and found the enemy, but that was not the fault of Constantinople. The normal, recalcitrant subdivisions within the city had not been created or intensified by the Empire. The commercial representatives of Venice and Genoa, with their own quarters and rights, the two major and feuding military orders, Templars and Hospitalers, the clergy and the king, all fought against the enemy at the end. The basic fault lay in trying to hold a few enclaves along a narrow coast with too few men and in the incessant peacetime quarrels among all the lords, commercial interests and military orders. With the arrival on the scene of an organizing genius, Saladin, the power of Egypt and Damascus, which Nureddin had already combined, was thrust against an inadequate force in Jerusalem. Only a low-temperature *jihad* needed to be preached, and part of it centered around the depredations of one wayward Christian feudal lord who had begun robbing Moslem pilgrims to Mecca, a religious outrage which the King of Jerusalem told Saladin he was incapable of punishing. The recapture of Jerusalem was retribution for anarchy rather than for ideology.

The Third Crusade, intended to rescue Jerusalem, was not quite such a complete failure as the one preceding it. The Crusaders' fortress at Acre was recaptured, but nothing else. Frederick Barbarossa, the Holy Roman Emperor, perished in a mountain stream and was to enter the world of German myth. Before his death he had experienced enough irritations at the hand of the Greek Emperor and was sufficiently horrified by a quiet pact that Emperor had made with Saladin, giving the Church positions in the Holy Land to the Greek Orthodox clergy, to call for an attack on Constantinople. Philip Augustus of France and Richard the Lionhearted of England quarreled, as men will do when their cause fails. Richard stayed in the Holy Land for some years, defeating Saladin on one occasion and negotiating a truce. He was even willing to give his sister in marriage to Saladin or to Saladin's brother in order to regain Jerusalem, a generosity which neither his sister nor Saladin reciprocated. On his way back to England, this great crusading hero was captured and held for ransom by the Duke of Austria, not an infidel but a fellow Christian. Both his brother John of England and his crusading colleague Philip Augustus of France were believed to have offered the kidnapper large sums of money, not to ransom him, but to hold him captive for a prolonged period so that they could go about their own quests for power without his interference.

Two things came out of this particular crusading effort. One was a decision to head for Egypt the next time. Conquest of that area seemed essential to control of the Holy Land. The other was a build-up of resentment against the Greek Empire's rulers. This stemmed basically from the original lack of agreement between the Eastern Empire and the Western forces, including the papacy, about the purpose of the crusades. The Greeks thought that the crusaders were to help the Greek Empire withstand Turkish assaults. The Westerners had five different purposes (adding the acquisition of land and feudal power to the four goals of Pope Urban) and only one of them coincided with the Greek purpose. Others conflicted with it.

Now the little annoyances which the crusaders had suffered from the Greeks built up into major enmities. The Church leaders, along with their original hopes of saving the Greek Empire from the Turks and uniting with the Orthodox Church, were pushed even further aside. Language difficulties intervened. Both crusaders and churchmen were slow to understand that propinquity could be the enemy of extremism. The attitudes of a people which have to live next to powerful neighbors are likely to be less intransigent than the views of people from distant lands. The Westerners had not learned to make allowance for this basic fact of international life.

Various sins of omission and commission were charged up against the allied but alien Greeks. Those people had irritated the lords of the First

Crusade by their demand of the oath of vassalage. They had neglected to send troops to aid in the siege of Antioch. They had refused to give the Westerners the secret of the napalm bomb of that day, the "Greek fire" which they had developed and which the Moslems had been able to discover. (These were balls containing a petroleum substance, hurled by a mechanical slingshot, and followed by fireballs which ignited the scattered petroleum. They were extremely effective against ships and siege towers.) A suspicion circulated among the crusading troops that the Greeks had directed both the poor men's crusade and a later one of nobles, intended to rescue captured Bohemund, directly into Turkish ambush. A Greek truce signed with the northern Turks in effect allowed the latter a free hand to attack Antioch. The men under Louis VII in the Second Crusade told stories of a charge against Turkish forces across a bridge, which ended with the Greeks opening the gates of a town to fleeing Turks. They told of a detachment of simple foot soldiers left behind by their nobles, men so frightened of being sold into slavery by the Greeks that they moved on their own, without leadership, across the desert and perished at the hands of the Turks. Louis VII himself was angered when his ships, returning to Europe, ran into a sea battle between Greek and Sicilian fleets, and the ship carrying Queen Eleanor was captured by the Greeks. Of course, the two great Arab leaders, Nureddin and later Saladin, saw their opportunity to divide the Western Christians from the Eastern Empire and had fun doing so. All vassals of the Greek Emperor were treated with a generosity which aroused the independent Franks to fury against the Greeks.

The Greeks, like the Frankish settlers in the Holy Land, were vulnerable to the accusation of having constant dealings with the infidel. They lived dangerously, with Moslem Turks all around them, pressing in on them. The Empire had never had any strong ideological urges to convert or exterminate Moslems. It survived by fighting invasion when that promised the greatest gains, by paying rewards to local Turkish rulers for keeping the peace when that was less costly. It had spent its ideological impulses on hounding Christian heretics, who were abundant in the area and who sometimes welcomed the invading Moslems with open arms as their liberators from an intolerable tyranny of mind. It was this Empire which passed on to Russia its tradition of Church subservience to the state, its sleeping-partner arrangement, which later assured Russian Czarist tyranny against criticism from the clergy on Christian grounds. Its most conspicuous virtue was its capacity for survival. For long years this Empire drew little appreciation from Western historians, who disliked its "religious politics and political religion." Described by the French historian Taine as "a gigantic moldiness lasting a thousand years" and reported in the West as a flowering of Levantine intrigue, a mixture of sadistic monarchs, contriving empresses, eunuch managers, mobs and ambitious priests, Gibbon, for one, wrote of it scathingly:

> But the subjects of the Byzantine empire, who assume and dishonor the names of both Greeks and Romans, present a dead uniformity of abject vices, which are neither softened by the weaknesses of humanity nor animated by the vigor of memorable crimes.[2]

The Greeks, in turn, had some solid reason to suspect Romans bearing gifts. They had learned after the Second Crusade that the Norman Roger II of Sicily had proposed an all-Western attack on Constantinople, which he chose to blame for the failure of the Second Crusade, and had received the approval of Louis VII of France and St. Bernard, who had preached that crusade. The Greeks had suffered a Norman devastation of Thessaly in 1157 and a Norman capture of Durazzo in 1185. They had been forced to get Turkish troops to help them defeat the Normans at that time. Their island of Cyprus had been captured by the Prince of Antioch. They had some cause for taking the crusades with salt and vinegar. Toward the end of the twelfth century they allowed their accumulated resentment toward these encroachments to be directed against Venice, whose fleet had been aiding the Normans in the Aegean, and canceled several of the considerable concessions for trade in the Greek Empire which that maritime city had enjoyed. This bit of petulance was to become the occasion of their undoing.

Crusades were harder to finance as doubts grew, time went on and failure seemed more certain. The Venetians, clever and ambitious people whose prosperity had increased with the crusades, used this shortage of crusader cash to gain control of the Fourth Crusade. They had two interests of their own, not included among the general interests of the papacy or the Western feudal lords or the Eastern Empire. One was to regain their predominant position in the trade with the Empire, to renew the canceled concessions. Another was to prevent their huge warehouses and trading establishments in Egypt from suffering in case the next crusade, headed toward a war with Egypt, actually got there. Their subversion of it was adroit in an almost perfect Levantine sense. They never argued their causes. Provide ships for the new Crusade? Of course. It would only cost half the crusaders' conquests and 85,000 marks. The crusaders' leaders accepted, went to Venice, found themselves without enough cash, asked for credit at the banks, were refused and then sat down to think about their money problem. The troops were eating up the sums they still had. Happily, some Venetians suggested a way out. There was, of course, no intention of diverting the crusade from Egypt, but the cash down payment would be reduced if the crusaders could be persuaded to subdue Zara, a port on the Adriatic Sea which had been causing Venice some trouble, on the way to Egypt. This was awkward because Zara was a good Christian community. The Pope would not like an attack on it. On the other hand, God's work could not be completely frustrated. The crusade had to get underway. Everyone who had come this far would be mocked if he went home without striking a blow against the infidel. A few impractical, idealistic crusaders broke off and went by themselves to the Holy Land. The bulk of them, however, went on to capture Christian Zara. The Pope interdicted the crusade at that point. At Zara, the same money problem came up again. The Venetians wanted the remainder of their cash payment, now a lesser amount, before they sailed the men to Egypt.

By another happy circumstance, just as the crusade was disintegrating, the son of an emperor deposed by a palace revolt arrived in Zara. This man, Alexius, asked the crusaders to help restore his father, Isaac Angelus, to his rightful throne. He promised to pay all the costs, and to give principalities and bounties to all who helped in this worthy task. The Venetians chimed in that they would supply not only ships but fighting men for such an effort.

The Fourth Crusade never got to Egypt, much less to the Holy Land after conquering Egypt. It did reach Constantinople. Isaac Angelus was restored to his throne. But Alexius was unable to pay off his glittering promises; transfer of lands from native subrulers to the Franks would have caused his father to be deposed again. These crusaders interpreted this as Levantine betrayal, as their predecessors had done. All the smoldering antagonisms between Latins and Greeks flared up again. In 1204, with the aid of the Venetians, the crusade sacked Constantinople. The Latin Empire of the East was then founded, with a king from Flanders and a religious patriarch from Venice. This conquest was to last fifty-seven years.

For a moment there was hope that, out of this amazing diversion of effort and perversion of purpose, the long-divided Christian Church might be brought together. The Pope blessed the conquest. But the local Greek hierarchy's objection to domination by Rome was too strong for Church unity. Not even victory could force ideological or managerial cohesion. The old Eastern Empire under its new name did not strengthen Western efforts to recapture the Holy Land. Instead, it drained off the supply of young Europeans who might otherwise have gone to free Jerusalem. Meanwhile, Venice was accused of misleading and maneuvering the Fourth Crusade away from Egypt in return for vast concessions and sums from that nation. While the Venetians argued that their rich concessions came after rather than before the event, the rest of Europe was now skeptical about this claim and many other things as well.

Much later, in 1228, men were amused and bemused by the eccentric adventure of the Hohenstaufen Emperor, Frederic II, a premature skeptic with Saracen troops and a harem. He delayed so long in fulfilling the crusading oath which had obtained the Pope's approval of his emperorship that his crusade was interdicted. In spite of this he succeeded, finding the same division between Damascus and Cairo that had made the First Crusade successful. Without killing any Moslems, he obtained a truce in 1228 which restored Jerusalem and other cities to the Christians. The Church disapproved so thoroughly of him and all he did that he had to crown himself King of Jerusalem. However, the people he left behind in the Holy Land did not understand that their continued occupation of Syria depended on continued neutrality between the two opposing Arab forces. They chose sides, picked the wrong partner and lost Jerusalem again, in 1244. It was not to be reconquered by Western arms until the First World War, in the twentieth century. Several other crusades were attempted and failed. The great fortress at Acre finally fell in 1291, and the Western encounter with the East was over until a while later, when the Turks moved to the Danube and threatened Budapest and Vienna.

When the Western encounter with the Middle East was resumed in modern times, it carried the additional handicap of Arab resentment at arrogant Western superiority, the "anything you can do, I can do better" view of a culture which had placed fatalism above human striving.

One of the most permanent legacies of the crusades to modern times grew accidentally out of the wealth in land which had accrued to the Church from gifts during the crusading years. This was a rule demanding celibacy of Roman Catholic priests. Even in 1967, when Pope Paul VI again insisted on the eternal sanctity of this custom, he seemed unaware of the manner in which it had been fastened onto the heritage of the Church. The idea had indeed been suggested in centuries long before the crusades, although neither the Apostles nor the early Church fathers accepted it for themselves. By the ninth century it was rather completely ignored, in spite of occasional admonitions from Rome. However, when the Church became the guardian of land for the crusaders away in the Holy Land, and the inheritor of vast acreages passed on to it by widows, the problem of priests endeavoring to provide for their children out of such gifts became an important one for the Church treasury at Rome. Little policing of remote parishes existed in those days, and priests and bishops followed the lay custom of seeking to hand on property to their children. In many cases they were not only Church lords but lay lords at the same time. The line between Church property and that of the clerics tended to fade into abstraction. The Church in that day thought it had an alternative between policing the land-ownership situation all over Europe, and forbidding the clergy to marry and have families.[3] So celibacy, a burden greater than many deeply religious men could bear, came back into practice and was in due time even enforced. Challenges to the practice and its by-product of occasional sinfulness were issued by the German clergy in the fifteenth century and even by the Emperor Charles V in the sixteenth, but without success. Although the Church has since those days established an administrative system which makes any similar appropriation of Church property impossible, the old decision of the twelfth century still limits the Church in its choice of men for the priesthood in the late twentieth century. Less of a worship of Christ than worship of a misunderstood past was involved.

By contrast, another and more useful practice of the Church during the crusading period and after it, has disappeared and did so partly because of the Church's heady excitement in diverting the impetus of the crusades to Europe, and to sanctified land-grabbing expeditions against dissenters and good Catholics on that continent. The Church was once in a position of moral authority over nobles and through the threat of excommunication could establish a "truce of God," or even a "peace of God," to put off limits the endless quarrels of nobles for land and power, their ceaseless pillaging of the poor. Sometimes a large part of the year was made safe for noncombatants. The power and readiness to do this was lost when the Church transferred the crusading idea, with its somewhat Islamic promise of heaven for those who died in a crusade, against Catholics in Europe.

One of these diversions was directed against a religious dissent in Provence in 1207. The victims, Catharans, held one conspicuously subversive belief: Church leaders should live in poverty rather than enjoy worldly pomp and pleasure. Men from northern France, graciously promised heaven for their acts and freedom to take land from heretics or the feudal lords protecting them, poured south. Provence was a more pleasant place than Syria. Good Catholic lords, sworn to protect their heretical vassals, did not accept the papal view that the lands of those vassals were suddenly free booty, and fought against good Catholic invaders. When one city, Beziers, was captured by the northerners, they slaughtered nonheretics along with the Catharans. These unfortunates were guilty by habitation and association, and no one was condemned to hell for killing them.

At this point the Church leaders seemed to have become captives of their own success. Once the killing of dissenters and good Catholics alike in the course of a crusade had been condoned, where could the line be drawn? Or why should any line be drawn? A process of escalation followed. In the 1260s a crusade against the Hohenstaufen rulers was proclaimed. They had possession of the Kingdom of Sicily and were constantly threatening to take over northern Italy as well. This would put the territorial possessions of the papacy in central Italy into a vise. There was no problem of heresy involved, only one of territorial expansion of which the papacy disapproved. Frederick II was excommunicated. After his death, Charles of Anjou, a French prince, was given crusading privileges to capture Sicily. He succeeded and, in defending it, killed off the last of the Hohenstaufen heirs. With that, the Holy Roman Empire ceased, for a while, to be a danger to the papacy. A later pope even excommunicated the Christian Aragonese, when they intervened during a revolt (the Sicilian Vespers) in 1282 against the French Charles of Anjou. But these were crusades and escalations with built-in boomerangs. Crusades in Syria were not the only ones which could have unexpected and undesired results. To eliminate the Hohenstaufens from the neighborhood of Rome was one thing. To bring in the French to supplant them, and to endow them with the prestige of crusaders, was another. Control of the tiara itself had recklessly been thrown into the maneuver.

The Church management was still unaware of the risks it had taken when it began to shift state powers around and to urge good Christians to kill other good Christians in the process, and to change the ownership of property in land. Pope Boniface VII was fresh from a magnificent celebration, in the year 1300, of the triumphs and glories of Christendom, when he was challenged by the strongest political power in Europe, France. Here was the confrontation which was to determine whether or not the papacy would be able to parlay its enormous prestige and past success into a position of authority over all rulers in Europe. It was not a prolonged one.

The incident which brought it on was the arrest, by King Philip IV of France, of a bishop who was, he claimed, inciting to revolt in southern France. That cleric was also as a matter of course charged with heresy and blasphemy. The King demanded that the Pope strip the bishop of his Church title so that he could be punished for his revolt by the state. The Pope refused and demanded that the arrested bishop be sent to Rome to be judged. In addition he called a synod of the French (Gallican) churchmen in Rome to deal with "the correction" of the King. The King, outraged, called his estates general together to advise him. At that moment the French armies suffered a crushing defeat at the hands of the Flemings.

Pope Boniface chose this opportunity to make a claim of Church superiority equal to any made several centuries earlier by Pope Gregory VII. In the bull *Unam Sanctam* he declared, defined and pronounced "that it is a necessity of salvation for every human creature to be subject to the Roman pontiff." He included all kings. This statement has been described as "the most absolute proclamation of theocratic doctrine ever formulated in the Middle Ages." In 1303 he threatened Philip IV, who was arousing French clergy against the Pope, with excommunication unless he made a complete submission. The King of France may have felt endangered. He knew what had happened to the Hohenstaufens after they had been excommunicated and crusades had been led against them. He knew of the earlier and forced submission of John of England to the same threat. Suddenly his men broke into the Pope's retreat at Agnani, in northern Italy, and took Boniface prisoner. Although rescued by indignant townspeople, the Pope died of shock within a month. With his death, the illusion of omnipotence burst. Its memory was cherished, its loss mourned, but it was never seen again in its full pristine beauty.

The temptation of sharing and then capturing political power had been too great for the Christian creed, and much too great for the Church which claimed to embody and advance it. Much of the mandate its early leaders had assumed, that of teaching men the Christian way of love and kindness on earth and of ennobling them in the process, was forgotten. It would be difficult to find any message to men in the medieval days which did as much to raise their hopes and increase their welfare as the Black Plague. That scourge killed every third or fourth man in Europe, but it created a labor shortage and raised wages and hopes for the lucky survivors.

With its seeking for political rule of the world, its use of crusades to obtain it, the Church lost much of its moral authority, many of the loyalties once attached to it. It acquired many enemies, produced many cynics. It moved toward the edge of a great schism and a humiliating Babylonian captivity.

The susceptibility of the early Church to the temptations of secular power and violence was a flaw of character which a large part of the Western world had to pay for during many cruel centuries. Neither the fatuity of trying to convert men by killing them nor any sudden awareness of the non-Christian character of persecution by the state in the name of religion brought an end to the custom started under Constantine. It was simply the weariness of people caught in an endless cross fire of death which put an end to the practice under which Catholic monarchs killed Protestants and Protestant monarchs killed Catholics and all possibility of community unity and purpose was being destroyed.

Perhaps the lesson for the later world is that any self-righteousness which leads to brutality needs to be reexamined by all concerned and checked as soon as it appears and as long as it exists.

The adventure into secular power was later to be accompanied by land acquisitions in huge amounts during and after the crusades, a passing of the clergy into the estate of noblemen, rivalry with worldly princes in display and ornament, alienation of many, including some of its own religious orders, neglect of the aspirations of its poorer members, and all the power problems of the secular states. Alliance with the state was one thing during the days of the Roman Empire, when only one important state existed. But alliance with a state when many rival kingdoms existed was something quite different and did not further any basic purpose of a church which claimed and sought universality. Later, when new forces and aspirations challenged a state's rulers from within, the Church's alliance with those rulers against their challengers created new doubts and confusions. The continued connection of the clerical hierarchy with the establishments in Brazil and Argentina even led furious priests to predict that, in case it continued, the Church would no longer exist in those nations in the 1990s. The lesson that an institution which bases itself even in small part on an ethic dealing with the relations of men to one another must itself remain consistent with that ethic, seems a hard one for some to understand, and the heritage of disruption when that lesson is omitted may seem to them to be a history which can still safely be neglected.

Two experiences which are useful even in modern times came directly from the crusades to the Holy Land. One is that men cannot expect that such crusades will accomplish their own objective if they go into them along with a host of different groups which have conflicting interests and purposes. The unifying task needs to be undertaken first, not after all the inherent disharmonies burst out and ruin the effort. No simple "God wills it" eliminates great divergencies, and perhaps particularly not when an idealistic aspiration is teamed with such rapacious and self-centered men as the Normans. The second experience, still useful, was a display of the inherent tendency of crusades to spread sidewards and to move against quite innocent targets. The rewards in prestige, land and power which the Church obtained during its crusade against the infidel Moslems in Syria, the original target, encouraged the clerical rulers to crusade against Christian dissenters, and to go on from there to crusade against good Catholic rulers who happened to be the rivals of Rome for worldly power. Some militant leaders of the black people in the United States, who saw themselves as crusaders, repeated the first of the two stages in this process when they turned against the Northern college students who had crusaded along with them for civil rights in a number of Southern states and suffered some wounds, but who were resolutely nonviolent and also white and therefore could be designated as objects of distrust and attack.

CHAPTER 5

The Disastrous
Victory

In the 1960s a great Church council was held in Rome—Vatican II. With that, a movement was begun to liberate the enduring institution from the shackles it had imposed upon itself in the past. Steps were taken, although hesitantly, toward a regrouping of all Christians into one body. Freedom of conscience was accepted as a reasonable concept. On that occasion the world's oldest clerical monarchy did not develop a permanent parliament of its bishops, but it began to listen to them. It was almost, but not quite as democratic or international as the great council assemblages five hundred years earlier. It considered many similar problems. Unfortunately, it was different in one respect: in the fifteenth century the councils had a chance to affect profoundly the rise and character of combative nationalisms, each with its own moral code and with its claims of the divine right of national rulers to do as they pleased. That opportunity was less open in the twentieth century. Five hundred unredeemable years had passed between the two major efforts.

When the internal Church revolt of 1414–1449 began, the tradition of one religion and the ideal of a single government were still strong. Most people still believed in a single, all-pervasive truth. To them, the life of modern man, in which everything is questioned—where a multiplicity of separate beliefs, conceits and views coexist and clash in the common marketplace of ideas—would have seemed shocking and

87

unbearable. Men entered the fifteenth century even more shaken than we have been by the Second World War and the nuclear arms race. They were still trying to recover their equilibrium after the greatest cataclysm that had ever befallen Europe. In the Black Death plague, a great multitude of people in Europe had died horribly. To the helpless survivors, the mysterious will of God became more important than ever. Strange, half-mad cults of flagellants appeared, scourging the evil cause of divine displeasure out of one another with bloody whips. Wild-eyed girls were burned as witches. Jews were slaughtered as scapegoats. Those who survived the plague in fear praised God for their existence.

Not long after that scourge there was another harrowing event, the Great Schism (1378). This carried over into the fifteenth century and started the audacious attempt to adjust an old church to new needs. The universal Church was moral arbiter, keeper of the key to salvation and eternal life, guardian of the natural law, preceptor of beliefs. Now the Church discredited and disgraced itself and began breaking into two hostile camps contending for the loyalty of all Christians. Each claimed true and full authority over souls, land, church buildings, monasteries and priests. No man could be sure anymore whether the priest who gave him the sacraments and absolution was entitled to do so, or whether the priest was an unwitting emissary of the devil. This situation seemed to everyone not only disgraceful but intolerable. Hence the organized effort to correct it.

At the very start of the movement to heal the schism of 1378–1417 the question was raised, "What are the purposes of this great institution, the Church?" Four of these purposes, it has been pointed out,[1] had been developed over the years but only one had received genuine, general approval: the Church as a witness to the world, bringing the Gospel to individuals and society. The other three purposes were challenged. One was the ideal of renouncing the world. Some orders of monks had accepted this; many but not all of the clergy had done so to the extent of celibacy. The mystics had attempted to achieve it; but they were criticized and banned because they believed they could find God through their individual strivings without Church aid. The second of the three challenged purposes was that of ruling the world. This was criticized as leading to worldliness, political involvement, intrigues and defeats. A third Church objective was to make the world produce wealth for it. This was a most vulnerable spot in its armor during the Middle Ages and even later. For here the conflicts between the City of God and the City of Man were fought out, between the worldly and other-worldly elements. In this struggle every other purpose of the Church became involved or suspect.

There had long been murmurings within the Church about its conflicting purposes, particularly about its ways of acquiring wealth. But there had been little serious attempt at thoroughgoing reform until the fifteenth century, when it was coupled with the effort to repair the broken Church body. A little while earlier, the Spiritual Franciscans had pleaded for a return to the days of apostolic poverty and had been found guilty of heresy because of it. Much of the popular criticism of the Church was directed at its taxes, tithes and other forms of raising income. The Church's estates in many areas included from a fourth to a third of all the land. At a time when land was the main source of income, these holdings were a visible limitation on the opportunities of laymen to survive or advance. Early in the century, a completely Catholic Parliament in England had debated seriously a petition that Church lands should be taken over to finance the nation's needs.

There were also criticisms of the behavior of the clergy, low and high. Northerners disapproved of what seemed to them a basic paganism among some of the Italian churchmen. But the explosions of conscience were touched off by something else: the new doctrine of indulgences. This seemed to many to vitiate the doctrine of salvation by works, observance of sacraments. People were misled into believing that, for a little money, they could buy complete remission of the penalties for their sins and get into heaven most simply. The devout poor were outraged at the injustice of this unequal form of salvation. It was less the doctrine than the sale of these indulgences to raise Church funds that originally aroused the indignation of Jan Hus in the early fifteenth century and of Luther in the early sixteenth. The money dispute rapidly moved on to disputes about authority and doctrine. The Church, first in Bohemia and then in northern Europe, was to divide in civil war.

Two remarkable men arose in the early fifteenth century, as demands for reestablishment of a single Church authority joined with demands for its reform. The first of these was an Italian, Baldassare Cossa, an adroit financial, political and ecclesiastical manipulator when there was intense competition in all of these fields. He was in time to be chosen as a third rival pope and to take the title of John XXIII. So many sins against the church, common morality and society were later laid against him that in the twentieth century another supreme pontiff took the same title as if to prove that the earlier John XXIII had been illegally chosen or deserved to be forgotten completely. Among historians there is general agreement that Cossa was so imbued with the corruption of his country and age that he could hardly understand, let alone meet, the challenges and obligations of the Church and society in this crucial period. Yet Cossa was the man who, by accident and out of fear, created the first opportunity for a parliamentary revolution by calling a General

Council of the Church at Constance. Through the same accident and fear he sent an indulgence peddler into Bohemia to raise money for his needs, provoking Jan Hus into open challenge of the Church. This led to the martyrdom of Hus and some years later to schism and religious war in Bohemia. Out of that came the second general Council of the Church at Basle and the second opportunity of churchmen to transform their absolute monarchy into a constitutional one. Cossa was the unwilling and unwitting mover of these great events.

The second remarkable character was Sigismund, sometime King of Hungary, elected but not accepted King of Bohemia, and elected King of the "Romans"—which, oddly, did not include Rome but meant the Germanies. He had been badly defeated by the Turks in Hungary in 1396. He was at odds with the people of Hungary and Bohemia most of his life and was foiled by German princes and cities in his unification efforts. He was a winner of tournaments, a Latinist, a patron of learning, a man of ideas, a believer in action; and, as Laffan graciously puts it, "His devotion to the ladies exceeded the generous allowance conceded to monarchs." At the same time the story was told that in one war he ordered 171 captured nobles decapitated, and that in another he had the right hands of 180 captured Venetians cut off and sent as a present to the Doge. It was this man who dragooned Cossa, the third pope of the day, into calling the first general council of the whole Church which had been held for centuries. It was this man, in need of Church help to settle the religious wars in Bohemia, who sponsored the second Council, called for Basle some years later. Two frustrated men of diverse ability unintentionally gave contemporary churchmen an opportunity to replace their absolutist ecclesiastical monarchy with a more representative and merciful form of government.

The cause of the original split in authority, which these two men were trying to heal, is significant. It was the take-over by the French of an institution which had been Italian but claimed universality. The first Frenchman elected as head of the Church (1305) stayed in France instead of going to the traditional seat in Rome. The self-perpetuating top bureaucracy of cardinals was then filled with Frenchmen, and chose more French popes. The Church capital became Avignon, in southern France, a pleasant place for relaxation. The Church stopped acting in behalf of all its members. It was used by France against the Holy Roman Empire, which in reaction became the spokesman of all the reformist and antipapal elements, particularly those favoring return to the apostolic poverty of pre-Constantine times. The Church's influence was also directed against England, which greatly resented it. Also, the Italian city-states felt the French pressure through the papacy; the city of Rome even declared a republic and chose an antipope of its own. It was not until 1367 that a pope briefly returned to a Rome which had, by some estimates, fallen to a population of 17,000 and become a social ruin. In 1376 the last French pope (Gregory XI) returned to Rome to stay.

That was not the end of the damage done by French control. The cardinals who moved back to Rome were still largely French. When the moment came to elect a new chief (1378), the Roman people rang the bells all night and stormed the building where the cardinals were holding their conclave. "A Roman, or at least an Italian!" was their cry. The curia chose a Neapolitan, Urban VI. Later he antagonized the cardinals, berated them, shouted them down, even villified them. They decided to replace him. They received assurance of protection from the King of France (Charles V) and then claimed that the election of Urban VI was invalid because it had been carried on under mob threats. The émigré cardinals then elected a second pope.

With this event, the Great Schism began. It lasted forty years (1378–1417). The French, imitating the Italians, had become accustomed to dominating the Church. They were willing to risk its ruin by electing a rival pope. After this experience with nationalistic control, the Church authorities might have learned one simple lesson in survival: domination of the Church by any nation (including Italy) prevented it from remaining universal and unified. If the lesson was ever read it was forgotten in the power struggles which followed. Even before the fifteenth century was over, the emerging nations began taking over control of Church affairs within their borders, and by the sixteenth century a series of royally controlled churches had emerged. By that time the concept of a common moral basis for society with a common mediating authority had been discarded, and the road was open for nationalistic anarchy coupled with religious wars.

But in the early fifteenth century it was not religious war but ecclesiastical anarchy which prevailed. As if two popes were not enough, a group of cardinals from both obediences dropped out and met at Pisa. A Church conference of sorts was held which deserved to be remembered perhaps only by protocol officers of modern nations. Apparently the English managed to win some degree of seating preference over the French by pointing out that they had been converted to Christianity through Joseph of Arimathea, against the unsuccessful French claim of having been converted by Lazarus, his sister Martha, and Mary Magdalene. The cardinals then deposed the other two popes and elected a third. He died within a year. As we have seen, his successor was Cossa, John XXIII. So the world was cursed with three popes instead of two, each attracting some allegiances, some funds, and rival colleges of cardinals. In these circumstances and on something like universal demand, the way was open for Sigismund, King of the "Romans," to do what a Roman emperor was then supposed to do, bring some order out of considerable clerical chaos.

Only "the whole body" of the Church in Council could restore the unity of the Church. With this in mind, he began negotiations with John XXIII, the third contender for the tiara. The two men were linked by events of their own making. Cossa was chased from Rome to Florence by King Ladislas of Naples. In Florence, seat of the Renaissance, he met a cold welcome. Meanwhile, his money-raising indulgence seller in Bohemia had provoked Jan Hus, popular rector of the University of Prague, to open protest; Sigismund was busy suspending sundry papal bulls that excluded Hus and his followers from the Church. Apparently afraid of what would happen to himself at the hands of Ladislas, Cossa started negotiating for help from Sigismund. To get that, he was forced to sign a bull calling a full general Church Council at Constance, an imperial city. Sigismund simply ignored the other two popes. Hardly had Cossa signed when his pursuer, Ladislas, died. Cossa wished to cancel his bull, but all Europe was busy making preparations to attend the Council; he could not do so. He was the victim of an accident in time—his enemy, Ladislas, had not died soon enough. So the great effort to reform and reunite the onetime universal Church could begin.

Into this Council (1414–1417) poured the churchmen and nobility of all Europe. This was the business of Europe. Among the churchmen were no less than twenty-nine cardinals, three patriarchs, thirty-three archbishops, a hundred and fifty bishops, a hundred abbots, fifty provosts and some three hundred doctors of theology. Thousands of people with Church business and more thousands of hangers-on joined the throng. Men had a sense of history being made.

First came the customary skirmish to pack the meeting. John XXIII (Cossa) thought he could flood it with obedient Italians to confirm his claim to power. He was adroitly turned back. Following the then current custom of universities, members were grouped into "nations" as voting units. All the Italians were grouped as only one nation among others: French, Germans, English. Later the Castilians made a fifth. Then cardinals were given equal status with the nations, on the principle that the Church was an international body not to be dominated by regional interests. The proposed new leadership was democratized. About half the clerical attendants were doctors of theology, who represented the lower ranks of the Church; their votes within each nation were as good as any others. The Church was to be not only international but more democratic.

The group went back to the practice of the very early days of the

Church when the councils governed. They voted to make councils a permanent institution, meeting regularly and automatically regardless of whether desired by any pope. This was a clean break with the closed, self-perpetuating hierarchical control of preceding centuries. The Council of Constance spelled out the thesis, which had prevailed at Nicaea in 325, that councils of the whole Church received their authority directly from Christ: Council decisions on dogma, ritual, organization, administration outranked the pope and curia. The Church's parliament controlled the Church's monarch, not the other way around. This was a revolutionary change, but because of the general desire to end the three-way schism, there was little dissent at the time.

Next, the key question arose. Which should come first: election of a true pope to replace the three rivals, or reformation of the Church? If a pope were elected first, the Council might soon be over. Indeed, the Council would then have a potential opponent. At this moment the Castilians arrived. They refused to join until it was agreed to elect a pope before reforming the Church. Sigismund wanted reform first. When the rumor spread that he planned to arrest opposition cardinals, they put on their red hats to show they were ready for martyrdom. The French opposed Sigismund because he recently had made an alliance with their enemy, the English king. Unfortunately, the brilliant English reformist, Bishop Hallam of Salisbury, died. These circumstances made the Spanish intervention decisive. The reforms-first group was voted down.

What to do with the three previously elected rival claimants to the tiara? No true pope could be deposed except for heresy. In the face of this difficulty, Jean Gerson and German theologians offered a solution: any pope who schismatically insisted on his differences to the point of breaking up the Church was thereby a heretic and as such could be properly deposed—even a truly elected pope.

Accepting this idea, the Council turned to the claimant nearest at hand, Cossa (John XXIII). After failing to pack the Council, he had fled disguised as a stable groom. He had obtained safe conduct from a neighboring lord and was waiting. He called his own cardinals to him, although their departure was forbidden by the Council. Finally, he was imprisoned and his cardinals returned to the Council; he offered to resign if given the papal power in Italy alone. This would have split the Church territorially permanently. He was deposed. One of Cossa's competitors was induced to resign when his support was withdrawn. Then the third claimant was deposed.

Now that a new pope could be elected, the principle of an international Church was stressed. Twenty-three cardinals were in Constance; to them were added thirty other prelates, six for each of the five "nations." The Council decided that election required not only the votes of two-thirds of the cardinals, but also four of the six prelates acting as special electors from each "nation." They elected one of the powerful aristocratic Colonna family of Rome, who took the title Martin V. The Church again had only one proper head. The schism was over. For the ordinary man, salvation was a little less of a gamble than it had been for the past forty years.

The Council of Constance is remembered for something it did without much thought. It tried Jan Hus of Bohemia. He refused to accept authority of pope or Council as against the Scriptures and his conscience. The safe conduct to Constance given to him by Sigismund was ignored. The Council did not stop to ponder the problems raised by his revolt. It was still medieval despite its small moves toward internationalization and democratization. The customary thing to do with heretics was to burn them, for their own good and that of the Church. So Hus of Bohemia set his conscience against the whole Church and paid with his life. He was burned in 1415. But thereupon the hills and valleys of Bohemia were swept with a fire of national indignation. Soon a religious issue had become a national cause, provoking a combined civil and religious war of the type that was to scar future centuries. Later another great council would be called and would try to undo the harm the first one had wrought so casually.

The Council of Constance did not reform the Church. From the end of that Council to the time of Luther there was still a century in which the Church might have begun to reform itself. But the Italians, who were again in charge, did not seem to be aware of how differently the Renaissance had affected other members of the universal Church than themselves. John Addington Symonds is one of the many who have stressed this difference. He found that the Italians encouraged a pseudo-pagan way of life, seeing no harm in "a golden age of epicurean ease made decent by a state of religion which no one cared to break with because no one was left to regard it seriously." But in the northern areas: "The touch of the new spirit which had evolved literature, art and culture in Italy sufficed in Germany to recreate Christianity. This new spirit in Italy emancipated human intelligence by the classics; in Germany it emancipated the human conscience by the Bible."[2]

Little was done to maintain the newly reestablished universality of the Church. Martin V was in the position several kings were to face in later centuries: he had been told to share power with a parliament under a constitution. The prospect displeased him. He had promised reform to the Council as the price of his election. But the fact that most reformers advocated conciliar control offended the new pope. He did call a Council as he had been instructed to do. That Council of Pavia

(1423) passed some minor resolutions and one on forceful extirpation of heresy. But when some French reformers pressed demands for major reform, the papal legates disappeared and that broke up the Council.

Martin had other problems. His first year and a half were spent in Florence because he could not get back to Rome. The Church, which had preached many crusades to recover Jerusalem, now had no safe home of its own. Rome was held by a general representing Naples. Between Florence and Rome other *condottieri* barred the way. Only an elaborate intrigue among these jealous men and the fortuitous deaths of two of them enabled Martin to regain the papal states and return to Rome. To provide Church income papal control of them seemed neces-sary. They had to be defended. This meant war or alliances with other city-states, France, Spain, or even the Holy Roman Emperor. War added to the expense, lowered the dignity, and divided the Church's purposes as well as its resources. One of Martin V's predecessors, John XXIII, had declared a crusade against Naples as he fled north and resorted to indulgence selling. Later popes were to be forced to call on the major military powers for help and become subject to them. No one at that time suggested the arrangement made in 1870 for a papal enclave inside of Rome. In the fifteenth century, when there was no united Italy, such an enclave might have been protected by an inter-national guard; then the Church might have avoided damaging single-nation control, as under the French from 1305 to 1417. Independence and financial reform could have resulted, with income from the papal states guaranteed by the major powers and title turned over to laymen. This alternative was not considered.

Would there ever be another meeting of the Church's new parlia-ment, the General Council? Martin hesitated as 1431 approached, the year appointed for it by the Council of Constance. He had been build-ing up and decorating Rome at a magnificent rate, creating needed employment for his fellow citizens and winning their praise. (His suc-cessor discovered that most of the papal treasury had found its way into the hands of the Colonna family, of which Martin was a member.)

Martin was forced to call the Council to deal with heresy. That sin would not disappear despite all his preachments, bulls, and orders for burning. Like Sigismund, Martin was the unwilling heir of the burning of Jan Hus at Constance. Armed revolt was sweeping Bohemia, peasants with flails and handguns and wagon stockades were fighting the Church with its own slogans. "If the sword might be used by divine command to preserve the Church, might it not be used by divine command to reform it?"[3] To make matters more difficult, two anonymous German nobles placarded Rome with the thesis that any pope who failed to call the Council on the specified day was a schismatic breaking Church unity, and therefore a heretic to be deposed. Martin called the Council. He appointed the able cardinal Julian Cesarini to lead a crusade against the Hussites. Then Martin died, in the same year as Joan of Arc, 1431.

The eyes of Europe were not, however, on Basle, where the new Council was to meet. They were on Bohemia, where Duke Frederick of Brandenburg and Cardinal-legate Cesarini with crusading armies were about to engage the heretical Hussites. A similar attack in 1427 had failed when the crusaders at Tachov ran without fighting. Since that dark day, the Czechs had been moving westward, garrisoning strong points, converting the poorer townspeople and peasants, and sending flaming proclamations into other countries. They acted as if they had the true religion. The avenging sword of God could not fail twice. But it did. When the great crusading army saw the Hussites advancing at Taus (August 1431), it also fled without fighting. It left behind rich loot and many prisoners.

So Europe had grave new business to transact at Basle in 1431. From the Taus rout Cardinal-legate Cesarini went directly to preside over the Council, convinced that unity could come only through conciliation. He was to become one of the great leaders of that Council and to oppose the new pope's efforts to dissolve it. One of the tragedies of the times was that Cesarini's desire for conciliation, and the faith of the Council's intellectual leader, the German Nicholas of Cusa, that the Church could absorb every positive intellectual achievement of mankind, were completely frustrated by a pope who thought only of retaining his absolute power. Such was Eugenius IV, another Italian, who was to have a long reign, but be forced to yield to kings that which he would not yield to his own colleagues.

The Church had every reason to remember the fatal consequences of its much earlier failure, under Constantine, to keep free from state control. Men were still alive who had seen the disaster of its control by France, and the long chaos before 1417. From the death of Hus in 1415 to the second rout of the German crusaders in 1431, churchmen had watched the merger of Bohemian political (anti-German) and religious (Hussite) movements grow into a new national religion. It was willing to defend itself against all comers in the name of its own image of Christianity and to kill with a religious zeal equal to any which could be brought against it. This was not merely armed heresy, it was national heresy in arms. What made this exceedingly important was that in this period kings and national states were displacing the feudal order and growing stronger rapidly. Would they not become successful competitors of the universal Church? Might not other heresies find their own nations, and other nations their own heresies, until the Church's goal of universality became impossible? Then what would be left of unity but pretenses and memories?

In the vast cathedral church at Basle five or six hundred churchmen sat in the Great Council. King Sigismund, its protector, was there occasionally, surrounded by the color and panoply of lesser princes and nobles. Much was expected of this Council: long-needed Church reform and an end to the schism in Bohemia. Safe conducts had been issued, prices of lodgings and meals had been agreed upon. When the Hussites were ready to come, streets were cleared of female hangers-on, dancing, gambling and gay dress were forbidden.

Hardly had the Council begun with piety and prayer than Eugenius IV, away in Rome, decided he wanted no part of it. The Council had invited the Hussites to confer. That was one excuse to dissolve it, for the proper way to deal with heretics was to refuse to yield an inch to them. Moreover, the Council professed the right to reform the Church from the papacy downward and the right to enunciate doctrine, two further reasons for dissolving it. During its first two years, Eugenius tried to replace it with another Basle council of his own henchmen or with a later council elsewhere. Healing the schism with the Greek Orthodox branch also seemed to him more important.

Cardinal Cesarini, who had narrowly escaped the rout at Taus, had to warn the Pope that the situation in Europe was not quite as it looked from the windows of Rome. Not only German and Bohemian nobles, but the whole clergy of the north would feel cheated if no serious attempt were made to end the Bohemian schism. Further, the Hussites would proclaim that other Catholics had been afraid to debate with them, an intolerable result. Only after the Council had tried to heal the schism could new money ever be collected for another crusade against them. Further, Cesarini pointed out that the attempt to heal the schism with the Greek branch of the Church would not come to anything. If the Pope recalled him from Basle, the Council would elect another presiding officer and proceed as before. More, if the Pope tried to dissolve the Council, there would be a new schism, for which Eugenius would be blamed. So ran his letter. It was ignored. The Pope's various drafts of bulls of dissolution, made public and then withdrawn under pressure, made the Council more determined than ever to reform the Church thoroughly.

What reforms were necessary? To most of the Council, smarting under Martin's dalliance with the project and under Eugenius' hatred of it, reform meant first of all that the Church parliament must always act as a check on extreme ecclesiastical monarchy. It issued solemn proclamations, restating the principles of Nicaea and Constance, that the real church was the body of believers as represented by the Council with which no pope could interfere. Also, reform meant more local control, less centralized operation; revision of the tax system, with more money spent locally; higher moral standards for the clergy.

Would these measures have saved the Church either from Hussite-type revolt and war or from the later Protestant Reformation? Would they have saved the Church in one nation after another from becoming the property of the king, claiming his divine right to rule as he pleased? The answer is far from clear. Especially, it is uncertain how far even local autonomy would have gone in meeting demands of rising individualism for tolerance of dissent or freedom of conscience. The English historian George Macaulay Trevelyan concluded that the following evolutionary reforms would have avoided the subsequent religious revolution in England:

> In the fourteenth and fifteenth centuries the Church refused every concession, effected no reform and called in brute force to repress heresy. If an opposite course had been followed: if the rights of sanctuary and benefit of clergy had been modified; if ecclesiastical property had been distributed more fairly to the poor parson; if priests had been permitted to marry their wives as in Saxon times; if the pope had ceased to job rich places of the Church for foreign favorites; if the ecclesiastical authorities had withdrawn their countenance from the sale of pardons and relics and other superstitious practices that revolted the better sort of laity, orthodox as well as heretic; if the Church courts had ceased to make a trade of spying on the lives of the laity in order to extract fines for sins; and finally, if Lollardy [Wycliffe doctrines of Scripture and conscience] had been tolerated as dissent, there would have been religious evolution spread over several centuries, instead of the religious revolution which we know as the Reformation."[4]

Of Trevelyan's seven requirements for peaceful religious development, the last probably was the crucial one. The Council of Basle is peculiarly interesting because it moved in fact, although not in theory, toward toleration of dissent. It came at the moment of conciliation with the Hussites, who were in a way followers of Wycliffe's doctrines and therefore close in spirit to contemporary English dissenters. The spirit of the Fathers of Basle reached forward five hundred years to that of a pope (John XXIII, 1961–1963) who could speak of non-Catholic Christians as "separated brothers." But Martin V, Eugenius IV and many others thought heretics were for burning.

Hussites wanted a church closer to them and holier. Some five years after the martyrdom of Hus, smarting under calumniation of their whole nation as heretical, the Czechs had formulated the Four Articles of Prague (1420). These asked that the word of God be preached freely; the sacrament of communion be administered to all the faithful; the clergy be divested of all riches and return to the apostolic life; all public sin (and public sinners of every rank) be punished. The chalice (for communion wine) became their symbol. What was the word of God that was to be preached freely? What the Czech University of Prague, using the Scriptures, thought nonheretical. To the head of the Roman Church these challenges to his authority seemed nonnegotiable. Consequently Sigismund could not be crowned King of Bohemia. Even the demand that the bread and wine representing the body and blood of Christ be shared with the laity seemed to question the special sanctity of the priesthood. Negotiations between the Hussites and the Fathers at Basle stalled when the former refused to accept the authority of the Council or hierarchy as final. They insisted that their cause be judged not by the Council, but by the divine law (the Scriptures) and by the practice of Christ.

The Fathers at Basle were willing to accept such a conciliation, while the pope of the day and his successors were most unwilling to do so. Yet the men of the Council were not willing to go beyond the immediate needs of the Hussites toward accepting the faith, represented by de Cusa of Germany, in the perfectible power of the Christian religion.

For a brief moment the Council modified the old doctrine that anyone who questioned the authority of the Church was, in effect, a heretic; it agreed, after a fashion and with many reservations and informally, that Hussites with their Four Articles could still be members of the Roman Church. The Diet of Bohemia approved; Sigismund signed his agreement with the Articles and was allowed to become king. Every succeeding Bohemian king for more than a hundred years had to swear allegiance to them. These remained the Czechs' *Magna Carta* until Hussite defeat in the Counter-Reformation (1620). Like other peoples with a basic document of rights, they did not always agree with one another about its meaning; there were some extreme adventures in interpretation. But the Czechs had achieved some degree of religious liberty much earlier than other Europeans, including the English. (Five hundred years later they were to hear a prime minister of England speak of them as "that faraway, little-known people," while he ignored their subjugation to Nazi terror.)

The fundamental question of the fifteenth century was this: Would the worship of the Christian God unite the people of Europe or divide them? The same question had arisen in the fourth century when churchmen obtained authority to hound their fellow Christians to death for differences of dogma and ritual. That resulted in many large heretical sects and the separate Greek Orthodox Church. Would the same process with the same results be repeated 1,100 years later? Meanwhile, the Renaissance had placed its humanistic accent on intellectual independence; and Hussites had been conciliated by the Council of Basle through allowance of an unconventional form of worship and partial acceptance of the scriptural guide to religious life.

When the papacy rejected the Council's slight reforms, the old fourth-century pattern of enforced conformity creating disunity reappeared. Consequently, the slowly emerging modern world would supersede in importance the Church, which chained itself to medievalism; nations would replace it as objects of devotion and sacrifice; wars between rival national gods would be prolonged because of the papacy's failure to look a little ahead—or far enough into the past.

After the schism with the Hussites seemed to be at least nominally healed, the Council turned to reform. For a moment it was free to do so without much interference from Rome. Milanese and Neapolitan armies were attacking the papal states (claiming they were acting on behalf of the Council); and Pope Eugenius under this pressure issued a bull approving all the Council had done up to that time. Still, he had to flee from Rome hidden under a shield in the bottom of a boat, disguised as a poor monk. No reform concerning the papal states which would have given him a little freedom from warfare had been undertaken and was not likely to be undertaken in his behalf by the Council. So the Council's work on other reforms went forward. Concubinage (licensed in England at the time) was to be penalized not only through the offending cleric but through the bishop or abbot who allowed it to continue. Some of the Germans remarked that the Greek Church allowed the clergy to marry, that was the way to remove this type of sinfulness. This change, they thought, would save some tens of thousands of good clergymen from hell each year. What evidence was there, they asked, that all of the Apostles and early Church Fathers had been unmarried? They were voted down. The reforming process took another direction. Synods were to be held every year or so in every bishopric; this would put a grass-roots democracy under the international republicanism of the Council. No nation was to have more than one-third of the cardinals. This was a blow at Italy's monopoly of Church power.

Then suddenly the Council made a major proposal which alarmed many and gave the Pope a new weapon. It voted in 1435 to abolish the annate system, which gave the Pope one year's full income from any benefice whenever a new occupant was appointed. Like other taxation systems, this was open to abuse. A pope could use one vacancy to multiply his normal income six- or sevenfold by moving around that many men. The Council talked vaguely about reimbursing the Pope from other sources, but did nothing concrete. So the Pope could charge with some plausibility that the Council was trying to destroy the papacy. He destroyed the Council instead.

Not all of the decisive battles of the world are fought with arms. The successful campaign of Eugenius IV to destroy the threat to papal absolutism was one of these decisive battles. He won the battle but lost a large part of the future in the process. He was followed by other popes who also enjoyed absolute power, saw no reason to share it, and were blind to its dangers to the Church. They were a remarkably inadequate group compared with some later leaders of the Church, particularly in the twentieth century. The comment of Lord Acton, himself a devout member of the Church, "Power corrupts, and absolute power corrupts absolutely," can be applied to most fourteenth- and fifteenth-century popes.

The tactics and strategy of Eugenius had more significance than the internecine strife of other institutions. He had early annoyed the Council by his attempts to dissolve it. When the Council's envoys helped to patch up the quarrel between France and Burgundy, he told them and Emperor Sigismund to keep hands off. He appointed as archbishop a notorious *condottiere* (Vitelleschi) who had killed the prefect of Rome. Later this assassin was elevated to the cardinalate despite a conciliar injunction against any such appointment while the Council was in session. The Council was being goaded to act in fury and folly. Its action abolishing annates was in that mood. This made many prelates wonder whether the Council members had any understanding of the difference between control of policy and day-by-day administration. A number of them began turning back to the Pope.

Then Eugenius led a trump card to pull more members away from Basle. He would hold a summit meeting to heal the schism with the Greek Orthodox Church. The Council had planned a similar meeting at Avignon, but the Greeks wanted to stay close to Constantinople. In Basle a minority supported the Pope in this matter. Rival bishops shouted down each other, and rival *Te Deums* were sung by their supporters. The Council's own seal was pried out of its box and affixed secretly to the minority's decree favoring the Pope's plan. When this fraud was exposed, the miscreants fled to a friendly reception in Rome. More prelates left Basle. Lesser dignitaries stayed, more antiabsolutist than before. Eugenius called a new council for Ferrara and denounced the Council of Basle as "the synagogue of Satan." He wrote to all the rulers, pleading his case. The Council retaliated (July 1437) by citing Eugenius to answer charges of refusing to reform the Church and causing schism by disobeying its decrees. Cardinal Cesarini refused to preside at this session and soon returned to Rome. When Eugenius ignored the indictment, the Council found him guilty of contumacy. Later the remnants of the Council decided to suspend him within four months and depose him within six unless he yielded. By this time, however, the Pope was safe; his conference with the Greek Church was underway, and he had Europe's attention as a potential hero-statesman.

Eugenius now reversed the democratic decisions of the Councils of

Constance and Basle. At Ferrara there was no "nonsense" about nations and internationalism, and little about representative Church government. Three groups were formed: one of cardinals, archbishops and bishops, a second of abbots and others, a third of doctors of theology. The votes of only two were necessary. So the lower orders of the Church were put back into their former place. The Italians resumed control.

Ferrara was one of the more ludicrous summit conferences of history. The Greek Emperor John VII (Palaeologus), along with the Patriarch of Constantinople, other patriarchs, twenty-two Orthodox bishops and many lesser prelates attended. The Emperor, like his predecessor in 1095, needed Western aid to protect his capital. In exchange for aid, he too was willing to consider reunification of the Eastern and Western churches. The patriarchs were, theoretically, subordinated to him. The Pope had given symbolic help (the Middle Age equivalent of a modern "trip-wire" force), a galley with 300 bowmen to help protect Constantinople while the Emperor was away.

Theological discussions began where they had left off long ago, as to whether it was lawful for one branch of the Church to add to the creed; and if so, was the addition at the time of Charlemagne, that the Holy Ghost had proceeded not only from the Father but from the Son, allowable? Here was an unrivaled opportunity for display of learning. There were many references to the Council of Nicaea and suggestions that important passages may have been slightly forged in some documents. After eleven months the Greek Emperor and his patriarchs were willing to accept, tentatively, the concept that the Holy Ghost had indeed proceeded from both Father and Son. Then the old question of authority came up. Did Rome really claim to have such control over the Greek Church that a patriarch could be ordered to Rome to stand charges? To that claim the Eastern answer was no! Greeks might be willing to consider unity but only with autonomy. Possibly the Greek marriage custom and its felicities influenced some delegates. Many began to slip away and had to be brought back by the Emperor's armed men.

After an interruption for the meeting to be moved to Florence because a Milanese captain was threatening to attack Ferrara, the question of defense aid was raised again. The Pope agreed to add two triremes, twenty other big ships and a land army, if necessary. The debate swung back to whether Rome would have absolute ecclesiastical authority or whether a federation would be satisfactory. When the Pope, despite the recent experience with the Hussites, insisted on completely centralized control, the Emperor gave the order to depart. A generalized formula was then found which covered much and solved little. On this document (July 1439) the Latins put down 115 signatures, and the Greeks only thirty-three.

Nothing came of that last effort to heal the ancient schism except increased bitterness. When the Eastern delegation returned to Constantinople, there was rioting in the streets and the Emperor, despite his peril from the Turks, did not dare promulgate the decree of Church union. His capital was captured by the Turks fourteen years later, and the promised papal forces were not present to protect it. But this summit meeting had served the Pope's purpose. By creating a rival conference, he had sabotaged the Council of Basle.

Nevertheless, the Pope could not wipe out all effects of Basle. His insistence on complete Roman doctrinal and administrative control of the Greek Orthodox Church was more incomprehensible than ever because in 1438 the French church asserted its autonomy. With the help of Joan of Arc's "gentle dauphin," who had become Charles VII, the French hierarchy accepted the Basle reforms and antipapal attitudes. The Pragmatic Sanction of Bourges combined those reforms with the independence of the French church. (In time the French kings were to wrest control of the national church from the French clergy.) The splitting up of Christendom was well underway.

Meanwhile, the Council of Basle, after calling Pope Eugenius IV to an accounting and failing to hear from him in 1439, followed its own logic of conciliar control of the Church. It deposed him. Eugenius ignored this. He had killed the Council's effectiveness; it had no way of making the deposition effective. It elected another pope anyway. This involved another schism nobody wanted. There were still to be some intrigues centering in Italy. But finally Eugenius found the right combination of bargains and promises; after nine years of exile in Florence, he was able to purchase his way back to Rome. Then it was only a matter of time until the Council of Basle—with all its republican and reformist hopes and its promises of an internationalized and non-absolutist church—would disappear. This was the last effort of the medieval Church to reform itself.

So by the middle of the fifteenth century all the important errors of commission and omission had been made. The course was set for the threefold Church defeat in the early sixteenth century: Luther's defiance at the Diet of Worms (1521), the sack of Rome (1527) and the English church's withdrawal from Rome (1534). The papacy had not regained the trust of the Christian world. It became more and more Italianate in character and style. It had not secured any guarantees of the independence of a safe home and would therefore be involved increasingly in little Italian wars, more and more dependent on major powers to help win them. Its huge landholdings throughout Europe still proclaimed its feudalism and worldliness, a provocation to the rising and hungry men of the day. The Church as the biggest landed proprietor and employer was also blind to the barest needs of the lower-income masses of Christians. Demands of these groups, for return to the Scriptures for rules of life and an apostolic clergy, became more violent the more they were ignored. As monarchs began taking over control of the Church piece by piece, the main task of the hierarchy seemed to be dealing with lay lords, while Christianizing and serving the serfs was more and more neglected.

The lower clergy's demand for a larger voice in the mission to which they dedicated their lives was ruthlessly suppressed, despite the split-off of the French church. Protests by some religious orders and many of the laity against raising revenues by the sale of indulgences were overruled. The German clergy, who had supplied some of the leadership at Basle, tried to follow the French Pragmatic Sanction and obtain a little autonomy of their own. But the new Holy Roman Emperor sold them out to the Pope for the privilege of appointing a few Church officials. With that, the reform movement began to collapse in the very nation where it had been strongest. Nevertheless, dislike of the Italian-controlled Church increased. Citing the Vienna Concordat (1448), in which the German imperial bargain was struck, Laffan comments:

> The papacy had temporarily broken the movement for reform by taking the princes into partnership. By doing so it increased the princely authority over the German church, an authority which two generations later, was to turn against Rome and, by canalizing the streams of a more vigorous reforming movement, to establish itself in independence of both Church and Empire.[5]

The papacy was soon to find out how much its victory at Basle had cost the Church. The first Borgia pope (from a family originally Spanish) tried to rally Europe against the expansion into Europe of the Turks from the Constantinople they had captured. But he found that French ships were held for a war with Naples, while others were reserved for a war with Genoa.

The next pope, Pius II, was a former advocate of the conciliar plan, a diplomat, scholar and humanist. When he called a conference to discuss the Turkish threat, he could persuade not one European monarch to attend. His ingenious plea that the now oppressed Greek Orthodox Church was not heretical but only schismatic left men cold. Crusades, anyone? No. Then he would go alone. Pius II was completely frustrated. King Louis XI controlled the French church without regard to the papacy and was being imitated by the archbishop-elector of Mainz in Germany. Pius had failed to reunite the separated Bohemian church, and King George there was imprisoning papal emissaries for calling the Hussites heretics. So the discouraged Pope set off for a crusade against the Turks. As he marched toward the embarcation port of Venice, he heard that Rome had revolted against him, that all the kings on whom he had counted for support were failing him. He had no funds to pay his tattered little force, and he fell ill. He suffered the further indignity of having the Venetian fleet sail up to ask whether his illness, like all the rest of his crusade, was a sham. It was not. Pius died on the scene of his failure. Twelve years later a papal fleet joined the Venetians for minor successes against the Turks, after which Western forces divided again and the failure was repeated. The crusades were over. The Church no longer had the moral authority to rally Christendom even when the infidel was entering its gates.

Pius II's successors were often able to live gaily and to decorate the Eternal City. Though they could not retrieve what had been lost by the costly papal victory over the Council of Basle, they did experiment in several directions. Sixtus IV (1471–1484) tried to use his nephews to build a Church dynasty among the Italian states. Alexander VI's son, Cesare Borgia, a competent papal *condottiere*, conquered several principalities and dominated Rome.

Julius II (1503–1513) utilized French forces along with those of the Empire and of Aragon against Venice. That city was guilty not only of being a republic but of a sin reserved for kings: it desired to appoint its own clergy. Later Julius II turned against France with the cry, "Drive the barbarians out of Italy!" A French Church synod (Tours, 1510) reassured the King that a war against the Pope would be a holy war and declared that a General Council of the Church should be called at once. Julius II was no more able than his predecessors to unify Italy or protect the papal states and their income. By driving out the French, he merely created a power vacuum which the Spaniards with "their rapacious poverty" rushed in to fill. For years Spain was to dominate Italy and the papacy.

The hundred years beginning with the Council of Constance ended with the reign of another Medici, Pope Leo X. To him is attributed the epigram, "What profit has not that fable of Christ brought us!" He, too, busied himself keeping the papal states together and adorning Rome. He sent another indulgence seller to Germany for funds to build St. Peter's in Rome. This was the moment when German resentment, conscience and nationalism were ready to boil over in Luther's challenge to the morals and authority and then to the doctrine of the Church. The same kind of revolt that the inglorious first John XXIII had evoked from Jan Hus in Bohemia, a cultured and luxury-loving Medici, Leo X, managed to arouse in Germany a century later by the same method, indulgence selling—as if no lessons were ever to be learned from any experience. With this event, a century of Church opportunity for unity through reform ended. The Protestant Revolution had begun. The dis-

covery that evil but rich people could apparently buy prior rights to a
heavenly hereafter which virtuous people could not obtain because of
their poverty was revolting. That the potential resentment at this un-
biblical inequality was overlooked, even after the Hussite wars, by the
Italian management was remarkable. Yet the Vatican, 500 years later,
must have been at least partly aware that its birth control veto (1968)
would bear more heavily on its poor, uneducated and docile parishioners
than on its educated and wealthier members, who would manage to
disregard adverse theological views on the subject, as they had in the
past tended to do.

This account of endeavor, conflict and defeat does not concern an
unimportant episode in an often forgotten age, for the unfinished tasks
of the early councils are still being faced by the Church in the twentieth
century. To appreciate the advantages which might possibly have flowed
from success of the fifteenth-century councils, it is only necessary to
remember the influence they exercised while they were in session and
the disruption and wars which followed their failure. During their meetings, when the reasons for limiting papal absolutism were being widely
discussed, royal absolutism was also on the defensive; it advanced rapidly
only after the Councils had been swept aside. While the Council of
Basle was in session in 1435, Sweden called for a general parliament,
which was to become the most democratic body in Europe. But after
the Councils had ended and kings had cheated the papacy out of its
reactionary victory by taking control of the churches within their
national domains, they received vital moral support from the subservient clergy for their own unrestrained rule. Kings obtained clerical
assurance that they had divine right to rule. It was then that Charles
VII of France freed himself from the parliamentary check of the Estates
General and that his son, Louis XI, first tried to take control of the
Church out of the hands of the French clergy. It was then (1461) that
the Yorkists, making Edward IV king of England, denied Parliament's
right to deal with the royal succession.

If the councils had succeeded in establishing for the whole community of believers a continuing, elective, international church body to
represent them, it might have been far more difficult for kings to institute the royal absolutism which oppressed Europe for many centuries.
The councils, as we have seen, sought to reconstruct the Church on a
democratic electoral foundation, to establish a representative, parliamentary ecclesiastical institution on an international basis. Inherited
Church doctrine might have been, in effect, the constitution, but one
adaptable to well-considered amendments as it finally became at the
Vatican Council of 1962–1965. With a large part of the fifteenth cen-

tury's educated classes participating in at least semidemocratic processes, there would probably have been little or no Church blessing for the divine right of kings. The pursuit of self-government could have been undertaken earlier. For the councils had probed the source of authority in a community and found it to lie in all the members. This was the doctrine of popular sovereignty, that authority was delegated not as a privilege but as a trust. The clergy's function was to worship God by saving men rather than by dominating them. These far-reaching findings affected the thinking of later men who prepared the way for England's Glorious Revolution in 1688, the American Revolution in 1776 and the French Revolution in 1789. Churchmen could have helped an earlier transition to constitutional monarchy and to republics. Heroes of the period could have included priests who stood against all absolutism in the name of human dignity and the Christian Gospel.

A more democratic Church also could have moderated the nationalism that turned Europe into a pool of prejudices, hatreds and wars for several centuries. People might have come closer to the teaching of St. Paul that in Christ there are no racial or national differences, no Gentiles, Jews, Greeks or barbarians. In quarrels between kings, the Church might then have found a popular demand for the revival of the truce and peace of God which it had once used effectively to mitigate or interrupt wars against lesser feudal lords.

If the councils had not been killed by the papacy, the Church might have been guided toward tolerance of man's individual search for a more meaningful personal relationship to God. Though that would have been asking a great deal, the proposed autonomous Church bodies would probably have been closer and more responsive to the new thought and aspirations of their members. The councils allowed Hussites to stay in the universal Church even when those dissenters placed new emphasis on the Scriptures as the key to conduct and the source of authority. A somewhat decentralized Church might have found bishops eager to suppress the provocative practice of indulgence selling on behalf of the beautification campaign in Rome. The peculiar arrogance of the Italian Curia of those days, when it had become a cultural backwater, remote from the mainstream of European intellectual development, might have been overcome by such bishops. Such a church would actually have found it easier than the papacy to emphasize St. Augustine's belief that faith as well as sacraments was a valid approach to God. Then Luther's belief that faith alone was the means of salvation might not have disrupted the Church.

Some regional bodies might even have found it possible to tolerate the Christian mystics. Those mystics were more interested in absorption in God than in theological doctrine. They felt little need of the sacraments. They saw no justification for enforcement of conformity, believing that a persecuting church could not be a true church. With this attitude, there might have been no more burning of men for heresy, a practice which some new sects also condoned.

When the councils of the fifteenth century failed, whatever hopes they may have originally held for the future of mankind died with them. Men narrowed the borders of their loyalties. A new parochialism developed among the believers and among the nations. The Reformation came, a major event in human history, but along with it came new persecutions and then the wars of religion. Their destructiveness set parts of Europe back for some centuries, and only after almost endless suffering did the exhaustion and fear of the people put an end to persecutions and death penalties, and bring some religious and civil liberties. There was also to be a very long period before the absolute kings could be replaced by self-governing peoples. Altogether, humanity found and traveled the hardest road toward its goals. While the councils of the fifteenth century could not, of course, have averted all the misery of later days, they held a reasonable hope that the causes of unity and freedom could have been achieved with less pain and sooner than they were.

More hopes and more grievous surprises were still ahead, however. The many-splendored, many-crevassed institution had been somewhat altered through the centuries by its struggles, victories and defeats. Now it was to observe an attempt by a major monarchy, one which had taken over control of the Church within its own lands, to convert the faith into a justification for imperial expansion, a major weapon in its own wars.

The attack on absolutism which we saw played out dramatically and disastrously in the fifteenth century is as modern as the efforts of indignant young men in Russia, Czechoslovakia and Yugoslavia to alter the absolutism under which they live, as current as the student revolts in the United States, France, Germany, Italy, Mexico and Spain against universities in whose purposes and functions they wish to share more vitally. The lesson is not that an institution can remain absolutist for 500 years, but that an absolutist institution loses support, perhaps even destroys its purpose of universality when it tries to do so. The vulnerability of this organization, which attempted to serve four somewhat conflicting purposes at one and the same time, also bears some witness across the centuries into our own times. We need only observe the difficulties which the United States has already encountered in some of the developing nations of the world. Its desires to promote stability but also to create more free, hopeful and democratic societies, come into rapid conflict with one another.

There is also an implicit admonition in this account about the danger to any international institution when it allows itself to be controlled by any one nation. The control of the Church by Rome was more enduring than that by Paris but both national controls of the Church made it suspect and retarded its efforts. A United Nations dominated by any one power or allied group of powers could be expected to invite similar reaction. The dangers to any organization which makes moral claims for itself but ignores moral obligations were already signaled in the previous chapter, and this later experience copies the earlier one. The danger that a remarkable opportunity will be ignored and never repeated was also demonstrated. The Church might still have become accepted as arbiter between nations during the fifteenth-century crisis. It had no later chance to do so. Even in those days the world could have used a universal ethic of conduct, when almost all men in the West were still members of one church. This accident of a single and irrevocable lost chance could be repeated at any moment in modern times.

There were also counsels for today and tomorrow in some of the lesser events of this period. For example, religious institutions do not necessarily perish as soon as some of their lay members are allowed to participate in their venerable rituals, ceremonies and practices. The Hussites, once granted the right of lay communicants to share the bread and wine with the priest, did not become less devout Christians, nor did the priests become less holy because they were no longer the exclusive celebrants of the Mass. The Church survived and will doubtless survive the efforts of twentieth-century members to obtain the same satisfaction of participation. Even universities will probably survive a sharing in matters of policy, administration and discipline with students.

The period also presented the modern world with a preview of the occasional sensitivity of the Christian conscience under sufficient stress. The Hussite revolt was stimulated in part by a practice which was already condemned by most thoughtful members of the Church, that of selling indulgences to the more ignorant people. They were somehow led to believe that they could have all past and future sins forgiven and thus escape purgatory and move directly into heaven through payment of some money. This was not justified by doctrine, and indeed represented a considerable heresy. However, the Pope at the time, like the Pope in Luther's time who repeated the error, needed money. The subsequent rebellion, partly attributable to this indecency, confounded the Church and made its road more difficult. Somewhat the same reaction of indignation from the incidental and unconsidered uses of mechanical power in warfare was later to be directed against the destruction of civilians and habitations by the United States and was quite as unexpected by its officials.

CHAPTER 6

Spain: Power and Ideology

 Spain—was that peculiar nation ever a great society? Today almost no one would group it among humanity's major achievements. Yet it was the most powerful political and religious force during one whole century, the sixteenth. It was the richest of them all, as well as the most arrogant, reactionary and internally frustrated area in Europe. Men of that period considered it great because it dominated and exploited much of the Continent, including the papacy, conquered and sweated fabulous wealth in gold and silver out of the Indians in Spanish America, and menaced England and France with its forces for long years. Ever since then the Spaniards have been obsessed by a remarkably durable sense of their inherent superiority.

Spain in its century of glory is much more than another riches-to-rags story. Its tilts with fate and fortune remain exciting today for two reasons. First, because it sought to do what many people still fear the Russians or Chinese will one day attempt—spread an outworn and outdated combination of intellectual tyranny, creed, and political obedience throughout the world by force of arms and wealth. Second, because it managed to convert many people outside its own borders to a belief in the very opposite of the combination it sought to impose—conformity of faith, intellectual blackout and Spanish power. Its leaders unwittingly perfected the technique of the international boomerang.

Even in modern times little Spain refuses to allow itself to be ignored.

The old limitations which members of its aristocracy imposed on their community obligations still prevail in much of Latin America. They are among the inducements to social revolution in a number of heavily populated, deeply deprived lands. Their colonials carried westward with them also the tradition of *personalismo* in political life which has thoroughly inhibited the development of parties based on programs. They took with them as well the arrogance of military men in the face of economic difficulties. In the 1930s Spain not only gave the world a preview of the Second World War, but gave it a forewarning of the possible fate of other societies which may be left outside the wealth- and welfare-creating processes of modern life. Misery, hope and the fear that life would never be allowed to become either free or good battled with fear that it would be changed too much, too irreverently and too rapidly. In their bloody civil war, the Spaniards expressed centuries of frustration and hate, and reached levels of barbarity that few have dared to equal. It was only in the 1950s that they found some course other than that of blaming their fellow citizens for their fate, and fighting them, and their slow movement into the modern world at last began. In the late 1960s Spain, no longer a complete outcast, seemed to have more young priests dedicated to the education of their elders in the reforming cause of the twentieth-century John XXIII than any other nation, as well as more elders who lacked that education. The younger men were beginning the long-neglected task of finding a place of usefulness and honor for the Church in society and of discarding a subservience to the state which was ancient, but had become dangerous.

Was Philip II, the Stalin and scourge of Europe in his century, correct in believing that an ideology can be imposed and maintained by force? Were his misfortunes simply due to avoidable bungling, or did he arrive too late in time, more than a century after people had begun to taste some of the excitements of freedom? In spite of his experience, are the bomb-it-out militants of the modern world ("Kill the capitalist imperialists!" "The only good Communist is a dead one!") correct in their conviction that some hostile or horrible ideology can be destroyed by armies? Modern rulers might well possess all the advantages which the Hapsburg monarchs of Spain had, a great treasure, competent armies and, above all, silenced citizens at home, without voice, afraid to discuss their ruler's activities because a crusade was underway—people who were told only that the wars abroad were going very well, but would soon begin to go much better. Would they do better today than the Spanish monarchs in the sixteenth century?

Although Spain was not one of the great cultures seeking freedom, brief glances at several of its interventions in world life during the impassioned sixteenth century may show that some of its discoveries remain pertinent to modern times. That age was one which held the past and future locked in tight embrace from its beginning to its end, never quite sure of either identity. It was the time of Michelangelo and da Vinci, of Elizabeth and her dueling partner, Mary of Scotland, of Luther, Calvin and Loyola, of white-plumed Henry of Navarre and Ivan the Terrible, of a boy who became a cardinal at fourteen. It saw the conquest of Peru, the slaughter of 100,000 Bible-seeking peasants in Germany, and European terror as the Turks hammered at the gates of Vienna. It poured out a mixture of arrogance and humility, genius and inefficiency, riches and squalor, piety and profligacy, individual martyrdom and mass submission.

The Spaniards' first discovery in the century was the difficulty of combining a political revolt with a social one, and the consequence of failure to do so. In their case, an excess of exclusiveness at a critical moment was to cripple the excluders for a century. The year was 1520. A young Hapsburg, Charles V, had inherited the throne of Spain. On the basis of the government's share—one-fifth of all the gold and silver from the new world—he borrowed enough money to buy election to the throne of the Holy Roman Empire. He appointed Flemish courtiers to high positions in Spain and left. Spanish nobles in Toledo rose in indignation at his contempt and neglect. Burghers and others joined in. An intercity junta actually ruled Spain for a while. The insane queen mother was captured by the rebels, the viceroy chased away, Castilian deputies murdered. Charles V, Holy Roman Emperor, ignored all demands for negotiation. He simply waited for class and regional rivalries to kill the revolt for him, which they did. When farm tenants joined the nobles and burghers and attempted to secure a little better life for themselves out of it, the upper-income groups had second thoughts and began to desert to the royalist party. Then the King's officials could move in. Royal *corregidores* were appointed to control the municipalities, whose ancient freedoms were slowly choked off. The provincial *cortes* from that time on obediently voted royal funds for adventures of which they disapproved. The one opportunity for a great national parliament, for a checkrein on royal absolutism, was lost in one moment of fright at a small threat to incomes, to status.

The second discovery by the Spaniards and their subjects in the Netherlands partly justified Lincoln's later observation, made in connection with Negro slavery, that once harm is inflicted on certain human beings by another group, nothing prevents the same harm from being inflicted on the initiators of the evil. The clerical Inquisition, under royal control in Spain, was accepted, although reluctantly by many bishops, because it seemed to be directed against the Marranos, Jews who claimed to have been converted to Christianity, but were nevertheless suspect. In due course, after a very few decades, nobles and clergy who expressed any novel ideas about anything at all found that they were not safe, that they too could and would be imprisoned, tortured and killed. In a slightly different atmosphere, the same process repeated itself in the Spanish-held Netherlands. In 1522 an Inquisition was established there, and the rich Catholic burghers saw no harm in it and some good, because it was directed only against the religious liberty of the Anabaptists, a cult which had the early primitive Christian concept of the communality of all property. Before long, the wealthy men discovered to their horror that the Inquisition seemed far more interested in the possible heresies of the wealthy Catholics (the property of any convicted heretics went to Inquisition officials) than to the heresies of indigent Protestants. Before they knew it, any discussion at all of religious matters by nontheologians was forbidden.

Ironically the King of Spain in due course suffered a not completely dissimilar reaction. The suffering inflicted on the Netherlanders by his Inquisition and his troops finally turned into rebellion, and the rich area was permanently lost to Spain.

The jovial, woman-loving Charles V made his own rediscovery of the fact that crusades with mixed motives, under mixed direction can fail and, also, that after a certain amount of time has been lost, even the most reasonable compromises can become impossible. In time, he was to become a true Hapsburg patriarch, a masterminding marriage broker for European royalty, dragooning youth and doddering age, beauty and beastliness, to mate and reproduce for the imperial Hapsburg benefit. But when he was younger he woke to the fact that he was a contemporary of a man named Martin Luther. In 1521 he heard the young Dominican monk at a session of his diet, or parliament, in the little German town of Worms. That monk dared to subordinate the vast, infinite authority of the everlasting Church to his own Christian conscience. Charles, who presided over a loose aggregation of divisive principalities and free cities, saw the danger of adding a religious difference to those already existing. He was suddenly rediscovering the peril of a state-church unity: Opponents of that church automatically became enemies of the government which supported it.

At that moment there seemed to be no great popular demand for a change in religious dogma. Luther's belief that faith was necessary for salvation had been expressed much earlier by St. Augustine and never completely disavowed by the Church. The popular demand that the laity share in the communion ceremony, that church leaders should behave more decorously than some did, that indulgence selling was deplorable and should be ended seemed not unreasonable to the Emperor. But he wanted Church support in heading off a religious division before it was too late, before German moral indignation at Italian paganism and self-interest boiled up into a new separatist movement. He suggested unsuccessfully a general council to the Pope of the day, Leo X. The papacy had learned to avoid councils like the plague.

When Leo X was followed by Charles' onetime viceroy in Spain, Adrian VI of Utrecht, Charles regained hope. Adrian seemed eager to help Charles hold the empire and church together. He even communicated his view of the current state of the postconciliar Church to his nuncio in Germany in these terms:

> From the head the corruption has passed to the limbs, from the Pope to the prelates; we have all departed; there is none that doeth good, no, not one.[1]

For this he was jeered by all who believed in brazening out the troubles in Germany, who thought any public confession of incomplete righteousness was aid and comfort to the enemy. Not unlike the old pagans who howled down the would-be reformer Porphry for trying to reform paganism in the face of the Christian threat, they denounced Pope Adrian. When he died, after two short years in office, Rome openly rejoiced. The doctor who had attended him during his illness was hailed as "the deliverer of Italy." Charles still needed help from the next pope, Clement VII, an Italian. That man made the mistake of siding with France against the Emperor, and then seeing the Spaniards defeat the French in the most important military event of the century, the battle of Pavia in 1525. After some later double-dealing by that Pope, Charles V allowed his armies to sack Rome in 1527. But precious time was being lost. The Lutherans were acquiring the support of princes and nobles in Germany. Charles felt unable to move against them successfully without support from Rome. He was even unable to get the necessary mercenaries, the famous German *Landsknechte*, for his contests with France except by consent of Lutheran princes in Germany.

For a few brief years Charles V had a little success. After a defeat of France and a truce with the Turks, he attacked and defeated some rebel Lutheran princes in Germany. The new pope, Paul III, who had been a cardinal at fourteen, loaned him large sums and 12,000 troops to accomplish this. But as news of the imperial victories swept into Rome, Pope Paul had second thoughts. A Church council had finally been called at the Emperor's insistence (Trent, First Session, 1545–1549), but it was completely dominated by Italians who did not think any compromise with the Lutheran theologians was necessary or desirable. Still, the Pope feared what a victorious Emperor might do at that council. He recalled his troops from Germany and issued enough statements unacceptable to the Lutherans so that all hope for unity, even under military pressure, was lost. The purposes and direction of the crusade against heresy had been too mixed and contradictory to bring success.

Charles bowed out after two efforts at reform. In 1548 he issued an imperial decree, the Augsburg Interim, which attempted the reconciliation which the Pope and Curia had refused to sanction. The Lutheran concept of salvation by faith was partially accepted, along with papal leadership of the Church. He provided for the marriage of priests and for lay communion in both kinds. Neither the old Church nor the new was happy with this. His slight attempts to enforce it in Germany failed for those reasons and because the populace hated the Spanish troops. In 1555 a Peace of Augsburg was drawn which left each German prince free to choose either the Catholic or Lutheran Church, but forced each subject of that prince to accept the prince's choice or emigrate. After Charles V abdicated in a grandly lachrymose ceremony in Flanders, no opportunity for reestablishing a common bond of Christian fraternity remained. Some years after his death in 1558 the final session of the Council of Trent (1562–1563) restated the medieval theology, thereby confirming the Church's continuing division.

The fourth major discovery became a tragedy. It rose from a crisis of conscience among the Spanish clergy stationed in Latin America. The priests there wanted to protect the converted Indians from inhuman exploitation. They looked at the forced labor, the long hours, the whips, the tiny payments, the early deaths and called the process slavery. Some refused Mass to the Spanish settlers and were chased out of their churches for that refusal. But a small group of Franciscans and Dominicans, including the famous Las Casas, persevered. Their detailed accounts of colonial barbarity impressed the Empress and then the Emperor Charles so much that a halt was ordered to new conquests in the Americas until the rights of the Christian Indians could be debated. At Valladolid (1550–1551) Las Casas defended the Indians. His opponent took the view of the settlers that they were natural inferiors, and cited Aristotle in support of his contention that such inferiors were destined to be slaves. The hearing came to no conclusion, but the settlers had the power, the support of officialdom, and Charles V needed funds badly. The brief revolution of conscience almost evaporated in the cold realities of the world, but not quite. Here and there a few priests still tried to protect the Indians, particularly in Mexico and

Paraguay, but most of the Indians became helots.[2] Then some of the conscience-stricken priests, including Las Casas, sought to save the Indians from their slavery by urging the importation of Negroes from Africa, who had, at that time, not been converted to Christianity and had consequently not earned mercy.

The Spaniards embarked on this venture in the West Indies rather slowly, not because of inefficiency but in order to keep the price of slaves high, the traffic profitable. When the English came in later, wholesaling began. Negro slavery became a custom of the country, and some hundreds of years were to lapse before the Americas could throw off the curse of it.

Two of Spain's encounters abroad under Philip II have some continuing interest. He was no compromiser like his father, Charles V. He wanted no negotiations with the freedom-seeking groups. He wanted only their destruction. Professor Dwight Salmon well expressed what Spain stood for in Philip's day:

> Religious conformity, political absolutism, aristocratic domination of society, economic monopoly, in short all the old privileges and the old traditionalism of medieval Europe. . . . He staked the existence and full strength of the Spanish Empire in the struggle to maintain those elements against the rising forces of individualism, the tide of the future.[3]

Philip was at least a century too late. Nationalism was already too strong, the promise of future freedom too attractive to be yielded readily. To amend Victor Hugo's hope-inspired suggestion that no power can stop an idea whose time has come, it may be that no power can gain lasting dominance for an idea whose time has passed.

The essence of Philip, "Philipism," was that of being more certain than anyone else that he was God's chosen instrument on earth and had divine assurance of success in all he did. No early success justified this heady view of himself. In fact in 1558–1560 he mismanaged and lost a huge international fleet and 10,000 men in a little attack on pirates in Tripoli. The Ottoman sultan saw this huge aggregation as a suspect overreaction to the pirate menace, sailed west, caught the fleet in harbor, captured troops stranded on a waterless island, made them slaves to row his galleys, and trailed the armorial crest of Philip and religious images in his wake back to Constantinople. Yet the indecisive man responsible for this major fiasco was not reluctant to manage himself the Great Armada's attempt against England thirty years later. He did no better with that, yet never lost faith in God or himself or, more accurately, in himself as God.

Never reluctant to see other men die for the sin-crime of neglecting to be members of his own religious sect, he allowed captured English seamen to be burned for their heresy. But he did not seem to see that what was acceptable and natural in Spain was considered outrageous in England. He consequently expected most of England to welcome his troops whenever they landed on that island. The English, quite to the contrary, expected to be burned should those troops ever reach their shores.

In France Philip II financed one of the world's most bitter contests of religion. He subsidized the Holy League, extremists within the old Church who demanded that all their fellow coreligionists accept and approve their own policy of murdering Huguenot neighbors, or be treated as fellow travelers with the Protestants. This provoked some Protestant extremism, and neither helped France. In spite of the fact that Spain was hated because it was an old enemy and had often defeated French armies, and in spite of the added hatred incurred by his efforts to control French political events through his army and his subsidies, Philip had the impression that he could persuade the French to accept his own daughter, born to his third and royal Valois wife, as their queen. The high court of Paris voted against letting any foreigner use religious hatreds to gain power in France. His own subsidy receivers in France finally had to tell him that Spain was as much hated in France as in England. Not the greatest army in Europe or the greatest treasure or the greatest arrogance was able to overcome the French determination to remain independent of Spain, that nation's ruler and executioner.

Finally, the Spaniards experienced the penalty attached to an excess of ambition and domination, much as the Romans of the later Empire had discovered it earlier. Spain had started off the decisive sixteenth century under several handicaps. The high culture which the Arabs had taken and fostered there had been destroyed. The managerial talent of the Jews had been driven out or killed off. An absentee king had not been offset by an effective and popular parliament which might have transferred some of the vast treasure from Peru and Mexico to the building up of agriculture and industry within Spain. For a century the national fifth of that enormous metallic treasure was not only squandered in domination abroad, it was used by other nations to build up supply industries with which Spain itself could not compete. It created a by-product inflation from which the poor of Spain suffered most.

Philip's hard-nosed belief that victories brought power, that there was no substitute for them, that no accommodation with the defeated was necessary in addition to military success, evaporated in the rapidly changing Continent. What use was it for Philip's lord lieutenant in the

Netherlands, the Duke of Alba, to encourage the burning of 8,000 heretics between 1568 and 1574 when the process led to the emigation of 400,000 Lowlanders, and the impoverishment of Spain's richest colony, and then to its wars of independence? What use was it for Philip to put so much relentless pressure on the colonists producing gold and silver in the New World that the whole process sprang leaks of loss and corruption at every joint in the pipeline, and in addition prepared Spanish America for revolts against the crown?

A few decades of momentum survived Philip's death in 1598, which came ten years after his top-heavy Armada had fallen victim to storms and to the low-decked English gun emplacements on their men-of-war. A silver age, not unlike that in Greece in the decades after its major disaster, came into being. The Spanish structure stayed afloat, as if by habit, and the pervasive spy system was one of the last parts of it to go. But in 1643 the army which had dominated Europe for a century was defeated by France, and then the financial and political bankruptcy of the nation became apparent to all. The hungry and hopeless turned to revolt then, and they were to do so many more times in the following centuries. One uprising in Catalonia, started in 1640, lasted nineteen years. Spain, which had once been the *muy brutal* bully of Europe, became a delinquent dropout from the march of progress which others undertook in the West.

Spain, where learning was suppressed for long centuries, remains an educational experience for the modern world. It has dragged its painful heritage of retardation and divisiveness into the twentieth century. It has left a deep imprint of social irresponsibility on many large and important areas of Latin America. Those who live in the shadow of that heritage seem the least likely candidates in the modern world for leadership in creating communities of common interests and opportunities, for obtaining the enrichments of personal freedom. It is a culture which lays great stress on self-respect but vitiates that value by insisting on respect for the powerful even when they fail to deserve it. It produces endless numbers of *caudillos*, men who attempt to reincorporate the "Philipism" of Spain's self-centered, conformity-hungry and brutal king.

Modern men can note some of the history of sixteenth-century Spain repeating itself in later tragedies. They can see the limitations of wealth and ideology in their contest with differing religious creeds, nationalisms and concepts of personal freedom. They can note that ideologies cannot be imposed or destroyed by armed forces over any prolonged period of time. They can note from Spain's later experience that social disunity produces both revolutions and military rulers. They can note the way in which the one revolution Spain needed, before Charles V and Phillip II wasted the wealth of the Americas in wars, was obstructed by the nobles and businessmen as soon as they saw it turning into a social revolution, one invading their own privileges and seeking improvement for the less fortunate people. They can note one of the events which Lincoln feared would take place in the United States, that any injury allowed by the majority against the few would probably be inflicted later on that majority. Religious persecution of converted Jews and Moors spread to independently minded Catholics in Spain, and in the Lowlands spread rapidly from Protestant radicals to rich Catholic burghers.

Modern also and perhaps eternally new is the power of greed to cause social havoc when it is allowed to work its way unchecked by scruple. The Church's righteous objections to the profitable enslavement of the Indians in Latin America were simply bowled over. This event, in turn, led to the introduction of African slavery into both American continents, and the bill for that consequence already exceeds by far all the wealth that Spain extracted from the Americas. In the sixteenth century, Spain had and lost its great opportunity to enrich and advance its people, and that was an irrevocable event, much like the one experienced by the Church in the fifteenth century.

CHAPTER 7

France: From Revolution to Empire

Two score authoritarian nations in the modern world, either military or Communist dictatorships, provide unhappy evidence that the goal of freedom and democracy is a high and difficult human ambition, that the penalties for failure to reach for it as well as those for failure to achieve it can be degrading, severe and prolonged. Long ago the French people, then the cultural leaders of the Western world, provided a memorable demonstration of what could be gained in the ennoblement of life through effort and idealism, how much could be lost in other ways. The tumultuous period of their course from revolution to empire declines to be ignored. The "national liberation front" movements of the authoritarians in today's underdeveloped and still partly feudal nations may be clocked, as the Bolshevik overthrow in Russia was, by French experience. Their major and confused opponents may still be unaware of the historic caveat which those days demonstrated for the benefit of eager military interveners from abroad. The road from feudalism to submission remains as open for much of today's world as it was for France.

The promising and fateful events began when almost everybody in the richest nation in Europe was frustrated and angry. The gods of authority brawled in public. Among the most vocal were nobles of the robe who presided over the high law courts, the *parlements* of France. Audaciously they accused the King of despotism and refused assent to his decrees, halting the whole governmental process. He, in turn, pointed out their crimes and suspended them, only to be forced to cancel that action by the popular demand. Nobles of the sword, some very rich and arrogant, many very poor, heard the King's own two obstreperous brothers loudly declare in their name that all nobles would refuse to pay if their tax exemptions were eliminated. Members of the first estate, the clergy, spokesmen for a Church which owned one-sixth of the farmland of France, also refused to increase their contributions to the debt-plagued government.

Angry, irritated and vocal too were the businessmen, bankers, land-owning peasants and professional men, making up a large share of the nation's human energy and stability, and proudly aware of their own value to that nation. They smoldered at their continued social inequality, their exclusion from the dominant sector of society, and feared that the loans they had extended to the government would be repudiated. The many peasants were being hard-pressed by objectionable and ancient feudal payments and services, by tithes for the Church, by taxes for the state which discouraged them from improving the land they tilled. Those who were only laborers on the land lived hazardously, meagerly, sometimes like animals, the lowliest of the miserables.

In the cities, exposed to the luxury and display of the very rich, the urban workers froze in the very cold winter of 1788–1789 and went hungry as the price of bread rose beyond the range of their thin earnings. Journalists and philosophers raised the level of their very old quarrels with court, nobility and clergy to a new pitch of bitter dissent. Almost everybody wanted change or reform of some sort, while no one wanted to pay much for it. The simple King and his alien, scandal-touched queen, Marie Antoinette, deplored the unhappiness and re-criminations among the people, although without any of the legendary advice that when they lacked bread they should eat cake. Grandson of a king who summarized his own career with the remark "After me, the deluge," Louis XVI was quite unprepared to prove his ancestor wrong.

Only a very few guessed in the spring of 1789 that the French people were on the verge of one of the world's most important revolutions. Their complaints and demands had not solidified into the type of revolutionary ideology to which the twentieth century has become accustomed. In spite of the formation of a republic in the United States of America, which the French had helped make possible, no republicans could be found at that time anywhere in France. Everybody was very shortly to be amazed at the speed with which a few small royal blunders could transform a general discontent into a great hope for change and then into an electric charge so powerful that it would explode and destroy many venerable and apparently invulnerable institutions, and stupefy the watching world.

The story of how King Louis XVI lost his welcome and influence and made himself the nonhero and then the villain of these tumultuous days, is not nearly so important as the account of several major misjudgments which were made by the leaders of the revolution after the King had done his preparatory mischief. The latter were the errors of thought and action which finally perverted and lost much of the triumph of liberty which had been won. But the King's mistakes ambushed his challengers. They were caught up in the underbrush and pitfalls in which his peculiar incompetence floundered.

Louis XVI did not seek to precipitate a social convulsion. He had the problem of a debt charge equal to half the expenditures, so large that recourse to additional loans was impossible. Since none of the three estates, or orders, of the realm planned to help him solve the government's financial problems at its own expense, he found himself forced to call a meeting of the Estates General, the ancient authority of France, which had not met since 1641. But he casually allowed his chief minister to decide that the third estate, representing about 95 out of every 100 people in France, would elect twice as many members as either of the other two estates, the clergy and the nobility. Suddenly he found himself, in May of 1789, following the advice of the nobles around him and ordering the three estates to meet separately and vote as units exactly as they had done in 1641. This meant that the two upper groups, representing together about five out of every 100 people, would always have a legislative majority of two to one. It was this decision which brought the third estate to the point of revolt. Its members could count. They did not want to remain in the role of a permanent minority in France or allow the vested interests of the nobles and clergy to continue to dominate the nation. Indeed, Louis XVI, if he had thought a little more deeply, might have feared the same result for the crown. Not only the commoners but the throne could have become helpless victims of that adventure.

The King overrated himself and the nobles and underrated the new men of France. He seems to have paid little attention to the huge outpouring of people—an exercise in almost universal suffrage—who took part in the three-stage elections to the third estate or to the lists of grievances which they all had to write for the guidance of their delegates. These were filled with clamor for a better life, fewer shackles of custom, fewer oppressions, more liberties, less autocracy, more participation in the life of the nation, more control of their own destinies. Ignoring all that surge of protest, he told the men of the third estate to remain the lowliest of a tripartite system. He had no idea that they would refuse. He had no idea that they would take it into their heads to call themselves the majority in France and to transform their own estate into a national assembly. So, on June 17, he repealed their decisions to do so and ordered them to behave as he saw fit. However, it was not for that they had been elected. They cleverly counterattacked with a law of their own, the only one that was sure to be obeyed throughout France. It was that no tax levied without their own consent needed to be paid.

The King yielded, somewhat dismayed, but soon found himself following the same self-interested and stupid advice of the nobles in his entourage, to meet the challenge of France's new voting majority by force. Here again he underrated the men who wanted a new constitution, a new arrangement for the affairs of the nation. He had not used troops against the third estate because at the moment only French soldiers were stationed in Versailles, and they could not be trusted to shoot at the leaders of the new National Assembly. But he had 10,000 foreign mercenaries along the border, and in July he called them to Versailles. At the same time he dismissed the one minister of state, the Swiss Necker, on whom the whole financial community was counting for a miraculous solution of the debt and taxation problem. People in Paris and throughout the nation understood him. He planned to suspend the new National Assembly by force, to go on trying to govern without the assent of most of his people and against their interests.

Three counter threats appeared almost simultaneously. First, the people of Paris, including many urban workers, gutted the city for arms and ammunition and captured the old prison, the Bastille fortress that would have been used by the King to dominate the city. They fought the King's garrison, and some French soldiers aided them. Second, the middle-class people of Paris, using the same agencies which had conducted the elections to the third estate, quickly organized a national guard to defend the Assembly against the King. These guardsmen did not swear loyalty to that King but to the nation. Finally, peasants in the countryside, stirred by their hopes at the time of the elections and caring little about the legalisms being debated at Versailles, began a process of undoing their feudal lords. After panicky moments of great fear, they sallied forth in bands and began hunting for the ancient books of record which recorded all their feudal obligation, and burned them. (The same desire to "go for the books" and destroy evidences of debt showed itself in the course of the lootings which took place in Washington in April 1968 after the assassination of Martin Luther King.) From burning the books, the French peasants went on to burn the chateaux of their landlords, and some of the more cruel stewards for these landlords were killed. Scattered throughout the countryside, these were acts which the King, for lack of funds, police and troops, was unable to stop. He called quits to his plans to intimidate the Assembly, canceled his summons to his foreign mercenaries, brought his popular minister of state back to Versailles, visited Paris and stuck the red, white and blue cockade of the revolution into his cap. It was pleasing, but not entirely persuasive. A few months later, in October, reports of French noble officers stamping on the same revolutionary cockade at a Versailles dinner for the royal family were enough to bring a marching mob of Parisians to his palace. Its members were suspicious, indignant and hungry. The price of food was rising sharply and the King was doing nothing about it. They slaughtered some of the royal guards. The Marquis de Lafayette, still trailing American-made glory, came up with the National Guard to protect the King, but could not prevent the whole royal family from being taken back to Paris, accompanied by the bloody heads of his guards on pikes. The angry nobles at court even accused Lafayette of being a Cromwell, coming to replace the King. Then they hastened to emigrate across the Rhine to a safer place. With the King's removal to Paris, followed rather unthinkingly by that of the Assembly, both crown and legislature had been moved into the one location where the urban and more extreme revolutionaries could exercise a large measure of influence and control.

So Louis XVI, who had in May possessed the moral authority to obtain the needed financial help from the Estates General at the price of a few reforms, had managed by October to become a semiprisoner. Failing to lead the nation's new majority, he lost much of the confidence and authority needed to survive. He had aroused suspicion about his interest in assuring the bulk of the French people an opportunity to improve their lives. He had allowed the transfer of the nation's hopes from the crown to the Assembly. He had shown them the weakness of his own armed forces in the face of popular support for the Assembly. More significantly, he had managed to set in motion two major forces, the peasantry and the urban workers, directed against the inequality of the feudal order which he had chosen to support. With this, he had helped to turn a mild political alteration of institutions on behalf of the middle class in the direction of a major social revolution. All this he had achieved within six months, between May and October of 1789.

Long, long before the United States watched one quick, small decision balloon and expand into an annual and not overly successful expenditure of $25 billion a year in Southeast Asia, the Legislative Assembly of France demonstrated the dangers of underrating consequences. It was searching for a way out of the financial difficulties of the King's government. It wanted to rid the budget of the enormous debt charges. It decided to confiscate the Church-held farmlands in order to use them as the credit base for an issue of paper money (*assignats*) with which to retire the debt. There was precedent for this action. Henry VIII of England had gained support for his rule by taking Church-held lands and dividing them among his nobles. German princelings had done the same at the time of the Reformation. The Church in France was vulnerable because of its foreign control, the contradiction between its spiritual and its feudal interests, the need of peasants for more land. A number of its hierarchy, deputies in the Assembly, voted for the land confiscation.

The next step in the escalatory process appeared promptly. Bankers and others were somewhat reluctant to accept the *assignats*, because the Church might at some time regain its properties. To make that less likely and to make the paper money more credible the Assembly voted to take over all responsibility for Church debts, the maintenance of Church functions, including salary payments to the clergy. In the process it doubled the miserable pay of the parish priests, cut the incomes of the richer and usually noble upper hierarchy.

But this led to still further decisions, all encroaching on the explosive area of state domination of the Church. The Assembly wanted the Church to be more efficiently operated and to be more democratic in character. In July of 1790 a Civil Constitution of the Clergy was passed. Bishoprics were confined to the same borders as the newly established eighty-three administrative provinces, a requirement which automatically retired and antagonized fifty-two out of 135 bishops. More, the parishes were allowed to elect their own clergy, and all the voting citizens within each parish were allowed to take part in such elections, regardless of whether they were parish members or not. These measures provoked a storm of opposition from the clergy and many of the faithful. So great was the outcry that the Assembly, in November of 1790, instituted a loyalty oath for the clergy. They had to swear to maintain the decisions of the Assembly with all their might. The Pope was actually urged by many of the French bishops to accept this Civil Constitution of the clergy. However, angered by the refusal of the Assembly to send troops to suppress a revolution in his own nearby land of Avignon, which was in favor of joining France, he denounced the whole change as anathema in April of 1791. So loyalty to the Church and loyalty to the state were set in opposition. A crisis of conscience was created.

Neither prelates nor poor parish priests knew which way to turn. In some parishes they were stoned by their congregations if they swore the loyalty oath. In others they were stoned if they failed to take it. A few years later, after the King had raised serious new questions about his own loyalty to the nation and after the legislature had raised new questions about its own humanity, the priests faced an even sharper

choice. Many of them who refused to take the oath became leaders of
royalist, counterrevolutionary activity, and many died for their acts. All
through the nineteenth century the clergy in France, frozen in reaction
to the demands and cruelty of the revolution, found themselves rather
automatically siding against every move and group which sought a more
democratic nation.

The National or Constituent Assembly, which had inaugurated and
presided over the first two years of the revolution, established a remarkable basis for personal liberty. However, it ended its sessions by taking
voting rights away from most of the people of France. There would be
liberty, but there would also be inequality.

The first Assembly will always be remembered for its Declaration of
the Rights of Man and of the Citizen. It was one of the first statements
in modern times about the dignity of the individual. It outlined the
realm of personal liberty, equality before the law, suffrage and taxation,
trial by jury, ownership of property and the sovereign rights of the
nation. The Assembly in its Constitution brought the administration of
the country together, and wiped out old provincial lines and privileges.
It abolished the nobility as a caste. It created a large, tariff-free market.
For those days these were startling and memorable achievements.

The Assembly lost some opportunities. It voted against a cabinet
form of government, with members chosen from the legislature. With
this negative decision, parliamentary government became practically
impossible. Here the Queen's proroyalist faction and Lafayette's king-at-
low-pressure group, made up a large part of the opposition. The Queen's
advisers thought that such a form of popular and parliamentary government might work and was therefore undesirable. Lafayette may have
been afraid that the Comte de Mirabeau, who was closer to the King,
would be chosen instead of himself as the King's first minister.

The Assembly also failed to provide for emergencies in its relations to
the executive branch of the government, a failing that had already
afflicted the Americans, who had neglected to provide adequately in
their own Constitution for a succession in case of presidential infirmity,
for a method of determining the outcome when votes were in dispute
within the states, and for the possibility that a small minority of the
population (voting as state units in the House of Representatives)
might be able to choose a president when none of three or more candidates obtained a majority in the electoral college. What the French
were confronted with was something different, an existing, hereditary
executive, who was, unlike a president, not subject to the electoral
process. Their first constitution gave that king a suspensive veto over
legislation which enabled him to delay action for six years. That

assumed a patriotic and sympathetic king, an extremely patient legislature, and a long period without national emergencies. None of these conditions prevailed. This check on the legislature was not balanced with one on the monarch, though the current king clearly needed restraint. When Louis was deposed a year after the new constitution was drawn, France was left without any constitutionally approved executive. The constitution had to be discarded, and then the legislature was left without any check on its own wisdom and activities. This unexpected default in governmental construction invited a semiauthoritarian state.

This first upper-middle-class Assembly could not leave the scene of its own triumph without striking two blows at the urban workers, men who happened to feel that they had served the nation and revolution very well by thwarting the King's attempts to undermine the Assembly. One consisted in cutting down the voting rights of these people by establishing a high property qualification for the suffrage. Over one-third of the people who had voted in 1789, and consequently thought that they had a right to vote, were cut from the rolls. The nonvoters were also excluded from the National Guard.

On top of that, the Assembly went some distance out of its way to show the urban workers that it cared little for their hunger and misery and would not in any way support their desire to obtain any improvement in their wages and hours through collective bargaining. These workers, in Paris, had been experiencing unemployment because of the flight of nobles and wealth abroad, which began with the peasant revolt and accelerated after the King had been brought to Paris, in October 1789. The poorer city people had hungered and frozen during two hard winters before that. The price of bread kept rising, lowering their already miserable standard of living. In Paris the construction workers requested a raise in pay from thirty to thirty-six sous per day's work. Some wanted a minimum wage. The employers were still autocratic, and workers were subject to a blacklist. They could not leave their jobs without their employer's consent on penalty of three years' imprisonment. The conservative middle class of Paris then controlled the Paris municipality, the Commune. That body decided against a minimum wage and prohibited all labor organizations grouped for the purpose of obtaining wage increases or shorter hours. The Assembly supported this in June of 1791 with the Le Chapelier Law forbidding labor organizations for these purposes. With these measures the urban workers were excluded from the march of the others into a better world.

These measures seemed to the middle-class members of the Assembly to insure their own dominance of the new order. To the urban workers and some poorer peasants these decrees indicated that their only remaining chance of gaining anything from the revolution was through direct action of their own. At this time there was no collaboration between the city workers and the poorer elements in the peasantry, who had also been excluded from the benefits of the revolution. The land taken from the Church had been sold at auction. Those peasants with money in their stockings could buy. However, one in five of the farm people in France was either a completely landless farm laborer or a tenant, who had no cash reserves and could not buy land. Many of them lived in conditions of squalor and hunger. Few were serfs, but many lived in submission, like serfs. Opportunities for corruption existed during the land sales, and reports of it further embittered these people. They were to be heard from later, when the church bells stopped ringing and the clerical issue became a royalist and peasant cause in certain parts of the nation.

In brief, the Assembly which had made the revolution had drawn a balance sheet showing some remarkable assets, but also some liabilities which were soon to become payable. In June of 1791, three months before the Assembly's three-year term of office expired, everybody in France was still a monarchist of sorts. There were almost no republicans. By July that had changed. Suddenly quite a number of republicans appeared. With one day's work, the blundering King had managed to turn a general disappointment and exasperation with himself into suspicion and disloyalty.

Revolution and counterrevolution change shapes with time and change one another's forms as well. By June of 1791, two years after the third estate had won its great initial triumph, three dissident forces were at large and active, and a fourth was slowly being recruited. The nobles and the King's two brothers who had emigrated to Koblenz, Aix-la-Chapelle and Turin, their partisans among the self-exiled prelates and their personal adherents and friends who had remained in France were the most important and well-financed group. The second group was composed of clergy who had remained in France. Many of the priests and some of the bishops who remained had been moving over to active opposition, and their followers were numerous in the countryside.

The King and his immediate court represented the third objecting group, the most visible one. The King, not a strong character, may have been manipulated by his stronger Queen, who was, along with him, busily engaged in correspondence with the émigré nobles and her brother, the Emperor of Austria, asking for help. But he held some strong feelings of his own, and one pertained to the respect due to the clergy. In the last days of 1790 the Assembly had voted to require all the priests and other clergy who were receiving state salaries to take a loyalty oath to the new constitution. In the early days of 1791 this requirement was extended to clergy who were members of the Constituent Assembly.

The penalty for refusal was deprivation of income. A number refused, and all felt uncertain of their obligation to both Church and state. The King resented being forced to approve these requirements, which he believed to be persecution of men faithful to himself. His delay in signing these decrees and his final act in signing them managed to please no one. He had followed the same procedure with decrees abolishing feudal duties in 1789. He managed to irritate his opponents first and then his supporters. The division of opinion and loyalty among the clergy as a result of the loyalty oath encouraged him to believe that most of the country outside of Paris wanted a return to the old days. The secret decision was made to attempt a flight across the border in order to return in triumph at the head of the émigré nobles and such armies as his fellow monarchs—the fourth dissident force—made available to him.

This flight, attempted in June of 1791, was a spectacular fiasco, complete with disguises, the Swedish Count de Ferson, Marie Antoinette's great and good friend, masquerading as coachman on top of almost the largest and most conspicuous cabriolet in the country, loyal dragoons roaming the countryside, thereby alerting citizens to something unusual, hours of delay over a hearty evening meal, and an arrest of the whole troupe of escapists at Varennes, a little short of the border. There followed a somber return to Paris, under guard, past huddled and bewildered multitudes who had up to this moment never thought of France without a king.

This was an educative and emotive event. A large number of members of the Assembly found that France could be governed without a king. (Louis XVI was suspended for several weeks, until in September he took an oath of loyalty to the revolution.) The workers of Paris and the lower middle class of tradesmen, led by certain journalists, moved over from suspicion to certainty and determined to get rid of the traitorous King and his supporters, including those in the Assembly. On July 15 of 1791 the Assembly exculpated the King of any charges of disloyalty. Two days later some of the skeptical citizens gathered on the Champs de Mars to sign or debate about signing a petition for elimination of the King and creation of a republic. A force from the National Guard (from which all those ineligible to vote had been excluded) moved in on them, perhaps without a proper display of the red banner signifying martial law, and killed thirty and wounded many more. This was "the massacre of the Champs de Mars" which the Parisian workmen saw, felt and remembered for years as evidence of the hostility of the middle-class Assembly to them and of the perfidy of Lafayette, who was in charge of the Guard.

The shouting and threats of the nobles across the border, the crisis of conscience among the clergy, the King's flight, this killing and the exculpation in July were within a short time all reconsidered and reviewed against the glare of the fourth dissident force, the crowned heads of Prussia and Austria. Only nine months later, in April 1792, France would declare a preventive war against their expected military intervention.

Nudged by the pleas of the émigrés and by the royal court of France, these two kings, both enlightened monarchs, discussed in July 1791 a joint statement to safeguard the French monarchy and limit the excesses of the revolution. England and Russia were not interested. For them the news that France was weaker and more divided than before was pleasant rather than provocative. Possibly Prussia and Austria preferred to have no showcase of constitutional government in the neighborhood. Leopold II of Austria, brother of the French Queen, made peace with the Turks. The French thought that he might be freeing his armies for later action against France in case its people maltreated Louis XVI and his wife. The two rulers made an alliance. This alliance worried some members of the Assembly, as did the republican demonstration in the Champs de Mars. They tried once more to obtain approval of a cabinet form of government, but failed again.

In late August of 1792 the two sovereigns issued a declaration from Pillnitz that the establishment of order (the older one) in France was a matter of common concern to all the sovereigns of Europe. This may have been intended simply as a bit of encouragement to the moderates in the French Assembly. Actually, it was a carefully safeguarded statement. No action against France was contemplated, it said, unless all the rulers of Europe agreed. Since the disagreement of England and Russia was certain, there was no serious immediate threat. However, the émigré spokesmen shouted for all to hear that it was a binding promise of support to the cause of the nobles and the prelates, a guarantee of intervention, an occasion for the complete roll-back of the revolution. While a number of émigrés, particularly those in London, saw that there was no such turning back to the old order, they were silenced by the bitter-enders. Those moderates were not heard at all. France chose to listen to its noisiest émigrés and to act as if it were presented with an actual urgent threat of losing what its people had gained in freedom, opportunity, land and status, and losing it at the hands of foreigners, with whom they had often engaged in war.

The French decision to declare a preventive war (with only seven votes in the Legislative Assembly against it) was the result of a peculiar mixture of conflicting motives. The King, Queen and royal party favored a war because they were sure that the French, deprived of the nobles as officers, would lose it, and the monarchy would then be restored to its former position of power. The Girondin middle-class majority in the Assembly, unable to forget the King's recalcitrance and his flight, thought that the war would unite the nation, help them shackle the King and provide themselves with the glory of victory. Lafayette thought that a limited war might help him to eliminate the more disturbing revolutionary elements from the Assembly. Some of the more solidly revolutionary groups in their Jacobin clubs throughout the nation accepted war at its face value, a defense of the nation against foreigners, of the revolution against monarchy, nobles and foreigners alike. Maximilien Robespierre, a lawyer who had once resigned a judgeship rather than inflict the death penalty on a criminal, already an outstanding leader of the Jacobin groups, voted against the war on the ground that it would produce a military dictatorship, ending the revolution. He was not allowed to live long enough to see Bonaparte prove the correctness of his judgment.

Given so many cross purposes for the same war, it was natural for some groups to be disappointed, and they were. But the Girondin desire to create a foreign foe in order to simplify their management of the revolution at home has had its imitators. Stalin constantly used the menace of "capitalist encirclement" to justify his dictatorship of Russia. Mainland China later used the same tactics, designating the United States as its menace, when it sought in the 1960s to impose a cultural revolution on top of the original one. None of these groups in France confided their basic purpose to their people, of course. The main Girondin leader in France, Jacques-Pierre Brissot, for example, delivered himself of this peculiar grab bag of justifications:

> The force of reason and of facts has persuaded me that a people which, after a thousand years of slavery, has achieved liberty, needs war. It needs war to consolidate its freedom. It needs war to purge away the vices of despotism. It needs war to banish from its bosom the men who might corrupt its liberty.[1]

However, the Girondins proved to be right on one score. The revolutionary gains of the French people by 1792 were adequate to unite the people against any foreign foe which threatened to take them away. The opponents of the revolution were sufficiently misled by their own memories and interests to scare their potential supporters within France by everything they said. Most conspicuously stupid was a manifesto written by the enraged émigrés for the Duke of Brunswick, commander of the Prussian forces, in the summer of 1793. He practically threatened death to anyone who had had anything to do with the revolution and destruction to Paris itself. He gave the Jacobin leader Danton the impetus necessary for a formidable defense within Paris against that danger. Years later the King's brother, the later Louis XVIII, issued a royalist proclamation from Verona which scared the life—or at least the pride of property—out of all the proroyalists who had managed to gain some land as a result of the revolution. The people of France had gained enough by 1792 so that they would fight to defend their gains. The émigrés and the rulers of Austria and Prussia paid for their failure to notice that they were now engaged in a war against a different kind of nation than France had been before the revolution. They were discovering the difficulty of countering a social revolution without offering anything better.

Given the cross purposes of the groups welcoming a foreign war, some ironic disappointments were a predictable outcome. Neither the main political party of the ruling middle class, the royal court, Lafayette nor the Jacobin group attained their hopes through the war, and many of them attained their early death. In their behalf it must be noted that those were still the days before total war—although they began the movement in that direction—and people had no particular reason to know in advance that wars can undo those who win them as well as those who lose them.

The major group desiring the war, the Girondins, managed to make itself peculiarly vulnerable to attack and overthrow. They did so by compromising themselves with a suspect King, who was soon to find his own hidden and carefully filed evidence of treason exposed, and in demonstrating their complete indifference to the inequality of suffering which the war produced among those least able to bear it. To their utter astonishment they were to find themselves forced into the ranks of the counterrevolutionaries, against whom they had sought to protect the nation.

The process of reversal began promptly with the war, when France went through agonies of defeat and apprehension. Within two weeks after it had declared war, in April of 1792, the nation began to echo with cries of treason coming from the front. In the first few encounters with the enemy near Lille, many noble officers deserted. Men ran, calling, "We have been betrayed!" This was shattering to public confidence. Only a few leaders were aware that the hard work of the army had always been done by non-nobles of lesser rank and that the first panic and chaos would subside as these men took over higher commands and the basic superiority of the French army, particularly in artillery, would be reasserted. Lafayette, who had been given command of one of the three armies in the north, could not forget his major fear, that the radicals would use the emergency to take power. He used the occasion of an armed invasion of the royal residence by groups of unruly Parisians in June, which included a humiliation of the King, to leave his command. He returned to Paris, demanded of the Assembly that it dissolve the radical Jacobin clubs. It refused. He then went to the National Guard of Paris and demanded that it march against those clubs and close them. It also refused. He returned to the front and secretly asked the Austrians for an armistice. They refused. In August the Jacobin minority in the Assembly asked his impeachment for deserting his post. This was disapproved. However, on August 19, the day that the enemy troops crossed into France, Lafayette made himself a war prisoner of the Austrians, refusing to join the émigrés. Within five months he had ended his usefulness to France. Later Frenchmen, who heard an American officer announce the arrival of American troops on French soil in 1917 with the happy phrase "Lafayette, we are here!" could only wonder what was to come.

The actual invasion was preceded by a Jacobin rally of Paris against the King. On August 1, the Brunswick manifesto was received in the city, and people feared a new St. Bartholomew's Day massacre of all those who had supported the revolution. The King's brothers, both in the emigration, were known to be behind that manifesto, a fact which implicated the King and Queen immediately. Robespierre now called for deposition of the King. He persuaded some 5,000 soldiers from the provinces who were passing through Paris to disobey their orders and stay in the city. They were militant republicans, who brought the rousing "Marseillaise" to Paris with them. They gave the republican people in Paris a sense of representing the will of the whole nation. They gave the Jacobins the muscle they had previously lacked to support their claims to power. (This measure to obtain friendly troops was later copied by the Bolsheviks in their successful effort to take over the government of Russia. They won the key Petrograd garrison to their side by promises that those troops would never be sent to the front.)

Things moved fast. Two days after the manifesto reached Paris, all but one of the forty-eight Paris sections petitioned the Constituent Assembly to depose the King forthwith. The Assembly ignored these demands and showed its support of the King by refusing the Jacobin request that Lafayette, the King's supporter, be impeached for desertion. That was on August 8. On the tenth, the Commune, now radicalized by danger, hardship and fear of betrayal by the Assembly as well as the King, invaded the Tuileries, took the royal family into its own custody in the Temple (the old headquarters of the Knights Templar), and received from the cowed Assembly authority not only to control Paris but to round up all men who might be suspected of antirevolutionary and antipatriotic actions. These people of Paris thought it was none too soon, for on August 19 the enemy forces crossed into France and took the fortress at Longwy. Worse, a few days later, Verdun fell, under suspicious circumstances.

Men felt surrounded by treasonous forces. The road to Paris was open for a moment. The invaders were stopped, somewhat fortuitously, in the Argonne, but a great fear prevailed in the capital and a major defense effort began. Rumor of a plot by political prisoners in the Paris jails, who were supposed to burst out together and support the invaders, led to a horrible massacre of many of them, including nonjuring priests, with only a pretense and mockery of legal process. Sadists had been given their opportunity and used it. The leaders of the Commune and Danton, the outstanding Jacobin moderate and a tower of strength in preparing the defense of Paris, looked the other way. This was the lowest point of criminality during the revolution. However, on September 20 the French general Kellermann defeated the Duke of Brunswick at Valmy, and a little later the Duke retreated across the border. Prussia, suddenly presented with the opportunity to expand, was more interested in assuring itself a slice of Poland than in fighting the French for Louis XVI.

To its own considerable astonishment, France now became a republic. Royalty was abolished on the twenty-first day of September in 1792, one day after the newly elected legislative body (called the National Convention because it was to draw a new constitution) had met. The King was deposed. Twenty-one years were to pass before another Bourbon was placed on the throne.

Although deposed, the King still had it in his power to discredit the Girondin royalists. They could also be discredited by their own generals. Both used that power. In November of 1792 the carefully preserved correspondence of the King conniving with the disloyal émigrés was found in a locked iron box in his former residence in the Tuileries. The letters proved his own disloyalty and the perjury of his oath supporting the new constitution. He brought himself to the guillotine in January 1793. He put into extreme jeopardy the Girondins who had supported him and who tried to save his life even after he had been found guilty of treason. After that effort failed, they continued in power only because their general officers were winning battles. Those generals, however, were engaged on a course which was ultimately fatal to the revolution and to France. They forced acceptance of their program and invaded the Netherlands. More, this invasion was followed by an opening of the Schelde River, an event which restored Belgium's long-lost trading position at the expense of Holland. These two occasions were accompanied by a promise of friendship and support, made by the National Convention, to all people wishing to recover their liberty. (Robespierre was heard scoffing about the welcome armed missionaries might receive.) And this was followed by an annexation of Savoy, which had been ruled by the Pope.

These several developments, taken together, changed the attitude of

Great Britain from one of indifference to one of alert attention. The British saw a French intent to occupy permanently and control England's old access to European markets through the Lowlands. England called up part of its militia and recalled Parliament. It was soon to become the great paymaster of one coalition after another against France until Waterloo ended French expansionist drives. Danton's efforts to proclaim a limit to French expansion at the old "natural frontiers" of the Alps, Rhine and Pyrenees came a little late and did not deal directly with the French control of the Lowlands.

The upper-middle-class majority in the Assembly had tied its fate to one general, Dumouriez, who had been the Girondin Minister of War for a while. They were living on his victories, a precarious nourishment. However, they refused a coalition with the moderate Jacobins which Danton proposed to them, which might have saved them, but which would have made Danton the leading figure in the government. Then, suddenly, Dumouriez not only failed them but practically killed them. He was defeated at Neerwinden in March of 1793, and all French troops had to retreat to the border fortresses again. This was bad enough, but in April, after trying in vain to get his troops to join with him on a march against Paris, he deserted to the Austrians. Here was treason in high revolutionary quarters, and all the Girondins were tarred with it, on top of being marked earlier by their prolonged support of the treasonous King.

The populace of Paris might not have risen against the Girondins, even after this evidence of treason and this guilt by association, if the Girondin leadership over its long period of power had shown a little compassion for the suffering in Paris. Those were men of principle, whose principle was that when you had achieved a free market it should remain free, regardless of the human consequences. So they had refused repeatedly all demands to limit the price of bread and to hold down rents, in spite of a severe inflation which lowered living levels day by day. The poorer people, who lived on bread, suffered disproportionately and in addition were conscripted in large numbers into the army. They saw fortunes being made in food speculation and smelled corruption. The Girondins did not offer to relieve the needs of these people. They were now overcommitted abroad and undercommitted at home.

At the end of May 1793, the Parisians decided to protect themselves against the National Convention, as they had once protected themselves against the King. The Paris Commune, which had become a center of both war organization and indignation, killed the National Guard commander in Paris, imprisoned city officials, and surrounded the Convention with several score thousand armed men and heavy artillery. Its leaders demanded and obtained the arrest of twenty-nine Girondin deputies and two Girondin ministers. Many others fled the legislature and the city in fear of their lives. One of the penalties of their fate was that, like the priests who refused to take the loyalty oath, once they had broken with the government in Paris they could discover no halfway point of opposition where they could stop. They found themselves, in spite of their commitment to the original revolution, fighting in the ranks of the extremists, the counterrevolutionaries.

Meanwhile, Robespierre, who had become leader of the more revolutionary Jacobins, moved toward power in the Committee for Public Safety, which had been established as the executive agency of the nation. He was far more sympathetic than the Girondins had been to the demands of the Commune, which included control of bread prices, a tax on wealth, and public assistance for the aged and the dependents of soldiers, as well as a purge of disloyal officials. When, in July, a Girondin devotee, a woman, assassinated the popular journalist Marat, the longtime enemy of the Girondins, and a plot on Robespierre's life was rumored, an open season on Girondin deputies everywhere was proclaimed.

Here was a hazardous moment when the interventionist armies might have succeeded in defeating France, for revolts against the Jacobin government in Paris broke out throughout the Rhone Valley and in Normandy and the Vendée as well. However, the English had marked Dunkirk as a potential second Gibraltar for themselves and marched their troops away from the other allied forces to capture it, a first-things-first decision which halted the other allied armies.

Under its Jacobin control, the Convention changed the constitution back to grant universal suffrage. It passed a law against food hoarding and attached the death penalty to it. A general maximum-price-limit law was also passed. With Paris quieted by these measures, the government proceeded to put down the revolts in the big cities of the South and in the countryside. In September those extreme measures were passed covering the arrest and trial of certain large categories of suspects which marked the beginning of the period of intimidation or terror, known and deplored throughout the Western world. Of 400,000 or so suspects arrested, some 17,000 were executed for counterrevolutionary acts. Possibly government forces put 40,000 to death altogether, although individual, unauthorized violence by individuals on both sides surely accounted for many, many more.

Five characteristics of this Reign of Terror are worth noting. Its brutality and injustice are only the most commonly observed. Many innocents were sentenced to death, including some children. Guilt frequently consisted of little more than past association with other suspects. This was a process which horrified the neighboring world and became the excuse for stopping reform movements abroad. The governments in other nations, in short, developed a guilt by association concept of their own, and all democrats became suspect of desiring terror. The injustice frequently perpetrated gave many suffering Frenchmen an enduring sense of revulsion at an unlimited executive power and buttressed their predilection for a weak executive, a powerful legislature. A second feature was the use of the instruments of intimidation against the very people who had insisted on them, the more radical leaders of the Parisian working class. One result of this was that those groups refused to support the Robespierre regime when it was challenged.

A third was the comparative brevity of the terror. It lasted from September 1793 into July 1794, some ten months, and then was brought to an end after a great military victory had eliminated the danger of invasion, defeat and punishment. Fourth, it was effective. It helped to put down the civil war which the counterrevolutionaries had opened and which was being encouraged by foreign powers and funds. It allowed for a mobilization of the nation's resources. By the spring of 1794 the French, conscripting men liberally, were able to put armies of superior strength on all the fronts. Finally, the delayed feedback of revulsion against the terror was directed largely against the urban working class and carried down with it all the hopes for a fully democratic and equalitarian republic. Some of their leaders had fallen victims to the terror, but after it was over the whole group was punished for the period through prohibition of its right to organize in self-protection and through elimination of the price-fixing laws which had supported its standard of living. The repeated exclusion of urban workers from the revolution, in spite of their several services to it, left the bewildered executors of the revolutionary estate with no group to whom they could turn for support except the army, when royalist sentiment revived three years later.

Some similarities to this Terror have been noted in modern times, while its victims have long since been outnumbered, for example in Germany in the 1940s, where millions of Jews and Slavs were killed by the government, and in Indonesia in the late 1960s, where possibly 300,000 dissidents were killed by the army and their own frightened neighbors, who feared them. A few months after the assassination of Marat by Charlotte Corday, a Girondin devotee, the practice of great staged public trials began. (In the twentieth century it would be used and then discarded by the Nazis, elaborated by the Communists under Stalin, and then imitated briefly by Fidel Castro in Cuba.) The purpose was not to discover the guilt of the accused but to convince the populace of their treason and to frighten the people with a sense of the pervasiveness of treason and its danger to them. When the accused

Girondin deputies were put on public trial (September 1793), 50,000 copies of the accusations against them were printed and circulated. Witnesses against them were in no danger of prosecution for perjury. Conspiracy against the nation could be established by mere proof of onetime association, however remote, between the royalists, émigrés or others accused of treason, and the defendants. For a moment, the right of an accused man to defend himself threatened to destroy the desired public effect; so the National Convention, intimidated by the Commune, gave the presiding officer of the courts the right to close the trials after three days if the jurymen declared that their consciences had been sufficiently enlightened. Accused people thereafter had no genuine right of self-defense. No French king had been quite so arbitrary. Girondin deputies were found guilty as charged and were executed in October 1793, only nine months after the execution of their king.

Possibly the death of 40,000 to 60,000 other people, not subjected to state trials but mobbed by their neighbors or killed by armed forces during the civil strife, had even more lasting effects on the French spirit than deaths inflicted directly by the tribunals. By the end of the period, hardly any of the active individuals of firm character in France had failed to discover the indifference of both revolutionaries and counter-revolutionaries to the dignity of life. The state killed, in the name of the people, on the flimsiest of evidence. Neighbors killed fellowmen who supported such a ruthless state, while other neighbors killed fellowmen who would not support such a ruthless state. Distrust of the state and of one another and need for a permanent attitude of *méfiance*, arm's-length suspicion of all others in society, became in effect a culturally inherited and transmitted characteristic.

When the Republican nominee for the Presidency of the United States proclaimed in 1964 that extremism in defense of liberty was no vice, too many people were reminded of Hitler and of his similar belief that the end could justify the means. They did the candidate something less than historical justice, for Hitler had no interest in advancing the cause of liberty. The memories that statement should have evoked were those of Robespierre and his Terror during the French Revolution. It was Maximilien Robespierre, executioner of thousands of upper- and middle-income people, who was the original and most eloquent advocate in history of the belief that extremism in defense of liberty was no crime. It was his undiluted creed which was, to the amazement of multitudes everywhere, revived in the world's most dynamic republic 170 years after a people bled white had taken their revenge on him for his endless extremisms of misguided devotion and injustice.

Shortly after the Girondins were expelled from the Convention under the Commune's guns, Danton withdrew from office. He was replaced on the key Committee of Public Safety by Robespierre, the idol of angry men of that day, the *enragés*. An even more vigorous effort to defeat foreign and domestic enemies began. In July 1793 the nation's plight seemed almost hopeless. On the northeast borders the armies were in flight, Mayence (Mainz) fell and then Valenciennes; the Spaniards were advancing. Toulon had been betrayed to the English fleet, and the Rhone Valley was moving into opposition under royalists and escaped Girondins. But with a mass levy of some 750,000 new troops and extreme effort of scientists, organizers and specialists in warfare, armies of the revolution began winning again at home and abroad. By October the immediate crisis was over. The Terror, however, continued.

The Jacobins under Robespierre were not sadists eager for blood or radicals eager for basic social change. In matters of property they were almost as conservative as the Girondins, but not quite. They believed that rationing of food and price fixing in wartime were justifiable. This concession to hunger, along with their determination to win the war and to whip the energies of the whole nation into shape to do so, won them the support of the Commune and the Paris working class. The extreme Jacobins accepted this support because it enabled them to eliminate the Girondins, execute the King, and depose Danton, their rival for popular support. Most of them did not, however, share the economic hopes of the workers. Strikes and labor organization were as strictly prohibited and severely punished, as under the Girondins. An example was quickly made of Jacobins holding more radical economic views.

Under a certain Hébert this group had been seeking support of the Commune, with the idea of taking power. It had created a consumer-worker-unemployed alliance of sorts and had forced on the Committee of Public Safety regulations to hold down food prices, authorize the armies to seize hoarded supplies, and to make trials of suspects simpler and shorter. It had placed some of its men in the War Ministry and was branching out. Also, it had taken up the cause of atheism. Robespierre accused the Hébert group of conspiracy to massacre members of the Convention. The leaders were rounded up, tried briefly and executed in March 1794. This clarified the government's differences with the Paris workers and broke its emergency ties with them.

France had to pay still another penalty for allowing Robespierre's faction to take unlimited power. Just a few months before the decisive victory which was to render the Terror needless, that group killed the one man who might have shepherded the republic through peace into some degree of unity. This was the venal but able Danton. He had yielded power to the extremists in the summer of 1793. He retired as one of the great organizers of the war effort. He thought his services to the nation had placed him beyond danger. He and the editor Camille Desmoulins began a campaign for mercy, at home and abroad. This was an extremely dangerous thing for them to do in the middle of civil and foreign war. Though Danton and his group had tolerated the persecution of Girondins and Hébertists, now it seemed to them the time had come to think again about national unity. Some support for this position was shown by the public. Robespierre, determined to continue the revolution and perhaps afraid of the competition, arrested Danton and Desmoulins. They were tried in the usual summary fashion. It now seems certain that they had been receiving foreign funds for their efforts.[2] A convenient rumor of a plot to rescue him from jail served as an excuse to cut off Danton's legal defense, which was impressing the court. With his execution in April 1794, France lost the last of her great leaders who might perhaps have sustained the revolution and also united the torn nation.

One of the ironies of Danton's death was that, through his Herculean efforts, he possibly had done more than anyone else to build up the government's authority and, except for Carnot, organizer of the armies, to achieve its military success. So when that government accused him of treason, its view was more readily accepted than if it had been weak. No open expressions of revulsion or rebellion were heard from the frightened witnesses of his procession to the guillotine, although his death gave many more men a sense that no one was safe.

With Danton out of the way, nothing stood in the road of Robespierre's continued dictatorship except his own excesses and a great military victory. He was omnipotent for a few months. He experimented with the idea of a theocratic government and organized a festival of the Supreme Being, possibly to offset any unfavorable impression the countryside might have gotten from the antireligious activities of the Hébertists in Paris. But he also kept pushing measures to insure his own dictatorship. Two days after this pretentious festival in 1794, he had the Convention pass an act (Law of 22nd of Prairial) which went far beyond absolutist monarchy. It has been called "the code of legal murder." Threats of assassination were cited to justify it. It suppressed the protections of ordinary law in all political trials. No time was to be wasted with witnesses or defense attorneys. All the usual formalities about arrest were also removed.

After passing this law, the cowed deputies discovered it applied to them no less than other people. Executions under it rose from an average of thirty-two a week to 196. With perhaps 80,000 in the prisons awaiting trial, Robespierre put through another measure to take the property of prisoners for distribution to the indigent and to deserving patriots. Prisoners were to be deported. This was an effort to help the poorest group of peasants to get some land in lieu of that which they had been unable to purchase at the auctions of church land in the first years of the revolution. However, the families of imprisoned suspects naturally feared that such a measure would add an economic motive to the legal process and insure more unjustified death sentences. The measure was resented, never enforced and then repealed.

Belatedly the people were beginning to rally to the cause of mercy which Danton had advocated. They had had enough. After the army's decisive victory at Fleurus (June 26, 1794), there seemed to be no reason to continue the intimidation. But Robespierre persisted. Blackmail was his weapon now. With about seventy of the moderate deputies in prison and their lives in his power, he believed he could force their friends in the Convention to vote as he dictated. So, confident because of his successful device of "treason" charges against the Girondins, the Hébertists and the Danton group, he discovered another "plot" and planned another purge. Once more the guillotine was to be moved into the breach.

But this time, alerted by Danton's fate, his intended victims failed to sign their own death warrants. They included hardened men who had themselves administered the Terror in Lyons, Bordeaux and Marseilles. To blackmailed members of the Convention they said, "Stand with us and your imprisoned colleagues will be freed, and you will never be blackmailed again." Tallien, one of the deputies marked for death, received from his future wife a note: "Coward! Tomorrow I am to be tried!" Suddenly all the hopes of 1789, for life, happiness and freedom, flared and fused together again. When Robespierre's close associate, Saint-Just, began a speech before the Convention calling for one last purification from the evil forces of counterrevolution, he was sharply interrupted by Tallien and others. Robespierre's protest was silenced. As his speech faltered, deputies cried out, "He is choking on Danton's blood!" They accused him of wanting to be dictator. In the uproar, his arrest and that of Saint-Just were moved and carried unanimously.

This in itself was not decisive. Armed sections of the Paris Commune could easily thwart the Convention, as they had before. They immediately released Robespierre and other arrested deputies of his persuasion. Tocsins were sounded, the city gates were closed. Thirteen of the forty-eight districts obediently sent troops. But significantly, the other ones did not. Going into emergency session, the Convention remembered the old adage, "When one strikes at a king, one must kill him." They annulled the Commune's insurrectionary orders and outlawed the released Robespierre and his partisans. Outlaws could be killed on sight. Some of the wavering Paris sections now swung over to the Convention. A force loyal to the Assembly broke into the city hall to reach Robespierre. He probably tried to kill himself—he was found lying across a table with a shattered jaw. Sixty members of the Commune and some police administrators were arrested. The guillotine, which had dispatched forty-five of Robespierre's opponents on July 27, took his life and that of eighty-three of his followers in the next few days. The only remotely amusing thing about this grim episode is that a rumor was promptly circulated that a royal fleur-de-lis, the Bourbon symbol, had been discovered on Robespierre's desk, which was assumed to mean that all the time he had been part of a great plot to restore the Bourbon monarchy. It was reminiscent of the rumors carefully spread abroad after the execution of Joan of Arc that she had been a witch and that the voices she had heard had been those of evil demons.

Now people wanted peace and freedom from fear more than anything else. They cheered when the Convention regained initiative, stripped the Revolutionary Tribunal of extraordinary powers and later abolished it. They applauded when the hated law for legal murder was repealed, when the Paris Commune was replaced by an appointed commission, and when Girondins were recalled to the Convention. In November the Jacobin clubs were closed down. In December, in the midst of a cold winter and rising prices for bread, all the limitations on prices were abolished, and social legislation was discarded. Unemployment and resentment grew. Out in the countryside the counter terror expanded against the Robespierre partisans. This, too, was horrible; again many thousands of people suffered for having supported or tolerated an injustice which they had been told was patriotic. Still, the guillotine was slowed down. The upper middle class had now used the popular demand for peace to take back the power it had yielded to the Paris Commune as a result of its own demand for war.

A third stage of the revolution began with the ending of the military crisis, withdrawal of Paris workers from their earlier participation with the middle class in the struggle, and realization that the wounds inflicted since 1789 were too deep to heal quickly. This stage lasted from late in 1794 to 1799, when Napoleon took over the power which others were too divided, weak and tired to carry. The interval of indecision, disorder, inflation and reaction aided him.

At first there was stalemate. Though the invasion threat had eased and Robespierre and his men were gone, the deputies were still distrustful and frightened of one another. They could combine only temporarily against royalist attack from one side or a workers' attack from the other. Suspicious Girondins, who had been invited back to the Convention, stared at the Jacobins who had voted to have them shot to death. Suspicious Jacobins stared at Girondins, who had joined a revolt against their government. Still, both feared a return of the royalists; this would mean that Jacobins who had killed a king, and Girondins who had not prevented him from being killed, might both perish. For lack of a leader who could bring them together to obtain peace and restore prosperity, the Convention was as impotent as Louis XVI had been before 1789.

The second difficulty was that its members could no longer count on the workers of Paris to protect them from the royalist opposition. The workers were tired of defending one set of middle-class leaders against another. Hungry again and angry again, they attacked the Convention in May and June of 1795, remembering the revolutionary coup d'état technique they had learned earlier. They were repulsed. Their attack and repulse encouraged a royalist rising. Royalists were revolting against the Convention's doubtful decision to perpetuate itself by requiring that the next legislative body include two-thirds of the members of the old Convention. An underemployed artillery officer with Jacobin leanings, Napoleon Bonaparte, who had recovered Toulon from the English fleet, was called on to handle the revolt. His "whiff of grape-shot" on the Rue Saint-Honoré on October 4, 1795, held the royalists in check for a while.

The three-year-old National Convention, which ended in 1795, had certain constructive achievements to its credit despite the Terror. Its predecessors had put the nation on a new road, opened up opportunity and freedom, provided in theory at least that justice should be available to all, brought the many regions into an administrative unity, freed farmlands from feudal dues, deprived the masters' trade guilds of monopolistic control of the nation's industrial life, created defense against the *ancien régime* by selling church lands, organized a parliament against great odds, and limited the monarchy. The Convention itself had abolished that monarchy, established a republic, announced the rights of all children to education at public expense from the lowest grades through the university, managed and financed a successful war, and finally had freed the national parliament from intimidation by Paris. These were no small achievements for six years of parliamentary beginnings. Napoleon was later given undue credit for some of them. A far more dubious heritage left by the Convention was still another new constitution. This established an executive branch of government to replace the king, a Directory of Five, along with a lower house (Council of Five Hundred) and an upper house (Council of Ancients). The new government, elected in 1795 on a restricted suffrage, contained two-thirds of the members of the previous Convention and provided that one-third of its deputies should be newly elected each year. The old quarrels continued, but Girondin and Jacobin antagonists were no longer afraid of being beheaded after the next election.

The continued wars and inflation forced the Directory, which had no direct popular support or mandate, to face financial insolvency. It dared not call back its numerous troops from their garrison or aggressive efforts abroad, since those forces were being financed by the nations which they had conquered. Returning home, they would simply add to unemployment and probably to new Jacobin or royalist movements. In addition, the generals, capitalizing their new importance in the financial and political scheme of things, insisted on continuing the wars abroad. So this mechanically improvised and isolated executive of tired, cynical and partly corrupt old men found itself back where the establishment of the Roman Republic had been, surviving on the loot of foreign lands and the mercy of its general officers. The Directory declared a national bankruptcy, possibly with the hope that only such a catastrophe would free it from dependence on its generals for funds. It lost many of its last vestiges of prestige in the process and was unable to realize its hope. Shortly after the declaration it sent Napoleon forth to conquer and loot Italy for the benefit of the treasury of France. He succeeded.

However, Napoleon's victories in Italy and those of other generals in the north brought no great popularity to the Directory. Rising unemployment and the worsening commercial situation were oppressive. Fear engendered by a communist (Babeuf) conspiracy, discovered in the spring of 1797 and ended with execution of its members, helped the royalists. New annual elections in May 1797, if accepted, would have brought into the two councils of government a majority of counter-revolutionaries and put one monarchist on the Directory. The gains of the revolution were again in danger.

The Directory then staged a first coup d'état of its own to upset the election result. With this act it gave up all claims to legality, all the moral sanction attached to an honest representation of the popular will. It put not only itself but the whole revolution under a cloud. Napoleon was again called in to help. In September 1797 he sent one of his officers, General Augereau, to quash the elections on one excuse or another in forty-nine departments. This kept the royalists out of office. The justification for this illegality was in the form of evidence of a monarchist plot, according to which a General Pichegru was to march his troops into Paris. A new repression of returned émigrés and refractory priests began. However, in the following year, the Directory staged a similar coup against the moderate Jacobins who won in the elections in 1798. Over 100 elected Jacobin deputies were prevented from taking their seats. No plot justified this action, simply fear that the Parisian working people, the old revolutionaries, who were now conveniently labelled "anarchists," would regain some power.

Suddenly with its claims to legitimacy in fragments, the Directory found itself facing another invasion. The allied coalition had finally found new generals, who pushed the French troops back to their old borders and prepared to move into France. The Directory of Five, which had survived on the basis of military success, now had no excuse for survival. It was blamed for the defeats, and an accumulated animus against its corruption and cynicism was freely expressed at last. Two of the five resigned and were replaced by Jacobins. They decreed a compulsory loan, actually a progressive income tax which fell heavily on their rich supporters, who protested. To mollify them, the Directory closed the Jacobin clubs again. But it had no large or effective popular support. Even after the new enemy threat had been repulsed, the Directory felt forced to turn to the generals again for help. They chose Napoleon Bonaparte, the most successful and best known of them, who had enough commitment to the revolution to preclude any interest in a Bourbon restoration. He had returned conveniently from Egypt at this moment. At some earlier time he might have been shot for losing the fleet there and deserting his army.

With his agreement, the Directory alleged the discovery of an anarchist plot. The legislative councils were persuaded to meet outside of Paris. Bonaparte surrounded them with troops and obtained the assent of the Council of Ancients to a change in the Constitution. The Council of Five Hundred, however, showed hostility and called for Bonaparte's impeachment. To persuade the troops to help Napoleon, his brother Lucien, who was presiding over this Council, proclaimed that the obstructing members of the Council were part of an English plot against France. Since that was still not quite persuasive, he drew a dagger and threatened to kill Napoleon if ever he did anything against the liberties of France. This theatrical performance seems to have persuaded the troops to storm in, and the deputies fled. A rump group later agreed to the establishment of a consulate, with the thirty-year-old Corsican officer as a member. He became the leader of a consulate of three, the new executive of France. In 1802, a referendum proclaimed him consul for life. In 1804, another proclaimed him emperor of the French. France had returned to a hereditary monarch who was also a military dictator. The revolution was over.

Once Napoleon had taken power, almost everyone began to hope that the period of indecision and inaction since 1794 would end. To the rich merchants, his advent seemed to promise stabilization of finances and an elimination of the war burdens. The unemployed expected jobs. To peasants and others who had acquired lands of the church and émigrés, his Jacobin views seemed to offer protection against a royalist return and loss of that land. Royalists, briefly, for some strange reason imagined he would restore the monarchy. The clergy expected an end to persecution.

His welcome was quite as enthusiastic and contradictory as that received by the Estates-General ten years earlier.

What France gained during its resort to military dictatorship was an end to revolutionary turmoil, a strong centralized government, coded law, sufficient breaking of class lines to allow men to advance in public life on the basis of ability, a reconciliation of sorts with the Church, a return of many embittered émigrés, a persistent denigration of political parties in the style later imitated by General de Gaulle, and a vast public-works program, beautifying Paris, which gave employment and profit to many.

What the French people lost was their ability to stop warfare and create conditions of peace in Europe. They found themselves helpless under the control of a man with the occupational disease of thinking that only through continuous military victories could he maintain his prestige and power in France. A prisoner of the Athenian cliché that there was no substitute for victory in battle, he completely misjudged both the French and the European longing for an end, a final end to his warfare. French power was spread from the heel of Italy to Hamburg, and eastward to the borders of Russia. To justify the imperial title he had demanded and obtained, Napoleon sacrificed a large share of French youth and devitalized the nation with that loss. Yet at best his dominion consisted of alliances with defeated or cowed nations waiting for an opportunity to break away, of thrones given to unworthy relatives who derided and betrayed him. When he was through, France had been pushed back to its prerevolutionary boundaries and was in danger of losing them. At home he managed an effective semipolice state, mitigated by high employment and glory.

The people of France had no say or veto when he made his great mistakes of invading Spain and Russia, whose nationals had been unprepared by revolutionary teachings to give him support, and lost an army of 300,000 in the first area and saw the whole Grand Army of 600,000 ruined in the second one.

Flushed with the arrogance of success and power, Napoleon neglected to foresee the possibility that his opponents might be able to change the game enough to frustrate him. The Russians did it by burning Moscow and leaving the French armies without food, shelter or a ruler conquered and forced to surrender. The Spaniards carried this a step further. They not only had no king who could surrender all Spain upon his capture, but elaborated the tactics of the Russian guerrillas who had harassed the French during their retreat from Moscow. The Spaniards attacked only when they had overwhelming numbers and disbanded when they did not. The French commanders were led into search-and-destroy expeditions with no help from the peasantry and into holding operations spread over vast territory, which then prevented them from massing on battlefields against the English. On top of all these unexpected tactics, effectively used later in Southeast Asia against the United States, Wellington found that the old British line formation could actually mow down and halt the charge in columns which had served the French well since 1793.[3] The Napoleonic steamroller was stopped.

Napoleon never understood the power of nationalism outside of France or the fateful paradox of imposing French domination in the name of a doctrine that proclaimed the liberty of people. Nor did he understand that Europe was already a community of interests much like France itself and, if pressed hard enough, might act as a federated group. As France finally summoned enough will and courage to stop Robespierre's domestic terror, so Europe finally united to stop Napoleon's international terror and impose a disciplined peace. That peace was oriented against French liberty, toward despotism, and ultimately played out its part in the First and Second World Wars.

The mystique of Napoleon's glory survived his defeats and became, along with the mystique of the revolution, one of the heritages dominating French thought and life.

The tragedy of this convulsive period went deeper than the loss of individual aspirations, the early death of many good and brave men who had hoped to stay alive and enjoy a better world. It struck at the core of Western society, the basic need for a trust men must have in one another's sense of justice and compassion in order to survive and to seek excellence together. A great ideal about human dignity and liberty and human brotherhood was stated, and while the surrounding world watched and waited for the new glory to unfold, the ideal was degraded, corrupted, almost discarded. In short, a revival of the most magnificent achievement of the classical Greeks was presented to the modern world, little by little, in the wretched and bloody rags of injustice, terror, venality, wars of despoliation and outright military despotism. Many in France and abroad saw only these outrages, turned their faces away forever, refusing to see more.

The conflict inside of France between those who abhorred and those who accepted the basic revolutionary goals continued throughout the nineteenth century into the twentieth. It was not decreased by three later revolutions. It continued into the desperate, stalemated days before the Second World War. It found one form in Marshall Pétain's regime of faith, order, discipline and family. The division between the noble "we" and the contemptible "they" was never quite overcome. General de Gaulle, in his day, sought very hard to varnish over these differences and the humiliation they had caused France to suffer in 1940 with memories of glory, new hopes for independence and grandeur. The task was enormous, for the true slogan of the French was never whole-heartedly "Liberty, Equality and Fraternity," it was always *"Méfiez-vous!"* Be on guard against your predatory neighbors! Their revolution in the name of liberty had not changed that, had even accentuated it.

Beyond the borders of France, the fears of similarly bloody internal conflicts and French conquest strengthened the reactionary elements for many decades. Almost no nation was left unmarked. The United States suffered its Alien and Sedition Laws at this time. In Spain a constitution drawn by the liberal Cortes of Cádiz in 1812 was nullified by Ferdinand II. The Inquisition reappeared briefly in Spain and Rome. Oppressive political police pervaded Austria and the Papal States in Italy as well as France. In England the habeas corpus act, the foundation of personal liberty, was suspended in 1817 and free assemblage in 1819. In that year some of the still frightened and reactionary victors over Napoleon issued the Carlsbad Decrees, which stated the obligation of all sovereigns never to yield to the demands of their people for any significant participation in government. The all-German Bundestag at Frankfurt laid upon all its princes and princelings the obligation to support one another against revolutionary movements and denied to any local parliament the right to refuse taxes to its ruler. The Czar of Russia, Alexander, tried to get the Congress of Vienna to undertake to undo any popular revolts anywhere in Europe and even in Spanish America. In France the Church was, for a while, given control of all education and sacrilege was made a crime. Savage rights to proscribe (exile) dissenting citizens were given to the king and were used. In Russia the pillaging, looting and burning of Napoleon's troops, as well as the Russian victory over them, consolidated all the classes of society in a remarkable way and increased the power and prestige of the Czar. For a decade or so after Waterloo, the field of Napoleon's last defeat, the forces of reaction seem to have "enjoyed more positive prestige and power than at anytime since the reign of Louis XIV," as David Thomson phrased it.[4]

In spite of some liberalization in the 1830s throughout Europe, the shock effects of the French combination of revolution and imperial conquest went on into time. After the abortive revolution of 1848, the older and more autocratic systems regained still another lease on life, and every liberalization effort was again identified with democracy and revolution. What Communism was to the twentieth century, the disorder and war of the French was to the nineteenth century, a means by which rulers could scare their subjects both into paying taxes for huge military expenditures and into acceptance of passive obedience to their defenders against new and disturbing ideas. The Napoleonic war machine created its counterpart in the Prussian war machine, and autocratic industry allied itself with that machine. Society in the German areas remained so stratified that a doctrine of class struggle became popular among the workers, as indeed it did in France. Excluded from most of the gains of the revolution in France, its alienated industrial workers led three later revolutions, in 1830, 1848 and 1871, and always failed to gain the participation, security and opportunity for advancement which they sought. Desperate and discouraged, they, too, drifted toward class-struggle doctrines and Communism, and then helped in the 1930s to make impossible any government sufficiently strong to withstand the renewed German threat.

The world lost one of its great opportunities to avoid a period of prolonged misery when the French middle class excluded its workers from the gains of its revolution. In the early nineteenth century the industrial revolution was really beginning to gain impetus, one of the most important events in modern history. If the French workers had been able to gain even such moderate measures as a minimum wage, a right to employment and a right to organize, and if these measures had been copied throughout Europe, many of the early cruelties of the industrial revolution might have been avoided, along with the class conflict. But the benefits to the world might have been even larger. Instead of waiting until the first half of the twentieth century for industrial managers to discover that large-scale factory production demands large-scale consumption and that a large public with adequate purchasing power is necessary for the success of an industrialized society, the discovery might—just possibly—have been made in France in the late 1790s. Better-paid workers could have purchased more products, industry could have prospered with the larger market, the whole long period of labor's misery could have been shortened, and the appeal and rise of authoritarian Communism might not have taken shape. The modern world might have been able to spend a large part of its current annual arms budget of close to $200 billion on its many neglected opportunities to eliminate poverty, hunger and illiteracy, and to make personal freedom an actuality instead of a remote hope throughout all continents.

Certainly tragedy gripped millions within and outside of France because the great revolution was so limited and so ridden by unexpected and calamitous by-products. But does the fact of tragedy provide adequate justification for characterizing the whole period from 1789 to 1815 as a failure? No one can fairly deny the leaders of that day some large measure of lasting success, an abolition of feudalism, a proclamation of human dignity, an establishment of personal liberty. The case for considering the period to be a failure of men to achieve far more lasting results lies in the avoidability of those actions which our advantaged position of hindsight allows us to call errors. Certainly no men are perfect, and no complete avoidance of actions which later turn out to be disastrous can ever be expected from any group of rulers. It is only when these seem unnecessary, more foolish than their state of culture warranted, that the errors may be called avoidable. So if the leaders of those revolutionary days had the physical, moral and intellectual resources to make the transition from one form of society to a much better one, but fell short of exercising their capabilities, their mistakes and the resulting tragedy can reasonably be ranked as a failure.

Their five major mistakes ended with national disunity quite as large and important a result as personal liberty. They aroused peasant revolts against themselves, largely through mishandling of the Church problem. They plunged into an aggressive war. They prevented industrial workers and, indeed, much of the lower-income population from sharing the major gains of the revolution. They instituted a most unjust reign of intimidation and death. They called in the war-prone Napoleon, who in turn neglected a number of opportunities to make peace in order to expand his empire. Were these five unfortunate actions avoidable? Were other options open to them at each point, and within their resource capacity?

We remember that the Church lands were confiscated in order to retire the huge national debt. This action then led to a state take-over of the obligation to pay the clergy, a loyalty oath, then dismissal of clergy who refused to take it, a schism of sorts within the Church, a peasant uprising stirred up, to a large extent, by the conscience-stricken clergy. Both the aggressive war and the Terror were later rationalized, in large part, by the danger to the revolution created by this clerical and peasant opposition which came on top of émigré efforts to undo the revolution.

Most of this turmoil could have been averted if the Assembly had simply undertaken the obligation to pay the Church, in compensation for its lands, a sum equivalent to the revenue from them and had kept the government's hands off all the problems of Church management and doctrine. The abolition of the nobility as a class, which took place in June of 1790, along with the loss of land, would have effectively reduced the objectionable arrogance and pomp of the higher prelates, who were all nobles at the time. The lesser clergy, unplagued by the loyalty oath and the return to the early Christian election of priests, might well have given a great deal of support throughout the countryside to the liberating aims of the revolution instead of opposing them. A number of clergy had done so, in the early days when they supported the third estate. It was within the historic knowledge of the leaders of the revolution that violent trouble was the usual result of state efforts to

control the Church, and vice versa, and it was within their sphere of
awareness that they could not afford to antagonize both the peasants,
for whom the voice of the priest was so often the voice of God, and also
the urban workers, at one and the same time, and still obtain any of the
social stability they needed for their success. Here there was an open
option and an avoidable error.

The second major error was that of plunging into war before actively
pursuing negotiations with Austria and Prussia to gain time. Then the
original mistake was compounded in three ways. The war immediately
became aggressive in the worst possible direction, taking the form of a
threat to British economic interests in the Lowlands. A defensive war
would probably have rallied the nation quite as much as an offensive
one. Next, the war was entrusted to generals whose interests were not
those of the governing majority. Lafayette wanted to march on Paris
and restore the King to favor. Balked by his troops, he deserted.
Dumouriez also wanted to march on Paris. Defeated and balked, he
also deserted. His treason played a large part in the downfall and later
massacre of the Girondin deputies. Finally, the war allegedly offering
freedom to foreign people was allowed to become a kind of international swindle. The slogans of the revolution gave the French troops a
welcome. However, their tax collectors, draft officers and demands for
heavy indemnities turned people against France and against the revolution, even before looting orders given to Napoleon, and his own
imperial ambitions, sickened them.

The third major mistake, that of neglecting and then throwing out of
the revolutionary parade the little people, including the industrial workers was also unnecessary. Too much worship of the gods of the free
market by their governors made these people the victims of high prices,
the prisoners of starvation, and the sufferers from the cold. They did not
even have feudal security in their jobs. When the nobility emigrated,
workers became unemployed. They were clearly an element of danger to
any indifferent parliament. They had, in addition, done much, as they
viewed it, to save that body from the King's threats. Under these
circumstances the upper middle class, the Girondin group, which was
running affairs, could have afforded to pay a little by way of subsidies on
food and fuel and public-works employment, so that these people could
have gained at least some security as a result of the revolution. It could
have left them the right to vote, which was taken away in 1792, and
granted the right to join in unions. It could have made these groups a
part of the emerging society and, incidentally, have saved the lives and
power of the Girondin leaders in the process. The lower middle class,
the Jacobins, who later took power with the military aid of these
workers, did only a little better by them. Neither governing group tried

to work out any method by which the lives and dignity of these people could be protected at least as much as landownership protected the peasantry. The punishment for this neglect, not dissimilar to the neglect of the Negroes after the Civil War in the United States, endured through the subsequent centuries.

This was an avoidable error, for the middle-class leaders, both Girondins and more radical Jacobins, had seen with their own eyes the rise of the working people against the nobles and King, their desire for protection from unemployment and decreases in living standards. It was within their knowledge that these people could shake the new order as well as the old. The money costs of providing them with some significant freedom from the exactions of their employers, some food subsidies to protect them against hardship, some breaking of the barriers against their illiteracy were small compared with the social costs of creating and maintaining an aggrieved minority within the new order. They were small compared with the cost of the continuing war abroad, which some of the Girondins had wanted as a means of retaining control of the population. Very little besides greed and smug self-content with their own new social status stood in the way of this option.

The way for the fourth major error, the Terror, was prepared by the three mistakes already mentioned. Without the controversy about the Church, which alienated many peasants, the neglect of the little people of Paris, and the war, there would have been no need for the Terror. The charter of personal liberties and equal protection under law, so proudly proclaimed in 1789, would not have been torn to shreds in so bloody a fashion. Guilt by association or by acquaintanceship would not have been raised to such juridical heights. Fewer of the independently minded people of the nation, fewer of the original revolutionaries would have perished so young. Alive, they might have been able to prevent the free grant of the whole nation to a war-prone Napoleon in 1799, which a few tired and scared old men perpetrated and, with that act of despair and moral bankruptcy, dedicated another million French lives to his wars and to France's ultimate defeat. The fate of the French people from those days on was that of being torn forever and indecisively between distrust of a strong executive, such as the one which managed the Terror, and the alternative of a strong, effective legislature, which their heritage of divisiveness frequently made impossible. They have paid for it.

It is not suggested here that once the earlier three mistakes had been made, some measure of discipline could have been completely avoided. Exile was a possible alternative to terror, which was simply the last link in a chain of four avoidable mistakes. Actually the lives it took were small in number compared to those which Napoleon required in almost every year of his endless wars. France had spent itself into financial bankruptcy paying the army's butcher bills even before he took power.

The fifth and final mistake was that made by Napoleon, of believing that only through continued and successful warfare could he keep his power within France. One of his more bizarre and impractical notions had been demonstrated even before power was turned over to him, that of defeating England by conquering the Middle East and even India. Once in power, he demonstrated another one, that of trying to force England to surrender by demanding of all his satellites and momentary allies, including the Pope, that they injure themselves by ceasing their trade with England. He had numerous occasions to make a nonimperial peace. He could have obtained it by neutralizing Belgium and the Netherlands. He had options. Although every step he made in the direction of peace was loudly cheered by the people of France, he continued the wars, unchecked by the submissive French people, and finally was defeated. France was forced back to its prerevolution boundaries and was allowed to keep those only at the expense of accepting a Bourbon king. The whole aggressive war process, even before his reign, had wasted the resources of France and forced it into bankruptcy. His own expeditions of empire lost France more than a million men, a loss from which it had not fully recovered before the end of the nineteenth century. His whole theory of a French empire which would forever dominate Europe was fallacious, along with his faith that he would always win. The repeated renewal of the coalitions against him should have demonstrated this to him long before those days when, exiled on St. Helena, he decided that he had been wrong and that brotherhoods of peoples in Europe were that continent's only and best hope.

All of these five major errors of judgment and action which brought so much tragedy were avoidable to some extent, at least. If even a few of them had been averted, not only France but the whole world of the nineteenth and twentieth centuries would have been happier and more hopeful habitations for men. Democracy, at one time the only acceptable successor of feudalism in the world's history, deserved a better introduction, upon its reentry on the stage of civilization, than it received at the hands of the French. They failed to rise beyond immediate self-interest to fulfill their obligation to their great opportunity.

Each generation brings a new view to the direct applicability of the French revolutionary experience to its own present and future. For example, several generations of Russian revolutionary underground seemed to agree that France had taught the lesson that a middle-class revolution for democracy was necessary before a proletarian revolution could possibly take place. Many of Lenin's fellows were consequently shocked when he suddenly drew a quite different conclusion and saw a pre-Napoleonic situation in the Russian defeat, demoralization, the nonrepresentative government and its noninterest in popular demands for food and peace, and lunged successfully at that point for power. Since much of the world's population still has its antifeudal revolutions ahead of it, the French experience remains important for all who are concerned with events in those less developed nations. Their prospective revolutions, however, may be altered in character by the fact that people are now offered the Communist formula as an alternative to the French formula, and since most of them are not French middle-class people, their revolutions may take a quite different form. The whole French experience, however, remains interesting and modernly significant because the United States, when it is not actively opposing any revolutionary change abroad which is even slightly tinged with violence, tends to represent the French idea of personal freedom over against the Communist formula. Meanwhile, the dominant local groups in industry, land, banking and government seem to wear with mandarin grace and arrogance the robes of the French nobility, determined to yield little or nothing to the men who seek change. It is around this contest of wills and interests that the third large problem area of the United States lies.

Men who seek change in those areas, peaceful or violent, in the name of freedom, can well pay some attention to all the errors listed above, all the options that were open to the French people, but not used. It is in them that any lessons which may be helpful to the future of freedom in the developing nations can be discovered. It is certainly not satisfactory to abbreviate the whole hopeful and tragic period into a summary that revolutions are never free from violence and stupidity, that both are regrettable and unavoidable, and that men will on occasion feel so strongly that they prefer to risk both rather than remain where they are. There is more to be learned than that, more which can be neglected only at the risk of participating in its repetition.

Just as exclusion leads to revolution, so it can during and after that event redivide societies which had been briefly unified. Double-dealing, apparent temporizing and retrogression, suspicion that the political authority is failing in its commitments, is lacking in honesty and integrity, can cause moral authority to be lost, and with that the nominal authority evaporates. Troops and police are no substitute for it. Still noteworthy is the danger to all concerned of combining a revolution and a war, or that of combining a counterrevolution with a war. The French had the former experience, the Austrian and Prussian interveners the latter. It was not wise of the French to allow their generals to dominate war policy. They found themselves in twenty years of warfare because these generals headed for the Lowlands. One political group tied its fortunes to the success of its officers, saw them defeated, and was ruined by their treason. The final consequence of relying on generals and asking them to undo elections was a military man's rule.

Since violence can be expected in every revolution in the less developed nations, and since the black leaders in the United States and some student leaders almost everywhere in the world have frequently been tempted to engage in it, either as a tactic of attention-calling and conscience-awakening or as retribution for neglect, the French experience with violence has a certain modern bearing. The violence of the peasants in the countryside was directed immediately at obtaining freedom from their feudal obligations. It was successful because no police or troops were available at that moment to halt or punish them. It also led to the abolition of the nobility as a caste. It was unsuccessful in another direction. The angered nobility was able to get a foreign intervention started, and the peasants paid for that in hundreds of thousands of their sons. The September massacre of prisoners, from which revolutionary leaders averted their eyes, disgraced the nation and like the official Terror which came later, helped arouse the private White Terror which slaughtered thousands outside of Paris. This was an act of major retribution. All these private and public acts of violence provoked reaction, prepared the way for the later restrictions on personal liberty and for the secret police of Napoleon and the two Bourbon monarchs who succeeded him. Meanwhile, the cause of liberty, in whose name some of this violence was carried on, was damaged by it both at home and abroad. Men were led to believe that liberty meant violence, injustice and private counterviolence and wanted none of the combination. Later, in three revolutions, violent attempts to gain participation and power by the working-class groups led to ferocious counterviolence, and then to the decision of many workers to stand in permanent Communist opposition to the republic. Ironically, while these internal recourses to murder and countermurder succeeded in adding to national divisiveness, Napoleon's foreign conquests, which killed far more Frenchmen and provoked repeated wars against France, have generally been considered great achievements by Frenchmen, evidences of the *grandeur* of their nation.

CHAPTER 8

The Peculiarly
American Tragedy

PART I

Disaster, as we have noticed by now, may come to societies in a number of different ways. An over-abundance of technological changes accumulating too rapidly—before people are socially prepared to live with them—is a frequently mentioned route along which the American community might be ruined. Historically, America has a record of its own in this sequence. The first time, it hit the American Indians of the Northeast. The British and French settlers sold steel traps and rifles to the Indians. This was a technological advance of no mean dimensions over the old methods of hunting animals and getting pelts. With these new implements the Indians proceeded to raise their tribal income somewhat, although most briefly. What they did in that process was to eliminate within three generations the beaver population of New England and the Mid-Atlantic states, their sole source of income from foreign markets. After this accomplishment of devastation, they felt forced to wage aggressive and exhausting wars in Canada, endeavoring to pirate or conquer that area's beaver supplies. In the process, their old agricultural and trading economy was severely damaged, their hard-won and peaceful intertribal arrangements were broken for good. Decimated and starving, they became weak people, later dependent mercenaries, hired soldiers, particularly for the French. The American colonists found them serving in that way in the French-Indian wars, which ended in 1763, less than thirty years before the United States was formally launched. The Indians had gained briefly but lost much in life and spirit when they accepted the offer of the Europeans to attain progress and prosperity through a new technology.

The colonists of those same early days happened to set a similar social mantrap for their own descendants, although in a different manner and area. Instead of starting off with an equivalent technological improvement, they began by importing cheap labor in the form of African captives to man the fields of cotton, tobacco, hemp and sugar cane in the warm South of the country. For that day this was an economically efficient form of production. The technological improvement—Whitney's cotton gin—which snapped the trap shut on the whole new nation, came later. However, the first elements of the conflict were assembled and the stage was set for the peculiarly American tragedy by the injection into colonial North America of an alien and backward race, along with the equally primitive institution of human slavery.

The drama was to play itself out from 1840 onward for more than a century, and in it the Civil War from 1861–1865 was only a heartbreaking second act. Human beings who had started their search for an excellent life with the Greeks, and who had suffered so much through the following ages from oppression, superstition and misused opportunities, had at last thought themselves rid of old obstacles in the New World. Instead, they found themselves caught in the fateful trap. Their efforts to free themselves and others from it, against bitter and violent opposition, nearly ended what once seemed to them the last, best hope on earth. It left the contestants diminished in spirit with their aspirations still far from achieved.

Greece had experienced servile insurrection; Rome had suffered servile wars, and slavery had helped to destroy the strength of its republic. Yet neither of those cultures had been plagued by all the fears, suspicions, racial and economic clashes between the demands of freedom and order that slave traders inflicted on America when they transported captured Negroes from Africa. Greek and Roman slaves had been people of their own race, victims of lost wars. Slaves of the Anglo-Saxons in North America were of different race, color and culture. They were victims of greed, of the unlearned lessons of history and of a Christian religion too late in recalling the admonition that all men are the children of God.

The tragedy which followed this importation of racial differences and slavery was not confined to Negroes, though they bore most of the wounds on their bodies and minds. Unchecked physical power over other men corrupts its possessors as much as any other kind of individual power. As Henry Clay of Kentucky said, Negro slavery was not only "a wrong to the slave, but a curse to the masters." Injection of alien race and slavery challenged religious belief and split the Christian churches. It became a persistent threat to survival of the nation, taking many hundreds of thousands of lives before its explosive potential could be smothered, even in part. Late in the twentieth century, it still was forcing Americans to test the reality of their vaunted creed of freedom, for they had tolerated its denial to millions of their fellow citizens. This, in turn, was detracting from America's support for the freedom of other peoples in the world faced by a new form of totalitarian slavery.

The combination of slavery and racial difference rather suddenly— within a generation—changed the early half-bucolic picture of American life. The process is comparable with the way discovery of nuclear energy and its immediate adaptation to warfare almost overnight wiped out the ocean barriers which had protected the United States during its period of growth, and then altered the whole concept of warfare. A vast accumulation of assumptions had to be painfully jettisoned.

When the nation was proclaimed in 1776 and established in 1789, there was no thought among its leaders that the combination of slavery and racial difference held any danger to its existence. Practically all of them, including the great Virginians, deplored the institution and believed that it soon would die out. In 1787 they prohibited it from entering the vast area around the Great Lakes. Slave trade with other nations was prohibited in 1808, so no new slaves could be imported. In the Constitution, slavery was never mentioned by name, although all states were called on to surrender persons escaping from servitude. Representation in Congress and direct taxation were based on a count of those in servitude as three-fifths of every man who was free. The Declaration of Independence had proclaimed that all men (not only white) were created equal and that all government rightly rested on consent of the governed.

The nation's founders believed they were creating a free society; in the Constitution they endeavored to protect both liberty and property. The national government had only those powers which the states granted to it and only the responsibilities which went with those powers. The Supreme Court was soon to undertake to inform Congress and the President whether the actions of those two branches of government were in accordance with the Constitution as the Court saw it. While the Constitution left opportunities for extended disagreement about differences between human and property rights, and about state and federal powers, it seemed to its creators free from any malignancy which might threaten the national life. Their task had been to create an acceptable political alternative to a loose and ineffective confederation, and they had achieved a remarkable result. The nation was to stay united and to prosper under its Constitution for more than seventy years before its unity was fractured by civil war.

The founders had not counted on the disruptive power of technological change. After Eli Whitney invented a cotton gin in 1793, a slave who had been able to clean only eight pounds of cotton a day suddenly could clean a thousand pounds. Within a few decades slavery became a profitable institution, cherished by those whom it enriched. Soon it dominated the political and economic life of the South. It changed the character and thinking of the people. All the small opportunities for disagreement left in the Constitution were pried open. The Union and the concept of freedom on which it had been based were endangered.

The full effects of Whitney's invention were even less foreseen by early-nineteenth-century Americans than their grandchildren foresaw the ways in which invention of the automobile would change their character and increase their problems. Given its dynamism by the cotton gin, slavery began to have an almost independent life of its own. It determined that the best Southern lands would be taken over by the 350,000 slave-owning families for plantations on which cotton, tobacco, sugar and hemp could be grown. Poorer farmers had to be satisfied with marginal lands. Living in the shadow of large slave estates with their concentrated economic, social and political power, these "poor whites" became more similar to European peasants than to the independent farmers of the North and West. Immigrants from Europe, shunning the degrading competition with slavery, flowed into the free states, increasing the population superiority of the North.

The relative power of the slave states in national political life, which had been equal or superior to that of the North when the nation was founded, consequently began to decline. With this Southern decrease in national importance, resentments which men always attach to a decline in power and status began to crystallize. To check this growing imbalance of population and power, Southern politicans tried to add new slave states to the Union, to rationalize such steps and to glorify the culture supporting the peculiar institution. During the first two decades after the cotton-gin invention, the political balance was maintained by adding slave and free states alternately. In 1820 the Missouri Compromise, which admitted free Maine and slave Missouri to the Union, seemed to open the way for slavery west of the Mississippi River, north of the line 36°30'. The aged Jefferson, who had drafted the Declaration of Independence, wrote that this action, like an alarm sounding in the night, had wakened him with fear for the fate of the Union.

The first notable peculiarity of this developing conflict was that it did not divide life vertically throughout the Union. The division was sectional. In the North and West, where climate and soil favored cereal crops produced by an independent farmer with his own labor, slavery could not thrive and was generally prohibited. In the border states it was on the defensive. But it flourished in the warm South, where cotton, tobacco, sugar and hemp needed plentiful cheap labor. So two diverse regions of economic and political power were developing under the same flag. This encouraged a sectional spirit, which in the deep South became a separate loyalty, even a new nationalism. As a result, a civil, or more accurately a sectional, war was possible and eventually probable. If slavery had been intrasectional, its explosive qualities might have been more limited. More men would have seen with their own eyes, and sooner, its threat to their livelihood and consciences; an overwhelming majority could have been counted on to eliminate it in one locality after another.

The second peculiarity of the developing division was that, even when men in both regions understood that slavery might lead to war, none of the political leaders was sufficiently bold to reach out for a solution in time. A way to prevent slavery from causing war was available to them. Early nineteenth-century governments in France were compensating some of the aristocracy whose land had been taken from them during the French revolution. England was compensating slaveholders in the West Indies for emancipation. Indeed, in the 1830s after the Nat Turner slave uprising, in which several score people had been killed, Virginia considered this possibility. This burden was too heavy for a single state. But was compensation to the slaveholders by the federal government, its credit supported by vast public land resources, impossible? The longer the problem was left unconsidered, the larger it grew. In 1860 there were about 2,610,000 slaves (over nine years of age) in the South. To compensate for an average investment of $600 per slave would have involved payments of about $1.6 billion ($5 billion in 1960 dollars). This was less than the first increase in the national debt because of the Civil War and a small fraction of the total cost of the war on both sides. But in 1860 the federal government was a small institution; about 30,000 mailmen and postal clerks and 6,000 other employees, with annual revenues of $60 million and a national debt of about the same. Creating a new debt twenty-seven times as large as the existing one, or as the revenues, was considered impossible—before war made it necessary.

Another barrier to the compensation solution was fear of a strong national government. The United States was not England or France, where one central institution could act in and for all its parts. It was a government of delegated powers, one in which the individual states guarded carefully their prerogatives against the federal administration.

Fear of states' rights opposition doubtless explains in part why some of the greatest statesmen of the prewar period never spoke publicly of their belief that compensated emancipation was the way to relieve the nation of the scourge which had been fastened on it. Two former Presidents, Jefferson and Madison, and two Whig party leaders, Henry Clay and Daniel Webster, all approved the idea privately, but none of them treated it as an alternative to civil war deserving full public discussion. Congress declined to approve a small step in this direction suggested by an individual member. Later, President Lincoln discussed the solution as a means of persuading some border states to back out of the war, but by that time it was too late. Even in 1862 he suggested to Congress that the United States might issue bonds to individual states to compensate slave-owners for freeing their slaves.

A third peculiarity of the conflict, and one which was also to shape the whole post-Civil War period, was the lack of understanding by the abolitionists. They failed to see that even this suggested action of liberation through compensation would leave a major problem of racial readjustment scattered like loose dynamite across the Southern areas. Fear of this grim prospect alone made many Southerners prefer war. Specifically, they feared what the South still dreaded a century later, job competition, social equality and interracial marriage. Somewhat more interested in eliminating slavery than in the individual Negroes and whites in the South, and not understanding the Southern fear fully, the abolitionists never felt the political need or moral compulsion to spell out what they intended to do with and for the Negroes whom they hoped to liberate; or with and for the poorer white men who would be placed in economic and social competition with the freedmen of another race. Yet there were five and a half million of these poorer white people who did not own slaves. They were consequently left with a choice between what they had, a precarious coexistence with slavery but social superiority, or alternatively the prospect of a humiliating and even frightening upheaval. They chose to support the former and to try to prevent the latter.

Possibly, with great difficulty and at some expense, a method could have been worked out to deal with this problem. The 350,000 slave-owning families receiving compensation for their slaves might have been required to settle the freed Negroes on some of the plantation land with a right to purchase it on easy terms, a period during which their civil and economic rights would both have special protection. At the same time the government could have also made credit available for the 1,400,000 poor white families to buy good land, as well as animals, tools and supplies. It could also have arranged to give both groups the advantages of education which their Northern and Western fellow citizens were obtaining. A period of somewhat painful adjustment, but one without major convulsions or intimidating violence might have taken place. However, neither the solution of compensated emancipation, coupling respect for personal rights and property rights, nor any arrangement for necessary racial adjustments was seriously considered on a high or low political level before the war.

But where no rational solutions for major difficulties are found, the field is opened for irrational ones. The Southerners gradually ceased deploring slavery as a necessary evil, as their fathers had done, and, instead, proclaimed it a noble institution, worthy of acceptance by freemen everywhere. This moved the defense over to a fright-creating offense, and moved the slave states over to the concept of expansion. Both moves challenged the self-interest and moral views of the nation and led to a division of the church bodies and to further sectional divisions within the political parties.

In the North, a strong abolitionist movement had developed early and in time became angry with the frustrations it encountered. Colonization of Negroes in Africa and Central America was advocated, but the freed Negroes considered themselves Americans; they did not want to go to alien Africa. Anyway, the project would have been too costly for private contribution and emancipation was not in sight. A few thought that the Constitution could be amended to provide for emancipation, but most people were forced to accept the conclusion that the slave states could probably always veto any amendment to obtain this result. The abolitionists' efforts at peaceful persuasion to eliminate slavery by voluntary action were blocked in several slave states. Their literature was kept out by local postmasters. Some laws were passed punishing those who taught Negroes to read. A senator from Mississippi warned a senator from New Hampshire that, if he tried to present the abolitionist cause in Mississippi, he would be hung from the highest tree.

Abolitionists were in the position of "ban the bomb" advocates in the 1960s, who were not allowed to reach the Soviet people. Some cursed the Constitution as a covenant with hell, as William Lloyd Garrison did. Others favored disunion, so that the blame for slavery would not lie on their own doorsteps. Some took part in freeing individual slaves through an "underground railway" from the South to Canada. Others helped these fugitives escape from authorities who were returning them to their masters. Among the extremists was John Brown. In 1856 he decided that he had the right in his own hands to kill four pro-slavery advocates in Kansas in retribution for pro-freedom people who had been killed by others. In 1859 Brown led a band of eighteen in a fanatical attack on Harper's Ferry arsenal to start a slave insurrection in Virginia.

The slaves did not rise. Brown and four others were hanged. He had become an abolitionist martyr at the price of solidifying the enraged South. Harriet Beecher Stowe's *Uncle Tom's Cabin*, a sentimental abolitionist novel provoked by the Fugitive Slave Act, was published in 1852 and sold some 1,200,000 copies in sixteen months. It lumped slave-owners together as moral lepers and enraged those who were kind to the slaves. Abolitionist propaganda was used by secessionists as evidence of a concerted Northern plot to obtain emancipation by fair means or foul. A cold war was turning warm.

This failure of communication and education produced diverse and ultimately disastrous results. For example, the basic fact of the whole dispute, that before the war the Constitution protected slavery wherever it existed and would do so for generations, seems to have been pushed out of sight by many expansionists and secessionists. Yet this legal barrier to emancipation was accepted by most Northern statesmen. Peaceful change could be obtained only by amending the Constitution. That document gave veto power over any amendment to one-fourth of all the states plus one. In 1860 there were fifteen slave states and sixteen free states. The fifteen slave states could veto any amendment until there were as many as forty-five free states committed to emancipation. Before that time came, some twenty-nine more free states would have had to be added to the Union, making a total of sixty. Any such proliferation of free states, while not impossible, was highly improbable. Slavery was therefore quite thoroughly protected where it existed, although its claims to expansion were not. One of the triumphs of the extremists in the cold war was to make the cause of expansion seem important to a majority of the Southerners, who actually had little to gain by the addition of a few more slave states to the Union. Those slave-owners whose coastal lands were being exhausted, however, had something to gain from it.

There was really only one way to lose for those Southerners who wanted to retain slavery where it already existed. This one their extremists found for them. It involved: first, withdrawing their members of Congress so that they no longer could challenge legislation there; then seceding and abstaining, so that the number of states required to pass unfavorable amendments to the Constitution would be decreased sufficiently to provide a three-fourths majority for an anti-slavery amendment, and finally, through insurrection, which would give the President emergency power to emancipate slaves as a war measure. All these things they did, and this result they obtained.

Before this, however, the Southern people had to be misinformed by the extremists, who deceived themselves as well. They made the error of believing their own propaganda. It was possible for them to do all this in the deep South without adequate challenge, because of the barriers of distance, editorial and official censorship and exclusion of opposition. With the help of these disrupted channels of communication, they could tell their listeners that secession was possible without war, the Northern military potential was small, the North had no deep convictions which would lead it to accept or endure a long war. So they said, although the probabilities were high that, if either Abraham Lincoln or Stephen A. Douglas were elected President in 1860, the Union would have been defended by arms. Instead of a costless, peaceable secession of the type promised, there would be, as Henry Clay, the Whig leader from Kentucky, had told the followers of Calhoun at the time of the Compromise of 1850, a "furious, bloody, implacable, exterminating war."

The extremists also misled the Southern people by telling them that, if war came, by accident and contrary to expectation, they would certainly win it. They would do so because their cause was just, because aristocracy (to which all of them were invited to claim affiliation) was superior to a commercial society, and because their men were better individual fighters. By the time this last argument had to be made, however, Southern Whigs and other moderates had been brushed aside. So there could be no adequate consideration of the probability of defeat inherent in the North's population superiority of more than two to one (more than three to one without the Negroes), and in manufacturing superiority of at least nine to one. Nor by that time could there be any cool consideration of the risks to slavery or states' rights if a war was started and lost. More important to the extremist leaders was the belief that time was running against them. The South's interest in slavery was larger then than it might be later. By 1880 there would obviously be less slavery in the border states, there would be more free states, and Northern population and industrial superiority would be greater. It was now or never.

Along with the underevaluation of Northern material superiority and devotion to the Union, secessionists erroneously discounted the inner convictions of their fellow countrymen on the subject of personal liberty. Southerners had been led to believe that, apart from the abolitionists, only the self-interest of the "free soilers" in seeking new land in the West was directly involved. But that self-interest was offset, it was said, by the self-interest of New England cotton-mill owners in maintaining peace with their Southern source of supply. And with this miscalculation about the strength of sentiment for preserving the Union, they also failed to understand the growing demand in the North and West, spurred on by the churches, for a higher social morality in the nation. It was this demand which created an audience for Lincoln in his debates with Douglas in 1858. He revived some of the enthusiasm for freedom and equality of the men who led the American Revolution and founded the nation.

As Lincoln saw it, a major temptation was being offered the people to go on their own prosperous way and forget about the human rights of the Negro. His opponent, Stephen A. Douglas of Illinois, leader of the Northern wing of the Democratic party and probable next President, invited the free states to let the material factors in life predominate at the expense of all others. The issue was, Douglas suggested, simply a matter of dollars and cents, and nature had made the new territories of the West unsuitable for slavery. He met the technical requirements for an appearance of democracy by his proposal of "popular sovereignty," which meant to him letting the first settlers in any territory vote on the fate of slavery in it forever. He urged others to follow him in refusing to care whether or not slavery was voted up or down by those settlers. The reward promised for such indifference was that the corrosive issue already dividing the Protestant churches and political parties, and threatening to break the nation into two warring elements, would disappear as a cause for disunion.

The case against yielding to such an insidious temptation was argued by Lincoln, also from Illinois. While in Congress, he had opposed the war with Mexico in 1848 as unnecessary, a maneuver of the South to acquire more slave states. He had supported the Wilmot Proviso, which would have prevented any land acquisitions from Mexico from entering the Union as slave states. While abhorring slavery, he was not an abolitionist. He believed in containment, holding slavery within its existing borders. At the same time, he believed that freedom carried certain obligations for those who possessed it. Freemen had to protect the personal liberty of all other men, including minorities, such as Negroes. Freemen, he said, could escape this obligation only through sacrifice of their own humanity and at the risk of losing their own freedom at some later time. No right existed to take away equal protection of equal laws from human beings who were Negroes, which could not later be used to deprive white minorities of their rights. (Thus Lincoln marked out what was to become one of the essential differences in the twentieth century between democracies and totalitarian nations, which also held elections but raised indifference to personal liberty and minority rights to the dignity of a dogma.) It was in support of this moral obligation that Northerners later sang, "As He died to make men holy, let us die to make men free."

Moderate Southern leaders who believed that secession could be invoked temporarily to obtain a better bargain, and then given up, did not understand that their first step committed them to the entire road, nor the extent to which the law of diminishing political returns was operating against them. Their extremists were clearly bent on going the whole way. In the summer of 1860 they split the Democratic party and nominated a sectional candidate of their own, Breckenridge. This ruined Douglas's chances for the Presidency. He accused the extremist leaders of wanting to elect Lincoln, the very event they were publicly deploring as a catastrophe and signal for secession.[1] In early December of 1860, before the remarkable last-minute efforts at another compromise, secessionist leaders addressed a statement to the Southern people alleging that all efforts at compromise and reconciliation had already been tried, and all had failed. It was an open falsehood. (One of these leaders would in April ask for the privilege of firing the first cannon shot at a federal fort in Charleston harbor and start the war.) It was the extremist group which used the word "revolution" for their goal, and in a revolutionary process the moderates are usually unable to step backward. That became impossible for them in the South. The extremists had their way in getting a separate nation for a while, but many of them were kept out of the positions of power within it.

Southern moderates also failed to see that Northerners were getting tired of going through the same harrowing process of threats, compromises and further threats which had taken place during and after the Compromise of 1850. The Northerners were absorbed with plans of their own for material progress, national development, social morality and democracy, and wanted the endless obstacles to them pushed aside. But they, also, were victims of misapprehensions of their own, which led to their surprise and military unpreparedness when secession came in 1860–1861. (More importantly, these early mistakes led to major errors of action and inaction in the postwar period, helping to blight the process of reunion.)

The people in the free states failed, first of all, to comprehend before 1860 how fully people in the slave states had developed a cause which to them seemed both rational and worthy of extreme dedication. It was not simply the self-interested slave-owners' cause of a small and rich minority; it was shared by the large majority who had no slaves. They were to fight for it in the name of freedom. While they meant by that elastic term the freedom of individual states to do as they pleased and the freedom of white men to rule over the Negro race as they pleased, they felt able to carry this impressive banner without inhibitions. In Northern eyes this seemed illogical, absurd, false and also irrelevant. Nevertheless, taken together and emotionalized by fear, resentment and pride, the sum became dynamic and greater than the total of its individual parts and was adequate to sustain Southerners through years of war and deprivation.

Behind this cause was a rationale developed by John C. Calhoun of South Carolina. It was to the effect that, despite creation of the Union to supplant an unworkable confederation of individual states and in spite of the absence of any authority in the Constitution for individual states to nullify that instrument of union, they nevertheless were free to do so whenever they believed such action necessary for their own protection. State sovereignty, he taught, could be interposed against federal action. Jefferson and Madison had sponsored a similar concept when the Federalist party passed censorship laws (the Alien and Sedition Acts) which resulted in jailing a number of Republican critics.

Between 1815 and 1825, however, the Supreme Court had ruled that it could decide disputes between the states and the federal government as well as find acts of Congress or of the executive illegal. It held that no state had power to supplant the Supreme Court in these functions or unilaterally to nullify (through state taxation, for example) any legal act of the federal government. The legislative and executive branches accepted this. Nevertheless, in 1832 Calhoun persuaded his own state to attempt nullification of a new national tariff act. President Andrew Jackson called this treason and threatened to send warships to collect the customs revenues. Congress modified the tariff somewhat and South Carolina then yielded. Calhoun revived this doctrine in the 1840s to include the right of unilateral secession.

Spread of this doctrine convinced the South that almost any unwelcome federal action was an infringement on states' rights, a further justification for revolt. Long before secession, many Southerners had been led to think of the federal government as an engine of oppression. "Freedom" began to mean to them not individual liberty but removal of national authority. It was this doctrine which the later leaders of the North believed they had so thoroughly and obviously destroyed through the sacrifices of the Civil War that they did not even bother to incorporate its destruction in the surrender terms they offered, nor did they even bother to obtain a clear Southern and national disavowal of it in the three postwar amendments to the Constitution which they passed. This was a crucial error of omission. This same doctrine, in the form of "interposition of state sovereignty," a hundred years later was invoked by several Southern states to defy federal court orders concerning the desegregation of public schools and state universities. Its survival was, in Arkansas in 1959 and in Mississippi in 1962, the cause for putting federal troops into those states to uphold the federal courts and the Union.

In the crucial 1850s, the doctrine might have made little headway had not the poorer white people been persuaded that emancipation was probable, that it would change their social status and force them into competition for jobs with Negroes. In evidence of this fear, they passed severe laws to compel freed Negroes to leave their home states. This was done by subjecting such Negroes to arrest, by forcing them to work for others without wages, and by auctioning them off to men who would guarantee to take them out of the state.

A similar concern with status was widespread in the North and West. A little more self-examination of their own society might have prepared people outside the South for some of the explosive quality of that concern in the South. Fear of being swamped socially and economically by white immigrants from Europe had created the American or "Know-Nothing" party, determined to make second-class citizens out of some of the newcomers. It had obtained power in some states. Lincoln wrote in 1855:

> As a nation, we began by declaring that "all men are created equal."
> We now practically read it "all men are created equal, *except Negroes.*"
> When the Know-Nothings get control, it will read "all men are created equal, *except Negroes, and foreigners and Catholics.*" When it comes to this I should prefer emigrating to some country where they make no pretence of loving liberty—to Russia, for instance, where despotism can be taken pure, and without the base alloy of hypocrisy.[2]

Few Northern and Western states allowed freed Negroes to vote. Some refused to allow Negroes to enter their borders. Workers occasionally declined to work along with them. Douglas had scored against Lincoln in the 1858 Senatorial race by suggesting that Lincoln's ideas would result in a migration of freed Negroes from neighboring slave Missouri into free Illinois. Professor Jaffa has gone so far as to suggest that "hatred of the Negro was almost indistinguishable from hatred of slavery as the dynamic of the Northern free-soil movement."[3] Fear of Negro competition in its double-edged form was particularly prevalent among the immigrant Irish, who were then at the bottom of the economic ladder. Yet, in spite of all this Northern concern with Negro competition and status, the Northern people were not psychologically prepared to believe that the Southern white worker's graver concern about status and livelihood could stoke a secessionist movement. It was not a unique blindness. Some seventy years later few people could foresee that the German inflation of the early 1920s would mean the loss of economic and social position for the bulk of the middle-class groups of Germany and would drive them over to the racially polarized Nazi movement and help to prepare the way for the Second World War.

A further explanation can be found for Northern failure to be prepared for Southern secession. Events of the 1850s seemed to have given the South an adequate advantage without resort to the extremist solution. Northern states had given up their veto power over the creation of new slave states out of territories acquired from Mexico, when they surrendered their Wilmot Proviso for the Compromise of 1850. That agreement had been broken in favor of the South four years later by the Kansas-Nebraska Act. Pledges of the Missouri Compromise of 1820, against slavery north of the 36° 30′ line, also were lost. Pro-slavery ruffians from Missouri had almost succeeded in their efforts to force slavery on Kansas by violence. A Democratic President had almost succeeded in getting Congress to validate a fraudulently obtained pro-slavery constitution for that territory. The Southern member of Congress who had caned Senator Sumner of Massachusetts on the floor of the Senate had been triumphantly reelected to office. A pro-slavery Supreme Court had declared in the Dred Scott decision (1857) a threatening doctrine that put property rights above human rights and which might force slavery on free states. A Southern governor had demanded reopening slave trade with Africa, closed since 1808. Slave smuggling into the South had been renewed, and Southern juries had refused to indict the arrested smugglers, let alone convict them. There had been Southern-aided filibustering in Central America and maneuvers to acquire Cuba. A Southern-controlled President had vetoed, as an alien socialistic measure, a Western homestead bill favored by Northerners as an encouragement to enterprise, independence and private ownership.

During these events the people of the North had been forced to watch, with humiliation and a sense of outraged humanity, the arrival of slave-owners in their own free cities to recapture fugitive Negroes. While observing their own policemen aiding these slave-owners, they could hardly forget that the scales of justice were slanted; United States commissioners received ten dollars in fees for finding that a fugitive belonged to a claimant and only five dollars if they found he did not. All this irritation and revulsion, coupled with their frustration at the impossibility of obtaining emancipation legally, made a few Northern leaders want to secede from the South. Memory of the fact that the secession movement of the 1840s had collapsed in 1850 also tended to leave them unprepared for the events to come.

The South during the 1850s was subjected to a masterful exhortatory process which stirred up all the old fears and resentments. Apprehensive people became convinced of a menacing force in the North, acting hypocritically and maliciously to pervert the Constitution and to establish emancipation upon election of a sectionally chosen Republican President. They were reminded of Calhoun's frightening prophecy of 1849 that continued resistance of the Northern states to Southern demands, coupled with the swing of political power to the free states due to increased population, would inevitably result in emancipation. That would include, he believed, overthrowing the white people's control of the South, creating bitter hostility between the two sections and promoting the Negroes over the heads of the whites to political power. The South would become the home of anarchy, poverty and misery. He thought this prospect justified Northern yielding to Southern demands; or, failing that, justified the Southerners "by all laws, divine and human" to repel the threat by any means, including secession.

There was fuel for Southerners' fears and resentments. They heard of the arms and settlers gathered to prevent slavery from being established in Kansas. They heard about John Brown's armed bands and his belief that he had the right to exact retribution by murder. They were told about Northern mobs which took fugitive slaves from authorities and freed them. They learned of Senator Seward's comment in Rochester that there was a higher law than the Constitution, that an "irreconcilable conflict" existed. They were alarmed by Lincoln's statement that a house divided against itself, a nation half slave and half free, could not stand, and by his expressed determination to find some way to set aside the Dred Scott decision declaring Negroes ineligible for citizenship.

To Southerners this sounded like a plan to override the Constitution and the Supreme Court and to impose emancipation by extralegal means. To some of them, the tariffs lobbied by Northern industry represented a burden which would be increased by any Republican electoral success. A blacklist was started against Northern manufacturers who supported abolition. John Brown's seizure of the federal arsenal at Harper's Ferry and Thoreau's praise of him as "an angel of light" horrified the South. The fact that the Republican platform of 1860 disapproved of Brown's act did not wipe out the fears aroused by that attempted servile insurrection.

As the secessionist cause gathered strength, accusations against the good faith of the Northern leaders became more severe. Even earlier one editor had argued that abolitionists were "committed to Socialism and Communism—to no private property, no church, no government— to free love, free lands, free women and free churches."[4] Of course, not everyone took all these charges seriously. But in the late 1850s more moderate men, those with most to lose, failed to present any less radical program than secession. How little some of them actually favored it, however, is indicated by a statement of Alexander H. Stephens of Georgia, future Vice-President of the Confederacy. He thought that a full two-thirds of the voters of his state had voted for secession with the expectation that it simply represented a brief withdrawal from the

Union to obtain a better bargain than the South could get without taking that step, after which there would be reunion.

Perhaps even the long campaign of secession propaganda might have collapsed if the press of the South, its educators, its planters and business moderates had felt free to discuss objectively the last-minute Northern effort to leave emancipation entirely in Southern hands. These proposed compromises, supported by President-elect Lincoln, deserved serious consideration. With the necessary two-thirds vote in each House, the outgoing Congress proposed this amendment to the Constitution for approval by three-fourths of the states:

> No amendment shall be made to the Constitution which will author-
> ize or give to Congress the power to abolish or interfere, within any
> state, with the domestic institutions thereof, including that of persons
> held to labor or service by the laws of said state.[5]

In earlier circumstances, this might have quieted the aroused South. It was an attempt to formulate an iron-clad anti-emancipation amendment, forbidding any change to the detriment of existing slavery for as long as any state wished to retain that institution. It would have been a revolutionary alteration of the Constitution. Lincoln, who supported it, and the members of Congress who passed it, were willing to pay this very high price to keep the nation safe from sectional war. But by the time this offer was made, the seceding states already were setting up their own separate government, the Confederate States of America. The proposed amendment was never submitted to the states for ratification.

That cold war, which was rapidly provoking hot war, had many similarities with the cold war of the mid-twentieth century. Persons within each feuding area were being persuaded by others that only violence could settle the contest. In the 1850s each side believed that the opponent was an active aggressor against its way of life. A curtain shut out full communication between the peoples. A broken peace "treaty" (the Compromise of 1850) cast doubt on the value of further agreements. "Aliens" (Negroes) were involved. Provocative extremists nurtured their opposites on the other side with loose threats. Moderates tended to become suspect. Each side tended to overrate its own virtues and capacities as a deterrent to violence and as a guaranty against defeat. Each side sneered at the other side's economic system as "human slavery" or "wage slavery." Each used the word "freedom." There was also open jeering at the morality of the other side. *The New York Tribune* called the South "a vast Negro harem"; Southerners were eloquent on the North's hypocrisy in cheering John Brown's murders and pretending to uphold the Constitution while they aided slaves to escape. The brush-fire war in Kansas, in which both sides furnished men and guns, gave a brief approximation of arms competition.

So the Civil War came to the United States because no way had been found to eliminate slavery peacefully without major political, economic and social injury to those enmeshed in it. A few bold men persuaded their fellows that the institution, along with their own fate, was threatened, that it could survive only by expanding. That decision, and the necessity to treat the peculiar institution as a noble element in society, put the Southern economic, social, and political system into conflict with the much larger Northern free society; it challenged the majority's deep loyalty to national unity and personal liberty. In that emotional atmosphere, the doctrine of disunion, of a state's right to secede, was accepted by the white people of the South as a rational basis for their own freedom to continue slavery.

With this rationalization raised to the sanctity of principle, further discussion of the moral issue involved in slavery or recognition of the effective protection accorded to slavery wherever it already existed was ignored. Meanwhile, Northerners had become convinced that they had an inherited obligation to preserve the Union. All the extreme states' rights claims seemed only to camouflage the basically disruptive issue of slavery. Unless that issue were forever eliminated, the Union and the free society never would be safe from new threats.

The American Civil War began in April 1861 and ended in April 1865.

Over a century later, in the late 1960s, some millions of people had purchased rifles and handguns in order to protect their families and property against any overflow of racial resentment into their neighborhoods. Meanwhile, more and more black people doubted that the apparently indifferent white society could ever be persuaded to grant them significant freedom, including equality of opportunity. This they believed to be theirs as a matter of right and law, refused for reasons of race. By then enough city areas had been burned and looted to put the city and state police and the nation's armed forces on almost permanent riot readiness and to tempt some extremists to argue for even more violent attacks on those interests and institutions which they viewed as citadels of hostility, illegality and indifference. These events had moved from pleas to flames during the years when the nation's leaders had shown their willingness to give a higher priority to a dubious military effort abroad than to social needs at home.

At this point the nation was surely moving, with a mixture of fear, indignation and uncertainty, beyond the edge of the first two of the great problem areas into the second one, mentioned earlier, which it had to cross before it could consider itself successful, pose its candidacy as one of the memorable societies of mankind. Clearly these two areas joined. Depersonalization and alienation were, at least for a large minority of the citizens, part and parcel of the second problem area of race and income distribution. As the national assumption that a military victory could be imposed on an antifeudal revolt in Asia grew more obviously preposterous, a sense of the absurdity of the society rose like smoke from a burning rubbish heap. Half of the costs of that war would have built a fairly solid road, for and with the more neglected people of our nation, out of their inequality and their poverty. The sheer, unexamined momentum of a course casually entered was again demanding its penalty, as it had so often before in history.

The pre–Civil War and pre-Reconstruction stories give some necessary background for an understanding of the problems which the nation inherited and is forced to deal with all over again a century later. Those were in a way our preadolescent years, full of idealism and hope, lack of adequate awareness of the plaguingly persistent character of early errors, the possibility that a life with so much freedom and opportunity for the favored people could contain so much tragic experience for all. These formative years covered many decades in the early life of the republic, for, like Rome, no hell is built in a day.

Those years give us a durable example of the futility of expecting a major injustice to disappear from the national scene if only we ignore it long enough. Again, they show how frustration—the inability of a society to agree upon or achieve any common purpose—leads to extremism, counterextremism, violence and counterviolence. They provide also an almost classic illustration of the ease with which moderates can be overtaken and overcome by far-outers in periods of helpless exasperation. Further, they illustrate the tactic, still in current use, by which extremists invite and help create the very menace they are claiming to combat. They remind us of the havoc that can be wrought when risks are underestimated, as they were by the Southern secessionists, how heavy the price of planlessness can be when moral indignation seems to be a sufficient fulfillment of moral duty, as it was with some of the abolitionists. They recall that the word "freedom" means quite different things to different people, and that this difference is vital. They put us into the middle of the debates between Lincoln and Douglas, forced to face the same moral problems, in new circumstances, and again in an atmosphere of impending but possibly avertible calamity. They show us how completely enmeshed men are in their past, even when their eyes strain to behold a less plagued future. They recall how small the costs of preventing disasters are compared to the costs of enduring them, as well as how reluctant today's men are to pay any remotely postponable bills in advance. They remind us that our own accelerated mechanization and automation may yet change the national character and future in ways which we cannot at present foresee.

PART II

It was sometimes called the American Civil War. It was sometimes called the War Between the States. In the four years of armed conflict (April 1861 to May 1865) there were probably more casualties than in any internal war in history up to that time. Union forces finally won the military victory, which meant that individual states had no right to secede and that slavery would be abolished.

Union victory did not, of course, change the view so widely held before the war that the Negro race was inferior to the white race. Nor did it convince the defeated white Southerners that individual liberty should apply equally to the former slaves and themselves. Amazingly enough, the surrender terms offered by Union General William Sherman to Confederate General Joseph Johnson seem loosely to have recognized continued property in slaves, an oversight soon corrected.[6] After Lincoln's assassination there was wrath coupled with planlessness. No one was really ready for peace. The road was consequently left open for dispute about the effects of the Union victory on liberty and equality, states' rights and states' duties; only the framework of that controversy had been altered by eliminating secession and chattel slavery. The nation was handicapped by its unpreparedness, its indecision.

The heroism, gallantry and brilliant tactics of soldiers on both sides have led to the writing and reading of thousands of books about the battles. Possibly this popular literary phenomenon represents in the present impersonal nuclear age a nostalgia for what Winston Churchill called "the last of the wars between gentlemen." More probably it represents a profound fascination with the drama of a great nation being torn apart and horror at the individual human tragedies involved. It was a war that left very deep wounds, not readily forgotten or forgiven as the postwar struggles for power and status developed their own animus. People of the victorious Union mourned an almost unbelievable number of their sons. They were angered by the treatment their soldiers had undergone in Southern prison camps. They were horrified by the act of a Southern fanatic in killing President Lincoln.

In the South there was disillusionment from beginning to end with all the extravagant promises the extremists had made—from no war at all to an English alliance to easy victory. They were outraged as the first sufferers of total war when Sherman's armies, marching through the heart of the Confederacy, burned and destroyed all they could find in order to cripple the Southern supply train and the will to continue. Rancor resulted from their own extreme states' rights doctrine: one state refused to let the Confederacy draft its men; during General Lee's last stand around Richmond, with his hungry men fighting in tattered clothes, a neighboring state hoarded for its own sovereign use large supplies of bacon and uniforms. Hunger and deprivation were so extreme that, months before the end of the fighting, men deserted by thousands to care for their starving families. Toward the last came the astonishing news that their own Confederate government, at General Lee's suggestion, was considering freedom for slaves in return for military service, which would have endowed them with an equality repugnant to the dogma of Negro inferiority.

At the close of the war, Lincoln, who was aware that the great task was to heal the wounds and reunite a badly torn people in a spirit of "malice toward none and charity toward all," was taken abruptly from the scene. Would the men who had seceded be treated as traitors, tried and hanged, or as misled brothers brought back into the larger community without humiliation? No one was sure.

Lack of responsible thinking before the war, about methods and costs of such a social revolution as the conversion of a slave economy into a free society, had led to underestimating the forces behind secession. Similarly, a lack of foresight of the magnitude of the same problems facing the nation at war's end blighted the postwar period. On the political side were problems of reuniting the severed states to the Union, of maintaining order in them, of determining the political status of the liberated slaves, and of establishing courts and agencies to protect such rights as they might be given. On the economic side were problems of restoring the destroyed farms and factories, transforming a chattel-labor system into a free-labor market and protecting the newcomers from abuse, feeding starving black and white people until the next crops came in, financing land ownership and reestablishing a banking system. On the social side were the problems of racial adjustment, education, training in responsibility and democratic methods, and preventing racial differences from leading to violence. To create a new order that included personal freedom for the Negroes would have been difficult in any case. To create it after four years of war waged by bitter men who, in spite of defeat, were still not persuaded that Negroes were entitled to equal rights, was a staggering task.

Yet, if the victors refused to accept a major share in the task, the completely bankrupted, hungry and angry Southerners would have to pay all the costs, carry all the burdens and run all the risks alone, geographically and psychologically separated from the prospering North and West.

Not fully understood at the time was the fact that a large measure of financial aid was needed as a first of several major steps—of the type taken by the United States belatedly after the First World War and more promptly and extensively after the Second World War to aid the defeated. Except for giving army rations to some hundreds of thousands of the starving, black and white, there was no major aid. The national government could have put credit guarantees behind land purchases by poor whites and liberated Negroes. This was badly needed because cotton-land values dropped to ten dollars an acre. A land-credit program, holding land values at thirty dollars an acre, would have put a floor under the whole sectional economy. Over the next twenty years cotton was to average nine cents a pound at the farm, and a family which undertook to borrow fifteen hundred dollars to purchase forty acres and supplies would have been able to pay off six-percent mortgages with forty pounds of cotton an acre, about a fifth of the crop. Once the banking system was reestablished, the mortgages could have been discounted, with the government required to put up little in actual funds. Probably less than one billion dollars in national credit to guarantee banks against losses on loans for land and equipment purchases would have been sufficient to end the South's postwar depression.

A very small move in this general direction had been made during the war, when Negroes fled from their owners to the small Union-held enclaves along the Atlantic coast and had to be fed. Army officers put them to work on abandoned or requisitioned land. A month before the war ended a Freedmen's Bureau was established by Congress to help the Negroes. A farsighted plea for a land-acquisition system was then voiced in Congress on the ground that, unless something of this kind were undertaken, "a generation of freedmen would be destroyed before a generation of free men could live."[7] The land-acquisition part of the army program turned out to be worthless, because the abandoned land leased to the Negroes was reclaimed by the original owners as soon as they were amnestied. No funds or credit for other land purchases were voted. Thaddeus Stevens, leader of the Republican Radicals in Congress, later twisted the concept of aid to Negroes into one of punishment for rebels. He urged confiscation of land of former slave-owners to establish Negroes on the land and pay off the national debt. That vindictiveness scared his own business supporters; once the idea of confiscating private property in peacetime started, no one could tell where it would stop. Congress might have returned to the unsolved problem, but then came a new Southern attack in savage and concentrated form, which opened the "dark, corrupt and bloody time."

Meanwhile, a major economic opportunity to help the freed Negroes was lost. During the following decades the government granted approximately two hundred million acres to transcontinental railroads, while only a few thousand acres in piney, infertile areas of the South were given as homesteads to Negroes. Instead of employing the freed Negroes, who were eager for work, the favored corporations imported many thousands of Chinese to lay the rails across the West.

The postwar effort to establish personal liberty among underprivileged and untrained Negroes in a racially sensitive area was riotous and unsuccessful. There were plots, intimidation, troop and civilian violence, and shifts in power at all levels of society. The engagements of the opposing forces were intense for twelve years, from 1865–1877, then were converted into rear-guard actions and gestures for another fifteen; after two generations they were resumed in the 1950s and 1960s. The long struggle over racial adjustment, like that over slavery before and during the Civil War, scarred the character of the nation.

During the Reconstruction period six groups faced one another across broken lines of communication, arid stretches of misunderstanding and deep marshes of hostility. In the South were ruined plantation owners, many of them ready to accept a new order; the vastly larger number of poor whites, who had fought the war to avoid the conditions that now engulfed them; and the liberated Negroes, who had not rebelled against their masters but had drifted away to Union armies entering the South. In the North and West many were willing to forget and forgive, and were disposed to let seceded states return to the Union without much change. But under the pressure of the new Southern attack toward the end of 1865, they divided into two groups. One was concerned about the fate of the Negroes but unready to do anything about it. Another group came to believe that only if the four million Negroes' human and civil rights were protected could the nation be free and safe from renewed challenges. In a third group were power-hungry Northern leaders who saw opportunities for their party and its industrial supporters to exploit the South for partisan advantage.

A misleading quiet followed the end of the fighting and the grief at President Lincoln's death. The Congress, which had told him that it wanted a far harsher treatment of the ruling powers in the seceded states than the one he had proclaimed, was not in session during the summer of 1865. Vice-President Andrew Johnson, who succeeded Lincoln, was a self-educated native of North Carolina, a tailor turned politician, a Democrat. He had served as a Congressman from Tennessee, then as governor before representing it in the U.S. Senate. During the war he was the only Southern senator loyal to the Union and was appointed by Lincoln to be wartime governor of Tennessee. When Johnson entered the White House, he intended to punish the secessionist leaders as traitors, but then thought better of it and quietly proceeded on Lincoln's lines to bring the South back into the Union. This meant having at least one-tenth of the previously registered voters (all whites) constitute new state governments after swearing loyalty to the Union. While this seemed to be a step toward one kind of peace and order, it was taken under a hovering cloud. The absent Congress had expressed an opposite policy, and it alone had the power to seat in its chambers any representatives from the seceded states.

In the autumn of 1865 the lull was ended with a great storm. While the Thirteenth Amendment, abolishing slavery and involuntary servitude, was being ratified by state legislatures, most of the Southern states startled the North with a countermove of their own. They passed so-called Black Codes or Black Laws to replace slavery with peonage, completely disregarding most of the personal liberties of Negroes. When Congress met in December, this challenge was lighted up by the burning of three Negro schools on the Eastern Shore of Maryland. This was the act of men who feared to lose possession of Negro children "bound out" to them to work for their keep without schooling. The Black Laws were most severe in states having the largest Negro populations. One or another of them provided for arrest of every colored person who stopped work before his year's labor contract was completed. Those who did so were labeled "deserters" and subject to arrest on sight. At a time when farm wages were less than 100 dollars a year, a Negro without steady employment was to be fined fifty dollars and imprisoned, then bound out to any white person willing to pay the fine, with preference given to his former master. In some cases, Negroes were forced to get licenses for any nonfarm work; in others, licenses to buy land. Insulting gestures, language or acts could draw a fine of 100 dollars. Local courts could "apprentice" children to their former owners on a showing of sorts that their parents could not support them; and the former owners were allowed to inflict "moderate corporal punishment." Testimony of Negroes was not to be accepted in court cases involving whites. Negroes were forbidden to serve on juries, vote or hold public office.

A five-point defense for these Black Codes was made then and later: First, the crops had to be made, or everyone would starve. The liberated people were wandering about, flocking to the cities where the army would feed them, unwilling to contract their services for the whole year needed for a crop, especially at the small wages offered. Yet the cotton growers absolutely required a dependable labor force. Second, the new laws were only a little worse than those for voluntarily freed Negroes before the war and those a century earlier in several Northern states. Third, educating the former slaves to understand such concepts as "contracts," "wages" and "democracy" would take a long time; the proposed peonage was a beginning, at least, and a substitute for chaos and pauperization. Fourth, the surrender terms had not forbidden this, and the victors had not proposed or made possible any alternative. Finally, this was the only way to maintain the tradition of white superiority.

However, what seemed rational in the South appeared irrational and revolting in the North. The Black Laws perpetuated slavery in disguised form. They provoked a Northern decision to give full citizenship and suffrage to the Negroes. Instead of producing general Northern awareness of the social revolution involved in the abolition of slavery and the need for common consultations, financial aid and other measures to ease the transition, the Black Laws strengthened those Northern leaders who believed that only federal troops and laws could settle the difficulties. So the Black Laws, suddenly and unexpectedly enacted, cut short any opportunity for a constructive process of reunion and for the long-term interests of the Negroes. Federal troops and laws failed to solve the problem. After twelve years of turmoil, ending in 1877, the Black Laws peonage system, with some modifications, prevailed.

Meanwhile, the challenge of the Black Codes was thrown at the new President. Did Andrew Johnson, who was vulnerable as a former Democrat from seceding Tennessee, favor peonage? Did he stand for liberty, or for a little of it, or none? Congress gave him numerous opportunities to develop an alternative to the Black Laws, but he declined them all. Congress thereupon passed a program of its own, despite the President. It renewed for a year the Freedmen's Bureau to protect Negroes in search for work at living wages. It passed a civil-rights bill to protect Negroes as citizens and gave exclusive jurisdiction over interference with those rights to federal courts. Johnson vetoed these bills, then both were passed over his veto by the required two-thirds vote. Republican Radicals, the largest group in Congress, did not have a two-thirds majority at the time. But moderates, knowing that they could not survive politically if they supported Johnson's failures to develop constructive alternatives, went along with the Radicals. To establish that Congress, and not the President, would determine reconstruction policy, that body denied seats to representatives from several states

Johnson already had reorganized. Congress also set up a Joint Committee on Reconstruction to examine matters of loyalty and abuse in the seceded area. Finally, to make sure that no change in Washington administrations would result in repeal of its Civil Rights Act, Congress passed the Fourteenth Amendment to the Constitution. This was sent out to the states for ratification.

The Civil Rights Act and the Fourteenth Amendment had been provoked by the hasty and embittered Black Laws of Southern states. But this federal reaction was also hasty, if not equally embittered. It was also less than clear and adequate. Consequently, the Fourteenth Amendment in time disappointed those who supported it, and was interpreted by the Supreme Court in unexpected ways.

What alternatives were there to the white-dominated, sharecropper, peonage system of the Southern Black Laws? There were several. England had liberated the slaves in the West Indies in the 1830s but had not given them the ballot (and did not do so until the 1930s). Lincoln had favored step-by-step suffrage; at first only for the 200,000 ex-slaves who had served in the Union army and for the few educated Negroes, meanwhile protecting all other civil rights of Negroes. The Thirteenth Amendment (1865) abolished slavery but did not guarantee civil rights and said nothing about the vote. Suffrage could have been conditioned on education (as was later done with immigrants seeking citizenship). Congress considered a proposal to guarantee all civil rights except suffrage, which would be postponed until 1876. Another alternative might have been to bring Negroes into the political community by age groups, beginning with those over fifty years old, and two years later those over forty-four years old, and so forth. That would have avoided the overwhelming Negro rush to support the Radical Republicans which occurred after the Fourteenth Amendment (1868) had declared them to be citizens.

Southern astonishment and opposition to this decision were understandable. The Negroes were illiterate. They had never participated in any important decisions, conducted any business or been entrusted with any major responsibility. As slaves they had owned no property and had paid no taxes. They seemed to the Southern whites to have brought no culture with them from Africa, and had been granted little opportunity to acquire much in the United States. Many had not been allowed to experience the responsibilities of family life. Their masters and poorer white neighbors could not see in them the potential of able lawyers, scientists, doctors, teachers, businessmen, literary and theatrical artists which some of their twentieth-century descendants became in fact. Except for a small group of house servants, Negroes were regarded as clods or clowns.

As Professor Dunning put it: "It was as inconceivable to the Southerners that rational men of the North should seriously approve of Negro suffrage *per se* as it had been in 1860 to the Northerners that rational men of the South should approve of secession *per se*."[8] In 1871 the Democratic minority of a Congressional committee investigating the Ku Klux Klan expressed Southern resentment in these words: "History, till now, gives no account of a conqueror so cruel as to place his vanquished foes under the domination of their former slaves."[9]

Charles Sumner, the famous abolitionist senator from Massachusetts who had suffered a cold-war caning, in 1866 argued the case for immediate and complete Negro suffrage:

> Without this you must have a standing army, which is a sorry substitute for justice. Before you is the plain alternative of the ballot box or the cartridge box; choose ye between them.[10]

These were not the actual alternatives, or the only ones. Though troops were required to get the vote for the Negro, after they left he lost his vote. The necessary massive aid for all parts of the population was never given, discussing and sharing the problems of transition with responsible Southern leaders never took place. When many of those leaders made a pilgrimage to Washington in the spring of 1867, to demonstrate their willingness to accept an amendment which made an education or property qualification a condition of Negro suffrage, the Fourteenth Amendment had already been voted by Congress and was in the process of being ratified by the states. It could not gracefully be withdrawn for rewriting. In that year General Beauregard and General Wade Hampton of the late Confederate army expressed a complete willingness to accept Negro suffrage if such qualifications were attached, in spite of the fact that many Southerners were opposed. They were disregarded. General Robert E. Lee, the beloved commander of the Confederate army, who was widely respected in the North, said the old order in the South could not be reestablished. But he was not consulted and, indeed, was not amnestied during his lifetime.

After the Fourteenth Amendment had been ratified (1868), there could be no further legal question about the political rights of the Negroes. They had been made citizens and had been given full civil rights by that act. They could, however, be cheated out of these by trickery or intimidation. Drafters of the Fourteenth Amendment thought that they had endowed the freedmen with all the privileges and immunities incorporated in the Bill of Rights, the first amendments to the Constitution; that the states were under a positive obligation to protect those rights and that, if the states failed to do so, the federal government assumed that obligation. Representative Bingham, author of the crucial first section, in 1871 told the House of Representatives that the words forbidding abridgment of privileges and immunitites of citizens "are an express prohibition upon every state of the Union, which may be enforced under existing laws of Congress, or such other laws for their better enforcement as Congress may make."[11]

This controversial first section (basis in the 1950s and 1960s for the Supreme Court desegregation decisions) reads:

> All persons born or naturalized in the United States, and subject to the jurisdiction thereof, are citizens of the United States and of the state wherein they reside. No state shall make or enforce any law which shall abridge the privileges or immunities of citizens of the United States; nor shall any state deprive any person of life, liberty or property, without due process of law; nor deny to any person within its jurisdiction the equal protection of the laws.

A second section provided that, if Negroes were refused suffrage in any state, the basis of representation in Congress should be reduced in direct proportion to the violation. This was never utilized, possibly because of fear that it might become an operating alternative to the first section. A third and much resented section prohibited anyone from holding state or national office who had been active in the secession, until amnestied by Congress. A fourth section forbade any assumption of public debt on account of the secession or emancipation. The fifth section gave Congress power to enforce all sections of the amendment.

The important first section did not say, "Congress shall have the power to prevent discrimination." It simply forbade states to discriminate. This was to grow into a world of difference. It did not say specifically that the Tenth Amendment, which reserved to the states the powers not granted to the federal government, was conditioned by this amendment. It went at the task negatively, by forbidding. Yet many in Congress who voted for the amendment thought it would increase federal powers to protect individual liberty, even overriding the powers of a recalcitrant state; those who opposed it in Congress agreed with them on this point. Later the Supreme Court used the difference between intention and explicit language to empty the amendment of much of its purpose and thereby to negate the Northern attempt to establish equal rights under equal laws for the liberated Negroes.

Meanwhile, events rushed on. Within a month after passage of the Fourteenth Amendment a peculiarly horrible event was allowed to take place. This, like the Black Laws, disgusted the North. It helped to convince them that the amendment should be ratified, that Northern troops should police the South, and that the Republican Radicals deserved support for more drastic programs. In July 1866, some white leaders from the North were organizing Negroes of New Orleans politically. They announced plans to hold a convention in a public building there. Opposition of the local white people to those organizational efforts was intense and loud. The city police were largely Irish, whose extreme antipathy to the Negroes was also well known. Under these circumstances, the military commandant there wired Secretary of War Stanton for instructions. Should he use the federal troops to protect the scheduled meeting from interference, or prohibit it as one likely to provoke riots, or what should he do? The message was sent and the officer waited. He had no idea that the message never reached the President, who did not know that an emergency threatened or that one of his cabinet had been asked for instructions. In New Orleans the troops were kept in their remote barracks. Without any interference a mob of armed people, led or joined by the city police, shot into the meeting. They killed sixty and wounded about 140, chiefly Negroes. The event had all the chivalry of a slaughterhouse. General Phil Sheridan, investigating later, reported that the police attacked "in a manner so unnecessary and atrocious as to compel me to say it was murder."[12]

The Northern public was unaware of the failure of communication. The innocent President's neglect to prevent the atrocity or to regret it publicly later seemed reprehensible to the uninformed North. This was viewed in the light of his plans for bringing the seceded states back into the Union under all-white control, possibly under revised Black Laws, and of his opposition to ratification of the Fourteenth Amendment because of the loyalty oath it required. In the November 1866 Congressional elections the voters swept out almost all of the moderates, giving the Radical Republicans a two-thirds majority in both Houses. It seemed to be an open mandate for a relentless, strong-fisted policy. When the last Southern rejection of the Fourteenth Amendment became known, Representative James A. Garfield of Ohio (a future President) took up the challenge with these words:

> The last one of the sinful ten [secessionist states] has at last with contempt and scorn flung back into our teeth the magnanimous offer of a generous nation. It is now our turn to act.[13]

In this spirit Congress in 1867 took control of reconstruction in the South, sidetracking the President and bypassing the Supreme Court. Under its direction, five military districts were created, their commanders under Congressional instructions to disregard orders from the President. They were ordered to establish new governments made up of whites who had not actively supported the Confederacy, and of Negroes. This eliminated most of the responsible men in the South from any participation in government. By late 1867 some 703,000 Negroes and 627,000 whites had been registered as voters. Congress also made ratification of the Thirteenth and Fourteenth amendments by the new state governments a condition of their return to the Union. As the Republican leadership did these things, while organizing its own racially oriented party in the South, it kept public opinion informed through hearings of the Joint Committee on Reconstruction. It was to this group that a letter was read from General Custer (still some years away from his final rendezvous on the Little Bighorn), saying that in Texas there had been 500 indictments for murder among disloyal men and no convictions. It publicized the report of an assistant commissioner of the Freedmen's Bureau in Tennessee (Johnson's state) that rural justices and juries still thought that Negroes had no rights a white man need respect. The report added that for thirty-five murders of Negroes by whites within eighteen months no one had been punished. This was red meat for the Radical Republicans in Congress. They dared anyone to condone murder. The alternatives repeatedly presented to the people as the true ones were murder or Radical reconstruction. Naturally, they preferred the latter.

Self-interest and honest idealism made a heady mixture in the reconstruction effort. Behind the Radical Republicans were industrial interests that wanted to keep the prevailing high tariffs and high interest charges, as well as the inside track on public land grants for their lumber and railroad ventures. They were afraid that the Southern states, once back in the Union and increasing their representation in Congress by counting every freedman as one, not three-fifths, would vote with Northern Democratic Congressmen against these privileges. So delay in readmitting the seceded states and also organization of Republican parties in those states were supported by Northern capital. Yet at the same time many Radicals idealistically wanted to do all they could, short of investing large sums, to protect the lives and liberty of Negroes. Reconstruction and its conspicuous later collapse must be viewed with these two overlapping and partly conflicting attitudes in mind.

Success or failure of that enterprise depended on the validity of the Radical assumptions about freedom and the social environment required for its growth. The controlling group in Congress believed that the Negroes were ready for active and responsible participation in government, that with the ballot they could protect their own civil rights. Also, it was assumed that two or three constitutional amendments and a number of enforcement laws would provide adequate aid for the Negroes, that the amendments restricting the states from discrimination would also restrain individuals from terrorist activities, that a free society and individual liberty could be established despite the fact that the large Negro group was left without economic freedom or security. None of these assumptions turned out to be valid under the material and psychological conditions prevailing.

Some Northerners ("carpetbaggers") migrated to the South to represent the Radicals; they reaped political and financial loot. Some Southerners ("scalawags") joined in. The higher-class agents of the civilian Freedmen's Bureau were misused by the politicians in this organizing task. That Bureau had been almost the only organization visible to the Negroes which was endeavoring to protect them in their search for work at living wages. Its staff had found and reported an arrangement among the owners of large cotton lands to hold down wages, to give former masters a preferential right to the labor of former slaves, and to control freed Negroes economically and politically. The Bureau staff was trusted by the Negroes and was consequently effective in organizing them into Union Leagues of voters. The Negroes registered and voted as a bloc for the Republicans, out of gratitude for their liberation, out of hope that the Republicans would in time give them land of their own, and out of fear that if the Democrats returned to power in Washington slavery would be reestablished. They made it difficult for any member of their race to become a Democrat without suffering ostracism or worse.

Short-term results of these organizing efforts were conspicuous. In the 1868 election—in which the war hero General Ulysses S. Grant was chosen President—the seven secessionist states which had rejoined the Union produced twelve out of a possible fourteen Republican senators and thirty out of a possible thirty-two Republican representatives. Grant won all but eight of the thirty-six states in the electoral-college vote. But in the popular balloting, even with some 600,000 or 700,000 Negroes in the South voting for him, the war hero had a majority of only 300,000. The Republican party had not received the majority support of the other voters, in spite of all its proud claims to have saved the Union, won the war, suppressed subversion and protected Negro rights.

This was discouraging. Despite some reluctance, it seemed necessary to the Republican leadership to obtain votes from Northern Negroes, possibly 500,000. The Northern states had not felt obligated by the Fourteenth Amendment to extend the suffrage to all of them. So Congress in 1869 prepared the Fifteenth Amendment, intended to give the vote to Negroes everywhere. Ironically, it gave or protected the vote for none in the South. Like the Fourteenth, it was drafted negatively and carelessly, although Congress had been warned on that score. The language approved by Congress and later ratified by the states reads:

1. The right of the citizens of the United States to vote shall not be denied or abridged by the United States or by any state on account of race, color, or previous condition of servitude.

2. Congress shall have power to enforce the provisions of this article by appropriate legislation.

Before this amendment was accepted by Congress, Senator Oliver P. Morton of Indiana had indicated how it could be circumvented, using language which was almost as valid a century later:

> This amendment leaves the whole power over voting in the states just as it exists now except for the three reasons of race, color and previous condition of servitude. They [Negroes] may be disenfranchised for want of education or want of intelligence. The states of Louisiana and Georgia may establish regulations upon the subject of suffrage that will cut out forty-nine out of every fifty colored men in these states from voting.[14]

It was not long before his prediction materialized. The Congressional majority had made a mistake in walking away from his challenge of their draftsmanship or their sincerity.

The Republican attack on the Black Laws and the peonage system did not end with the three postwar amendments, the Civil Rights Act of 1866, and the several reconstruction acts. It went on in 1870–1871 with a bill to outlaw the Ku Klux Klan and similar terrorist organizations, and with two enforcement acts. With those acts, Congress considered the job done. The enforcement act of 1870 was notable because it was directed against lawless individuals as well as against recalcitrant state officials. It was intended to translate the Fourteenth and Fifteenth amendments into practice. It put jurisdiction over offenses against Negro voting into the federal courts. Offending individuals, including election registrars, were required to pay a 500-dollar indemnity to the person whose rights were violated, as well as a fine of the same amount. This law also sought to offset the obvious economic coercion which had been taking place. It imposed a fine of 500 dollars on any person guilty of threatening disemployment or eviction for the purpose of intimidating and preventing anyone from voting. The second law, in 1871, put supervision of Congressional elections under federal deputy marshals. The anti-Ku Klux Klan law was supported by a number of the Southerners because that organization had become the center of much indiscriminate criminality. The law allowed the President to suspend habeas corpus where Klan activities or those of other organizations represented rebellion. President Grant did so in nine counties in South Carolina. Some hundreds of arrests were made and over eighty people were fined or imprisoned. In the 1870–1880 decade several thousand arrests under the three laws took place, largely in Mississippi, the Carolinas and Tennessee. Some estimates put the total convictions at 1,200.

Much effort was spent on purging the legislatures and trying to enforce the laws and amendments. A desegregation law was adopted in 1875. A premature note of triumph was sounded by the reforming Republican senator from Missouri, Carl Schurz. After the enforcement act of 1870, he reassured the nation that:

> Neither a state nor an individual shall deprive any citizen of the United States, on account of race or color, of the free exercise of his right to participate in the functions of self-government; and the national government assumes the duty to prevent the commission of the crime and to correct the consequences when committed.[15]

Such contented optimism was shattered by the Southern counterrevolution, aided by the depression in 1873; popular disgust at corruption of the Grant regime; the political leverage which some major industrial and financial interests of the North found in Southern willingness to trade for power; several Supreme Court decisions; and the shift of national interest from old battlefields to the new excitements of economic growth.

To understand the sectional success Southern leaders wrung from this combination of events, it is necessary to recall the early postwar period. That it was one of destruction, impoverishment, neglect and uncertainty has been indicated earlier. Also, there was lack of adequate self-criticism. As before the war, the North was blamed for almost everything. Actually, much of the misery was due to their leaders' failure to arrange for a peace after Atlanta had been captured in September 1864. This was before mass desertions began and while Lincoln was still alive and eager to put an end to the fratricidal conflict. It was before unconditional surrender had become an established policy. Methods for a peaceable transition to a free society might have been incorporated, after discussion, in the peace terms. Yet there was almost no Southern criticism of their own leadership for this error. Similarly, those who passed the Black Laws, an ill-judged joint action which roused the harsh retaliation of Radical reconstruction, went without criticism for many years.

The first Southern grievance came when the Radical Republicans changed Lincoln's plan for reunion. Under that plan the secessionist states were to be allowed to return to the Union after at least one-tenth of the previously registered voters (all whites) had sworn loyalty to the Union and constituted a new state government. When the Radical Republicans decided on the different policy of completely new state governments made up only of whites who had taken no active part in the Confederacy and of Negroes, this seemed to be a breach of faith.

Federal troops, who might have been accepted as a temporary police, became an army of occupation; the sense of being a conquered and controlled people increased.

Exclusion from political life of those leaders who had been active in the war, and substitution for them of outsiders and of Negroes, upset the tradition of authority to which the South was accustomed. This process added the peculiar bitterness of discrimination because only Southern Negroes, not those in the North, were being enfranchised. It was not until 1870, when the Fifteenth Amendment was ratified, that all Negroes throughout the Union were given at least the nominal right to vote. Southerners resented particularly the loyalty oath which their leaders had to sign before being allowed to take office, even after they had been amnestied. This was their excuse for refusing to ratify the Fourteenth Amendment. As the new state governments—chosen by carpetbaggers, scalawags and Negroes—began to rule, resentment and bitterness increased. Respect for government was destroyed. Many new officials, particularly Negroes, including judges, could not read or write. Their concept of freedom was often the life they had seen lived by the plantation owners, a life of luxury paid for by the toil of others. Legislatures and governors were frequently grossly corrupt. Those who had never paid taxes found it easy to impose backbreaking burdens on others, who had practically no voice in the government. This seemed intolerable to those who had lost half their capital through emancipation and now were being forced to sell their farm land for as little as ten dollars an acre.

The necessary respect for government, which was being destroyed in the South, was not being cultivated in the nation's capital. Thaddeus Stevens, leader of the Radical Republicans, was assailing President Johnson as "an alien enemy, a citizen of a foreign State . . . not legally President"—jeering that compared to him Caligula's horse (reputedly made a consul to mock the broken Roman Senate) was respectable. The reformist orator Wendell Phillips was classing the President with Aaron Burr and Benedict Arnold, and announcing that Andrew Johnson had taken Jefferson Davis' place as head of the Confederacy. The President's attempts to retort in kind hardly raised the level of political discussion.

More significant were the Radicals' successful efforts to cut legal corners. By act of Congress, the Supreme Court was excluded from considering the legality of reconstruction measures. The president's power of appointment and dismissal had been arbitrarily limited. Commanders of the five military districts had been ordered to take no instructions from him, only from Congress. The President was forbidden to change the status of General of the Armies Ulyssess S. Grant or to move him out of Washington. Several Tennessee legislators were arrested by troops in order to obtain a favorable government there, while the commander's request for instructions from the President was held up for three decisive days. In 1868 an attempt was made to remove the President by impeachment, for little other reason than that he failed to obey Congress, a new crime. The few Republicans who dared to vote against this effort were vindictively hounded out of political life. Under President Grant an era of conspicuous corruption began. None of these developments set an impressive example for Southerners or encouraged moderation.

Feeling oppressed and excluded, Southern leaders resumed the counterrevolution begun in 1865 with the Black Laws and then interrupted. This time it was to succeed. It involved, first, the use of all available powers to regain control of their state governments. Since they had little political power, they used economic pressure and intimidation. These were more than adequate to offset the efforts of local Republican party leaders and the 10,000 federal troops in the South. Republican failure to provide Negro security through land ownership left them the prey of those who wished to exploit them financially and to reduce their political and other civil rights. A sharecropper system replaced chattel slavery. Negro sharecroppers were supplied with seed, tools, poor shelter and food; in return they had to grow cotton, for which they received little more than enough to pay for their supplies. Estimates of the interest they paid on the materials supplied to them go as high as forty percent. There was no feudal security in this system; they could be chased from the fields at will. After the Freedmen's Bureau was closed, they had little effective opportunity to defend their claims in court.

The utterly necessitous man was not free and could not become free. Economic pressure was the great weapon with which their political freedom was reduced. On top of this came secret white organizations to enforce a merciless law of their own. Negroes who persisted in political activity were threatened and not infrequently killed. Their Union League meetings were disrupted. Negro attempts at armed resistance were few and were met with massacres. One at Colfax in Louisiana in 1873, resulting in the death of about fifty Negroes and a few white men, produced a notable Supreme Court decision in 1875. It was a dark and bloody period.

The national government had too few troops in the area to control the situation. Violence was always distant from the troop locations. The enforcement act of 1870 tried to dole out punishment for the use of economic pressure to destroy political liberty. It tried to punish individuals for intimidation. But indictments and convictions were hard to get. Not everyone condoned intimidation when carried to the point of killing or accepted the later version that all these acts were motivated or justified by a disinterested passion for racial purity. Former Confederate General Wade Hampton, soon to be elected Governor of South Carolina, appealed to the people against the Ku Klux Klan: "No cause can prosper that calls murder to its assistance or which looks to assassination for success."[16] He tried to persuade Negroes to enter the Democratic party and to obtain some degree of political cooperation between the races in that way.

With Negroes being induced by Republican politicians to join only that party, an opposing all-white Democratic party grew in most of the secessionist states. White people were threatened with social and economic ostracism, even tar and feathers, if they voted Republican. In spite of all the efforts of President Grant and the troops to keep Republican legislatures in power, political control began to fall back into white hands. In 1871 this was accomplished in Virginia, North Carolina, Georgia and Tennessee; by 1874 in Arkansas, Alabama and Texas; and by 1877 Mississippi, Louisiana, Florida and South Carolina had completed that list. Meanwhile, Radical Republicans were losing power in the North. In the 1870 election they lost their two-thirds majority in Congress. In 1874, after the financial panic had started, there was a Democratic majority in Congress. Reaction against the Grant administration almost elected a Democratic President in 1876 and gave the Democrats a popular majority.

With return of Democratic Congressmen from the South, their power expanded to national affairs. They were aided by the financial panic and depression of 1873. While they had joined in 1872 with their Northern colleagues in party convention in voting to confirm Negro emancipation and enfranchisement, and "to oppose any reopening of the questions settled by the 13th, 14th and 15th Amendments," by 1874 their acceptance of that position was less clear.

In 1875, after a Congressional investigation of the remarkable postwar building of Washington as a capital city, Congress changed the governmental structure of the capital area. Negro suffrage, which had been granted in 1867, and also white suffrage were lost in the process (neither was to be restored until 1960, and then only in part). The event seemed to justify Lincoln's fear that what might be done against some human beings because they were colored could also be done with equal justice against human beings who were not colored. In any case, after 1875 Washington was no longer a symbol of enfranchisement. A bill against Negro segregation in certain public facilities was allowed to pass in 1875 in honor of the late Senator Sumner, who had advocated it for many years; but Democratic Congressmen predicted that it would not be observed in the South, that it would only cause trouble for the Republicans elsewhere and probably would be thrown out by the Supreme

Court. All of these predictions proved to be accurate. More importantly, however, Southern Democrats in Congress began to vote with the Northern city and farm Democrats and independents on such crucial matters as soft versus hard money. With these moves they recreated a fear in the industrial and financial North which was shortly to prove exceedingly valuable to them.

Before the highly controversial Presidential election of 1876, the Supreme Court began to tear away the protection which postwar Congresses had tried to erect around Negro civil liberties. The process was reminiscent of the way in which, eighteen years earlier, another Supreme Court, in the Dred Scott decision, had destroyed the barriers against the expansion of slavery into new territories. The Court in 1875 had under consideration a case arising from the Colfax massacre. It was brought under the Enforcement Act of 1870, which heavily penalized interference by individuals with the voting rights of other people. That law rested on the Fourteenth Amendment, thought by its authors and supporters to protect citizens against their fellow citizens. Chief Justice Waite disagreed. He thought the language did not give to the United States this right or duty, which properly was the function of the state governments: "The Fourteenth Amendment prohibits a state from depriving any person of life, liberty or property, without due process of law, but this adds nothing to the rights of one citizen against another."[17] The majority of the Court agreed with him. This decision threw Southern Negroes back upon the protection, or absence of protection, provided by their state governments. Only a large voting opposition to state inaction against individual intimidation could prevent its continuation or spread. But it prevented Negroes from voting and consequently left the state governments free to ignore private economic and private physical intimidation.

Once this major protection to civil rights had been torn away, and most of the Southern states had returned to all-white control, and the Democratic party had obtained control of Congress, much of the reconstruction effort was endangered. It remained for popular revulsion at the corruption of the Grant administrations (1868–1876) and resentment over the economic depression to bring the rest of the civil-rights structure down to the political marketplace where it could be traded off for power. This came in the vote for President in the fall of 1876, when the Republican Hayes of Ohio and the Democrat Tilden of New York were the candidates. A popular Democratic majority of 250,000 was counted. First returns calculated in electoral-college votes indicated that Tilden had 185 electoral votes, one short of the majority needed. Uncounted at that point were the votes of Louisiana, South Carolina and Florida. Their election boards at first indicated majorities for Tilden from all three, which would have insured his election. But these states were still under Republican control supported by troops.

Both Republicans and Democrats in those states had stuffed and manipulated ballot boxes. Republican election officials were now put under increased pressure. Hopes for high rewards were created. Florida officials decided that a preliminary count giving Tilden a ninety-vote majority should, after deliberation, be an actual majority of 925 for Hayes. In Louisiana the preliminary count of some 6,000 majority for Tilden became a 4,000 majority for Hayes. South Carolina also produced a majority for Hayes. Democratic officials on the election boards turned in opposing figures. All this was done under the watchful eyes of the public. A crisis in the Latin-American style seemed imminent, for the Constitution had made no provision for deciding contested election returns to the electoral college. A special commission was set up by Congress which included five justices of the Supreme Court. On a partisan basis, it declined to "go behind" official returns from the states and declared Hayes elected President. While bitter charges of bribery and threats of trouble were heard, there was actually no attempt to alter the decision by any disorder in or outside of Congress.

A quiet bargain had been struck. The view taken of it by most earlier historians of the period is typified by Professor Dunning's observation: "Generalized, this famous bargain meant: Let the reforming Republicans direct the national government and the Southern whites may rule the Negroes."[18] In fact, troops were promptly removed from the last three states, the Republican governments fell at once and were replaced by white Democratic administrations. In a more recent study, Professor Vann Woodward concludes that more than immediate political power was involved in the long negotiations. The South, he believed, in return for the free hand with the Negroes which it received, pledged support for all the sectional interests of Eastern industry "which were reflected in new statutes regarding taxes, money, tariffs, banks, land, railroads, subsidies, all placed upon the law books while the South was out of the Union."[19] It was at this point that the North-South conservative coalition, which became so important in the twentieth century, seems to have taken shape. Not until 1957, after Negro emigration to the North had created important marginal enclaves of Negro voters, did any further legislation on Negro personal liberties pass over objections of that coalition.

Three more blows were aimed at civil-rights protection before it disappeared from sight and almost from memory. In 1883 a case under the Enforcement Act of 1870 came to the Supreme Court from Lexington, Kentucky. An election inspector, a state official, had refused to count votes of several Negroes who had not paid a city capitation tax. Chief

Justice Waite only echoed the warning given to Congress years earlier
when he wrote:

> The Fifteenth Amendment does not confer the right of suffrage upon
> anyone. It prevents the states, or the United States, however, from
> giving preference in this particular, to one citizen over another on
> account of race, color or previous condition of servitude.[20]

In short, there was no apparent limit to barriers states could raise
against Negro voting so long as they were not openly based on one of
the three forbidden grounds.

In view of this decision, some Southern leaders concluded that, as
long as a friendly Supreme Court supported them, they were back in the
days before the Fourteenth and Fifteenth amendments with complete
jurisdiction over the civil rights of Negroes. They moved on from there.
In the 1890s they passed all-white state primary laws imposing poll and
other taxes and constructing jigsaw puzzles of educational requirements
Negroes could never solve, however well educated. These measures
came at the time when small white farmers of the South were rising
against political control by larger landowners. This control had continued beyond the reconstruction period because Negroes who worked
for the larger landowners and were allowed to vote, obediently supported the landowners' candidates. The smaller white farmers, economically emancipated, had, after 1865, acquired better land and, for the
most part, had prospered. Elimination of the Negro from the political
community was desired by them to reduce the large landowners' political power. In the 1890s they gained local power at the expense of the
Negroes, much as the Republicans had done in 1877 on a national
scale.

Along with this second blow came a third—the Southern segregation
laws, which were extended by Congress to the capital city of Washington, thereby repealing an antisegregation law Lincoln had signed. After
these three actions, little was left of all that had been attempted in the
name of personal freedom during the reconstruction period. What remained were "bloody shirt" campaigns for power in which veterans were
reminded "to vote as you shot" and in which campaign gestures were
made vowing allegiance to liberty and justice for all and to enforcement
of all the amendments.

From 1877 until the 1950s it almost seemed as if Douglas had at last
won the debates of 1858 with Lincoln, that the people had decided they
did not care whether Negroes had civil rights or not. They were busy
with other affairs, particularly with Western development and Eastern
industrialization stimulated by the war. They seemed to think they had
tried everything they could and that the Supreme Court prevented

them from doing more. Many accepted the Southern view that the Negroes were not ready for political or economic equality. Some admitted that they did not know how to solve racial problems and therewith absolved themselves of further effort. The issues which had broken many spirits and taken many lives seemed to have been forgotten in the very areas where they had once caused most concern. Lynchings stirred a young maverick in the House of Representatives, Henry Cabot Lodge, to introduce a bill in 1890 to enforce the old Civil Rights Act, with troops if necessary. It passed the House; but the Senate found a dozen more important matters to consider first and was able to tap a wealth of sentiment against arousing long-sleeping differences and opening up old wounds. No civil-rights laws affecting Negroes were to be approved by Congress until 1957.

So the nation chose to neglect the personal freedom of the Negroes in the South for more than eighty years. Its leaders resolutely looked the other way, tired and exasperated with the upheaval, eager to turn their energies to less difficult, more profitable enterprises. This was not a uniquely American reaction. The seventeenth-century English, after the Cromwellian convulsions, had also rushed into forgetfulness of the goals for which they had once battled. As Lord Acton described it, "the country confessed the failure of its striving, disavowed its aims, and flung itself with enthusiasm and without any effective stipulations, at the feet of a worthless king."[21] Americans did no less, no more.

During these decades most of the Negroes in the South found economic and political barriers erected solidly against their individual and group progress. They became, in effect, a colonial people living under state rather than national imperialism. In spite of much individual kindness and fairness on the part of some of their white neighbors, they suffered from a burden of social, economic and political inferiority, which was added to the old racial difference. The Negroes found that a number of Southern whites were imitating John Brown's idea that individual murder could be justified by personal belief. Juries of white neighbors would not indict or convict the guilty. While lynchings were gradually stopped, occasional individual murders of Negroes suspected of violating local patterns of conformity continued. Meanwhile the Negroes were not given the opportunity to learn civic duties or the discipline of individual enterprise, nor were they educated or trained, for the most part, in any way which would have allowed them to compete on a basis of equality. They were consequently, even in the second half of the twentieth century, to be the last to be employed, the first dismissed, the lowest-paid. Worse, they were the least favored as members of churches, labor unions or neighborhoods. With the weight of generations of handicap loaded on them, they had to attempt the task of the ancient Greeks, of obtaining respect in order to be accepted as full members of a community and doing so under conditions in which even self-respect was difficult to achieve.

The change in their situation which created hope, and with that an almost revolutionary demand for more rapid improvement, can be credited to two events. One was the demand for labor which caused large numbers of them to move North and West during the First World War and again in the Second War. More moved out of the South when farm mechanization cut off work opportunities. Away from that area, they were allowed to vote freely and became an important swing group to which political men had to listen. In the late 1960s the inner sections of many large cities had Negro majorities or the early prospect of them, while the more affluent whites moved away to the suburbs. Slums, ghettoes, exploitation and crime rates rose together in the inner cities. One of the many ironies of history is that the Northern and Western sections of the nation which had chosen to forget the Negroes in the South should have to pay the delayed bill for their earlier neglectfulness.

The second event which altered Negro prospects for the better was not caused by their own fate and misfortune or even by a public conscience outraged through television broadcasts of scenes of their maltreatment by some Southern sheriffs and police. It was a gradual change in public opinion about the relative effectiveness of two concepts of freedom. The older one was that of residual liberty for the individual— what was left for people after their stronger neighbors had used their own rights and powers, while the government stayed aloof, refusing to intervene in the workings of economic or social institutions. The second was a concept of structural freedom which contained the idea of opportunity for everyone. It was one which could on occasion be increased by the government's intervention in the functioning of the other sectors of society. The two had been illustrated and contrasted after the Civil War. The abolition of the institution of slavery had visibly increased the sum total of personal liberty. The government's later lack of action in protecting personal rights resulted in a diminution of them, leaving the Negroes in the South only a small residual.

However, it was not awareness of that particular post-Civil War contrast between structural and residual liberty which increased the hopes and prospects of the Negroes in the mid-twentieth century. Much of the change in public opinion which took place can be credited to the Great Depression of the 1930s, another of the nation's major moments of frustration. Then a considerable majority of the people decided that positive government intervention was needed to free them from the impoverishment and humiliation caused by a breakdown of the non-governmental forces in society. This decision was renewed after the Second World War when social and economic maladjustments, neglected for two decades, snowballed into frightening size. A large fraction of the population was evidently inheriting and transmitting poverty as a way of life. The rush to the cities was creating problems of crowding and transportation too large and endless for the cities to manage alone. Slums, crime and despondency were apparently feeding on one another and growing beyond control. The nation's leaders, concerned with the possibility of a class-ridden and crime-cursed society, began to see that the important question which a democracy in a modern industrial complex had to ask itself was not "Is any national action necessary?" It was, instead, "Does any proposed national action increase the total amount of personal freedom and opportunity?"

So the process of liberating people from both hardship and enforced inequality of opportunity could begin. By 1954 it was possible for a Supreme Court to find unanimously that the inferiority which accompanied segregated schooling affected both the freedom and opportunity of the Negroes, and to order a change in the practice under the authority of the Fourteenth Amendment. By 1957 it was possible for Congress to pass a law giving the Negroes some protection in their civic rights and by the 1960s even to help them toward attaining the suffrage promised by the Fifteenth Amendment in 1870. By then it even became possible for the government to mount an attack on the causes for continuing poverty, among both Negroes and whites, instead of confining its activities to the after-effects of uneradicated causes. Amid such changes in attitude, it was possible for the Negroes to move forward, easy for them to demand even more rapid progress, and easier yet for them to divide on methods for achieving it.

A hundred years after slavery had been abolished, the most affluent and powerful nation in the world was still not quite sure of when it would be able to end the peculiarly American tragedy and be able to think in earnest about the creation of a memorable society.

This dark and bloody period tells much about the vulnerability of a society in which men cherish opposing views about freedom and, since they still do so, its experience remains important to us. Even the revered Constitution turned out to be vulnerable to disregard and manipulation. Something like a French adventure into legislative sovereignty was undertaken, and the President and Supreme Court, both given power to act as a check on a rampaging Congress, were efficiently sidetracked, not during but after a war. The fact of this event may be overlooked today, particularly at a time when the President, through his war powers, can act almost alone. But the question posed about who and what can prevent a recurrence of such a procedure still remains unanswered.

We can usefully note also the unpreparedness of statesmen for completely foreseeable events, such as a cessation, sooner or later, of warfare. Our leaders, worn out by war, were as unready as those in Sparta and Athens to translate an end of fighting into a dynamic stability worthy of the name of peace. A military victory can apparently mean internal disruption almost as much as a defeat. Lincoln, whose persuasive voice had been stilled by assassination, had not been able to convince either the nation or the Congress that "malice toward none, charity toward all" was a viable attitude. Without any approval from Congress, he and then Andrew Johnson began a program of taking back states into the Union. When Congress repudiated it, the Southerners quite naturally claimed a breach of good faith. The French were to feel aggrieved and deserted in the same way, for the same reason, less than six decades later. At that time Congress failed to consider President Woodrow Wilson's mutual defense pact with Great Britain and France. The stilling of Lincoln's voice, and his succession by a less capable and more handicapped man, spelled out for the nation the danger inherent in the political practice of choosing a Vice-President on the basis of his sectional or group appeal instead of on the basis of his capacity to preside over the nation's destinies.

The lack of creative thought and action during the latter war period and early postwar months—including the failure to use the open option of providing national credit to underwrite a restoration of the whole ruined Southern economy—raises the question of whether men are actually more insighted and farsighted today. Today also sees the equivalent of the Southern wreckage in the racial, urban ghettoes, the vast pileup of unequal education and training, housing and job opportunity all over the North. Yet today's nation also hesitates, although it is far more confident of doubling its income within twenty-five years or less than were the men of 1865, who had the vast public domain of the West to use as their credit base. The rage which the Radical Republicans of that day expressed at the Southern Black Codes might properly have been directed at themselves for failing to give the Southern economy an adequate, secure alternative to those codes, insuring dependable labor while protecting the freedmen from the vagaries and heavy-handed manipulation of the free labor market which took place. In today's world some of the rage men feel at the burnings and lootings of their cities, which are also almost inexcusable, might properly also be directed in part at themselves. Sins of omission seem to father sins of commission.

But the main values which can come from an examination of this period of failure on both sides of the Mason-Dixon line apply to the third major problem area confronting the modern United States. This covers the relation of this nation to the expected antifeudal and anti-hunger revolts in the most populated areas of the world. The American interest is clearly that of helping them to survive both independent and possessed of personal freedom. What have we learned about how to make men free? The problem arose in South Vietnam. It will arise quickly in other areas, perhaps much sooner than we are prepared for it. In spite of our post-Civil War tragedy, there is little evidence that we are prepared to understand what freedom means in such areas, and particularly how it can disappoint and disappear. This is a matter of far more than charitable or kindly interest in the starvation and fate of hundreds of millions of other people. This is also a matter of national disunity on a new and frightening scale. One loss of over thirty thousand men and seventy billion dollars may not completely tear the nation apart although it can start the process, but a consecutive series of them, with most ending in disappointments or defeats, can do it. Much like the Germany of the First World War, we do not expect, we resent defeats.

How do we help to establish the conditions under which personal freedom can endure and, by enduring and functioning, give men the desire to fight for the continued independence of their nation? We eliminated a slavery system in the name of freedom. We did not substitute a feudal system for it. That system usually has some security built into it. The peasant under the feudal system could not be chased from his land, he had opportunity to advance his fortunes by hard work, as long as he paid his dues, his rent. Instead, we allowed a peonage system, one without any security or opportunity, to replace slavery. High interest on goods furnished in advance of the crops put men in debt. Debt prevented escape. Powerful neighbors then made it practically impossible for a man to maintain any civil rights, any voting rights. The farm tenant or sharecropper was sometimes less sure of getting food regularly than he had been as a slave. In short, this was not an effective freedom, only a nominal one, hardly a varnish over oppression.

The situation we encountered in South Vietnam, one which we can expect to encounter elsewhere in Asia and in parts of Latin America, is a cross between the feudal and peonage systems. Heavy debt, with loan-shark rates of fifty percent annually, immobilizes men. Excessive land division impoverishes them, closes down opportunity. A revolution takes place. Farm people are given free grants of land which is the property of large landowners. They are promised liberation from the corruption which lowers their meager incomes. They are promised a break up of the mandarin, or *hombre rico*, group which has kept them from advancing. They are promised education for all to make them equal to their earlier masters in skill and ability. At this point the status quo group gets help in money and then armed forces from the United States to protect law and order, defend the nation against possible or actual foreign invasion on behalf of the revolution. What happens then? The United States troops clear the revolutionaries out of some area. The landlords, loan sharks return under American protection, claim back and new rents due, back and new interest on loans. The people find their income is one-third less than it was before the United States troops came in to protect their freedom. At this point the pacification program breaks down. Political freedom, the combination of civil liberties and the right to vote in honest elections, even if the governing group allowed it, seems less important to people who were given land of their own than the reestablishment of the old masters, the large landowner and the money lender, the decrease in their incomes. The revolutionaries obtain more rather than less support. The United States is again, as in the post-Civil War period, supporting a nominal and diminishable rather than a significant freedom. It can expect both actual and post-victory defeats, or a semipermanent engagement of its troops to police the nation for the benefit of a hated group. Very few of the makings of success, very little protection against internal disunity at home, lie in such a course, little effective and constructive opposition to the spread of Communism. The tragic era of Reconstruction suggests that something quite different is necessary today and tomorrow whenever the United States seeks to promote freedom abroad more effectively than it did at home.

CHAPTER 9

Russia: Reaction
Against Reaction

 The conquest of Russia by the Communists might possibly have been averted. However, such an outcome would have required first a Czarist regime which had prepared a democratic alternative to itself, and then a more alert and able governing body than that which actually was put into place to deal with the catastrophe of the day. No such thoughtfully conservative Czarist regime existed, and no adequately functioning inheritors took its place. One of the world's most completely reactionary establishments opened the road for one of the world's most radical counterreactions, after the inheritors of the Czarist group lost or spoiled their few remaining opportunities.

A very few opportunities did indeed exist for the men who briefly inherited the Czar-made catastrophe in 1917 to stave off the Communist attack. To those occasions attention may properly be called, without any intent of exaggerating the chances for success, because other governments under stress may find themselves caught in similar positions in the course of time. Some belief even exists that the anti-Communist military interventions of France and England coupled with a somewhat less aggressive American troop presence, during the civil war which followed the Communist take-over of Russia were the key errors which allowed the Communists to retain control of Russia. In view of later events in Southeast Asia and the expectation of other antifeudal or hunger revolutions accompanied by military interventions, this view may also be worthy of recall.

No ambitious effort to explain the Russian people then or now will be found in these pages. They have bewildered the rest of the world—and possibly themselves—before this and may do so again. For example, they probably did more to fractionalize the opposition to Fascism before the Second World War than any other nation. Yet they also did as much or more than any other to defeat the Nazi-led Germans. They brought the world to the edge of a nuclear war with a reckless attempt to place nuclear weapons in Cuba. Yet they shattered the theological unity of the Communist nations and the faith of their true believers by announcing that wars against non-Communist nations were neither always inevitable nor desirable. Claiming to be the original and only genuine lovers and practitioners of peace, they armed the Arab nations before the Arab-Israeli war of 1967, but after their defeat disclaimed all responsibility for all Arab belligerence, and then rearmed them.

The whys and wherefores of all this is beyond the scope of this brief account. It deals only with the inability of the more reactionary forces in old Russia to foresee or forestall revolution and the subsequent failure of the more democratic forces to prevent that revolution from being captured by known authoritarians. The account of that conquest may remain current history in every underdeveloped nation where privileged groups deny human dignity, rights and opportunity to their fellow citizens. The sequence of events throws a little light on the debated question of whether it is a weak and ineffectual government or a strong and competent one which is more vulnerable to a Communist attack. It may serve to provoke second thoughts among idealistic young men in trouble-prone areas, by reminding them that their own passion for social justice and freedom can be converted into a new tyranny by a very few men who are less scrupulous and humane than themselves.

The ancient idea that imperial absolutism was a God-given right, that abnegation of any part of it was both a crime and a sin, prevailed in the Court of Czar Nicholas II during a crucial part of the early twentieth century. It was the most backward court in any of the major powers of Europe. The ancient idea played out the last years of its life against the background and activity of a high-level, Western-oriented culture in the urban centers, and a much more widespread low culture of illiteracy and superstition among the millions of neglected peasants. Then, very much as armies at war imitate one another's worst barbarities, so the Czar's ultimate successors imitated his absolutism.

The leading actor in the first scenes of the century, Nicholas II, was an authentic nonhero. He followed stronger men who surrounded him. He had trouble distinguishing between cause and effect. When he experienced an unprecedented wave of popular revolt in 1905, due to a severe depression and a humiliating defeat by Japan, he was still willing to believe his secret-police reports that only a few agitators caused all the trouble. After his troops had shot down several hundred men and women, some with children in arms, who had expected to witness a grand moment of reconciliation between the Little Father and his obedient people, when the nation was horrified by the unnecessary brutality of his troops, some terrorists blew up the Grand Duke Sergius in the Kremlin in Moscow by way of retaliation. It remained for Nicholas II to inquire, "But why this horrible crime?" In early 1917, when the war was coming to a close for Russia, troops were deserting by the thousands, the population in an uproar of indignation, he expressed his concept of the proper duty of a people by asking the British representative: "Do you mean that I am to regain the confidence of the people, Mr. Ambassador, or that they are to regain my confidence?" He was hardly aided by his wife, who wrote to him when he was in the field with the breaking armies, to be strong, summarizing her understanding of the disappearing world around her with the explanation, "Russia loves to feel the whip."

The ruling powers of imperial Russia, large landowners, nobles, army leaders, courtiers, some industrialists, can be charged with no more than six major errors of judgment and action during the first seventeen years of the century. But they were large ones and sufficient for the destruction of all involved.

The first grand mistake was to allow a war with Japan to start during a severe depression, about a cause (possession of Korea) for which the people cared nothing, and then to lose it in a humiliating fashion. Multitudes were angered by both events and many were incensed by the government's sponsorship of a number of brutal pogroms against Jews. Russia had more martyrs to freedom in the nineteenth century than any other nation and many more young students who sought the redemption of the serfs or semiserfs from their degradation. A wave of demands for freedom swept the nation. So many hitherto mute and cowed groups, including past supporters of the Czarist regime, demanded personal liberties, freedom of press and assemblage, an elected constitutional assembly, that court circles finally yielded. Their acceptance of open elections came only after an effective general strike. The story was current that the Grand Duke Nicholas had threatened the Czar that he would blow out his brains in the Czar's office unless those elections were called.

The second major mistake of the ruling group was that of refusing to make the elected Duma, the legislature, a responsible partner in government. Instead, it was ignored and villified, its members persecuted, its meetings closed by force. The wide-open elections had produced an antiadministration majority, with the professional and middle-class party

(Cadets) in its lead, then the peasants' party (Social Revolutionaries), then the Social Democrats, representing the industrial workers, which had boycotted the election. To prevent the Czar from revoking any of his grants to the people, the Duma wanted to start writing a constitution. The Czar wanted nothing of the kind. Indeed, he had been reminded by his religious adviser that he had sinned against God in giving up some of his prerogatives and should do penance by recovering them. So he proclaimed some Fundamental Laws, reaffirming his exclusive control of the government, and created a rival body to the Duma, an Imperial Council. In the countryside his troops and the terrorist Black Hundreds, whom his police organized systematically, harried supporters of the Duma. When that body censured the Czar's Chief Minister for refusing its request for an amnesty for the 75,000 political prisoners in the jails and then, after a massacre of Jews at Bialystok, demanded an investigation, the Czar responded by throwing troops around the Tauride Palace and dissolving the Duma. Judicial proceedings were started against 180 deputies who fled to an area of greater rights in the province of Finland and asked for civil disobedience. They were also forbidden to run for reelection.

Intimidation did not produce a pro-Czarist majority in the second Duma, elected in 1906. Before those elections, 337 newspapers were suspended and 167 editors were accused of crimes against the state.[1] The opposition still won sixty-eight percent of the Duma seats, only one percent less than before. It was this time more oriented toward the workers and peasants than it had been, while the middle-class group lost its preeminence. This unexpected result of the government's suppression did not give the Czarist centers any pause. The Chief Minister, Stolypin, charged that some of the Social Democratic deputies were plotting against the Czar's life. Secret-police connivance in plots and even in assassinations was so widely understood at this time that his charge was not taken too seriously. The Duma decided to conduct an investigation of its own. That outcome was intolerable to the Chief Minister, and the Duma was again dissolved, in 1907.

Where intimidation had failed, outright deprivation of the vote did not fail. In the 1907 elections city deputies were cut in number from twenty-five to seven, while those from large landholdings were increased. Poland and the Caucasus were also cut and Central Asia was deprived of all representation. With these acts, a new Duma (1907–1912) showed a solid third for the Czar, another third for the moderates who frequently supported him, and a third covering workers, peasants and nationality groups. In this body and the succeeding Duma (1912–1917) the regime could usually obtain any action or inaction it desired. The first revolution of the century was now lost.

All this maneuvering not only led to increased distrust of the Czar and those around him and convinced many more, including students in the universities, that only a complete revolution could ever change the character of the government, but it also left the men who would in time succeed the Czar without training in policy formation or administration. It also left them without solid roots of support in the nation. All these lacks later took their toll.

Not long after the First World War began, the unpreparedness of Russia for a modern, total war became evident. It lacked enough artillery, shells and machine guns. It used up soldiers to plug those holes. It had some able generals, obedient troops, a fairly unanimous public opinion at first, determined not to be oppressed by the Germans. Some of the intelligentsia told one another that they would move through victory to revolution. At that time nobody foresaw that there could be two revolutions, and instead of obtaining freedom they would end up with a regime that hated that concept as much as the Czar's men did. Some victories were achieved, but were followed by defeats. The industrial plant soon began to wear out. Refugees poured in from the regions invaded by the Germans and added to the supply and lodging problems. In 1915 the armies were pushed back, yielding Poland, Galicia, Lithuania, at that time parts of Russia.

The major mistake of entering the war unprepared, of substituting lives for guns, was compounded in 1915 by the Czar's sharp refusal of the Duma's request for a coalition government and "a cabinet of public confidence." Responsibility was not to be shared, even when war demanded every available bit of support from everyone and inefficiency was general and conspicuous. That error was again compounded by a decision which sent the Czar himself into the field as supreme commander of the armies, while the Duma was abruptly disbanded, told to get out of the way. The Czar replaced the generally respected Grand Duke Nicholas. This was Russian roulette on an imperial scale. The Romanov dynasty would allow its fate to be determined by the Czar's ability to turn a series of defeats into victory. When the decision was announced, the Foreign Minister of the moment, Sazanov, reportedly remarked, "Now there is nothing left for us to do but go drown ourselves." Few who knew the Czar had any confidence in his military ability, his capacity for leadership. He produced no miracles on the battlefields.

The Czar's departure from the capital, Petrograd, meant that his unstable wife became his representative in the government and that the capital would soon begin to leak suspicions of treason, corruption and dishonor out into the countryside. The Czarina was captivated, perhaps somewhat hypnotized, by her notorious "holy man," Grigori Rasputin. Neither priest nor monk, he gave the royal couple a sense of being linked through him to the "Dark People" of the old countryside. They thought that he had saved the life of their son, who was suffering from hemophilia, and were grateful. A debauchee of note, his bedchamber was believed to be a necessary station stop for major political appointments. As self-respecting and indignant officials resigned, his men took their places, and he became the regent for the Czar's regent. Nothing like it had been observed before north of Constantinople. Indiscreet letters from the Czarina and high court ladies were passed from hand to hand and read and repeated with loathing. The story that Rasputin demanded and received advance reports of all troop movements so that he might pray for their success was circulated and believed.

A Duma leader finally presented two unpleasant alternatives to the nation. He recited a long list of logistic and military failures, and after each one of them asked reasonably, "Is this stupidity, or is this treason?" His speech was censored out of the press but circulated privately, and no one liked either alternative. The Chief Minister resigned. Rasputin was belatedly killed by some outraged nobles. But then the Czar thought it was more necessary to console his wife for the loss of her confidant than to fight the war, and returned to the capital. Government practically stopped for a while. At this point, toward the end of 1916, the death toll of Russian soldiers had reached two million, the count of wounded at least four million. Corruption and the possibility of treason within the imperial court itself had been displayed to a people who could not bear much more defeat, suffering and degradation.

While the honor of making the final two fatal errors of the Czarist group would fall to several of his loyal generals, the Czar closed out his rule in the high style of a man who refuses to learn anything from change. He reverted to the old maxim of absolutist rulers before him, "When the people protest, issue more bullets to the soldiers." The January cold in 1917 went to forty below zero. One-third of the workers in Petrograd were out on strike for higher wages to meet rising living costs. Here and there shortages of fuel and food appeared. The people of Petrograd came out into the streets, some joining the strikers, some calling for immediate peace, some raiding the bakeries. The Czar's police shot. Then everybody came out. The Minister of the Interior, charged with internal order, was oddly busy in séance with the Czarina, trying to consult Rasputin's spirit for guidance. The President of the Duma told the Czar, who was at the front again, that at long last the nation must have a ministry, a cabinet, it would trust. The Czar denied that request, suspended the Duma again, and ordered his generals to put down the revolt. This time, however, the garrison troops in Petrograd shot at the police, not at the crowds. The Czar was told by the high nobles and generals that this was the end, he must abdicate, and he did, in March 1917. The world joined the Russians in cheering and rejoicing. Hated Czarism had come to an end. A new world of hope and freedom could now begin.

Rarely in history has any group been presented with such an overwhelming task as that which fell to the inheritors of the fallen Czar that spring. The German armies were advancing toward the bread basket of the Ukraine. The Russian troops were being induced to fraternize, experiencing the inner hesitation which comes from knowing personally today the men whom you will be ordered to kill tomorrow, and began deserting in ever larger numbers. Worn-out factories were unable to stay in operation, the supply of guns and shells dwindled. General and other army and navy officers were still loyal to the deposed emperor. Supplies of food and fuel were being withheld by the peasants, who could buy little with the rubles they received in payment. Actual power to get things done had moved into the hands of workers' committees (soviets) in the cities. However, responsibility remained in the hands of the Czar's inheritors, a committee of the Duma. Its members had been elected by a limited number of voters in 1912 and could hardly claim to represent anybody or anything in the war-weary nation except legitimacy. All around them rose fervent demands for peace of some sort and land for the peasants. A Constitutional Convention to establish democracy and distribute land and make peace was called for, almost unanimously, although not by the Czarist group.

So much was moving inside of Russia at this time to reshape the foundations of the society, to rid it forever of tyranny and war, to give all men freedom and opportunity, that no inheritor of the old days could really do much without a very wide and deep basis of popular support. Chaos has rarely been the happy birthplace of democracy. Yet there were some opportunities to gain that support, to ride out the storms of defeat, need and land hunger. A few errors of omission and commission could probably have been avoided. Their consequences could have been prevented from snowballing into new masses of disorder and distrust. Hindsight allows observers to separate out six of these between March and October of 1917.

The provisional government could have issued a call for an immediate election to a Constitutional Convention, to take place in May. With that call made, it could have presented itself to the people as the temporary but essential guardian of the national purpose until that Convention established a new and truly representative government, made peace and distributed land. Instead, it let itself be put off by the opposition of the old guard, who wanted no constitution, and by the bureaucrats, who demanded more time to prepare for the vote. The Convention did not actually meet until January 1918, long after the democrats had lost control of the government and nation. The Bolsheviks (the revolutionary wing of the Social Democrats) used troops to close it down quite as ruthlessly as the Czar had closed the Duma with troops eleven years earlier.

The Duma government could also have handled the disruptive cause of land distribution more effectively than it did. It had promised land to the peasants, and a considerable amount of distribution began to take place at the local level. This fact led many young villagers in uniform at the front to desert in order to get home and protect their rights to land. Here was a hemorrhage of troop strength which could have been halted. By setting an early May date for the Convention, and then by insisting that only the Convention could legitimatize the land distribution, and by making proof of continued and adequate military service a condition for rights to land, the desertions might have been halted. In the same way, the peasants' refusal to supply enough goods and fuel to the cities might have been met by making land distribution dependent on continued deliveries of food and fuel to the cities. The power to divide land among people who had longed for it for centuries and felt cheated by the distribution process of 1862 was sheer gold to any able government, enormous power to any group which used it well.

Again, the new government knew that it had responsibility without real power to get things done long before its Foreign Minister brought the fact out into the open by the awkwardness of his double-dealing. The power to get supplies to hungry people, to get employees to work, to defend the city had all passed to the committees of workers. Most of them were still democratically oriented in the spring of 1917, when they demanded a peace without annexations or indemnities and an end to the war. With that, Russia gave up its claims to the Dardanelles and Constantinople, agreed to in secret treaties among the European Allies. In sending out this notice to the foreign ambassadors, the new Foreign Minister, former head of the Cadet party, slipped in a personal note advising the ambassadors to pay no attention to it, that Russia's old war aims remained unchanged. This double-dealing was discovered, and he was forced to resign. He had lost a large measure of credibility for the government. It was not the government but the soviets of Petrograd who prevented a popular uprising from overthrowing the government at that time. The soviets ordered the troops to stay in their barracks. But it was not until that show of strength that five representatives of peasants and workers were brought into the government. They, in turn, made the mistake of entering it without demanding a voice in all military decisions and were, with all Russia, to suffer from their neglect.

The government also neglected to use some means at its disposal to avert the suspicion of treason which was later to engulf it. It left many old Czarist officers in charge of troops who mistrusted them completely. Some shuffle in high commands, some retirements, some ceremony of officers swearing an oath of loyalty to the democratic rule in front of their troops might have altered the men's suspicions of their commanders. This was not done. Instead, a new Minister of War, Kerensky, who became dominant in the altered government, even extended—although vaguely and therefore dangerously—some of the functions of General Kornilov, an old Czarist officer who was soon to show that he saw no difference between democrats and Bolsheviks and aided the latter. With the matters of peace, land, supplies and troop morale all at loose ends, under the urgings of Allied officers and labor-union officials from abroad who had no understanding of the extent of demoralization among the Russian troops, Kerensky ordered an attack in July of 1917. Hardly anything could have been more self-defeating and ultimately disastrous under the prevailing circumstances. After the attack gained a little territory, the troops stopped fighting and withdrew. The Germans poured through open holes in the lines. After this folly and defeat, there was little hope for the government. A brief Bolshevik attempt to take power in Petrograd, immediately after this disaster, failed. Some loyal troops were recalled from the front for security, but were then sent back. Petrograd was left with a praetorian guard of garrison troops, whom the Bolsheviks were convincing that only through their efforts could the soldiers be saved from duty and death at the front.

At this point possibly a Russian request to the Germans for an armistice, leaving the bread basket of the Ukraine to Russia, might have rallied the Russian nation to fight defensively at that line. By this time the United States had entered the war and the long-term chances of gaining back any other Russian territory had improved. But the government, in spite of a rising Bolshevik campaign to become the government of peace, failed to act. It felt honor-bound by its agreement with the Allies to fight together until the end. The Allies still did not understand that this could be an act of suicide for a new democracy, nor did the new Russian government.

All the omitted actions about peace, land, supplies and military loyalty cumulated into cataclysm when the Czarist General Kornilov, dismissed in September, feeling angry and misled, decided to attack Petrograd. This was counterrevolution on behalf of the old regime and was so understood. (This was the fifth of the six errors earlier assigned to the Czarist ruling group.) His effort was stopped by a refusal of the railway workers to move the trains with his troops and by men from the Petrograd soviets who convinced advancing cavalrymen that they were being misused. Arms were distributed from the arsenals in the planned defense of the city, and the Bolsheviks obtained a large number of them.

The troops followed the attempted counterrevolution by arresting and on occasion murdering officers suspected of disloyalty in both army and navy. More importantly, Kornilov's attack fathered a belief, which the Bolsheviks spread widely, that Kerensky and with him the provisional government had shown themselves to be in favor of counterrevolution. They were enemies of the people, who deserved no further trust. With this, the last of the government's small remaining store of credibility evaporated into thin air. The Bolsheviks were now able to present themselves as the only genuine defense against Czarist counterrevolution as well as the only party which really wanted peace.

From then on, it was only a matter of time before the Bolsheviks would take over. They had carefully kept clear of all responsibility for meeting the immediate needs of the nation, much as the Nazi deputies to the Reichstag were later to absent themselves from all voting in 1932 when that body had to make unpopular decisions. The Bolsheviks smugly blamed all the hardships of the day on their rivals, the more moderate group of Social Democrats and the Social Revolutionaries, representing the urban workers and the peasants. They capitalized upon every discontent. They waited until the demand for a strong, effective government was irresistible and led people to believe that they alone could put such a government into place.

By October the end was in sight. The democratic representatives of the soviets in the government had resigned. German troops were getting closer in the Baltic area and threatened Petrograd. Food shortages were more frequent. The Bolsheviks had won over most of the soviets of workers and soldiers. The Petrograd garrison had received new pledges from them that they would not be sent to the front. A workers' militia of Red Guards was formed. The garrison then formally refused obedience to the government. On October 23 the Bolsheviks took over some government offices and the whole communication system. Kerensky fled to the front, vainly seeking loyal troops. On October 25 the Bolsheviks occupied the Czar's Winter Palace without resistance, and began governing. A small resistance by military cadets a few days later was suppressed. All over the nation people rushed into Communist hands under the impression that they were obtaining democracy and peace.

The Duma government had no monopoly of mistakes. The democracy-minded leaders of the urban workers and peasants might have prevented Lenin's disruptive activities in the spring of 1917. They had learned to know him as a potential Napoleon long before then, to recognize his lack of scruples, his conviction that his goal justified any

means, his contempt for the democratic process. They knew that he had
been brought to Russia by the German military command willingly, that
he believed a German victory would lead to a proletarian revolution in
Russia, while an Allied victory would mean a democratic revolution. But
most of these leaders of workers and peasants had for decades been a
hounded and harried group. They were not even a part of the government at the time of his arrival and his first denunciation of them as
traitors to the workers' cause. They also believed in a free press and did
not want to be the men guilty of reestablishing the hated Czarist censorship. In bewilderment mixed with respect for him as an old anti-
Czarist, they allowed him to function and to subvert, sometimes in
Finland, sometimes in Russia. He confused many of them with solemn
pledges, such as one that the Bolsheviks would conform to any decisions
the Constitutional Convention arrived at. But when the time came for
that pledge to be honored, he did not allow the Convention to survive.

Here Lenin was only repeating himself. Leaders of the workers and
peasants had been brought up in a constant underground warfare
against their cause by the Czar's secret police—who were ubiquitous and
infiltrated the workers' and peasants' organizations—and by the Black
Hundreds, hoodlums who used violence against dissenters from the
Czar's rule. In addition, terrorists, men who wanted to fight fire with
fire, government violence with the assassination of government officials,
had also infiltrated their ranks. Then a group under Lenin's direction
began a series of bank robberies. Both the terrorist acts and the robberies gave the Czarist government some excuses for violence. The
Social Democratic party voted to stop all the expropriations, as the bank
robberies were called. But Lenin, playing a lone hand, ignored this
decision. In 1911 he was censured by the party for continuing the robberies in spite of the decision and for using the funds to build up his
own faction against all others. It was a triple accusation of disloyalty,
disobedience and theft.

Bitter because of the Czar's execution of his brother, convinced that
only a major revolution could succeed, Lenin had the rare quality of
organizational ability to add to his acute perceptiveness of human needs.
He saw that, in the 1917 chaos, promises of peace, bread and land were
more effective than those of personal freedom. He saw also that men
sought for a new integration into society, a new function for themselves,
and led them to believe they would find it in a workers' rule. From the
French revolution he had learned enough about both the Commune's
and Napoleon's use of troops in seizing power to know that the Petrograd garrison had to be won over to neutrality at least, to support if
possible.

The antidemocratic government which he had in mind was well

known to the other leaders. It had been the subject of endless debate. As early as 1903 one of his opponents, later an important lieutenant and still later again an opponent, Leon Trotsky wrote, with the same prescience of a Henry Clay predicting the outcome of the South's demands for the expansion of slavery:

> In Lenin's scheme, the party takes the place of the working class. The party organization displaces the party. The Central Committee displaces the party organization, and finally the dictator displaces the Central Committee.[2]

Here was the path Stalin later took. In the same vein, one of the more famous old-time leaders of the Russian Social Democratic party, Plekhanov, said that Lenin was "confusing the dictatorship of the proletariat with the dictatorship over the proletariat," and Martov, another democratically minded man, had attacked Lenin's idea of party members behaving like soldiers under orders of a high command as a proposal for martial law.

However, in spite of all this open disagreement with his views and lack of scruples, few foresaw that he would dishonor his public support of a Constitutional Convention. He had made the pledge, "Even if the peasants still follow the Social Revolutionaries, even if they give that party a majority in the Constituent Assembly, we will say: So be it." They did not imagine that he would imitate the Czar and close the doors to the elected members of that body. Of 707 elected delegates, the Bolsheviks had only 175, less than a quarter. Even under threats of reprisals, intimidation and earlier arrests of Social Democratic delegates, the remaining delegates refused by 237 to 136 to transfer all power from the Assembly to the Bolshevik-controlled soviets. This was Russia speaking against the Bolsheviks on the last occasion it was allowed to speak at all. It voted them down 64 percent to 36 percent. Russia was the first nation conquered by Communists with the use of troops.

This brutally Czarist type of action against the popularly elected Constitutional Convention, along with a quick suppression of all freedom of press and assemblage, led to civil war. The peasants' party, the Social Revolutionaries, raised an army against the Bolsheviks and fought. Nobles and other members of the old Czarist regime did the same. War went on from 1918 into 1920, and possibly a million men were killed, while many others starved to death in the bloody process.

Here the French, coupled on this occasion with the British, made the third of their unfortunate interventions in Russian affairs, and the old Czarist generals made the last of the six errors of that group. The French had in 1906, at the very time when the Duma was seeking some degree of popular control of the government, loaned to Czarist Russia a sum equal in values of the late 1960s to a billion dollars. That loan prevented the Duma from exercising the old power of Parliament in England over wayward monarchs, that of refusing credit until it was exchanged for partnership. The loans were canceled in 1917 because they had done exactly that. With those loans, the French paid for all the havoc of the war with Japan, for all the police costs of putting down revolt in 1905, for all the subsequent Czarist brutality and pogroms. Then, in the summer of 1917, British and French officers had strongly urged the fateful offensive which Kerensky ordered and which did so much to end the chances for survival of the provisional government. Now, in the civil war, they made the third mistake of putting French and British forces into Russia to overthrow the new government, arousing and uniting all the sentiments of nationalism against themselves. (Some American troops were also briefly involved.) Worse, the French and British financed old Czarist generals, whose aim was not a democratic government but another Czarist rule. These last two foreign errors (as old as Sparta) were thereupon compounded by their subsidized Russian generals. The latter let it be known publicly that they planned to give back the land to the large landlords, the former owners, which the peasants had already received, even before the Bolsheviks took over. This was their only payment for years of suffering and for the loss of several millions of their men in war. At that point, the Social Revolutionaries could no longer ally themselves with such reactionary and unacceptable concepts. They disbanded, stopped fighting.

These foreign and old Czarist errors allowed the Communists to wrap themselves in the mantle of Russian patriotism and to discredit their rivals as Hessians of foreign imperialism. The same response to the same errors was to be echoed in Vietnam in another civil war fifty years later. The American diplomat and historian George F. Kennan later described the Western expeditions into Russia as "little sideshows of policy, conducted absentmindedly" by men preoccupied with more important matters at Paris. But the Allied military efforts, however casual, he wrote:

> served everywhere to compromise the enemies of the Bolsheviks and to strengthen the Communists as well. So important was this factor that I think it may well be questioned whether Bolshevism would have ever prevailed had the Western governments not aided its progress to power by this ill-conceived interference.[3]

The Russian people discovered something which the Germans were not yet aware of fifteen years later, that the vast mechanism of modern society can be mobilized to make a recapture of lost liberties almost impossible. Food, shelter and life itself can be refused to dissidents, and a secret police even more ubiquitous than that of the Czar's can turn a nation mute, pervert all idealism into plots against the totalitarian state. They also found out that they had no chance to prevent major errors in foreign policy or even a rule by assassination. Under Stalin almost two-thirds of the Communist governing class in Russia was destroyed, mostly through mock trials following accusations of treason. A new obstacle to necessary change and reform throughout the nonauthoritarian world was raised. All reactionaries could claim that all reformist efforts were Communist-inspired, and much of the world's current backlog of undone tasks accumulated under the burden of such claims. While Russia experienced its new terror, the peoples of the rest of the world were also cursed with a new distrust of one another. With their absolute loyalty to a creed which superseded all humanism, the Communists did much to destroy the cement of trust among men on which other societies were based. The quality of life was debased as it had not been since the sixteenth and seventeenth centuries, during the wars of religion.

Still, in a world where power counts most, the Communists obtained it for Russia. The peasants and workers, defrauded of the land, civic rights and factory control they had been promised, were sweated sufficiently to produce the capital necessary for an enormous industrial expansion. Enough industrial plant was in place to repair the great German destruction in the Second World War. By the later 1950s Russia was the second most powerful industrial and military force in the world, one that others were unable to ignore or pity.

How much, if anything, did the Russian people gain by their forced acceptance of Communist control and creed? It is almost impossible not to yield to the temptation of speculating about the fate of that nation and the world if the Constitutional Convention had been called for May 1917 instead of January 1918, long months before the Bolsheviks had become strong enough to close it by force of arms.

At the end of 1918 Allied victory returned the Ukraine's food and mineral resources to Russia. With a democratic Russia seated as a major participant in the peacemaking at Paris, the devastating civil war, Allied intervention in it, the war with Poland, financed by France, which took several million Russians into Poland, might all have been avoided. Industrialization would probably have been speeded somewhat by foreign loans and by trade with Germany, which needed food and raw materials badly and could have swapped machines for them. Russia might even have found its way toward the no-riches-no-poverty pattern of the Scandinavian nations. Living standards might have risen about as much as they actually did, approaching in the late 1960s the levels of Czecho-slovakia—no mean achievement. Peasants might even have retained control of the land they had received before the Bolsheviks took over, instead of having to watch five million of their ablest people separated from the land by force and exiled or killed. The communalization of the land might have been avoided. Without the Communist menace to serve Hitler's purposes and to scare the necessary funds from the pockets of unforesighted German industrialists, the rise of the Nazis to power might have been checked, then reversed. Even if it had not been checked, a Russian army could have been ready to stop its expansion some years before Munich and would have been welcomed by England and France, perhaps even by Poland, instead of being cold-shouldered. The Second World War, which was to cost Russia and many other nations so many millions of lives and so much devastation of material and spirit and to produce so much endless tragedy for the Jewish people in Europe might well have been averted.

Since no people anywhere during several generations will be quite immune to the after-effects and success formulas of the Russian revolu-tion, some features of the process of overthrow are worth their atten-tion. In the less developed areas, many impatient men have already been tempted to move out of the group of hopeful reformers into that of the revolutionaries. In the modern industrial societies, other men will either be participating in efforts to prevent or defeat revolutions or be engaged in observing, perhaps deploring, the excesses and brutalities of all parties to the event.

One overall feature of this period of revolution may be stressed. It is that revolutions made in the name of personal liberty and democracy can become so devoid of both that they amount to swindles of those who support them. Not only did Lenin, once in power, break his pledge to respect the democratically elected Constitutional Convention, he actually closed it with troops. Freedom of press and assemblage, which had allowed him to come to power, were almost immediately sup-pressed. A secret spy organization, then called the Cheka, was created which equaled the Czar's spy organization and hunted down dissidents. The workers, who were promised control of factories and management of the state, were soon to become the regimented troops of the new managerial bureaucracy. Peasants, given land even before the Bolsheviks took power and fighting against Czarist generals and foreign troops on behalf of the Bolsheviks because of that grant of land, later had much of it taken from them and communized. The tactic of confusing and mis-leading people about the purpose and significance of the revolution continued long after its original stress on freedom had been lost in Russia. In the 1950s and 1960s, for example, spokesmen for that revolution told people in India that Russia had started from the unbelievably low living level of India and had moved to much higher levels because of the revolution. This was not so. Compared to the miserable huts, the one or two kitchen pots and a chair which made up the poor man's ménage in India, the Russians of 1917 were already enormously advanced.

To be noted also for the future is the value to a revolutionary group of a well-developed mystique. In the case of the Bolsheviks, it was the claim that the scientific study of history determined that the workers were destined to take control of all societies. It had the additional attraction of calling on men to work for the good of their fellowmen instead of for the less satisfying self-interest. It promised peace throughout the whole world when the revolution of the workers and peasants had taken over all societies. To this mystique were added definite promises of material and status gains to various groups. Then, under foreign attack, the whole cause was wrapped in nationalism. All this would still not have been enough if the military defeats of the Czar's armies, the heavy toll in dead, wounded, hunger and hardship had not presented the revolutionaries with an original opportunity they never expected to find. The democratic group was uninventive, underrated the emergency, cumulated too many unnecessary mistakes in too short a time. So the machinery of the society was visibly coming apart when the Communists struck. They could make the additional appeal of being the only group which really wanted to end the war, really establish a new order. They had an advantage over their democratic rivals in being able to stand clear of all responsibility. They were free to tar their rivals with accusations of all crimes in the book as those unhappy people had to take one unpopular step after another to try to overcome the national emergency.

Men who create the conditions for an authoritarian take-over and men who allow or encourage it must apparently be ready to see an absolutism managed by a group turn into one-man rule. Lincoln at one moment pointed out that there was no limit to secession. Once it had started, the seceding group might expect to split again and again into smaller and smaller fragments. A somewhat similar process seems to be in the nature of the authoritarian organization. It tends toward one-man control. That man can be or become a paranoiac, savage in his brutality, able to order the murders of many former associates. Stalin and Hitler both demonstrated this inherent tendency of the system, and with that demonstration cast new doubts on its capacity to observe the requirements of peace in a weapon-loaded world.

Something is also worth remembering for tomorrow about the determination of the Czar and his court to hold on to an old order too long. Apparently, in a nontotalitarian nation whose people know something about personal freedom and democratic participation, absolutism cannot be maintained forever, particularly not when the nation is forced to endure a series of shocks to its welfare and conscience. This is not true of absolutism in a totalitarian state, since modern methods of food distribution, transportation, communication and employment, as well as the monopoly of major armaments, give such a state the power to starve men into obedience and silence and to prevent attempts at overthrow. Czarist Russia was absolutist but not totalitarian. The important by-product result of Czarist violence was not simply the counterviolence of bomb throwing and expropriations it evoked, but the grinding away of the moderate and democratically inclined forces of the undercover opposition. Every pogrom, every brutal act of the Black Hundreds gave the new authoritarians within that opposition a new lease on life, a new justification. Force-loving parents bred children in their own image.

Immediately after the Bolsheviks had taken power, Russia gave the world a useful lesson in the futility of a foreign military intervention which sought to undo the gains of a revolution. They repeated the French experience with similar interventionists some hundred and thirty years earlier. They wrote once again a record which their followers have used in Southeast Asia and will presumably use successfully everytime and everywhere that a foreign power intervenes against revolutionary gains with military force. It will be recalled that the land of the large landowners had been distributed to the peasants before the Bolsheviks took power. This was an enormous grant to the peasants, one longed for over many decades. When the Germans took the Ukraine, they gave the land back to the landlords and acquired additional Russian hate for that act. The peasants' party (Social Revolutionaries) had taken up arms against the Bolsheviks in the name of democracy. Then the Czarist generals, supported actively by the French and British, less actively by the Americans (who were under orders to be neutral), copied the hated Germans and announced that an anti-Bolshevik victory would also involve a return of the land to the large landowners. At that point, the peasants' party stopped fighting, and peasants became guerrillas with a cause and harried and hounded the anti-Bolshevik armies. The civil war, with its famine and hundreds of thousands of dead, soon ended. The cause of democracy was defeated by military men who understood nothing beyond military action.

The futility of trying to beat a horse with no horse has generally been recognized. However, the futility of trying to counter an authoritarian revolution without competitive appeals still is awaiting recognition. It received a little after Chiang Kai-shek in China had refused to rival his Communist opponents by granting land to the peasants, as they were doing. He lost power. However, after his flight to Taiwan, he realized the consequences of such an oversight, and land reform in Taiwan began promptly. It moved rapidly, for the land-reform officials showed the large landowners on the island the newspapers from the mainland, full of announcements that this or that large landlord's head had been chopped off. Their counterparts on Taiwan were offered a choice: Do you prefer to lose only your land, or both your head and your land? Their response was unanimous, and they were paid fairly, out of future crops, even more fairly than in Japan, where they were paid in yen, which rapidly depreciated in value. So men occasionally do learn from their mistakes.

Returning to 1919, Russia, then considered a social pariah and menace, was not invited to be present when the victorious allies, the United States, and the Germans, all in their separate ways, began the process of risking then losing the opportunity to establish a durable peace in Western Europe.

CHAPTER 10

Fifteen Years of Avoidable Anarchy

(*Germany: 1918–1933*)

Germany in 1933, like Russia in late 1917, gave people living in freedom-oriented nations the shock of discovery that every democratic rule everywhere which failed to meet its challenges well could be supplanted, that nobility of creed did not guarantee immunity. Inability to end a war in Russia, inability to ride out a depression in Germany were only the final demonstrations of weakness and inadequacy, the funereally engraved invitations extended to totalitarian overthrow. The event in Germany was the more striking of the two, because it occurred in a more Western and middle-class nation. Both, however, suffered alike from the same spiteful rising against democracy at the crucial moment by old and powerful antidemocratic forces. In Russia this took the form of a military attack by a former Czarist general on the brief democracy that inherited the Czar's turmoil. In Germany it was an attack by leading industrialists combined with a refusal of support by the old General Staff. Both risings helped sweep the new authoritarians into power. The most reactionary forces in both nations were the best allies of the most radical ones.

The fifteen years in Germany between 1918 and 1933 indicate again, as other turning points in Western history have, that alternatives to catastrophe are usually available, that avoidance of a few mistakes, a little more serious attention to past human experience might have brought an entirely different result. They picture again the vast differ-

218

ence between the cost of prevention and that of reconstruction. They demonstrate how one obnoxious extremism can be utilized to scare innocent people into acceptance of a different but equally vicious one. They show how victories can be gutted of their content and sacrifice and how men can be hypnotized into new folly by their passion to avoid repetition of an old one which they misunderstand. They tell of the internal Munich of the Germans—an event which ruined them twice over—long before the rest of the world became ashamed of the other Munich.

The peoples of Europe laid down their arms in November 1918, at the end of the First World War, with an enormous passion for peace. Most of them had suffered long and cruelly. But they looked at one another with amazement. The Germans came out from behind the curtain of their military censorship under the impression that they had been surrounded, attacked, had fought only in self-defense, had beat off the primitive Russians, had been offered and had accepted an honorable armistice. People in the Allied nations came out from under their own curtains of war censorship sure that they had been the ones attacked, they had fought only in defense against unwarranted aggression, that the Germans were only half-disguised Huns who had cut off babies' hands and raped women all over Belgium, and who chose churches and hospitals as favorite artillery and bombing targets. These mad dogs of Europe were not to be trusted under any circumstances. Perhaps they were to be somewhat pitied for their passive submission to the Hohenzollerns and the tyrants of the German General Staff, but not much. Only armies could keep them from breaking loose again. The patriotic propagandists on both sides—some of them certainly lying in their teeth—had done so well to win the war that they had managed to jeopardize the peace.

This atmosphere of distrust carried over into the preparation and signing of the Treaty of Versailles in 1919. The Germans had not been allowed to discuss its effects on Germany with their victors. They had been told to sign it or see their country occupied. They were not even allowed public comment on its conspicuous variances from the armistice terms. Premier Clemenceau of France taunted President Wilson for showing signs of commiseration with the defeated Germans, suggesting that he might be pro-Bosch. In that atmosphere, a great many fine men who had died on the battlefields lost what they had fought for, democracy and peace, a world mobilized against war.

That war, it will be remembered, had lasted four years, from August 1914 into November 1918. The loss of men had been enormous. France, along with Russia, had suffered most severely. While France had been able to muster 240,000 men in the class which came of military age in 1914, in the crucial year of 1936 it was able to muster only 120,000 in that year's class. It had been dealt a severe blow. Its relative power in Europe had been reduced. In April 1917 the United States entered a stalemated trench war. In the fall of that year Russia withdrew from it. Germany surrendered in November 1918 without having been invaded or destroyed.

The first mistake, to which an earlier reference has been made, was that the United States, whose help was greatly needed by England, France, Belgium, Italy and Russia, was allowed to enter the war by its President and Congress before its prospective allies had agreed with the United States on the objectives of the war, the kind of peace to be arranged by the victors. The importance of obtaining such an agreement had been signaled by the coolness of both sides to a no-annexation, no-indemnity peace proposal which originated among the Scandinavian neutrals in 1916. Even in April 1917 President Wilson was not completely stopped from obtaining such an advance agreement by the German resumption of U-boat warfare. He had promised war against Germany if that activity was resumed. He might, nevertheless, have delayed the actual declaration of war long enough to obtain such an understanding from his prospective allies. Neglect to use his brief power put him into the position of becoming only one pleader among other special interests at the 1918–1919 peace negotiations. Later, he made the additional mistake of not taking with him as advisers any of the major Republican leaders of the United States Senate, which would have to approve any treaty he brought home. Since the Republicans had gained control of Congress before he went to Paris, this was a serious oversight.

The possibility of repeating the war-without-advance agreement error —as old as Pope Urban II at the beginning of the crusades—can become greater as calls for United States help in feudal and hunger-ridden nations increase in the coming decades. Since nations once fully committed to war can no longer influence their allies, it is even possible to foresee the absurdity of a small dictator turning the very nation which subsidizes and aids him into a dependent and servant, even to rebuke it publicly for not sacrificing more of its resources and men. Possibly in the early 1960s an advance agreement with a prospective ally in Saigon, along the Eisenhower line of aid-only-in-return-for-performance, might have affected favorably the amount of fighting undertaken by the South Vietnamese army, the amount of personal freedom allowed by the government, a diminution of the feudal burdens it sought to reimpose on rebellious people, perhaps even the possibility of a peace.

The second mistake was made by French leaders, who were naturally and belligerently determined to protect France from still a third invasion by the Germans. They obtained President Wilson's signature to an American-French-British treaty which committed the United States to put armed forces into Europe in case of a German attack on France or England. Clemenceau, the French Premier, insisted on this, because he did not see in the draft of the Treaty of Versailles, or in the League of Nations Covenant incorporated in it, any automatic defense for France against German aggression. With this signed tripartite treaty in hand, however, he withdrew the original French demand that the Allies keep a permanent occupation force in the Rhineland, along with some armed bridgeheads on the right bank of the Rhine, so that any new war would start on German rather than French soil.

This represented a major error of understanding about the state of American public opinion and about the power of an American President to get any treaty which he signed ratified by two-thirds of the United States Senate. At the end of the war in 1918, the Americans wanted peace and yet were quite uncertain about underwriting any border defense in a Europe which seemed to be accident-prone. The newspapers had given the people a vivid picture of major quarrels between great powers in Paris, of a rough handling of their President by the statesmen of their Allies, of heavy reparations levied on Germany, of secret treaties, published by the Russians, dividing up some of the spoils of war.

The French had ample warning that the United States Senate might not ratify either treaty. The British had given that possibility a red alert by inserting in the tripartite pact a condition that their own adherence depended on ratification by the Senate of the United States. Not only had the 1918 election shown that President Wilson no longer controlled Congress, but such prominent Republicans as former President Theodore Roosevelt and Senator Henry Cabot Lodge had been freely informing Europe that the President could no longer speak for the nation. All this might have been enough to make the French leaders seek another way to obtain security for France. This objective was not impossible.

A more alert French leadership might have noticed that the Treaty of Versailles could go into effect without ratification by the United States. They could have put into that treaty a conditional clause to this effect: In the event of United States ratification of both treaties, military occupation would be minor and brief. In the event of nonratification by the United States of the tripartite pact, the occupation of territory within Germany would be large and prolonged.

This alteration might even have produced a German plea to the United States to ratify the pact. As it was, the Senate refused to ratify the Treaty of Versailles by seven votes, and then neglected to consider the tripartite pact at all. The British then put salt into French wounds by canceling their own adherence to the pact. France was left alone, isolated and diminished on the Continent without its past ally, Russia. Fear, fury and a sense of betrayal swept through that nation. An ultranationalistic majority was elected to its Assembly for the first time since 1871. Soon Poincaré was to become Premier and to begin that process of irritating and weakening Germany which later earned him some claim to the parentage of Hitler. American absence from the Continent delayed any effective moves toward postwar neighborliness, goodwill and peace.

The third mistake was shared by the Allies and the United States. It was that of giving the Germans cause for belief that they had been defrauded of honor and of money. They had surrendered on the basis of an armistice which did not attach to Germany sole responsibility for starting the war. While it envisaged German reparations for damages incurred, it did not include pensions for the families of Allied soldiers. But when the Treaty of Versailles was submitted to them—on a take-it-or-accept-occupation basis—it contained a clause laying sole responsibility for the war on Germany. This was an affront to fact, but more importantly it was an affront to all that the German people had been sedulously taught by their guided press for four years. It led to a wave of indignation in Germany, the resignation of the cabinet, a preparation to refuse to sign the treaty and accept occupation as more onerous but more honorable. The Allied blindness to this almost unanimous protest, the readiness of the victorious powers to judge Germany and to exculpate their own military and political leaders, was to handicap all Germans who wanted to conform to the other and more essential parts of the treaty. In addition, the Allies laid on the already hard-pressed Germans a demand that their reparations payments include pensions for the families of Allied soldiers. This again, because it had not been suggested or accepted in the surrender terms, seemed a fraud to the Germans. Pressure on the Germans to sign was accentuated by a blockade of food supplies. The victors never seemed to consider the possibility that too cruel a victory might boomerang.

A fourth mistake, with a built-in explosive charge, was made by victors and vanquished in combination. The Allies overlooked the need of a young democratic republic for a loyal and republican army. The Germans, in turn, were blind to the potential unscrupulousness of their General Staff and the danger that could represent for the republic. Between the two of them, they managed to leave Germany without the support it needed in its upcoming moments of crisis.

The Allies did their part somewhat casually. The size of Germany's army seemed more important than its character, and they put the allowed limit at 100,000, permitting long-term enlistments. Marshal

Foch, head of the French forces, proposed 200,000, to be conscripted, but with only one-year terms of service. The French Premier, who lost no love on Foch, vetoed this and the British concurred. The Americans were indifferent. The decision had important effects. A conscripted army meant that all of German opinion would be represented in the army, that it could not readily become the private weapon of the General Staff. A professional army with long-term enlistments meant that the Staff could choose men with its own views and prejudices. Here, in fact, the noncoms were trained who later officered the millions of German troops in World War II. Neither in 1920 nor toward the end of the republic's brief life could the democratic forces count on the army as a support against all forms of attack from within.

The Germans who wanted their republic to function never had the audacity to confide to the public any details of the somewhat indifferent record which the famous German General Staff had produced during the war. They knew that after 1915 the Kaiser had been superseded as a governing force by two leading general officers, Ludendorff and Hindenburg, who had made their reputations in defeating the Russians. Those two had run the nation, not only its supply system but its political life. It was at General Staff insistence that neutral Belgium had been invaded in 1914, an act which brought England into the war promptly. It had botched a favorable opportunity to capture Paris in the first months. The two heroes had transported Lenin into Russia in April 1917, thereby increasing the long-term Communist threat to Germany. They had opposed the no-annexations, no-indemnities measures of 1917 and had made them ridiculous and even hypocritical by the harshness of the terms they imposed on Russia. They had renewed the U-boat warfare against the United States in early 1917, which brought that nation into the struggle and provided the decisive margin for Germany's defeat. They had underrated the capacity of the United States to put an army into the field rapidly. They had supported a course of financing the war through loans and currency printing rather than adequate taxation—a "victor take all" gamble. They had allowed themselves to be so hypnotized by the prospect of retaining for Germany the rich farmland of the Ukraine that they left a million men in the East to police it—probably enough to push their successful western-front offensive of March 1918 all the way into Paris. It was not a great record. But in their hour of defeat the Germans needed to cling to some heroes (much as the Egyptians clung to Nasser after their defeat by Israel in 1967) and these two were hallowed. Both were consequently protected and left free to make their not inconsiderable later contributions to chaos. Like the later German worship of Hitler, it was a most expensive form of idolatry.

The trusting liberals and prodemocrats who found themselves put in charge of the German fate in late 1918, by direction of the German General Staff, were first to experience a truly royal double-cross by that group. In September and October of 1918, Field Marshal Hindenburg informed the crown council that he had to have an armistice. Turkey and the Austro-Hungarian forces were crumbling, the Allied offensive in the west had finally gained momentum. War-weariness and hunger had moved from the civilians to the troops. Naval mutiny was around the corner. He was impatient and said on October 2 that the army could not wait forty-eight hours. To meet President Wilson's demands for a new image for Germany, Hindenburg requested and obtained a new cabinet with progressive faces, gave Prussia the equal suffrage it had long demanded in vain, made the Chancellor (Prime Minister) responsible to the Reichstag for the first time, detailed an officer to tell the Kaiser to abdicate, and told the new cabinet to negotiate the armistice. The new men were to be the public front of surrender while the General Staff would stay in the background under favorable conditions of low visibility. The American President had stated that any attempt to have a surrender negotiated by the Kaiser or the General Staff would result in a demand for an unconditional surrender. With the armistice signed, the German troops were marched home in orderly ranks and demobilized. The Allies began their peace discussions in Paris.

While they were so engaged, Europe began the first of its postwar convulsions. In Hungary the Communists held Budapest for a while. The Austro-Hungarian Empire broke up into its several parts. The Communists in Russia were busy with a civil war. In Germany disillusioned soldiers and sailors began forming soldiers' and workers' committees. They wanted a radical revolution, eliminating the agricultural feudalism of the Junkers in the east and the industrial feudalism of the coal and steel barons of the Ruhr. The stability of the newly formed German government was threatened. The new political leaders needed army help to keep order. At this point the new army commander, General Groener—the man told to order Kaiser Wilhelm II to abdicate —made an informal arrangement with the new prodemocratic Chancellor, Friederich Ebert, who was to become first President of the first German Republic. It was that the army would help retain the new administration in power, provided that the new men would not interfere with the army.[1] Here Ebert made the same error that a crusading Pope and a President had made before him. He did not get his agreement with a potential ally spelled out to cover all contingencies. He did not make it public. Nor did he demand that all army officers swear an oath before their troops and the nation, offering loyalty to the republic at all times. Ebert had given up his right to form a republican militia in return for a promise that could be broken at will.

The first occasion for a welshing on that promise came in 1920. In

March of that year, armed semi-irregulars (free corps) who had been organized for service on the disturbed Polish and Baltic frontiers were used in an attack on the republic's government in Berlin. They were martialed by one of the Kaiser's more reactionary generals (Lüttwitz), and led by a minor official (Kapp). The government had to flee Berlin. The Republic's commanding general (von Seekt) simply sent himself on leave, shirking all responsibility. A general strike called by the labor unions throughout the nation ended the rebellion. When officials called in von Seekt to ask why he had failed to carry through the General Staff's promise of protection, he passed the question off with arrogance. "What? Order Reichswehr [German Army] to shoot at Reichswehr? Preposterous." Even when faced with this evidence of the army's bad faith, and with the whole labor-union movement mobilized on their behalf, the Republic's leaders failed to seize the demonstration of a broken bargain to create a republican militia which would really protect it. Here was a major mistake.

It was in November of the same year, 1920, that Field Marshal Hindenburg himself reached for the jugular of the new republic and gave the Great Lie a plausible parentage. The background for his action needs to be recalled. He had himself demanded the armistice, and had demanded it long before November. Announcement of the peace terms and the sole-responsibility accusation came in the late spring of 1919. The Chancellor of the Republic had resigned with his whole cabinet in indignation. He was the Social Democrat who had proclaimed the Republic. Indignation meetings had been held all over. At one, attended by members of the Catholic Center Party, its leader, Fehrenbach later a Chancellor himself, had prophetically told the Allies to look out for a later generation of Germans dedicated to breaking the chains of slavery imposed by the Treaty of Versailles.

At the crucial moment when the civilian German government seemed ready to reject the treaty, Generals Hindenburg and Groener conferred. The latter telephoned President Ebert that no prospects for a successful defense existed, since the armies had been demobilized. Hindenburg avoided a direct contact and personal commitment. Yet if he had said or even suggested, "Don't ratify," the civilians would have rejected the treaty and accepted occupation. The democrats now made a further fateful mistake. They trusted in the legendary mystique of officer honor in Germany and neglected to get a signed request from both general officers that the peace treaty be accepted. Instead, members of the Reichstag were quietly informed that the army command saw no alternative to acceptance, and thereupon voted to ratify it. At no time did the General Staff officers expose themselves and their activities to public view.

It was before a Reichstag Committee of Inquiry that Hindenburg, still many years away from his later senility, remarked that the German armies had not really been defeated by enemy armies in the field, but had suffered a *Dolchstoss*, a dagger stab in the back, by civilians over-eager for peace. He left it at that, in low key, without further explanation, but his plea in avoidance was enough to allow all haters of the new Republic to conclude that noble, heroic and undefeated Germans had been betrayed by pacifists and republic lovers. They soon made the most of it. The early 1920s were bloodied with the assassination of outstanding prodemocrats. Yet Hindenburg's statement was contrary to all evidence, to all his own activities. Such was his aura of monopolized superpatriotism that he could not effectively be called to account. Hitler was later to base half his campaign for power on charges of treason against the "November 1918 criminals." Hindenburg had effectively armed reviving German nationalism and directed it at the jugular of the Republic. While some nations can be born through defeat, few can survive charges of treason on top of defeat, and Germany was not one of that number.

With these various moves, one of the major supports and symbols of old semifeudal nationalism had been restored to its prerepublic position of authority and power. It now became the function of the General Staff to demonstrate to such eager learners as Hitler the vast possibilities of international, as distinct from national, deceit. The limitation of 100,000 men placed on the army was evaded by creation of a Black Reichswehr, supposedly a labor corps, but one armed and trained in military formations. Then General von Seekt promptly set about evading other obligations of the peace treaty by secret rearmament both in Germany and in Russia. Elaborate arrangements were made for testing new tanks and fabricating grenades in Russia. In 1926 the Social Democrat Scheidemann exposed some of these matters in the Reichstag. He was howled down and denied by nationalists and Communists in unison. That year the Allied Arms Control Commission made a 500-page report on its work in Germany, which was never to be published. Many years later the English Brigadier General J. H. Morgan wrote that the report said in essence that "Germany had never disarmed, had never had the intention of disarming, and for seven years had done everything in her power to deceive and 'counter-control' the Commission appointed to control her disarmament."[2]

As a consequence of all this maneuvering, evasion and deceit, in 1932, when it was a matter of life or death, the German Republic could not trust the army to protect it against the Hitler forces, Hindenburg would be President and could not be trusted to ask the army to do so, and he would, in fact, turn the Republic over to Hitler, who had vowed its death and who despised the idea of freedom.

A still later consequence would be that the proud army command, after a decade of politicking and cabinet making, would fall into a position of complete obedience and subservience to Hitler's wildest whims. The command would see him promote and unmake generals and field marshals, order them dismissed, have them killed out of hand by his gangs. They would see him walk into the feared two-front war, and then make decisions in favor of holding on to every inch of ground once occupied, and with those orders invite the defeat of whole armies, and finally the expansion of Soviet Russia into Western Europe. The officer corps would finally be as helpless and humiliated as the republicans whom it had hoodwinked.

The fifth major error, one of misunderstanding about the linked requirements of peace and democracy, was of joint German and French make. It led to the galloping inflation of 1923, oddly enough manipulated by a Chancellor from the business group, who poured out more tons of paper money during the Ruhr crisis than Germany could stand. This impoverished and disoriented the middle and professional classes, and separated many of them from their earlier support of the Republic. Worse, this shock was so severe that avoidance of its repetition in the early 1930s seemed more important than the task of saving the Republic. The Germans were traumatized by it in much the same way that the surrender at Munich in 1938 was to affect a British Prime Minister in 1956 at the time of Suez, and officials of the United States during the Vietnam War. At no cost could it be repeated.

By 1923 many Germans had been led to believe that they had been victimized by their victors. Extreme nationalists had been busy explaining that they were being treated as incorrigible delinquents by a court whose fairness was in doubt. East Prussia was cut by a Polish corridor. Plebiscites in Silesia which showed a desire of people to remain inside of Germany did not prevent several areas from being allocated to Poland. On top of all these annoyances and burdens, the government of the Republic had lost prestige through the prolonged disorder of 1918–1919 and the ignominious flight at the time of the Kapp Putsch in 1920. In the subsequent 1920 elections the main support of the moderate Republic, the Social Democrats, lost half their strength, dropping from eleven to 5.6 million votes. The relatively small split within Germany which began with the signing of the Versailles Treaty had by 1923 widened considerably and ominously.

Nationalistic extremists, in addition to their assassinations, attempted to blame the Jews for all Germany's postwar difficulties. Anti-Semitism had lurked in the German subculture for years as in that of Poland and Russia, and now found a new opportunity. Germany had never had any

Lincoln to convince people that every justification for injury to one group of men could and would be used against all other groups. It had never had any Mazzini or Jaurès to excite people about the concept of personal freedom. Germans, who had never felt strongly enough about that concept to stage a successful revolution on its behalf, now began to consider the Republic itself as an alien institution, imposed on them by its conquerors, obedient to them in disregard of the true German interests.

The confusion was heightened when French and Belgian troops marched in to occupy the whole Ruhr area—the heart of industrial output—in 1923. The propriety of their occupation was put into doubt by an English refusal to join. The cause for this action was a German failure to meet all its reparations obligations—those in lumber, coal and railroad equipment—promptly and adequately. The Germans had asked for a delay so that their industrial output could be geared to the demand, but had been refused. Along with this occupation came horrifying rumors and reports that Frenchmen were trying to break the Rhineland off from Germany. The German government, then under Chancellor Cuno, a representative of one of the parties oriented toward industry, entered on a campaign to make the occupation unsuccessful. Sabotage was subsidized. Production was diminished in the Ruhr and disarranged throughout most of Germany. Currency was printed as freely as newspapers.

Inflation had been underway even before 1923. In 1919 the German mark was worth only a fourth of its prewar value. After the reparations demand had been announced in January 1922 (the then astronomical sum of 32 billion dollars), it fell to one-thousandth of that value. Late in 1923 four billion marks were required to purchase the dollar, which could have been bought before the war for four marks. Here was the world's most spectacular inflation. The purchasing power of wages dropped. All pensions and fixed incomes were practically wiped out.

In the cold autumn nights in the Ruhr and Rhineland daughters of the impoverished families sold themselves to foreign soldiers for a bar of chocolate, because it was food. Their fathers went to work for a bagful of government paper notes that would buy a loaf of bread in the morning, but only half a loaf in the evening. Farmers (as in Russia in 1917) refused to bring their products to market for worthless paper. Children no longer got milk. The savings and pensions of workers, civil servants, teachers, doctors, lawyers, clerks became waste paper. This process did not merely demoralize people, it derationalized them. Nobody could plan for the future or even for the next day. Was this order? Was this justice? Was it the promised democracy? It made no sense to work or save. It made no sense to obey the authorities who allowed such chaos. Some young people began to speak of themselves as "wanderers into the nothingness." The middle class was not so much proletarianized, as the later able Chancellor Stresemann believed, as it was torn away from its old moorings of faith, trust and respect.

Industrialists and landowning farmers, however, were able to pay off their debt with the depreciated currency and thereby became wealthier by far than they had been before. At this moment few sensible men would have wagered any small coin on the survival chances of the Republic.

During these crucial years from 1919 through 1923 the United States, the only nation which had, after the Civil War, experienced intimately the results of neglecting a defeated but unconvinced people after a total war, stayed out of Europe. Talks about loans to Germany had been begun, but they did not turn into funds (the Dawes Plan loans) until 1924. Stabilization came only when the German government wanted it to come, in late 1923. It could have come earlier.[3] For lack of gold reserves, the mark was based quite simply on the nation's real estate. With Dawes Plan loans a spectacular boom began and lasted until 1929. For the moment, the Republic was saved. But the United States financial cavalry had not charged onto the field until after a large part of the German population had been wounded, disgusted and demoralized.

The year 1923 was also marked by a preview of what lay ahead of Germany in any new political and economic crisis. Bavaria, a state in the southern part of the country, opened the public press to a new hero of the racial and ultranationalistic groups. Before his career of antidemocratic action and anti-Communist sloganeering to make his aims acceptable had ended, Germany would be invaded and divided far more decisively than after the First World War, and the Communist armed forces would stand within a hundred miles of the Rhine. In Bavaria, Adolf Hitler brought to the old nationalist cause the idea of gaining mass support by socialistic appeals to the workers. He managed to establish a personal dictatorship, a one-man rule, over a little group which was later to be called the National Socialist German Workers party, soon abbreviated into "Nazi." When the inflation grew, he accused the Republic's government of robbing the workers. When in September 1923 a new Chancellor, Stresemann, ended the German resistance in the Ruhr and promised to pay all due reparations, Hitler and others cried treason. Stresemann put the Minister of Defense and the Commander of the Reichswehr in charge. Separatist Bavaria reacted by putting in dictatorial charge of that state a monarchist (von Karr) who refused to recognize the Reich's emergency decrees.

Danger of civil war was evidenced by the capture of several of the Republic's forts by rebellious Black Reichswehr. Karr refused to replace the army commander in Bavaria with one loyal to the Republic. Hitler tried to organize the ultranationalists into a march on the Munich government. Ludendorff was with him. Police fired. Hitler escaped unwounded, as did Ludendorff. Goering, later to be Air Marshal, was wounded. Sentenced to five years in prison, Hitler was let out after nine months. He had become famous. The Bavarian officials who had, up to a point, joined in his conspiracy, were not even prosecuted.

Even after 1923 the Communists continued their attacks on the Republic. The German Communists, with some exceptions, were under Russian tutelage throughout the postwar period. Their two major contributions to the downfall of the Republic and the breakup of peace can be considered Russian rather than *echt deutsch* (truly German) errors. They had not tried to make a revolution in 1923, although, through mistaken orders, a small revolt was started in Hamburg. Significantly, in that year one of their Russian leaders (Radek) had spoken on the same platform with German nationalist leaders, possibly in the hope of obtaining their support for a closer Russian-German alliance than that suggested by the Rapallo Treaty of 1922.[4] He horrified the true believers. In 1924, however, the Communists, renewing an old fight on the Versailles Treaty, attacked the Dawes Plan loans from the United States.

In 1925 they made an even more serious mistake. They played the game of the reactionary antirepublicans in the Presidential election. General Hindenburg was the candidate of the nationalists and the industrialists. The Republic's supporters had nominated Wilhelm Marx, a respected but hardly charismatic leader of the Center (Catholic) party. After the Ruhr and Bavarian troubles of 1923 and Stresemann's contested decision to pay reparations in full, a close election was expected. At that point, the Communists entered one of their Russia-dominated leaders (Thälmann) as a third candidate. He drew off enough votes to allow Hindenburg to be elected President. The old General received 900,000 votes more than the republican Marx, with the Communists polling 1,500,000. With Hindenburg's election, the wartime regime was given new strength, hope and opportunity. In due course he was to give the Republic his own version of a stab in the back. From 1928 on, the Communists attacked the Social Democrats as "Social Fascists," withheld criticism of the reactionary forces, and voted with the latter in the Reichstag and in the Prussian Landtag (assembly) against the supporters of the Republic. They saw their assigned task as that of discrediting the Social Democrats so thoroughly that they could take power away from that group. After that, the Communist party was supposed to become the inheritor of all labor-union strength. They misjudged Germany and the nature of the coming crisis quite thoroughly. Their suicidal role in the German drama was that of masquerading as the hero-champions of the working class while actually serving the ultranationalists and anti-democrats as an excuse for their own subversion of the Republic. In that particular tragedy anti-Communism sheltered the fascist groups most effectively.

The final disruptive error of misunderstanding was about essential priorities. It broke out within the German Establishment. A number of its important leaders failed to comprehend rapidly enough that the depression which started in 1929 could create a successful revolution against the economic order as well as the political one.

Five years of prosperity (1924–1928) and the belated acceptance of Germany into the community of nations with membership in the League of Nations granted in 1926 had given the prodemocratic forces a new mandate. In 1928 the parties supporting the Republic won the Reichstag elections by an overwhelming vote. The industry-oriented conservative groups lost two million voters between 1924 and 1928, the Nazi party dropped to 810,000 votes. In the Reichstag the outright antirepublican forces of Communists and Nazis held only thirteen percent of the seats. The republican majority seemed at that time adequate to cope with all imaginable crises to come.

The world depression began in 1929. Germany, living on borrowed money, was among the first to experience its hardships. New loans stopped abruptly, old loans were called. Contraction started. Farm prices dropped, and farm people became militantly vocal. Factories closed, and the unemployed rioted. Customer nations, including the United States, raised tariffs, diminishing German exports. By January 1930 the jobless total had risen to 3,220,000—an increase of forty-three percent over 1928. By January 1931 unemployment reached 4,890,000. It climbed to 6,040,000 in the following twelve months. Mines, farms, factories, stores, services all pushed out unwanted men and women into the streets. The relentless, apparently endless process of disintegration, hunger and helplessness not only ground down the hopes attached to the Republic, but brought the once prevailing confidence in the liberal economic system into question, the whole existing order of things. If the democratic government could not bring this disaster to a close, who could?

The depression had not been caused by Germany, but that nation was to become its most conspicuous victim. Neither Germany nor any of the other large industrial powers of the world understood at that time how thoroughly their economies were interlinked, how quickly the misery of one nation would spread to others. No common defense lines had been built or even planned. National sovereignties and protective tariffs were still the order of the day.

Few Germans faced their combined economic and political crisis with quite the reluctance to see the government intervene in it which marked the early years of the depression in the United States. As long ago as 1881, the Iron Chancellor, Bismarck, had asked the Reichstag of his time: "Is it not rooted in our entire moral relationship that the individual who comes before his fellow citizens and says, 'I am physically fit, ready to work, but can find no job,' is entitled to say, 'Give me a job,' and the state is obligated to provide a job for him?"[5] This concept, still seriously questioned in the late 1960s in the United States, was in the background of German thinking and feeling during the crisis of the early 1930s. Hitler, who had blamed the government for inaction during the inflation of 1923 was now excoriating it for allowing the new and greater misery, and was gaining adherents with every new month of hardship, with every bit of street fighting in which his gang and supporters of the Communists (Red Front), industrialists (Stahlhelm), and Social Democrats (Reichsbanner) clashed. The Communists began gaining a little at the same time, at the expense of the Social Democrats who were in the government. In the 1931 elections the Nazi members of the Reichstag increased from twelve to 107, the Communist members from fifty-four to seventy-seven. An election in 1932 brought the Nazi members up to 230 seats out of the total of 608. This was not yet a majority control. Three years of continued depression had made this antidemocratic and racist revolutionary group the largest party in the German parliament.

At this point the storm warnings were up. The German state, suffering from its own and the West's economic collapse, had to act to save itself. Public works and large credits to create goods and jobs were proposed. They were opposed because they seemed to involve a depreciation of the mark. In this crisis, the trauma of the 1923 inflation froze the bones and minds of officials. They worried more about saving the German mark than about saving the German Republic. The cabinet, which was at that time largely Social Democrat and Christian Union, but with a Finance Minister from one of the more conservative parties, had an adequate parliamentary majority in 1930. The Finance Minister, however, caught up in this fear of inflation, suggested cutting the unemployment compensation benefits in order to help balance the budget. Under pressure of increasing unemployment and misery, the Social Democrats, whose strength was largely in the labor unions, objected. Industrialists and their party leaders pressed for the cut. The Finance Minister threatened to resign. On this small issue the last coalition of men committed to keeping Germany democratic broke up.

Heinrich Bruening of the Christian Union party became Chancellor with a conservative cabinet and made an unwise promise to hold new elections shortly. His program was to save the mark first and then to do something about unemployment. He proposed higher taxes on medium and large incomes, a cut in salaries of civil servants and in unemployment compensation. He could have taken less deflationary measures. He could have devalued the mark a little, as England had already devalued the pound sterling, and regained some lost export markets. He could have forced the creation of credit to finance employment on public works. He could have compromised on unemployment-compensation reduction and won back the Social Democrats' 153 important votes. Instead, he decided to "put the economy through the wringer," to deflate. This turned out to be not simply a bad decision but probably the worst.

A long record of assassinations, bullying, racist provocations, slander and street killings was by this time available to convince everyone— liberal, Catholic, industrialist, farmer, worker and unemployed—that no laws or rights would be respected if Hitler took power. The hemorrhage that was bleeding off support from the government had to be stanched. Bruening's insistence on applying in such an emergency the methods of orthodox financing useful for normal times brought plaudits only from those without responsibility for the survival of the Republic, and perhaps no major interest in it. The industrial groups saw to it that their representatives and their press made it as impossible as they could for him to use either old or new techniques to overcome the economic disaster. Some of them had already begun to finance the Nazis, others would soon do so. The Communists also sabotaged.

The parliamentary majority broke down as early as 1931, with the advent to the parliament of an additional ninety-five Nazis and twenty-three Communists. The joint revolutionary opposition had become thirty-two percent of the total. These two groups voted together against the administration on almost every occasion. To carry any measure, the government needed seventy-three percent of the other members, but the opposition of nationalists and conservatives made this impossible to obtain. Bruening had to turn the effective power back to the President, who was Hindenburg. After that, he could govern only as long as Hindenburg approved decrees put before him. The old General approved nothing that the more reactionary members of his entourage disliked. The mark was saved, but after unemployment went above six million in early 1932, the Nazis elected their 230 members and became the wave of an unhappy future.

A process of demoralization of the pro-Republic's parties set in. To prevent the worst, they felt obligated to vote for people and measures they despised. They lost morale and support with every vote. The Social Democrats, far less socialistic than democratic, felt this embarrassment keenly. In the early days of the Republic, they had not dared to unseat the semifeudal lords of the Ruhr and East Prussia estates or to break their dependence on the General Staff or to discredit the other reactionary and militaristic institutions which were helping the rising dictatorship directly or indirectly. In 1932 Social Democratic deputies voted for Bruening's deflationary measures, which they abhorred, because they feared any other course would lead to Hitler. But that course also led to Hitler. For the same reason, they had supported Hindenburg for President, although they knew he was approaching senility and was dangerously reactionary. The alternative was Hitler, who received thirty-seven percent of the vote in 1932. Similarly, Bruening's divided Catholic party decided it had no alternative except to work with the conservatives for deflation and for reelection of Hindenburg, whom they distrusted. Their own Chancellor Bruening was summoned into the presidential presence and dismissed like some maid caught stealing the household silver.

After Bruening, two Chancellors representing more conservative groups had an opportunity to rally remnants of the old institutions against the extremist threats. The first was von Papen, who came from the old nobility. His popular support was slight. He called the disastrous elections of July 1932, in which the Nazies got 230 Reichstag seats out of 608. He was succeeded by General von Schleicher of the officers corps, who at least realized that he needed some popular support and began discussions with the labor unions. This split his conservative support. Time was running out. Von Schleicher then tried to end a scandal involved in governmental subsidies to the large junker landowners in East Prussia. This cost him Hindenburg's favor. The Nazis, with their huge representation in the Reichstag and their active organization pushing and threatening in every corner of the nation, demanded the chancellorship. A palace vendetta began; the clique around the feeble, senile old President started bargaining with Hitler. They supported him on the theory he could not last; that after failure in office, he would be voted out and his whole movement would collapse. They did not understand that Hitler never would allow himself to be voted out of power. They did not comprehend, even with the Russian Bolshevik example before their eyes, that a dictatorship party which gains control by terrorizing and eliminating all opposition can govern, however badly or cruelly, indefinitely. They let Hitler become Chancellor in January 1933. The era of the one-party, authoritarian state soon began.

But before this happened, the parties which had founded and supported the Republic paid the penalties of inaction in the form of further compromises and frustration. Every Nazi success helped to create further disorder and to bring them closer to power as saviors from disorder. Election of 107 riotous and contemptuous Nazi deputies in 1930 speeded the withdrawal of foreign credits. Their street fighting intimidated supporters of the government and the government itself. Their extreme nationalistic slogans bought them some influence within the officer corps and made it even more hostile to the government. By the end of 1931, only a government willing to use the full national credit and the army could have won against the Nazis. But none of the republican parties could count on President Hindenburg's support, or that of the General Staff, for use of the army against these terrorists.

Possibly the dangerous corner of unemployment could have been turned by Bruening with a little more time, or by the two Chancellors who succeeded him, if some major German industrialists and financiers had not subsidized Hitler. Those men, who held in their own hands briefly the remaining chance for a free society in Germany, made huge contributions to him. They enabled Hitler to conduct a continuous whirlwind campaign by plane (then a novelty) in every corner of Germany. He piled up successes in municipal and state elections. Those funds also financed the continuous street fighting and intimidation. With this financing, these industrialists (not all) signed the Republic's death warrant, by acts of commission as others in the political field had done by acts of omission. Doubtless, many gave this support as insurance against Communism. While that fear was not imaginary, much of the Communist threat resulted from votes of the industrialist group in the Reichstag against state action which would have dampened the depression and decreased unemployment. Their own representatives had voted with the Communists against the Republic for some years. These supporters of Hitler had their own interests, which were not exactly his. They apparently obtained his promise that he would drop the Socialist part of the Nazi creed. This he did, later on, though it led to the organized murder in 1934 of many lesser party leaders in the Storm Troop section (S.A.) who believed in that part of the creed.

The supporting industrialists wanted a corporative state in which their influence could not be challenged by the electorate. They were promised some offices; Hugenberg, one of their leaders, was a member of the first Hitler cabinet. They thought they could control Hitler. Once their parties and the Center had voted plenary powers to Hitler, however, those hopes were ended. They gave this vote, although he already had shown he would not protect their interests.

No group reacted effectively to the danger of an authoritarian state which was in the making. The Social Democrats, who still in 1932 had control of Prussia and its state police, allowed themselves to be ousted without a fight. The Christian Democratic party, the Catholic Center, failed repeatedly. It was unwilling or unable to persuade its own Chancellor Bruening to abandon the deflationary policy. It tolerated his imitation of the Nazis in blaming the Allies. People were sure that, if a stiff stand against the Allies was all that was needed, the Nazis would be better at it than the Catholic Center. Leaders of this party also made the gross error of accepting an unwritten pledge from Chancellor Hitler that he would retain the multiparty system. On that dubious basis, its naïve and cowed deputies voted him full emergency powers. By that time the Communists, Hitler's decoys, had been expelled from the Reichstag. Only those Social Democrats who had not been jailed voted against plenary powers. The non-Nazi political parties were soon disbanded.

Following the Reichstag vote giving Hitler full powers, he was able to do as he wished with all German political, social and economic institutions and laws. He no longer had to consider any opposition from outside his own party. He boldly used the very economic measures from which Bruening and sound-money men had flinched. He established a controlled economy. Without major gold reserves, he reestablished almost full employment within a few years. The Germans were grateful for this. In addition, he gave them a sense of purpose, a national "occupational vocation," of making Germany the leading nation in Europe and of creating a new order. Germans then had no intimation that Hitler would carry this to the point of a war or that the Western powers would allow him to do so. Nor did all the people who voted for the Nazis and the guidance principle (*Fuehrer Prinzip*) understand that, when they cast off their individual responsibility to one another and left this to the state, they would no longer have any protection from either the state or individuals. They would have to accept without protest any amount of state brutality against others and finally against themselves. Their fear of Communism and of chaos had led them to accept, unwittingly, a major characteristic of the Communist society.

With Hitler's assumption of power in January 1933, the last major postwar mistake of the 1919–1933 period had been completed. The Allies and the United States had actively or passively participated in five of them; and those five mistakes had helped to magnify all the many serious failings of all the German groups from left to right, from rich to poor, which finally enslaved the Germans in a new totalitarianism.

The German experience with the rise and consequences of fascism cannot be written off as the unique and inimitable peculiarity of a politically backward people. It can be repeated elsewhere in the world, whenever and wherever major disorders in society provoke so much alienation and revulsion that people prefer the offers of reestablished law and order to such personal freedom as they possess. They may even fail to see in advance that they are necessarily yielding the one for the sake of obtaining the other. Their transition from a democratic to an authoritarian society is not necessarily a self-conscious one. They may know only that they want the disorder ended, and that the men who promise to end it for them do so in the name of the nation. Hitler's basically nationalistic appeal to stand up for Germany was strong and was widely accepted, and can be repeated in any language.

The United States is not immune to a fascist government. The four problem areas described in Chapter 1 all involve potentials of disorder and failure. By-products of both invite accusations of incompetence, strong arm methods, organized efforts to subdue opposition, dragoon acquiescence, close off free discussion and smother democracy.

The German agony is far from irrelevant to the people of the United States during the last part of this century. The assassinations of President John Kennedy, Martin Luther King, Jr., and Robert Kennedy had their counterparts in the murder of several great and able German liberals in the early 1920s. The frustrations and sacrifices of a war that was not won according to expectations, and the later pressures on the middle classes and workers exercised by diminishing status and street disorders were not entirely dissimilar. Those objectors who wrapped themselves in the flag had an advantage over those who did not. In Germany the Communist minority, seeking to serve Russia or the world proletariat, actually served the fascists well, providing a conspicuous cause for fear, an excuse for terror and for the decisive financing of the fascists by industrialists. In the United States the black and white militants, with their violence and nihilism seem unaware of history, or indifferent to it, and so occasionally appear willing to serve brutal reaction in much the same way.

Other similarities may be recalled. The Germans of the 1920s and early 1930s had cause for disappointment and complaint. Their older institutions had led them into war and defeat, had later managed to manipulate a demoralizing inflation and to checkmate the Republic at almost every turn. Yet the Germans, young and old, did not turn against those who caused their basic troubles, they turned instead against the new and democratic Republic and made it their victim. It was there and it was vulnerable. They accepted without too much questioning the vague promises of the Nazis that order and the old glory would be restored. Most of them surely never expected to see a complete police state, one-man government, another war, or the murder of a whole minority race, as the results of their support of those who promised this return to greatness, law and order. In the United States young people also have some legitimate cause for disappointment. Many of them see around them a society which has substituted the search for power, comfort and wealth for any pursuit of higher ideals and goals. The national demand in the 1960s that they kill and be killed in a war which they consider both immoral and futile—violating both schools of American thought in one blow—makes life a kind of horror for them. The national decision to downgrade domestic programs which would eliminate slums and create opportunities for the underprivileged in order to finance that war, disgusted many. They listened to the frequent sneers at "do gooders" coming from adults who faithfully attended churches dedicated to the spirit of the greatest doer of good in history, and detected the corrupt odor of hypocrisy. They have some cause to be concerned with the future and character of their nation, particularly with the rapid polarization of fear around the black minority.

This concern and disappointment hardly free them from the obligation, intellectual and moral, to do better than the Germans did, to learn from history how fascism grows, to weigh the chances for obtaining a better life under a democracy as against those under an authoritarian or even a semi-police state. Nor does it free them either from the obligation to protest and alter injustice and stupidity wherever they find it or from the human obligation not to lead their followers into the jails of a police state under the impression that they are entering a brave new world. Yet young black and white militants alike had already in the late 1960s been engaging in activities for which the most backward-yearning elements in any nation would probably have paid them well, if that had been necessary or possible. Burning and looting, forcible disbarment of white teachers from schools, demands for racial resegregation, openly expressed contempt for the majority on racial grounds, all somewhat explicable in terms of past and current grievances and neglect, are not tactics which have any historical record of encouraging or even permitting peaceful and necessary social progress.

In turn the student resort to violence, along with the police violence which provoked it, or which it evoked, and along with attempts to halt and degrade the political process by preventing candidates from speaking, have about the same relationship to the creation of a more satisfying society as the violence used against a village in Vietnam has to converting its surviving inhabitants to the virtues of democracy. Some history cannot be ignored, and has to be learned before the time for learning is passed. The semi-civil war in the German streets in the early 1930s, where armed gangs of Nazis, Communists, Social Democrats and Conservatives fought one another and the police, all ended with irresistible demands for law and order, a strong government which could end the violence. Even in Czarist Russia, where multitudes hated the system, the terrorists of the 1880s managed to persuade many people that it was preferable to their own rule. In later decades the tactics of violent confrontations, bomb-throwing and bank robberies, always manipulated by a few determined individuals who evaded control of the political parties they claimed to represent, helped to discredit all democratic opposition to the Czar. Incitements to violence can always be expected to come from those who hate democracy and seek to destroy it. But when it comes from those whose study of history has informed them that mankind can only survive if its institutions are changed to meet new challenges, and that democracy offers the only road to peaceful change, violence can be as fatal as it is stupid.

CHAPTER 11

The Munich
Syndrome

 The word "Munich" has in time come to mean an unnecessary and disastrous surrender on the part of men and nations who were able to prevent aggression and subsequent war, but failed in their duty to their nations and civilization.

In an effort to be guiltless of any similar default of courage and spirit, a British Prime Minister, Anthony Eden, saw the Egyptian leader Nasser—who had seized the Suez Canal—as a new Hitler, and joined British forces with Israeli and French troops in an attack. This was in 1956, and it shifted world attention from a merciless Russian reconquest of Hungary. At that time neither President Eisenhower nor his Secretary of State, John Foster Dulles, could see Nasser as another Hitler and objected to the attack. The Russians joined the Americans and even rattled nuclear artillery. Ten years later the bad word "Munich" came into usage again. It even seemed possible that American officials would find the challenge of Munich not only in Vietnam but in every other corner of the world (except the Middle East) where national sovereignty or even internal order was threatened. It also seemed possible that other parts of the world would be as skeptical about the analogy as Eisenhower and Dulles were in 1956.

Whether in the form of armed invasion or in that of foreign-fed subversion and revolution, the confrontations of the future will continue to evoke memories and invocations of the events before, during and after

Munich. The world's current competition in ideology-fed powers practically insures such a practice, and the growing contrast between a deprived, overpopulated and retarded southern hemisphere and an advantaged northern hemisphere may increase rather than diminish the opportunity for and number of those encounters and comparisons.

Some parts of the dramatic and tragedy-loaded events at Munich are well known. Some are not, including the evidence of Russian willingness to prevent any surrender at Munich, and the French and English reluctance to invite that nation's help. The episode was accompanied by a really remarkable obfuscation of public opinion by political leaders in England and France, as well as a discovery that the self-determination of small nations could lead them to weakness rather than strength, and their neighbors to the temptation of conquest and loot. The mindless repetition by the British Prime Minister, Neville Chamberlain, of the papal and presidential error of failing to gain prior commitments from potential allies again demanded its built-in penalty. The subsequent moral Munich of the German churches, the cynical submersion of creeds by Germany and Russia in 1939 in favor of national advantage also need to be noted. Nor should the element of luck be disregarded, the somewhat casual and accidental way in which Hitler made it easy for the United States to enter Europe to defeat him, the remarkable way in which French weakness tempted German arrogance into eventual defeat.

The causes for Munich go back to the errors made by victors and vanquished alike after the First World War, which have been noted in the previous chapter. Those continued to work their effects into the crucial late 1930s, at a time when the Western nations were still being debilitated by the historic depression of those years, while Germany was mastering it and being invigorated by that success. The failure of two great powers of Europe—England and France—and of the United States to counterattack that somewhat earlier economic threat with all the seriousness and resources they would have applied to a war, left them weak of will, confused by a sense of guilt toward Germany, almost convinced by the evidence of their own incompetence at home that they had no competence or interest in the safety of other nations, the peace of the world.

The fragile structure of Western international law and order began splintering even before Nazi terrorists in Austria had murdered Chancellor Dollfuss in 1934. Collapse of the world's peace machinery had begun in 1931. In that year the League of Nations was unable to halt a Japanese aggression against Manchuria, duplicating the failure of the special Great Powers treaties (to which the United States was a party) for China's protection. An investigation, report and admonition were all that the League could produce. In 1932 German reparations payments, one ladder by which the Nazis had climbed to power, simply disappeared from the picture. International trade had almost come to a stop. With the disappearance of reparations, Allied payments of war debts to the United States also stopped. That was interpreted as willful breach of contract and reenforced the old American isolationism.

Also in 1932 a disarmament conference, which had begun inauspiciously when Japanese guns were shelling Shanghai in China, failed either to produce any major disarmament or French-British unity. At the conference France tried to squeeze out for itself every ounce of security; while Germany, harassed by the Nazis, tried to squeeze out every pound of equality with the other powers. After Hitler took control in 1933, he told the West that Germany must have 300,000 troops instead of the 100,000 allowed by the Versailles Treaty, plus the large paramilitary formations of the S.A. (Sturm Abteilung, Storm Trooper section, Brown Shirts) and those of the S.S. (Schutzstaffel, élite guards, Black Shirts). By 1934 the German budget openly showed large expenditures for rearmament, in violation of the Treaty. No effective protests were made. The French-British split opened wider when England made a naval treaty with Germany. Amazingly, this allowed Germany to concentrate its new naval strength in submarines. Ten years later those very U-boats almost strangled England and nearly won the war for Germany. This separate treaty with Germany violated the spirit of the understanding (Stresa Pact) among England, France and Italy to treat with Germany together, not separately. The French felt betrayed, the old picture of perfidious Albion was dusted off and hung again in the French parlor.

Suspicion that Nazi Germany was getting ready for expansion was first registered by Italy and Russia. Italy was concerned directly because it had a joint border with Austria and indirectly because it wanted a free hand for imperialistic adventure of its own in Africa. With Germany instead of Austria on its border, Italy would not have that free hand. As an opening gambit, Rome suggested to London and Paris that all three nations encourage Germany to expand into Poland instead of into Austria. This would violate, of course, their commitments to the League of Nations. Besides, France had a defensive alliance with Poland. Nevertheless, French indifference toward its East European allies was rumored. So Poland signed a nonaggression pact with Germany early in 1934. The rising Nazi power had received the first official recognition of its strength. This pact disturbed the other allies of France.

It was on January 30, 1934, that Hitler said: "The assertion that the German Reich intends to violate the Austrian state is absurd, and cannot be substantiated."[1] In July the Nazi underground in Austria murdered the Chancellor, took over the government radio briefly, and called for an armed uprising to make Austria German and Nazi. France immediately announced that an *Anschluss* meant war. Italy moved troops up to the Brenner Pass. Thereupon Hitler gently proclaimed that he had no aggressive designs. For the moment Austria was safe. However, after that expression of determination by Italy and France, the great split in the West began. What Italy had done to keep the peace in Austria it immediately proceeded to undo on a grandiose scale. Mussolini's Italy had noted that Germany had not even been reproved when in early 1935 it repudiated the Treaty of Versailles by announcing creation of an army and navy regardless of treaty limitations. Italy concluded that it also could violate the League Covenant with impunity. In the fall it attacked impoverished, underdeveloped, helpless Ethiopia. This was an uncomplicated aggression. The Emperor of Ethiopia promptly appealed to the League for protection. The world sat up with a start. If not only Nazi Germany but Fascist Italy could ignore all the agreements which bound them, then the peace of all Europe would be jeopardized.

At about this time the Soviet Union also saw the danger to itself of an aggressive Germany. It reversed its earlier efforts to weaken Western Europe. It instructed its subservient Communist parties abroad to stop calling the democratic Socialists and liberals "Social Fascists," and to make a "popular front" with them. The Soviet Union also joined the League, and there became the most vocal opponent of aggression. It also signed a defensive alliance with France in 1935.

Italy's attack on Ethiopia presented France and England with an awkward choice. If League sanctions (embargoes, blockades, armed force) were voted by the League and succeeded in stopping Italy, Mussolini would be more likely to cast his lot with expansionist Germany. If France, Britain and other League members showed themselves incapable of preventing aggression, all the world would know their impotence, the League would disintegrate, and Hitler's road would be opened wide. Neither choice was free from risks, in either case Germany would be the *tertius gaudens*, the jeering third-party beneficiary.

The watching world saw that the decision to be made by England and France was crucial. Either the League would justify itself by stopping this aggression, or it would fail as a peace-keeping body. The French position was complicated by the dealings of Premier Pierre Laval with Mussolini. On a visit to Rome that spring, he apparently promised a free hand to Italy in Ethiopia in return for Italian support for French claims in other parts of North Africa. Many believed so. Further, there was no interest in Paris or London in toppling Mussolini from power by frustrating his desire to imitate ancient Rome. But local and world opinion demanded that some action be taken. After long cabinet discussions, the British Foreign Secretary, Sir Samuel Hoare, announced to a League session: "The League stands, and my country stands with it, for the collective maintenance of the Covenant in its entirety, and particularly for steady and collective resistance to all acts of unprovoked aggression."

Cheered by this clear British commitment, the League voted to impose some sanctions on the Italian aggressor, although no embargo on oil. But these brave words turned out to be part of a process—possibly not deliberate but one repeated with increasing frequency—of raising people's hopes only to disappoint them a little later. The best of men could be turned into cynics by it. For a while discussions went on as to whether Italy would wage war or be incapable of doing so if its Achilles' heel were wounded by an oil embargo. Then a purposeful Paris leak to the press deflated the English pose of righteousness. This revealed a secret Hoare-Laval agreement to appease Italy with a major share of the territory of the little nation it was invading. While public indignation at this duplicity led to Hoare's resignation, it did not result in any oil embargo on Italy by the League. Mussolini consequently was able to fuel his ships, planes, tanks and trucks, and to complete his conquest of Ethiopia with mustard gas and aerial bombing.

The democratic nations in Hitler's eyes now seemed as spineless, ineffective, incapable of unity and survival as the democratic parties he had destroyed in Germany. So the next year he risked a large venture of his own. Hitler timed this when the French Chamber had voted out one administration, the people were waiting to elect another one, and no one in France was really responsible for anything, let alone the peace of Europe. France was to pay endlessly for the fear of a strong executive which had created this particular immobilism. It was also a moment when the British people, if not their government, were furious with the French for, as they thought, frustrating the oil embargo and pulling the League down in humiliating helplessness. They were not inclined to press their leaders to help France at that moment.

The Rhineland was the peril point. It was the legally demilitarized area which gave the French their only assurance that another war would be fought on German rather than French soil. In January the outgoing French government had asked Britain what it would do if Hitler moved in troops to occupy that part of Germany. London replied by asking what the French proposed to do. There was no answer, for by that time the Paris government had fallen and no new one had been elected. So there was no concerted plan to prevent Hitler from altering the entire military and political balance of Europe by occupying the Rhineland. There was nothing in Hitler's way.

On March 7, 1936, Hitler sent his troops into the Rhineland. It became known later that they had orders to retire if they met resistance. There was none. They met only a complete default of national self-interest and international responsibility. At that moment France and her allies, Poland and Czechoslovakia, had at least twice as many fully equipped divisions as the Germans. The French Chief of Staff, General Gamelin, added to the French cabinet's indecision by claiming that he would need to have a complete mobilization in order to throw even a few divisions into the Rhineland. Any determined Premier could have overruled that preposterous assertion. Poland, almost alone, saw the significance of the German move and offered its troops to France. Days later two members of the French cabinet journeyed to London to ask Prime Minister Baldwin what he could do to help. One of them (Flandin) later reported that Baldwin had told him that, even if the risk of war was only one in a hundred, that was too much for unprepared Britain.[2] Still, France might have acted alone. It underrated the dangerous momentum which successful arrogance lends to imperialistic expansion and did nothing except protest.

March 7, 1936, was the decisive day in the twenty-year interwar period. From that day on nothing went well fror Britain or France. German troops on the Rhine, plus a heavy flight of gold from France managed by the financial community, crippled the newly elected Popular Front government there before it could begin to function. With hostile forces in Italy and on the Rhine, Paris felt more than ever dependent on London for leadership.

In May 1936 the Spanish Civil War began. That army revolt, supported at first by Italy and then by Germany, threatened to put hostile forces on almost every land border of France. Even by faithfully following Britain's indifference toward the Spanish conflict, France ended up with hostile forces on three of its borders. There seemed no way out. The French people began to believe that their Maginot Line of defensive fortresses was their best hope, possibly their only one.

To make matters worse for France, its 1935 defensive alliance with the Soviet Union now appeared worthless. Russian purges, public treason trials and executions followed one another from 1936 through 1937, when a number of Soviet military leaders were executed, and continued into 1938. Russia seemed to be on the brink of a complete breakdown of morale and production. This encouraged pro-German activity in the eastern areas nominally allied to France. Russia looked so weak that Hitler spoke publicly of the wonderful opportunities which would be open to Germany if it possessed the riches of the Ukraine and Urals. This bit of hungry audacity brought an immediate response from Russia that it was ready for war at any time. However, the rest of the world felt free to doubt it. France, almost surrounded by hostile powers, seemed quite isolated, and the English officials, in spite of an alliance covering an attack on France's own frontiers, seemed willing to leave France in that insecurity.

Gazing happily on this disorder abroad, Hitler called his general officers into conference in Berlin in November 1937. His analysis of the situation was that neither Britain nor France would fight if Germany took over Austria and Czechoslovakia. He announced to his officers his intention of seizing those two nations by force, or by agreement with London and Paris. He believed there was no determination to stop him and no policeman able to do so. Earlier in that year, the Belgians had come to much the same conclusion. They had withdrawn from the Locarno Pact commitments made to Britain and France. They sought such refuge as might still exist in neutrality.

After Hitler's November statement, the world was less than two years from war. The significant moves toward it were marked by fantastic German triumphs. The first came in Austria. The plan for its annexation had been laid aside after the 1934 murder of Dollfuss brought Italy and France into open opposition to Germany. But the situation had changed greatly since that year. The successful Nazi effort to obtain control of Austria began in February 1938. Hitler summoned the Austrian Chancellor to Berchtesgaden and delivered an oral ultimatum. As a result of this threat, Dr. Schuschnigg appointed the chief Austrian Nazi (Seyss-Inquart) his Minister of the Interior, the agency in charge of public law and order. Immediately subversion removed its masks. Uniformed gangs marched through the streets shouting *"Ein Reich! Ein Volk! Ein Fuehrer!"* and demanded that the Nazi swastika be displayed on public buildings. The doubtful saw the way the wind was blowing and joined in subversion. The Chancellor had inherited a divided nation. Three groups disputed for power: the Christian Social (Catholic) party, the Social Democrats and the Nazis. The nation was governed under a form of semiauthoritarianism with clerical support. Social Democrats had been shot down by the hundreds. Still, Austrians were not fanatics, independence from Nazi Germany was important to many, and the Chancellor believed that up to eighty percent of the people would oppose *Anschluss*.

Would anyone help? France had once said that *l'Anschluss, c'est la guerre!* Italy had once marshaled troops in 1934 when Dollfuss was murdered. Britain had once insisted on Austrian independence. But since then its pro-League of Nations Foreign Minister, Anthony Eden, had resigned because of differences with Prime Minister Neville Chamberlain about appeasing Italy and Germany. Chamberlain now uttered the chilling words:

The League as constituted today is unable to provide collective security for anybody. . . . We must not try to delude small weak nations into thinking that they will be protected by the League against aggression.[3]

In spite of this warning, Chancellor Schuschnigg acted. Suddenly he ordered up the police, forbade further Nazi demonstrations, and called for a quick plebiscite on the question of Austrian independence. He thought it would show the world that Hitler's claims that the Austrians wanted to join the Nazi Reich were false. He expected a vote for independence from sixty to eighty percent. This was intolerable to Hitler. It would have made a mockery of his claims to expansion on grounds of self-determination. At this crucial moment the French government resigned. Hitler seized the occasion to act quickly, as he had done two years earlier when France had also voluntarily decapitated itself. He ordered the Austrian Chancellor to postpone the plebiscite, under threat of invasion. Schuschnigg was forced to agree. Then he was ordered to resign in favor of the Nazi leader Seyss-Inquart, to give two-thirds of the cabinet positions to Nazis, and to allow freedom of the streets to Nazi violence. Schuschnigg decided not to shed blood. He denounced as lies the German contentions that the disorders were out of his control, prayed God to guard Austria, and left. His resignation did not protect Austria from invasion. German troops marched in on March 11, 1938, moving to their appointed billets with clocklike precision. German police followed after them, herding thousands of listed anti-Nazi Austrians to jails, concentration camps and death. A strategic area had been lost for the West. All this came less than ten months after Hitler had told the credulous world: "Germany neither intends nor wishes to interfere in the internal affairs of Austria, to annex Austria or to conclude an *Anschluss.*"[4]

With this seizure of Austria, it might have been clear that a tiger was loose in Europe, that no one was safe, that heroic measures were needed at once. German troops now were on the borders of Italy and Czechoslovakia. France was separated farther from her allies in Poland, Czechoslovakia, Rumania and Yugoslavia, by forts and armies. Still, there were statesmen who thought that possibly Nazi Germany would be satiated by the conquest of Austria and would stop there. Others, however, remarked that England was in danger of what it had struggled against for centuries—the domination of Europe by a single power.

The fine principle of self-determination of small nations, which President Wilson had advocated in 1918, was turning into an advantage to expansionist Germany. The old Austro-Hungarian Empire had split into a large number of smaller political units, and Hitler could pick them off one by one. Wilson knew that these nations needed at least some degree of economic cohesion and wanted to see them create an economic unity. That wish was not fulfilled. The result was a new balkanization in Europe. Hitler was soon to move from Austria to Czechoslovakia and then to Poland. The bewildered observing world was to see Wilson's peace principles converted by Hitler into excuses for aggression. He managed to persuade Germans and others that some people of German extraction were being badly treated in each country and that he was, in the name of self-determination, rescuing them from oppression. At a time when much of the Western world was still suffering from a lingering sense of guilt about its treatment of Germany after the war, this statement found some listeners abroad.

However, the people of Britain and France probably were more willing to take strong preventive measures against any further German or Italian aggression than their political leaders believed. It was recalled that in England in 1935 a private "Peace Ballot" had been taken. That was shortly after Germany's unilateral repudiation of the Versailles limitations on rearmament but before Italy's attack on Ethiopia. Eleven and a half million people took part in it, about half the total number of voters in public elections at that time. Over ten million voted in favor of stopping aggression by nonmilitary means. The vote for stopping it by military means was 6,784,000, or eighty-four percent of those voting on that particular question. In the general election of that year all parties re-endorsed the League of Nations. The Conservatives won again, and the genial Stanley Baldwin was again Prime Minister. He yielded place to Neville Chamberlain in May 1937. The 1935 election, the last before the war, did not show reluctance to use either economic or military sanctions to prevent aggression in Europe. Yet only shortly after this election the Hoare-Laval agreement to give Italy a part of Ethiopia was discovered. Only a few years later Chamberlain, who had certainly been given no mandate from the electorate to do so, decided that German domination of Europe was negotiable.

After Austria had been taken by the Germans, in March 1938, the Soviet Union showed an interest in preventing any further German expansion eastward. With that conquest, German troops had moved to the border of Hungary, one step closer to Russia, and posed a threat to Russian ambitions among the Danubian nations. Those troops made Czechoslovakia vulnerable on a new border, one which the Czechs hastened to fortify. Shortly after the coup in Austria, Soviet Foreign Minister Litvinov proposed to England and France that they consult on practical measures to prevent further aggression. Unfortunately, the Russian record had not been conducive to trust. Soviet emissaries had been active for years in stirring up revolt. At the time of the Italian conquest of Ethiopia, the Soviet Union had been the most eloquent of the protesting nations and had demanded rigid sanctions against Italy. Yet it continued to ship strategic materials to the offending nation.[5] So the sudden efforts of Russia to contain Germany, in cooperation with France, Britain and the Eastern European nations, seemed spurious at worst, undesirable at least to most Western statesmen who heard about them. They saw in the Russian move only an effort to push the Western powers toward war with one another. This, they feared, would result in the destruction of the capitalist system, after which the Soviets would move in.[6]

In any case, neither the United States nor the Soviet Union was invited to take part in the events which soon led to Munich and beyond it to war. To Russia's March proposal that measures to stop aggression be developed at once, Chamberlain replied coldly that "a conference called only to organize concentrated action against aggression would not necessarily have a favorable effect upon the prospects of European peace." This was a most remarkable assertion. He followed it up by refusing to make any commitment to protect exposed Czechoslovakia, although France and Russia did so. He was unwilling to face Hitler with a coalition of nonfascist nations, but he was willing to appease German demands for more *Lebensraum* and more power. Normally a battle royal could have been expected in Parliament on this Chamberlain position, but it did not take place. This was avoided because the Prime Minister told the House of Commons he had received definite assurances from Germany that the integrity of Czechoslovakia would be respected. His statement was not completely accurate. However, it reassured the British in the face of Hitler's record of double talk on Austria, and postponed the full attack on Chamberlain's policies which Winston Churchill and others had prepared. It also delayed a British decision to rearm, although rapid German rearmament was well known.

Meanwhile, March, the month in which Austria was occupied, ended with Hitler calling in the supposedly independent Nazi leaders of the Sudeten region of Czechoslovakia. He ordered them to begin disorderly pressures on the Prague government; Konrad Henlein, chief of those henchmen, interpreted Hitler's orders to mean: "We must always demand so much that we can never be satisfied."[7] He understood the basic Nazi strategy in Europe, which the Western statesmen did not comprehend.

The elaborate machinery to destroy Czechoslovakia was shifted into high political and military gear. Capture of Austria had been accompanied by the claim that Austrians were really Germans and naturally wanted to join the greater Reich. The attack on Czechoslovakia was preceded by the claim that the German-speaking minority, living in the

Sudetenland, adjoining Germany, was suffering grievous injustice. While Nazi leaders there were creating "evidence" of such injustices and demanding redress, Hitler launched a campaign to divide Western public opinion on the subject. In April the extreme-right press of France favored the Nazis. In addition to its normal scurrilous attacks on Paris officials, it publicized the slogan: "Do you want to die for Czechoslovakia?" A year later, after that nation had been lost and Poland was the new target, the slogan changed to: "Do you want to die for Danzig?" At Karlsbad the spokesman for the Nazi Sudetens, Henlein, put forth eight demands of autonomy. They included no suggestion of secession to Germany. The Henlein demands led to a conference in London between the French political leaders and the British inner cabinet. French Premier Édouard Daladier argued that a firm statement of intent by both of the Western nations might avoid a war. Chamberlain replied that Czechoslovakia was now almost surrounded by German troops, that the other eastern allies of France were weak, and that Britain was not ready for war. Clearly, England would give Czechoslovakia no help.

Two men who thought that peace could be obtained by making small grants of power to Hitler were in positions where they could affect events and opinion seriously. One of them was Georges Bonnet, Foreign Minister of France. The other was Neville Chamberlain. Neither had any feeling that the Czechs, "the little-known people" as the Prime Minister once described them, had through two decades of democratic life won a moral right to continue existing as a nation. They seemed to be an obstacle in the way of peace in the West. On May 7, 1938, the British ambassador in Berlin told the Germans that Britain and France were urging the Czechs to settle the Sudeten grievances. A little later, foreign-press correspondents in London were quoting Chamberlain's private conversations that neither France nor the Soviet Union, and least of all Britain, would fight for the threatened little nation and that it could hardly survive in its present form.

These views were not arrived at without German encouragement. Hitler brought to the effort to destroy the Western world's power system more skill than the Communists had formerly used, and fewer handicaps. His authoritarian society had, for example, put industrial leaders and publishers under strict state control but had not eliminated them. It had taken over their function without destroying their status or their capacity to earn profits. It was managed by men from the middle class, as the Communist society had been to some extent in its early days. However, it carried the banner of nationalistic dynamism instead of proletarian revolution and working-class control. It did not fit neatly into any preestablished pattern of fears and revulsions. This facade of respectability made it possible for a Chamberlain to convince himself that Nazi leaders might believe in the sanctity of contracts, that they had only normal political aspirations for glory and power and might be legitimately concerned with the fate of German minorities in Czechoslovakia and Poland. Italian Fascist leaders, by contrast, were far more aware of the difference between the reality and the facade. In a telephone conversation with Hitler in September 1939, a little before the long-scheduled German attack on Poland, Foreign Minister Ciano, with complete cynicism asked Hitler what day had been chosen by Germany for its discovery of a finally intolerable outrage by Poland against long-suffering Germans in that country.

The demoralization process was far from complete in May of 1938. During the municipal elections in Czechoslovakia, Sudeten-inspired riots broke out. German troops were on maneuvers near the Czech border. Tension grew rapidly. The Czechs ordered partial mobilization. They were ready to defend themselves. They had twenty-one first-line divisions, fifteen to sixteen reserve divisions, and modern front-line fortifications equal to France's Maginot Line. Czech decisiveness changed the picture abruptly. France spoke out: her troops would move if the German army crossed the Czech frontier. Russia spoke out. London told Berlin it could not remain uninvolved. That show of strength did it. Hitler backed down—for the moment. He ordered his Sudetens to negotiate quietly for a while. But he sat down in frustration and wrote his order for Operation Green: his "unchangeable purpose to destroy Czechoslovakia through military action in a foreseeable period." He fixed the deadline for October 1.

Hitler understood that, despite the May demonstration of Allied unity, the links between Czechoslovakia, Russia, Britain and France were weak. He set out to break them. To dissuade the French, Hitler ordered fortification of the Rhineland. The French were to worry about the number of lives they could lose there. In England, he needed to do little. To the astonishment of many, Chamberlain had seen in the effective May unity not strength but only danger.

The Prime Minister on July 18 recommended to the Czechs that they accept his colleague Lord Runciman as arbitrator, or at least as counselor, in the Sudetenland negotiations. The Czechs objected that this would raise the Sudeten Nazis to a governmental level. The Paris cabinet divided over it at first. However, the French were pleased that Chamberlain was taking the responsibility for solving the problem, relieving them of it. So they joined in pressuring the Czechs to accept. This forced the Czechs to do so—a fatal mistake. Then they were amazed by Chamberlain's three statements to the House of Commons on July 28 which seemed to them to have no relationship with the truth. The Runciman Mission, he said, had been sent "in response to a request from the government of Czechoslovakia"; the British government had not been pressuring Prague; there was now "a relaxation of that sense of tension which six months ago was present." At the same time, the Czechs heard from Paris that, while Premier Daladier was using the expected phrases about France honoring its Czech alliance, Foreign Minister Bonnet was informing all and sundry that neither France nor Britain intended to resist the aggressive German policy.

These developments were not to the liking of the Russians. They stepped back onto the stage. They had repeatedly told the Germans and Czechs that they would fight for Czechoslovakia if France, too, honored its own alliance. But this promise had always had an air of unreality about it. Russia did not border on the threatened nation; its troops could not help the Czechs without crossing Poland or Rumania. The Poles, who in 1920 had taken several million Russians and Ukrainians, refused to allow Russian troops to enter their area for any purpose. Rumania at first had adopted the same position. However, on September 11 in Geneva, Soviet Foreign Minister Litvinov informed Bonnet of France in the presence of Rumanian Foreign Minister Comnen that Rumania had agreed to allow Russian troops to cross to aid Czechoslovakia as soon as the League of Nations declared the latter country a victim of aggression.[8] In order to make such a declaration by the League effective, Litvinov suggested that it be called into session at once. This development threatened a two-front war against Germany. It was the one eventuality which the German General Staff was bent on avoiding, and the one area of strategy where the generals still had a veto over Hitler.

This sudden opportunity to reverse the danger came a little late. Demoralization had been carried on for several months. On September 4 Czech President Beneš (after being let down by Chamberlain and Bonnet) had told the Sudeten negotiators he would grant their demands. Amazed, they hardly knew what to ask, for their orders from Hitler were to drag out discussions until a date as yet unspecified. Beneš took his pen in hand and said: "Dictate, and I will take it down." He granted everything they suggested except their demand for a profascist foreign policy. He agreed to full autonomy. Notably, they made no demand for cession of Czech territory to Germany. Hitler had ordered a crescendo of Sudeten revolt to peak after his forthcoming speech at the Nuremberg Nazi Congress beginning September 11—the day Litvinov made his crucial statement to Bonnet. On that same day, Chamberlain again confused the situation. While he told the world that "Germany cannot with impunity carry out a rapid and successful military campaign against Czechoslovakia without fear of intervention by France and Great Britain,"[9] he refused to tell the French officials what, specifically,

Britain would do in a military showdown. His silence told the French more than his public words.

Probably neither the English nor French publics were aware at that point of how thoroughly committed Chamberlain and Bonnet had become to their appeasement policy, or how completely closed their minds were to the new situation and opportunity. Carefully considered, Chamberlain's public warning had simply told Germany to avoid using provocative military means when less violent means might do. Chamberlain expressed, in a way, an esthetics of surrender. Bonnet, supposedly the bearer of the good news of the Russian-Rumanian agreement threatening a two-front defensive war if Hitler attacked, was significantly unvocal. Bonnet over a period had undercut what little determination his Premier had occasionally mustered. Now Bonnet minimized to the French cabinet the significance of the Litvinov lifesaver. He reported only that the Russians and Rumanians had "wrapped themselves in League procedure." To that deceptive remark, he added that they had shown little eagerness for action.[10] The one new factor which might have stopped Hitler without war may not have been known to Premier Daladier. It was not known to the French and British people.

The fateful day for Europe is frequently fixed as September 13, 1938, although in this account it is March 7, 1936 (the day when Germany took the Rhineland). September 13 was the day following Hitler's Nuremberg speech. On that occasion he had made his intentions clear. He charged that the "noble," German-speaking Sudeten people were being mistreated by the "contemptible" Czechs and that justice had to be done. Europe realized that, after such a challenge, unless France mobilized to protect its ally the Czechs were deserted. The French cabinet met. Six were for mobilization, including Daladier; four against, including Bonnet. Because of this division it was decided to let Chamberlain settle the Czech-German dispute as he saw fit. The French government defaulted on its treaty pledge and on its responsibility. This opened for France a troubled road of guilt and humiliation; in the course of time it would wander through Compiègne, Dienbienphu and Algeria, and change the life of France.

Chamberlain thereupon acted with dispatch. He accepted a recommendation by Lord Halifax never previously suggested. It was for immediate transfer to Germany, without even a plebiscite, of all frontier areas (including fortresses) of Czechoslovakia having a majority of German-speaking people. For such a far-reaching proposal, Britain's unwritten constitution warranted consultation with His Majesty's Opposition. None took place. Chamberlain persuaded the French to accept the Halifax recommendation with the provision that, after Czechoslovakia had been dismembered and defortified, the security of the truncated remainder would be guaranteed by Britain, France and Germany. The guarantees of defense which Britain had refused even to France for twenty years it was now offering to a defenseless fragment of a nation far away from its lines of communication and the possibility of help. The British historian P. A. Reynolds has observed:

> It was indeed a somewhat fantastic procedure—to strip a country of its strategic frontier and the powerful fortifications without which it could not defend itself, and then to guarantee the defenseless rump. All was staked on Hitler's good faith.[11]

The worthlessness of Hitler's word was well known by this time. So when this course was broached to the Czechs, they protested vehemently. Where were decency and honor? But the Anglo-French pressure on them was severe. Bonnet insisted: *"Acceptez! Acceptez!"* The British told the Czechs that, if they resisted this dismemberment, Britain and France would stand aside in case of a German invasion. The Czechs naturally understood this to mean that they would be blamed for war if they resisted, but if they agreed, then Britain and France would protect them from invasion. On September 19, in Paris, Daladier and Bonnet dared not at first show the full note to the Czechs to their cabinet colleagues, and Beneš refused to agree. He offered to arbitrate the differences with Germany under the 1925 arbitration treaty. He was told not to be frivolous, Europe's peace was at stake. At Geneva, Litvinov repeated publicly the Soviet Union's pledge to respect its treaty. In Prague, the Russian ambassador assured Beneš that Russian troops would be allowed to race across Rumania to the rescue as soon as the League was formally apprised of the aggression (instead of waiting for a League decision). That meant at the moment when German troops crossed the Czech border. But Anglo-French pressure was too strong. On September 22 Beneš submitted. Bonnet tried to make it appear that the Czechs had asked for French pressure as camouflage to justify their own desire to surrender sovereignty. Throughout September the French leaders neither consulted their Chamber seriously nor suggested to their people that France's safety was deeply involved with the fate of Czechoslovakia.

Britain was still poorly armed. Even German occupation of the Rhineland and Austria had not changed that. Chamberlain spoke for a nation which had not been standing still in the rearmament race, but slipping backward at an alarming rate because of Nazi speed. He went to Godesberg to meet Hitler on September 22. He offered the whole Sudetenland and its fortifications without any plebiscite, apparently believing that he was meeting all of the German *Fuehrer's* requirements.

But, since neither France nor Britain would defend Czechoslovakia,

Hitler increased his demands. He listened to Chamberlain's surrender and replied: "I am really very sorry [*es tut mir furchtbar leid*], but that doesn't suit me anymore." What he now wanted was all that area with its fortifications, arms, munitions, cattle and raw materials plus an occupation by his own army within a few days—an invasion. This was too much for the Czechs. It was too much for the British cabinet. Even the French, in spite of Bonnet, rejected the Godesberg terms. Jan Masaryk, son of the Republic's founder, wrote the Czech rejection: "The nation of St. Wenceslas, Jan Hus and Thomas Masaryk will not be a nation of slaves."

All this looked like united, successful resistance. But the demoralization process had gone so far it now had vested interests in appeasement. A bewildering sequence of events followed. When the British Foreign Office declared that, "if a German attack is made upon Czechoslovakia, the immediate result must be that France will be bound to come to her assistance and Great Britain and Russia will certainly stand by France," Bonnet in Paris told the press corps this was not official, that he had no confirmation of it. Still, the British navy was mobilized on September 27, the auxiliary air force was called up, the people started digging trenches in London parks.

But on the day after this outward show, Britain told the Czechs that their borders would be crossed the next day and that now they had sole responsibility for peace in Europe. Even while President Beneš was trying to understand this note, another British communication proposed military occupation by the German armies and an Anglo-German-Czech border commission. This note contained the chilling words: "The only alternative to this plan would be an invasion and dismemberment of the country by force, and . . . Czechoslovakia, though a conflict might rise which would lead to incalculable loss of life, could not be reconstituted in her frontiers, whatever the result of the conflict may be."[12] A more terrible threat could hardly have been contrived by London. Many millions of deaths later, German General Staff files showed that a number of German generals had been far from certain they could overcome the strong Czech border fortifications. The Czech army officers at that time were also sure that their solid and mechanized defenses could not be taken.

On the very day that Britain's threatening words went to Beneš, Chamberlain was writing to Hitler, "I feel certain that you can get all the essentials without war and without delay," and invited himself to the city of Munich. The Czechs and Russians were not invited to the conference there at Munich on September 29. The Germans, Italians, French and English met to settle the fate of Europe. The once repudiated Godesberg memo was now revived and endorsed, with a few minor changes. The historian Charles Loch Mowat has described the proceedings:

> Czechoslovakia was betrayed and handed over, gagged and bound, to Hitler's mercies; the Czech representatives were called into the conference room after the dictators had left and told to accept the terms; no comments were expected or allowed. . . . Hitler had got all he wanted, and without firing a shot; Czechoslovakia ruined, Britain and France humbled before himself and in the eyes of the world, Poland exposed to attack, Russia isolated, Hitler himself raised to a pinnacle of power and success among his own people . . . and 800,000 Czechs, a new oppressed minority, and any anti-Nazis among the 2.8 million Germans in the ceded territories, had to face inquisition, torture and murder at the hands of Nazi storm troopers and the Gestapo.[13]

So great was the longing for "peace" in the West that Chamberlain on returning to London was hailed, and accepted the acclaim. Daladier on his return to Paris had the grace to be ashamed at the crowd's ignorant cheers. Winston Churchill was not among those London crowds cheering Chamberlain's claim that Munich meant "peace in our time." A few days later Churchill rose in Parliament to explain the Munich agreement:

> We have sustained a total and unmitigated defeat. . . . Do not suppose this is the end. This is only the beginning of the reckoning.

Clement Atlee, future Labor Prime Minister, agreed this was one of Britain's worst defeats, that Hitler had won dominance over Europe without firing a shot. But the government policy was approved by a vote of 366 to 144. Most Britains accepted Chamberlain's assurance that Hitler would now keep the peace. They wanted very much to believe this.

German dismemberment of Czechoslovakia was more brutal than Chamberlain and Daladier had expected. Hitler insisted on using a 1910 census which would give him more territory instead of a 1930 census. The Czech protest was ignored by Britain and France. Poland and Hungary wanted some of the splintered land. The British and French members of the border commission were disregarded. The territory demanded was "awarded" to the two claimants by the German and Italian members. The British did not even bother to protest this violation of the agreement.

Success led to more arrogance. In March 1939 Hitler conveniently forgot all of his earlier remarks about limiting his conquests to people of Germanic origin. Only five days after Chamberlain informed the pleased House of Commons that "Europe was settling down to a period of tranquility," Hitler ordered the Slovakian and Ruthenian states of

Czechoslovakia to put themselves under German protection and with-draw from Czechoslovakia. The new Czech Prime Minister (Hacha) was summoned to Berlin, where Hitler and Air Marshal Goering bullied him into a treaty putting the rest of his country under German "protection." Six hours later German troops occupied Prague. What was left became a German protectorate; the German secret police (Gestapo) and its machinery of death moved in on March 15, 1939, five and a half months after Munich.

German military occupation of Prague and of the rest of Czechoslovakia was an obvious violation of the guarantee given by Britain and France. London protested mildly, but was told not to bother—this was now purely an internal affair; since Germany and Italy had never signed the international guarantee, it did not exist. The difference between wishful hoping and reality was written large, for only a few days after Munich Sir Samuel Hoare had told the House of Commons that the guarantee "will be more effective than either the France-Czech Treaty or the Soviet-Czech Treaty . . . and may make the new Republic as safe as Switzerland has been for many generations."[14]

So ended the twenty-year story of the life of Czechoslovakia as an independent nation. Did the Czech leaders underestimate the anti-fascist forces stirring feebly in the Western world? Many Czechs have wondered about this, have suggested that the spectacle of little Czechoslovakia being tortured and bombed by huge Germany would within a month have made the French disown their leaders, redeem their pledges. Then Russia could have raced across Rumania to help, and the prospect of a two-front war might have led to Hitler's elimination by German officers. This sequence was not utterly impossible, but was not certain, either. One of the ironies of history was that Chamberlain, only a year later, after people had seen the dismemberment of Czechoslovakia, gave the much less democratic nation of Poland the opportunity to say no to Hitler, which he had refused to Czechoslovakia, and with that the power to start the Second World War.

Occupation of Prague had hardly disturbed the complacency or conscience of Britain and France before another blow was heralded. Six days after the Nazis took Prague, Foreign Minister von Ribbentrop moved against Poland. That nation, because of the occupation of Czechoslovakia, was now confronted on the south as well as on the west by German forces. Von Ribbentrop demanded cession of the old Free City of Danzig and alteration of the Polish corridor separating part of East Prussia from the remainder of Germany. The usual rumors of German troop movements began to circulate. The Lithuanians, similarly under German pressure, ceded the city of Memel. Evidently the process of combining organized local subversion with international bullying, so successful in the rape of Czechoslovakia, was to be repeated in Poland and the Baltic states. After the invasion of Prague, this finally shocked the West.

There had been another reason for shock. Within two months after Munich, a young Polish Jew, grief-stricken over sufferings inflicted on his family by the Nazis in Germany, killed a minor official of the German Embassy in Paris, a Baron vom Rath. With that incident the Nazi leaders bought for Hitler his own freedom from the fear of assassination. Immediately a Nazi-organized pogrom was scheduled in Germany and carried out by the S.A. (Brown Shirts). It lasted fifteen hours. Scores of Jews were killed, more were badly injured. Thousands were dragged from their homes to concentration camps. Synagogues throughout Germany were desecrated and burned. Jewish shops and stores were sacked and destroyed. Fines of about 150 million dollars were levied against the Jewish community. Its members were forced to pay the government for all the damage the government had inflicted on them. All Jews were barred from the economic life of Germany. They no longer had any right to work. With this "Crystal Night," as Nazi romantics called it, any would-be assassins of Hitler (Christian, Jew or atheist) were put on notice that their efforts would result in the death not only of thousands but possibly of millions of innocent people.

Another explanation of this horror suggested by the English historian A. J. P. Taylor needs to be considered. He wrote:

> The great pogrom of November 1938, following hard on the victory of Munich, was the test mobilization of German morale. If the Germans could stomach that, they could stomach anything.[15]

He added that not a single Christian church in Germany had opened its doors to give sanctuary to the Jews. The advance of Christianity may perhaps be measured by the fact that during the peasants' crusade to the Holy Land, 800 years earlier, Cologne churches had, in fact, opened their doors and protected Jews against the savagery of men who believed that their mission was to destroy all non-Christians. The moral Munich of the German churches had begun.

This 1938 pogrom was the fifth of several outbursts of illegality before the war which might have warned the Germans that no life would be safe, no sense of decency and no law would prevail whenever the Nazis achieved power or so long as they retained it. The first was the series of assassinations by right-wing nationalists in the early 1920s. The second was when the Hitler minority in 1933 began arresting and imprisoning Reichstag members in order to gain a majority and full powers. No one charged the Nazi party with illegality at that time because no one was left free to do so. The third was the 1934 Blood Purge, in which Hitler paid his debts to the industrialists for their financial contributions to his party by massacring the leaders of the S.A. who had believed that he meant to establish some form of socialism. This was a completely lawless procedure, a directed group assassination without benefit of courts. General Schleicher, former army commander and Chancellor, was one of those conveniently eliminated in that purge, with his wife. The fourth was the cold-blooded murder of the Austrian Chancellor Dolfuss by Nazi agents, also in 1934. The 1938 pogrom was the fifth in that series.

With the war in 1939 the extermination of Jews throughout conquered Europe, the maltreatment and starvation of Slav prisoners of war and the selective killing of Polish leaders began. By that time Hitler no longer needed to concern himself with the conscience of the Germans. He was their church and their conscience. Censorship of news even prevented heroic martyrdom from having its legendary effect in arousing people to resistance. Nobody ever heard about the martyrs. In Poland, however, he had to salve the conscience of the army officer corps. It showed some unwillingness to engage in the murder of selected civilians in that conquered country. Hitler handled this by detailing that brutality to the Schutzstaffel (S.S.) under Himmler. Later he took his revenge on the squeamish officer corps by forcing it to accept the S.S. as part of the German army, its officers the coequals of all others.

No evidence is available to indicate that Hitler and his closest entourage ever doubted the logic and propriety of their violence. They were extreme nationalists. Ever since its early beginnings nationalism had tended to inculcate a sense of superiority to others, to people of other nations, other origins, other faiths. Hitler carried this process along the path of its own logic: all Germans were completely superior to all other people by virtue of origin and history. As superiors it was their right to treat inferiors within their own nation and conquered nations harshly, even to enslave and kill them. Rights were duties. The Nazi government was custodian of all rights and duties of all Germans. Its duty was to deal with any minority groups as it thought best, even to eliminate them by forced migration or death.

The fury with which Hitler attacked the Czechs for daring to oppose him and his open racial contempt for them were early indications of his feeling of superiority over all Slavs. The war would show more completely the extent of his contempt. The 1938 pogrom was only an indication of what he would do when free to kill six million Jews throughout all of captured Europe. The teaching of the German philosopher Kant—that humanity-in-persons, respect and kindness toward others, was "a demand lying like an absolute at the heart of Western civilization," as Hocking phrased it[16]—was to be utterly denied. All respect for individual rights and dignity, even for mere human decency, was to give way to the dictates of this savage racist nationalism.

During the war possibly two million Slavs in labor camps were treated so brutally and allowed so little food that they died.[17] The Reich Commissar for the Ukraine expressed succinctly the Nazi view in 1943: "We are a master race, which must remember that the lowliest German is racially and biologically a thousand times more valuable than the population here." Hitler's deputy, Hermann Borman, spelled out the wartime policy: "The Slavs are to work for us. In so far as we do not need them, they may die." Hitler in an order to the German Governor-General of conquered Poland stated that "all representatives of the Polish intelligentsia are to be exterminated."[18]

This attitude toward human dignity, freedom and life, coupled with the Nazi drive for power over Europe, created a virtually unprecedented challenge to Western civilization. Every Christian scruple was confuted. Until the November 1938 pogrom, even the German people were not aware that the Nazi concept of the heroic life, which the leaders reiterated endlessly, involved suppression of every element of personal decency and responsibility for others. Western ideals of personal freedom and national independence were being buried. Basic hopes were being smothered in violence and panic. Europeans seemed almost ready to accept a monstrous master and his lash. Unless they found wiser and braver leaders soon, their subjection by the "master" race seemed certain.

Europe's statesmen had little time left. Poland was the announced next German target, and after that could come Scandinavia, the Balkans, the Lowlands, or France. Western leaders still had four pieces on the chessboard which could be moved. Czech fortifications and divisions had been given away. Gone also was any faith in British or French treaty commitments. The remaining four pieces were these: Russia's fear of German troops on its own border after a Nazi conquest of Poland; Moscow was calling for a Bucharest meeting of all threatened nations to develop practical defense against further aggression. The second was possible conscription and rearmament in Britain. The third was to take advantage of the German General Staff's opposition to a two-front war. The fourth was to make the Western publics aware that appeasement had not prevented war but invited it. These were not powerful pieces, but they might have sufficed for a while if a Clemenceau or a Churchill had been in position to play them.

But against these pieces the Germans had an impressive array of their own, together with the cumulative dynamism of repeated success achieved without resistance. Hitler could tell his generals, "I have met those miserable worms [Chamberlain and Daladier] at Munich, and they will go only as far as a blockade, no more"; and this silenced the doubting generals. By the readiness test, the Germans had the largest and best-equipped army in Europe and a growing air force. Working for them was the venal sector of the French press, creating doubt of their own government's ability and suspicion of its integrity.

The Germans also were aided by the West's moral uncertainty about Poland's semifascist dictatorship, its possession of the onetime German Danzig, the rationale of the Polish corridor which separated two parts of Germany, and Poland's 1938 seizure of part of Czechoslovakia at Hitler's invitation. Such reservations about Poland's cause were coupled with an underlying Western conviction that no one, not even Hitler, would be willing to expose his nation to a second world war after experiencing the losses of the one which ended only two decades earlier.

Moscow was suspicious that London and Paris wanted a German-Russian war and were capable of a super-Munich at Russian expense. This was accentuated by reports of private Anglo-German negotiations for a large private loan to Germany. This news became public in July 1939, just prior to crucial military negotiations with the Russians. Finally, and this was their biggest and most negotiable asset, the Germans could offer more than the Allies to Moscow. If worst came to worst, Hitler could buy off Russia with shares of future victims in Poland and the Balkans.

The dangerous diplomatic game was played out badly for the West. Chamberlain suddenly in late March gave a unilateral guarantee of support to Poland. It was without any conditions. It was made without consulting Russia. It was made by an appeasement government which could not get troops or ships or planes to Poland in case of war. So it was not taken seriously. Four days after Chamberlain's guarantee was given, Hitler sat down to write his instruction on Operation White for the August invasion of Poland. Eight days after Chamberlain's announcement of the guarantee, Mussolini invaded Albania. A month later the leader of the Labour party, Clement Atlee, opposed Chamberlain's belated proposal to institute conscription.

The United Kingdom had avoided repeating one of its 1914 mistakes. This time Germany, at the last moment, had been warned that Britain would fight. But the situation had changed radically since 1914. Britain was no longer able to deter aggression by threatening to fight. Few believed Chamberlain anymore, and all knew that Britain was very weak. The key question was whether Britain and France could obtain support of either the Soviet Union or the United States. In July French Ambassador Coulondre in Berlin informed his government:

The prevalent opinion at the Wilhelmstrasse [German Foreign Office] is that if Poland stands firm, Hitler's decision will depend on whether the Anglo-Russian Pact is signed. It is believed that he will risk a war if he need not fight Russia, but if he knows that he will also have her against him, he will draw back rather than expose his country, party and himself to destruction.[19]

At this point Chamberlain's irresponsible impetuosity posed a difficult problem for the Western powers. The first key to discussions with the Russians was the attitude of the Poles toward letting Russian troops cross their borders to help protect them. Chamberlain had received no such promise before giving the guarantee: the Poles, with his guarantee in hand, felt no compulsion to give the promise. In London, Winston Churchill and former Prime Minister Lloyd George saw the gap. The latter urged Chamberlain to retrace his steps and to force Poland to let the Russians help. The strategy involved—that, if Warsaw made the promise, the Russian troops probably would never have to go through— was never accepted by the Poles. Their triumph in 1920 in taking in so many people from Russian areas now jeopardized their survival.

Everything depended in these last weeks on getting an Anglo-French-Russian agreement. London and Paris knew that Soviet conversations with the Germans had been resumed under the new Russian Foreign Minister, Molotov, who was more acceptable to the Germans than the Jewish Litvinov had been. Though the Western Allies now had an active competitor for Russian help, a relatively low-level diplomatic and military delegation with no power to sign anything was sent from London to Moscow for the negotiations. They did not fly, but leisurely went by ship. They and a French general met sharp questions at once. Soviet General Voroshilov put two to them at once: Could they obtain immediate Polish and Rumanian consent for Soviet troops to cross those borders in case of an armed German attack on Poland? Could they guarantee that Britain and France would put into the field forces equal to seventy percent of the Russian military strength, if Russia were attacked first? If they could, Russia would put the same proportion into the field in case France was attacked first. The Western officers were unable to meet either condition. What the British could do came out slowly in the course of the discussions. After six months they could put only six divisions into the line, and more later. The Russians, who had perhaps 100 divisions ready, thereupon retorted in much the same language Anglo-French statesmen had used to President Beneš a year earlier: this was no time for frivolity, the peace of Europe was at stake.

The Anglo-French attitude in these negotiations in Moscow increased Soviet suspicions that the Western powers were not serious about a pact. The Russians did not understand that Poland and Rumania, clients and debtors of France, could refuse to behave as France desired. Moscow saw the possibility of a Russo-German war in which France and Britain carried only a very small share of the military burden. Meanwhile, the Germans had been pressing Russia ever more insistently for plenipotentiary discussions. On August 22 Voroshilov broke off the military talks with the Western powers. He told them that his delegation "could not recommend to its government to take part in an enterprise so obviously doomed to failure."[20] On that same day the German U-boat fleet quietly left its harbors to take its positions around Britain. For Germany the road to war was now open.

On the day following termination of the Anglo-French-Russian talks, German Foreign Minister von Ribbentrop arrived in Moscow by plane with full powers. A political agreement was signed rapidly. To it was attached a secret convention. This divided Poland and the Baltic nations between Russia and Germany. The next day the German people, who had been taught to abhor Russia as the great threat, and the Russian people, who had been taught to abhor the Nazis as the great threat, woke up to find out that they were friends and allies. Communists throughout the world had a bad time of it. They had been arguing that Communism was the world's only determined opponent of fascism. On August 25, after German U-boats already had encircled the United Kingdom, the French Communist organ *Humanité* proclaimed that the Nazi-Soviet Pact was a "tremendous contribution to the peace of the world."

From this bargain, sometimes called "the thieves' pact," the Germans obtained a great advantage. They had a free hand to fight Britain and France without fear of being attacked from the east. They could mass all their troops in really effective units in the west, once their *Blitzkrieg* had overwhelmed Poland. They also obtained assurance of a steady supply of raw materials from Russia for their war against the west. The Russians were not losers, either—not at once. Their share of the bargain was a large slice of Poland, a free hand in the Baltic states and some new rights in the Balkans. Also, they had insured Russia against a Nazi double-cross: if the Soviet Union later was attacked by Germany, the Western powers would by then be completely involved in the war and unable to shift the main burden of the fighting onto Russia. A week after the Molotov–von Ribbentrop pact was signed, the Second World War began, on September 30—on the schedule Hitler had established months earlier.

The Poles had been expected by French officers to fight for six months. However, their troops were relatively few, badly equipped and inadequately organized. After six weeks of heroic individual fighting by soldiers and civilians, they were overwhelmed. The Germans used the new attack techniques of concentrating vastly superior power on one point and breaking through, then spreading out behind the rest of the lines. France did not move out any troops from behind her line of forts to help Poland, though the latter believed France had promised to do so. Consequently, the Russians believed that France would have betrayed the proposed pledge to Russia. That nation, as Hitler's ally, had time to rearm and to push its frontiers across Poland and the Baltic states farther to the west.

Then the great accident, which may have saved Western Europe from generations of Nazi rule and continued racial murder, occurred. The two Western allies, acting separately, managed to turn the "thieves' pact" into a catastrophe for Germany and a tragedy for the Soviet Union. That pact had split the French workers. After it was announced, the French Communist leaders thought they had to be on the side of Russia's new ally, Germany, since their intellectual, moral and political tutor was Moscow and their loyalties were with Russia. France's internal division already had been deepened by the defeatism of its old generals, the infirmity of its political leaders and the avowed preference of certain prominent Frenchmen for Hitler's Germany as a uniting force in a badly divided Europe. France became almost paralyzed. The German army attack circumvented the French fortresses; the French troops were overwhelmed. Help from England was heroic but small. French leaders did not even have the energy to move the Paris government to North Africa. They surrendered on June 21, 1940. The Germans occupied northern France, including Paris. A corporative state was established, under an aging hero of the First World War, Marshal Pétain, submissive to Germany.

This rapid French collapse took the Russians by surprise. They had expected the French to go on fighting for years, as in the First World War. Now France, by failing to prolong the war, liberated the huge German army, organized and equipped for an enormous struggle. Meanwhile, Britain found a magnificent leader in Churchill, who revived its heroic tradition. Alone, with no help at all from Europe and only some weapons from the United States, Britain continued the war. The Germans calculated that Britain would surrender after France fell. But isolated Britain continued to fight in the air and at sea. So a long war loomed. It became clear that Hitler needed time to build an invasion fleet, or enough rockets or enough new planes, to conquer Britain. The German army would have to wait until the scientists and the factories did their long and sometimes uncertain tasks.

With his vast army idle, Hitler guessed that sooner or later the Soviet Union would discover, as Britain belatedly had done, that a Germany dominant over all the rest of the Continent would appear dangerous to its interests; that Russia then would attack Germany. Hitler decided to be clever and attack first. He had the army for it. His great successes, not only in Austria and Czechoslovakia but in Poland and France, went to his head. He apparently thought that nothing could stop him. On December 18, 1940, he ordered preparations for an attack on Russia.[21] In spite of warnings from London and Washington that Hitler was about to attack, Stalin still trusted him. The German attack, delayed six weeks by a Balkan diversion, began on June 22, 1941. Unprepared Russian border forces and forts were overrun. Misjudging the vast distances into which Soviet forces could retreat, far from German bases, and discounting the Russian spirit and the cold winter, Hitler counted on victory in three months. Here was the two-front war which the General Staff had opposed ever since 1918. However, since Hitler had outguessed the Staff regarding the weakness of Poland and France, it could no longer veto the successful *Fuehrer*.

Even with the Soviet Union and the United Kingdom engaged together against Germany there was no certainty that Germany would be defeated. All the rest of Europe was working to supply Hitler. When ambitious Japan was safe from any flank attack by Russia, it assaulted the American outposts in the Pacific; and Hitler declared war on the United States, which had been aiding Great Britain with arms and ships. With this the probabilities of victory shifted. While the United States would probably have entered the war at some point, its entry in late 1941 speeded the German defeat. Hitler had compounded his great blunder of underestimating Russian strength by contemptuously discounting American power. Yet entry of the United States into the war did not automatically guarantee Allied victory. A year's delay by the German military bureaucracy in preparing rockets for use against England and in reequipping the U-boat fleet allowed England to survive and to become the staging area for an invasion of the Continent. Slowly Germany had to engage armies in huge numbers in the east, in Africa and in the west, and began to lose battles, even to despised Slavs. Its people and territory were gradually engulfed and exhausted. Altogether, in World War II twenty-five million people are reported to have died as a result of direct military action, while another fifteen million perished from enforced starvation, disease and execution. The direct and planned mass murder of six million Jews and the direct and indirect killing of two million Slavs who were prisoners of war or civilians gave this war a depravity which other military conflicts in modern centuries had been able to avoid.

When the war against the Nazis had been won, the people of Europe knew that they had escaped a fate which had never before threatened them. They were not to become industrious helots in the service of Nazi masters. They were not to be forced into a primitive intellectual, religious and ideological conformity. They were not to be compelled to connive, on penalty of death, in an endless racial murder of their neighbors, a continuous pursuit to the death of resisters and heretics.

The bloodstream of Europe was poisoned and the Second World War prepared during the years 1919–1939, a short moment in human history. Altogether, at least ten opportunities presented themselves—and have been mentioned in this chapter and the preceding one—for men inside and outside of Germany to prevent the virus of racial fascism from attacking the young democracy so successfully. In each event more favorable decisions could have been made. A little more sense of common humanity and mutual interdependence, a little more awareness of the vulnerability of democracy, a little more willingness to make sacrifices in peacetime instead of hoarding them all for a later war could have saved Germany from its submission to the new barbarians. And even if all laws of probability were broken, as they were in fact, and no favorable decisions were made, and the Nazis had obtained power within Germany, quite a few opportunities were still open between 1919 and 1939 for the victors of the First World War and Russia, separately or together, to prevent the Nazis from capturing the Rhineland, Austria, Czechoslovakia and Poland, and with those acts inaugurating the Second World War. In the structural weakness and disunity of Europe after the First World War and in the additional battering, fear and poverty inflicted by the crack-up of the world's economic structure in the early 1930s, all of these further opportunities were also wasted.

This disheartening picture of nations unable to act together to prevent disaster to democracy or the destruction of peace is relieved by the very different decisions of men and nations after the Second World War was over. They had learned. None of the earlier attempts to treat the defeated Germans as permanent delinquents, to punish them endlessly for the crimes of their masters, to squeeze war costs out of them was repeated. Marshall Plan aid from the United States to the extent of 17 billion dollars was given to rebuild the productive plant of friend and foe alike in Western Europe, to give men new hope for a free future. Democracy, in all Western Europe, including France and Italy, was given the economic foundation necessary for survival.

Real progress was made toward creating an economic unity within Europe, a common market, to end the economic nationalism that had long cursed that area, to give people everywhere a higher standard of living. In addition, a joint military force (NATO) was established, complete with the English and American troops who had been missing after the first war, to protect Western Europe from any new attack.

While endless difficulties accompanied each effort and France later withdrew from NATO, a remarkable set of men had managed to avoid most of the mistakes made before. The lessons may have been excessively expensive, but they were learned, not ignored, at that crucial time. No new sequence of chaos and fascism or of chaos and Communism appeared. Free men could move forward again, could try to create a more foolproof society, perhaps even a nobler one.

Munich, much like the cities of Athens, Rome, Paris and Leningrad, has become a textbook town for all manner of lessons, quite diverse, but all studied earnestly by men who know that it was a major political and moral defeat. Not only was it the last in a series of shock waves which destroyed the foundations of hope underlying the League of Nations, it was a demonstration of the complete inadequacy of the only alternative and substitute for the League, the haphazard balance-of-power arrangement in Europe. Munich remains important for many reasons. One is that today's world is also living with a similar accumulated awareness of the weakness of its United Nations Organization and with a realization that its multipower balance of nuclear terror is subject to a similar demonstration of inadequacy whenever any chief executive of those powers, or of any other acquiring this capacity for terror, is seized with a Hitlerian passion for indignation, expansion and glory, and a willingness to risk his nation's fate.

The fact that Munich means quite different things to different people was revealed in the 1960s when United States officials stated that they saw a Munich-type danger in Southeast Asia, while very few of the officials and commentators in any part of Western Europe saw any similarity at all, and most of the people of Europe, who had suffered from Munich, objected to the American action in Vietnam. A somewhat oversimplified lesson of Munich is frequently offered: "Never surrender any friendly territory to save the peace, for you will only have to surrender again and again, and finally have to fight with less strength than you had originally." This statement accurately reflects the progression from the Rhineland in 1936 to Austria and Czechoslovakia in 1938, to Poland and the Second World War in 1939. It does not explain why the powers in the areas surrounding Germany, and vulnerable to its later aggressions, failed to show, in advance of the consequences, some awareness of the probable cause-effect result of their separate and then cumulative defaults.

Why were the defense alliances between England and France, France and its allies in Eastern Europe, including Czechoslovakia and Poland, so weakened by English and French official doubts, deprecations, differences and denials? Their statesmen were speaking for nations which were still staggering from the losses of the First World War and newly groggy with the blows of the depression. They felt poor in funds, dispirited in aspirations. They had not found the German way or any other way to gain full production and employment, to derive a dynamism of will from economic success and community unity. But at the same time, while they were standing motionless, Germany was moving into full employment, high production, huge military expansion. Formerly parallel lines now began to intersect. Power corrupted German decency and humanity, while weakness corrupted the will and good sense of the French and the English until the West went from national to international demoralization and Russia retreated into savage retributions.

Meanwhile, one of the major rules of the peace game was altered unilaterally. Leaders of the two democracies, responding to the war weariness and peace hopes of their own people, were slow to realize that in Germany that particular counterweight to war risk had been removed. After 1933, no Germans were allowed to speak out against anything which Hitler did or sponsored. In short, the democracies underrated the capability of an authoritarian state not only to develop its full potential output, but also to discipline its people and silence their peace hopes. Later, in 1941, most military commentators similarly underrated the capacity and will of another authoritarian state, Soviet Russia, to produce and continue fighting after severe initial defeats. So the causes for Munich, always more important than immediate incidents, go back beyond the events and errors in Germany, described briefly in the preceding chapter, to the difficulties of the democracies in mastering their internal problems. They go even beyond them into the failure of all members of the League of Nations to make that new institution as much a national obligation as fire departments in their cities, to obtain for it not only the military force it needed but the constantly pledged loyalty of all who wanted to prevent another war threat from moving into actual warfare. The causes went even beyond that default to the dropout of both the United States and Soviet Russia, participants in the First World War, from the defense arrangements of postwar Europe and their absence from the League at the start of its precarious life.

Two striking similarities with the pre-Munich syndrome in Europe are present in the later part of the century. The first is the sense of helplessness which people feel as a result of their individual incapacity to control their fate. In the pre-Munich days people were not informed accurately by their governments or the press about what their leaders were doing, or why, nor could they make any informed judgment about the wisdom of that course until long after the crucial decisions had been made. In more recent times, when a hundred million or more people in each of the superpowers and many others elsewhere have become hostages to the restraint and wisdom of a very few rulers, those millions know little more, control their rulers no more adequately, and again feel themselves to be objects in a society rather than the civilized, masterful individuals once promised to the world by the advances in the physical sciences. Nor can they make any judgment about the wisdom of the course pursued by sheltered bureaucracies until much later. Now as well as then a sufficiently strong and prevailing sense of helplessness can demoralize men.

The other similarity which stands out is the general unawareness that continuing weakness in any major developing area invites cancerous foreign attempts to expand and control, and that men need to remedy those weaknesses before the opportunity to do so is lost and war alerts start flashing. Cuba may remind them. The weakness of Germany after the First World War brought in the Nazis. The weakness of the rest of Europe, including England and France after their struggles with the economic depression of the 1930s, invited the German attack on Austria, Czechoslovakia and Poland. The fact that all three were actual or threatened military attacks has dominated our thinking about Munich. However, in the future other attacks due to weakness may be non-military, and because of the nuclear threat they are likely to be non-military. They can simply take the form of strong and well-financed efforts to use the growing sickness and weaknesses of important developing areas in the world to obtain control of them. The probability of hunger revolutions mentioned in Chapter 1 suggests a time table for such efforts.

Successful non-military takeovers in a number of important developing areas mean that the balance of power has shifted. With any serious shift, the danger of war is increased. In such circumstances the competitive use of troops, complete with bombs and napalm, can be expected to fail to cure the illness which invited the attack. After the power has once been shifted, troops are neither preventive nor post-operative medicine, they are simply punishment. Wars rarely turn the clock all the way back. Before the Second World War Czechoslovakia was under the Germans. Even after that war it was not free, it was under the Russians.

Until all the people who are products of Western civilization become aware that their own fate may depend on their success in curing the weaknesses in those important areas of the world where hunger grows and hopes are frustrated, and on their ability to do so before it is too late, they will not have learned enough about the meaning of Munich to them. By now, however, we have glanced at the unfortunate fate of enough societies to know that perhaps the most difficult truth men can learn is that humaneness in their relations to their less privileged fellowmen is not simply charity and nobility but may also be a necessity for their own survival and that of the institutions they cherish.

CHAPTER 12

Yesterday's
Tomorrows

Men will stagger under the enormous accumulation of challenges to their moral, physical and intellectual resources in the decades ahead. It is during those years that much of the inherited structure of world oversight and neglect may start crashing down into rubble and death. A few more shortsighted decisions, a few more nostalgically medieval trials by combat, a few more stubborn refusals to outgrow old clothes and customs may well lose men their best chance to create a magnificent world in place of their present home of contrasted poverty and riches, of fear and hostility. For this task they will need all the hard-earned wisdom they can glean from the past, as well as a far greater creativity than they have so far demonstrated. Yet they now have as much capacity to foresee and rebuild as to kill and be killed, to cause suffering and endure it. They can now also summon to their service great resources of compassion, an ingredient often missing in the past.

As they undertake the vast tasks they cannot safely avoid any longer, the past can be useful in helping them to see what is constructive and what is not, in releasing them from a sense of frustration and helplessness as their great opportunities, difficulties and dangers grow. In particular, these accounts of past defeats can remind them that men always had better options than they used, that a greater degree of humaneness might have saved ancient civilizations and more recent societies from many of their troubles. Those accounts have now covered nine crucial turning points in the lives of eight important Western societies. In these particular periods, men were too tied to their past and present to create a much better future. Their defaults did not simply leave society where it had been, but retarded it, sometimes for centuries. They had no copyright on this procedure. It can be repeated.

These brief views of crucial moments in history do not justify more than a normal degree of pessimism about the ability of men to blunder and societies to dig their own graves. History is equally replete with accounts of good fortune, both accidental and earned. For example, we may think of what civilization would be like today if Philip II of Spain had been able to sweat an additional billion dollars in gold and silver out of the wearied Indians of Spanish America, had subverted or bought English and French armies, had branded all of Europe and both Americas with his hatred for liberty, and had established firmly the practice of punishing all incipient scientists at the inquisitorial stake. The Chinese might now be waking the West from a long nightmare and debating among themselves how to aid three underdeveloped continents. Or we may think of what the present world would be like if there had been no challenge to racial injustice in the United States in the mid-nineteenth century, and that nation had comfortably rationalized its passivity and had stepped onto the world's scene in the twentieth century as the greatest of racist and possibly fascist powers.

Even more vividly, we may think of the consequences if England, fighting alone, had not found its heroes or been able to equip them with fast planes and radar. It might have surrendered in 1941, instead of battling on alone, and the Nazis would have become dominant throughout an enslaved Europe, with their open-end commitment to authoritarianism and racial massacre. Nor is any great effort of imagination necessary for us to guess what a barracks state the United States might now be if the Russians had been able to sweep to the Channel in the late 1940s, unhalted by Marshall Plan aid to Europe or by American weapons. Along with the opposite, men have had their moments of reward for effort and their pieces of good fortune. No particular reason exists to believe that they will have fewer of them.

What parts of the painful experience undergone by men and societies in these particular dark periods of the human past can be useful to us both today and tomorrow? Certainly not everything, for history does not repeat its surrenders or its dramatic confrontations in the same form; it only persists in presenting the same basic problems of society and civilization for more adequate solutions. Dynamic men are still searching, as they have for more than 2,000 years, for ways to live together in peace, to humanize the quality of life, to provide the significant freedom men seek, the occasion to be useful to others as well as themselves, to create communities and a life of which they can be proud. Today and tomorrow they can be expected to carry forward that search in spite of the legacies of past neglect and error. They will have to do so amid the havoc with which the scientific revolution—despite its gift of wealth—has newly littered their lives. To it can be attributed much of the overpopulation of the world, the upcoming hunger revolutions, the competitive nuclear terror, the threatened loss of the individual in the mechanized and huddled mass, the acceleration of time, the diminution of opportunities for gradual change, the urgency for undertaking tasks which were neglected and pushed out of sight.

In facing that future and undertaking their search and action, men probably have more cause for confidence and optimism than for their opposites. For the first time in the world's long history, men can produce enough to provide protection for everyone against hunger, illness, ignorance. Today more men have personal freedom—in a limited but large area—than ever before. They have also demonstrated their capacity to learn from the past. What they might have learned from the post-Civil War days in the United States was later learned expensively from the anarchy of Europe after the First World War, but their knowledge was applied, and with great success, after the second one. Also, the deep and personal psychological needs of men for freedom and for a democracy which will allow them full expression of that freedom is on their side. Not even the authoritarian nations seem able to repress it forever. Today's and tomorrow's people can only benefit from the gradual crumbling, at least in the West, of the world's latest messianic theology, Communism, and some dulling of its cutting edge. The world may yet avoid more wars of political religion. On man's side, too, is the growing awareness throughout the earth that its people are in fact a single community in the making, that the fate of everyone touches everyone else, sooner or later. Growing also, although more slowly, is the absurdity of allowing any rulers to retain a power which no ancient kings or tyrants ever had, even in the darkest and earliest days of the race, that of destroying most of life on earth through the use of nuclear weapons.

Because errors which create great social tragedies are not made in a vacuum, but are due to the attitudes toward life and society underlying the arenas of conflict, one important factor in our future is the speed with which those basic attitudes can change for the better. Five unequal but very important changes within this century indicate that attitudes do accommodate themselves to pressures and that yesterday's remote ideal can become today's visible and accepted necessity. For one, white indifference to the welfare of the black minority in the United States has been declining. Next, men who endured the hardship and humiliation of helplessness which accompanied the Great Depression actually did put a floor under the economy so that later generations could be spared any repetition. Again, in Russia the Communist managers of affairs have been finding out that state ownership of industry was no panacea, that the competence of industrial organizers, labor productivity and attention to consumer demands for quality were more important factors in distributing and producing output and well-being. One source of ideological differences between the closed and open societies seemed to be drying up. Next, some of the menace to international trade inherent in a gold supply which could not possibly be increased as rapidly as the trade it was supposed to support has been removed through international effort. Finally, and more importantly, in most of the industrialized Western world the ancient struggle between classes was altered in character by the insistence of large-scale industry on gaining the advantages of low-cost production. This required an expanding purchasing power, which meant higher wages for the workers. The interdependence of all industrial managers and all workers was recognized. With this change the modern world broke out of a potentially death-dealing trap. All of these changes were accompanied by a shift in attitudes, a greater willingness to master man's fate, a stronger determination to attain freedom from the bondage of older ideas, to foresee rather than to regret later. These illustrations give some added justification for the belief that the four great American problem areas, some shared by other great nations, can be approached with some reasonable amount of hope.

Meanwhile, the temptations for pessimism can hardly be ignored. Men do love to sweep unpleasantness under the rug and try to forget it. They do prefer to enjoy the present and let the future take care of itself. They do find it easy to ignore the high unemployment among Negroes and their social exclusion in the United States, the explosive pile-up of neglected refugees and of arms in the Middle East, the semifeudal conditions of poverty, illness and ignorance under which most of the world still labors, and to slight the increasing alienation of the young from the values of their elders. In many parts of the world, the haves still rationalize and glorify a certain amount of pure piggishness, and designate all efforts of those who have nothing and want more as subversion, probably foreign in origin. Men are slow to chain down the propensity of their leaders in wartime to villainize their enemies and make peace more difficult because of the hatred they have increased. They are reluctant to move from effects to causes, from crime on the street to the roots of degradation, from a fear of Communist symptoms in the world's riotous areas of neglect to construction of a viable and competitive democratic alternative. They ignore the past experiences of mankind too readily, misinterpret them too often, repeat and even escalate methods that have proved inadequate, gain time only to waste it, tend to do too little and be too late. Yet, in spite of all these slovenly and very human traits, they can occasionally rise in crises to something approaching greatness.

Can some of these brief but still revealing glimpses into other men's failures enable us in any way to surmount our own crises, master the difficulties ahead? Have we gained from them and from other studies of the past a sense of history and avoidable tragedy which can actually be useful for our present and future? Have we learned to recognize errors and their causes with sufficient certainty to allow us to refuse, quite deliberately, to build inadequate assumptions and inherited mistakes into the structure of our own society? If we have come to that point, then much blood, sweat and tears may be avoided, hope can be more confidently nourished, an enrichment of many lives expected, the gradual transformation of a large nation into a memorable community be considered possible. However, if we do not come to that point, we may even find to our astonishment that in this rapidly moving and competitive world we can lose, as the Church did in the fifteenth century, Spain in the sixteenth, our single and then irrevocable opportunity. We may then become so embroiled in the momentum of several combined follies that we no longer will see clearly where we are going or know why, or be able to keep options open for ourselves or avoid the final humiliation of discovering, like the Romans of the Empire, that our pretensions have become absurd.

By way of answer to the question asked, we may test for ourselves the current and future value of these past experiences which ended in failure. We may even do so twice. The first test can deal with two problem areas mentioned earlier, which are interlinked. The first concerned the growing depersonalization and alienation of individuals, the second covered racial and group conflicts about the meaning of freedom. A later test can deal with the other two problem areas, which are also interlinked. The first test of the usefulness of the past will be confined to a single statement of fact and a single question.

Several choices of methods for eliminating poverty—a significant factor in some individual and group alienation—have been presented to the nation for decision. One of them is that of continuing the present relief system. The second is that of transferring some income from those above the poverty level to those below it. The third is that of establishing a right to employment, with the government as the employer of last resource in case no other employer offers work. Each alternative has a different money cost. The question is this: Has our examination of past failures led us to see that something more than varying money costs is involved in the three choices, that the whole character of the society may be profoundly affected for better or worse by the alternative chosen?

We have noticed some evidences of alienation in the past. For the Greeks, whose personal lives were entwined with that of their communities, it came after their cherished institutions had failed to provide them with the expected peace and protection of their freedom. For the Romans, it came after the break-up of their republic, the disappearance of the old sense of a unified community, the inadequacy of the ideals of material wealth and imperial power. The early Christians, breaking away from Rome, prayed that it might perish. Other Christians were later alienated by their own sect's persecution of them, aided by the Roman legions. Still later, the whole Protestant movement expressed an alienation from the corruption and intellectual absolutism of the dominant Italian element in the Church.

In Spain we saw less alienation in the underdogs of that day than despair and occasional revolt. In France the industrial workers fought hard in a series of revolutions against their exclusion from the benefits gained by the middle class, and finally expressed their alienation by moving toward the Communists. Bitter division rather than alienation marked the pre-Civil War period in the United States and the dark postwar era. In Russia, however, the alienation from Czarist absolutism of whole generations of students was marked. It was accompanied by nihilism, anarchism and recriminatory bomb throwing. The process took a different but also tragic shape in Germany, when the extreme nationalists first began hating the newly created Republic, again when inflation broke away part of the middle class, and finally when unemployment and depression humiliated millions and pushed them into rival extremist parties, and fascism could ride to victory on a wave of accumulated resentments. Germany produced a youth movement, and some members of it called themselves "wanderers into nothingness." We know also, although not from these accounts, that the "playwrights of the absurd" appeared in France only after the humiliation of France in the war and during the moments of defeats in Indochina and Algeria and an officers' revolt against authority.

In our own country, individual and group alienation seem to be more affected by mass crowding in huge cities, the downgrading of old skills to the level of machine tending, the depersonalization of the employment and work process, fear and mistrust of unknown neighbors, hatred of the competition for survival and promotion called the "rat race," horror at the new barbarities of warfare, disgust with the television fodder of sex and violence, the dichotomy between religious teachings and actuality, the rivalry of conspicuous consumption, the absurdity of poverty in a rich society, fear of nuclear war. All or most of these have a modern twist, if not character, and lead a number of people to find the whole system objectionable, to withdraw into themselves in disgust, helpless and frustrated, or strike out in desperation. A notable increase in recent years in the number of those called "insane" and hospitalized accompanies the alienation. When whole groups feel that there is no hope for them in the society and pull away from it, the society faces even greater troubles.

Some relationship between group exclusion and group alienation obviously exists. Most of the tragic periods we have glanced at show a conscious or tolerated exclusion of others by the dominant group in society. Most of them show that the dominant group suffered quickly or belatedly for its act of exclusion. When the Spartans made helots of some of the people they conquered and dispossessed, and turned some into second-class citizens, they made the decision which determined that Sparta would become a permanent police barracks and step out of the march of Hellenic progress. Athens in time lost heavily after it excluded its many small allies from a voice in its empire and decisions and denied them the right to seek Athenian citizenship. The persecution of dissenters by early Christians weakened the Roman Empire, which approved it. That undertaken by the medieval Church brought on the Protestant Revolution. The elimination or degradation of Moors and Jews in Spain lowered the competitive capacity of that nation in Europe, while the chase of heretics in the Lowlands lost to Spain the productive capacity of several hundred thousand skilled craftsmen and then the whole rich area. In France, the exclusion of the growing middle and professional class brought on the elimination of the caste of nobles, while the exclusion of the workers led to repeated social upheavals, later to an active and obstructive Communist bloc in the legislature.

The nominal inclusion but actual and often brutal exclusion of liberated Negroes after the American Civil War, due in part to a confusion and difference about the meaning of freedom, took a heavy toll for a century and may take a greater one in property, life and reaction against democracy than it has levied so far. Similarly, the exclusion of Indians in Spanish America left that continent with endless scars of resentment. Czarist Russia was marked by class barriers against most of the peasantry, depriving them of opportunity and education, while much of the very literate population was excluded from power. The violent reaction of both groups helped end that system. The treatment of Germany and Russia as pariahs after the First World War helped to bring on the second one and exacted a heavy retribution.

Exclusion may be conscious and purposeful, as it was in Rome. Or it may be the result of indifference, financial interest and misunderstanding, as it apparently has been in the United States. In either case, it means two things to the excluded groups: they do not possess an equality of opportunity to advance or to protect their families against hunger and other forms of want. As a consequence, they never stand any chance of obtaining the esteem of their fellowmen as a result of their efforts. They will always be looked down on. Pride may be a grievous sin in religious doctrine, but man's need and desire to have the respect of the whole community, to be and possess something of which he can be proud, is an exceedingly valuable attribute for any nation. The wisdom of Athens in using its aristocratic tradition to build its social structure on the earning and acknowledging of respect cannot be casually ignored.

The American misunderstanding about the intimate connection between the demand for opportunity and the need for respect was demonstrated most vividly, as we saw, in the mid-nineteenth century. The earlier confusion about the meaning of the word "freedom," demonstrated in the conflicting claims of Sparta and Athens to its possession, reappeared in new form. Men in the Southern states used it to mean their liberty to retain other men in slavery, while Northern men used it to mean civil and political rights for Negroes. A similar confusion has continued into modern times when United States officials loosely spoke of a "free world," which happened to contain a conspicuous number of areas in which personal freedom hardly existed. They meant a world in which the member nations were independent of Communist control, and could have avoided complaints of hypocrisy by saying so. But in the period after the Civil War, the Northern assumption was that personal freedom and the suffrage were all that the liberated slaves needed to insure the survival of those grants. Few opportunities to advance were opened to them or ways by which to earn the respect of the whole community. No security was provided against rapacious neighbors, who then took the framework of rights and participation apart, piece by piece, and put something approaching peonage in its place.

This event remains exceedingly important for the United States, and the vulnerability and emptiness of unprotected personal freedom are still not fully understood. People did not actually have to wait a generation to hear Justice Oliver Wendell Holmes observe that "the necessitous man is not free" in order to know that freedom needed additional supports, including security and opportunity, in order to stay alive. Yet it was a shock to many in the third quarter of the twentieth century to find that the black people had incorporated the idea of equality of opportunity into their concept of freedom. They expressed a desire to move up freely and equally into the currently restricting suburbs, and also to climb all educational, economic and social ladders in the same way. In those suburbs they found that the national debate echoed the 1850s. It was then that Stephen A. Douglas proposed "popular sovereignty" for the territories. The spread or nonspread of slavery in such areas was to be determined by the first residents, excluding then and forever after the voice of the rest of the nation in a matter which affected the whole character of the nation.

The search for respect and for an opportunity to gain it are large and significant parts of this demand for equality of opportunity. Here we may usefully recall that both the totalitarian ideologies of the twentieth century gained supporters by promising the lost and helpless people a new place and function in their own societies. Part of that fact of life roughly called "the white backlash" can be explained by the post-Civil War heritage of ignorance about the respect which black people could earn. The white middle-class people who object strongly to the movement of Negroes into jobs and suburbs want them to earn the missing respect before they move in and up. The black people, smarting from a thousand bruises and wounds, insist that the movement in and up is a necessary means for earning the respect they desire, if not a recognition of the respect many of them have already earned for themselves as individuals. Some labor unions have opened the same before-after box as the suburbanites. Indeed, it presents much the same dilemma as the high-school dropout often encounters: he cannot get a job because he has had no experience; he cannot get experience because he has no job.

Extremism has already been bred by this freedom-opportunity-equality-respect relationship. At this point, the past tragedies of the Western world have taught something about the limits and dangers of the insistence that only one idea is the full truth and that all others must be combatted with violence. Almost no effort of the world to move forward has been free of extremism. Each variety regularly and monotonously nourishes its opposite. The Communists and Nazis provided each other with excuses for violence in the Germany of the 1920s and 1930s. Before that, we noticed the Holy League in France in the sixteenth century, whose members were so intent on killing Protestants that they were willing to kill fellow religionists who questioned this purpose, and saw also the violent Protestant reaction to this extremism. We saw how the extremists who wanted the South to secede were incited by the extremists of the North and vice versa. We also saw the spoiling techniques extremists devised. Marie Antoinette's success in revolutionary France in defeating the one measure which might have produced a stable government led her and the King to their deaths. The Southerners, who said that they feared the election of Lincoln above everything else, did all they could to insure that election by nominating a second Democratic candidate. Douglas, their victim, saw and said exactly what they were doing, but was helpless to stop them.

That extremism provokes counterextremism was shown again in Russia. The violence of the Czar's police and Black Hundreds called into being the bomb throwers and expropriators of the underground, who got completely out of the control of their political groups, and the Czar and his violent opposition both prepared the way for the Bolsheviks. We can go back farther into time if we choose and recall the terror and counterterror in France, the effect of Napoleon's endless wars in preparing a rule of reaction in Europe. Caught in the middle, the moderates always seem besieged and are frequently overcome by their more single-minded opponents. The process is as old as Athens, as new as the surge of black militants in the United States against the nonviolent leaders of the Negroes.

As the national debate about freedom, equality and respect goes forward, we may listen to some warnings from the past about the unchecked momentum which small decisions gain from neglect. Unexamined, unconsidered, they move from small beginnings into very large consequences. The "we are stuck with it" situation Pericles described when he admitted that the Athenian empire had become a tyranny, but observed that it was now too late to give it up, has been repeated throughout time, but may become even more frequent and dangerous as modern nations move toward a principate form of government. In the perilous pre-Munich days, we noted some remarkably secret and undiscussed moves by Chamberlain in England, some quite secret dealings by Laval with Mussolini, some significant silences by Bonnet in regard to the Russian offer to send troops through Rumania. The parliaments remained unaware of them at crucial moments. Since then, the nuclear threat, with its half hour or less of warning time, seems to have transferred almost all power over warfare and the national fate from the legislature to the executive. Then the legislature tends to abdicate. Modern nations are unwittingly being forced, without much consideration of the consequences, to watch the growth of one-man rule, to see his decisions acquire enough self-generated momentum to outrage their hopes, imperil their democracy.

It was the sheer momentum of an enterprise once started but checkable only by the executive which allowed nuclear bombs to be dropped on Japan at a time when that nation was already extending peace feelers, an abortive expedition to Cuba to continue, and the dreaded land war in Asia to escalate up to the level of half a million men and seventy billion dollars. This may possibly be a quite different form of absolutism than the men who established democracy ever expected to encounter. It seems to be inherent in the authoritarian societies. The unchecked momentum of the cult of German racial superiority led to the world's most despicable mass murders of the racially different and did so under the guidance of an unchecked executive who was a devotee of that cult. The new cult of black power and black self-segregation may not be immune to the momentum of similar assumptions about the undesirability and guilt of white people, and the outcome could also be murderous. This type of momentum is not completely different from that hallowed by venerability, such as the practice of priestly celibacy, which, as we saw, had long outgrown the needs of medieval property accounting which provided its original justification.

These accounts may also serve to remind us that nations which postpone their problems and seek to evade them sometimes have to pay a heavier bill for their procrastination than they would have paid for prevention. The slavery story will be recalled, also the policy of no help to the ruined Southern states, no land to the liberated slaves, and also the comparative costs of preventing and fighting the Second World War. We may remember the German reluctance to spend a few hundred millions in 1931–1932 to lower unemployment enough to allow the Republic to survive, and then estimate for ourselves the savings in life and resources that action might have obtained for Germany and the world. Someday the neglect of the United States to disavow feudalism in South Vietnam and so obtain a chance to gain popular support before it decided to fight there, may be listed as another illustration. However, the bill for postponement and evasion may not only involve money sums but may include revolution and war, or civil strife. A refusal to spend money to remedy some neglect does not mean that a nation is saving money; it only means that the costs are being shifted from one generation to the next.

Perhaps nothing stands out so clearly in these various accounts of effort and disappointment as the frequency with which men perverted or lost their objectives through the repulsive means they used to obtain them. We have seen the Athenians not only losing their empire but their democracy and ultimately Greek independence through callous attempts to force obedience, on pain of death, from very small towns, to gain the power to starve all others through a far-off foreign conquest. We have seen Roman patricians obtaining wealth by taking the old common lands from villagers and thereby insuring that their generals would confiscate the patricians' properties in order to pay the soldiers' pensions, which formerly had come from those commons, and killing those who objected. We have watched the early Christians, seeking the safety and power of the Church, tie themselves to a moribund Roman Empire, then absorb its autocratic blood and, with that, forget large parts of the simple and appealing message of its savior, which dealt with the redeeming power of love in society. We have observed a pope, engaged in the good purpose of rebuilding and decorating Rome, raise money in Bohemia (modern Czechoslovakia) through the despicable practice of indulgence selling at the very time when such a violation of decency was most likely to arouse Hus and his followers to war against the Church. Then we saw another pope do the same thing all over again in Germany, at the very time when that travesty of religion was most likely to offend German conscience and, with that, losing much of that area to the Church. We saw the conciliar reformers spoil their own efforts to limit papal absolutism by an ill-conceived attempt to limit Church financing.

Almost no one seems to be exempt from punishment for this error. The men of the Spanish Lowlands might not have risen against Spanish rule if Philip II had not used the means of the Inquisition and its torture to obtain religious as well as political obedience. We saw all the different political objectives sought by Lafayette, Marie Antoinette and the middle-class Girondins through a declaration of war ruined by the conduct and demands of that war. We saw the hoped-for revolutionary and liberating impact of the French Revolution on its dynastic neighbors thwarted by means used to impose the national will of France on them through taxation, indemnities and conscription. The Southern moderates might not have lost their deplorable objective of retaining slavery in those states where it was already established if they had not chosen to accompany their extremists down the hazardous road of secession and war.

In our own century, we saw the victors in the First World War, interested in absolving their own nations from all blame for that war, forcing a newly democratic Germany to accept the sole guilt for starting it, managing a hunger blockade and threatening occupation if it failed to agree to accept the sole guilt. We saw how those means helped Hitler to capitalize a resentful old nationalism. More recently we noticed how Southern sheriffs, in the pursuit of their malicious objective of depriving Negroes of their civil rights, used cattle prods and police dogs in front of television cameras, means which caused a moral backlash throughout the nation and insured the passage of the very civil-rights law they wanted least.

The suggestion made by Walter Lippmann to the universities of the nation, mentioned earlier, that they concentrate their teaching of the future rulers of the nation on the vital interrelation of means and ends, is obviously not pointless. Perhaps the particular moments of defeat described in earlier pages are sufficiently tragic and pertinent to the present and future to allow that suggestion to be carried one step further. Possibly all students in schools and colleges should be taken off their frequently dreary diet of dates and names, and be presented instead with a quest for the causes for the great successes of humanity, of which there are many, and of the several failures, along with the options open but not chosen, as well as the always present and interlocking means-objectives syndrome. They might then become somewhat more prepared for today's burdens and tomorrow's challenges than they are at present.

The pertinence and usefulness of the past to the present is at this point subject to the first test with which we presented it. This was, it will be recalled, in the form of a question about which of three alternative ways to eliminate poverty—one cause for individual and group alienation—now seemed preferable to the others. If some new awareness has been acquired that each alternative has profoundly different implications for the future character of the nation and that much more than a money calculation is involved in the choice, the past has met at least one part of its test.

If, in addition, we are now able to see more clearly than before that, of two alternatives, one involves the creating or maintaining of a dependent group within the society far into the future, while the other does not involve such exclusion nor the ancillary resentment on the part of both givers and receivers, but offers instead some elements of equal opportunity for men and women to earn both a living and the necessary respect of fellow citizens, and that the transformation of the nation into a community of proud people with common ideals is more likely to result from it, the past can be considered to have met the most important part of its test of current usefulness. Whatever we have been freshly reminded of—about the relative costs of prevention and later cure, the historic price of group exclusion, the follies and horrors to which extremism and militant ideologies may lead, the perils to national hopes of unreexamined decisions which acquire their own momentum and life, and the propensity of men to destroy their objectives by the means they use—can also become pertinent to our choice of alternatives and can allow the past not only to meet its first test, but to do so with honors.

Are these accounts of past defeats also relevant to the last two problem areas which the United States must with success traverse before it can lay claim to becoming a memorable instead of a grandiose society? This is the second pragmatic test to which we may subject them. The first of these last two difficult realms covered our interest and involvement in the fate of the less-developed areas, those expected to endure antifeudal and antihunger revolts in the near future. The second covers our ability to contribute usefully to an elimination of the danger of another world war, particularly a nuclear war, in which completely innocent peoples and nations would perish along with us. The two areas are interlinked.

An illustrative test of the potential usefulness of the past to the present in these two problem areas—our second one—may be limited again to one question: Do men's past defeats and experiences with ideologies and power competitions enable us to plan more freely and boldly than before how to avert more Vietnams, Munichs and world wars by engaging in action decades before such disasters are allowed to commemorate our impotence, our failures of understanding, compassion and creativeness?

A few simple facts from these accounts are worth recalling in connection with that question. One is that societies and civilizations can and do disintegrate, great nations do occasionally become very unimportant ones. Another is that catastrophes such as Munich and the Second World War do not usually happen overnight. That one was built up by twenty years of default and blunder on both sides of the Rhine. Neither the ruin of the Roman Republic nor the disintegration of the Roman Empire was built to its climax in a day. Still another fact is that almost every one of these great failures was profoundly influenced by the society's neighbors. No one of those considered made all of its errors in its own isolated vacuum. Still another observation is that nations which allow their people to believe that they are invulnerable and indomitable (Athens, Sparta, Rome, Spain, Napoleon's France, Wilhelm's Germany) seem even more likely than others to take dangerous risks, even more likely to traumatize their people with the shock of defeat when it finally comes.

The shock of unexpected defeat led to cries of treason in Germany and aided Hitler to move the nation toward fascism. The United States, which was also undefeated on the battlefield for a century, stood similarly vulnerable to shock and trauma. In 1948 and thereafter, an administration was accused of the crime of losing China, which this nation had never possessed or even remotely controlled. It had only been aiding it in various ways. If the United States, weary and sick of its involvement in South Vietnam, were to retreat from all the other areas it has been aiding, and if its ideological and power rivals were then to move in, a great temptation to those who think only in terms of military force would certainly be offered.

Since the nonsuccess of arms in South and North Vietnam to achieve social and political objectives may overshadow the whole great challenge of the areas of the world which need food, schooling, doctors and industrial capital before they can move into a productive stage, two things need to be noted which made that situation abnormal.

The first is that a really massive neglect of relevant history demanded a huge price. The second is that a quite different approach than the military one stood a fair chance to gain for the nation everything the United States sought. The past errors which were negligently repeated have all been noted in the earlier accounts. The Spartans as well as the interveners in the French and Russian revolutions made the first error, which we repeated. It was that of identifying with a small, unpopular clique, of aiding those who sought to take away gains already achieved. In South Vietnam the main gain was a grant of land ownership. We repeated the error made during the crusades to the Holy Land, again by President Wilson and again by Prime Minister Chamberlain at crucial moments. It was that of failing to get solid advance agreements from potential allies about the amount of effort they would expend, the goals to be achieved on the internal and foreign fronts alike. The third error repeated was that made when Germany was burdened with the "sole guilt" for starting the war of 1914–1918. North Vietnam was held solely responsible for starting and conducting the war, even in the face of a large organization of South Vietnamese (the National Liberation Front) which had been the only existing administration in large parts of that nation for a decade. Since many of its members would have been humiliated and might have become hostile if Hanoi had accepted any such sole guilt or credit, Hanoi was asked to do the politically impossible. The fourth repeated error was that of allowing the momentum of a process once started to carry the nation from an involvement of a few thousand advisors to half a million and more armed men without adequate recheck by executive or legislature or public of the value of the purposes or the effectiveness of the means. The failure to avoid the error of creating the same kind of credibility gap which demoralized the people of England, France and Czechoslovakia before Munich is the fifth repetition. From the questioned Gulf of Tonkin incident on, through a hundred dubious boasts of actual triumphs and promises of final ones, the public was turned into doubters and cynics. The sixth mistake was that of ignoring the potentially important side-effects of a practice of terror. In this case, it took the form of a much higher slaughter of civilians in relation to soldiers than in any other war. It became a village bombing process of liberating people for the good life by destroying their habitations and the people themselves, a finding of guilt by location and association, punishable with a nondiscriminating death sentence. Public reaction to this mechanized, depersonalized cruelty by men who were not personally cruel was strong at first in Europe, later in the United States. The horror seemed to be even without the justification behind the city bombing in the Second World War, that the enemy was doing the same thing. Here the ancient mistake of ruining a good intention by an unacceptable means was repeated. The seventh historic mistake repeated was that made by Rome long ago, by the Girondins in France, by Czar Nicholas II when he waged war against Japan in 1903. It was that of ignoring the needs of people at home and turning instead to a war which was not primarily in defense of the nation. In this case, a fairly large and necessitous segment of the public, which had been promised much, was given to understand that its needs and hopes ranked low in the scale of things. Not only an administration's credibility but its whole scale of values came under fire.

The chances for creating conditions which will provide a constructive alternative to another world war and the fate of the hungry and revolution-prone areas of the world are connected. The function and character of the future United States are involved in both areas of action. Possibly the United States will learn from its experience in Southeast Asia what its leaders neglected to learn from the earlier failures of men to achieve the progress, freedom and peace they sought. Suggested earlier was the possibility that the United States might have achieved all that it wished to help South Vietnam obtain—democracy, personal freedom, protection from foreign attack—in ways which would not have involved the massive military confrontation and destruction which took place. A little closer attention to the distinction between cause and effect would have been useful. The cause for the weakness of the Saigon government was its mandarin opposition to the demands and needs of the people for a modernization of the prevailing feudal and excluding regime in all parts of the society. This weakness invited revolution first, then invited also the aid to the revolutionaries which North Vietnam provided. The cause was exclusion from opportunity, the effect was aggression to aid revolution. Aggression was not the cause of the war, but the effect flowing from a different cause. When the United States chose to make the effect the target of its attack, no great popular support in its behalf could be aroused.

The revolution-prone, hungry areas of the world can be expected to present a somewhat similar occasion for confusing cause and effect, with or without the added ingredient of intervening neighbors. Unmet demands for opportunity and food will lead to disorders, attempts by revolutionaries to take control. American efforts to undo the effect, the power lunge by the revolutionaries, without eliminating the causes for that effect, can again waste many lives, many more billions.

A serious attempt to eliminate the basic causes for revolution, and along with them the temptation of neighbors to intervene, might have been far less costly in Southeast Asia and may be far less costly in other areas where the social structure remains oppressive and vulnerable. A careful calculation shows that the cost to the United States in 1967 of replacing the feudal structure of South Vietnam and of gaining the enthusiastic support of most of its people would have been no more than the cost of three months of its fighting there, about six billion dollars. For this sum, every rural family could have received title to the eight acres of good rice land it could farm. The large landlords would have received in payment one billion dollars in the stocks of new industrial plants in the nation. The pervasive loan-shark system, with its interest rates of fifty percent a year, could have been replaced by credit cooperatives. A widespread educational effort could have provided the men who could participate in management and government without their present handicaps. People would have been able to obtain personal freedom. The law to imprison all dissenters could have been repealed. Really free, open and honest elections would no longer have been feared by Saigon. With some restrictions on the flight of capital, that little nation might have been able to continue its modernization process quite as competently as it could have done after two decades or more of rigid obedience to an authoritarian regime. None of the slaughter of dissident farm people, of the type which took place in North Vietnam, none of the executions of village headmen by the Vietcong, which took place in South Vietnam, would have been involved, nor much of the destruction of the war. North Vietnam would have been hard put to it to find a moral justification for an attempt to undo either the land distribution or the modernization of the nation. The people, having gained most of what they needed, could well have invited North Vietnam to go and stay home.

If these accounts of past defeats and our more recent experience with ignoring their warnings have given us an awareness that dominant but excluding groups cannot expect to survive unchanged and that societies have a limited time in which to act constructively before their exclusions and neglects immobilize or ruin them, we may be able to look at the oncoming antihunger and antifeudal uprisings with fresh attention. We may see a new significance in a remark attributed to Che Guevara, the Cuban revolutionary who was killed in Bolivia. It was to the effect that revolutionaries should engage at once in so many revolts at the same time that the United States, trying to be the world policeman, would be unable to help the old order repress any of them effectively. If the United States tries only to suppress such revolutions without using the time still available to alter the basic causes for such revolts, it may indeed find itself in a situation where its aid is spread so thinly that no military or other assistance can help people gain or retain personal freedom. Man's future would be far more hopeful if all assistance to those who will be starving and to those who are seeking to transform their marginal social systems into productive and satisfying societies could be internationalized. Human misery should never be allowed to feed the power conflict.

Here the world may turn out to be dependent on its younger generations, those who are not yet enthralled by many practices and habits of modern life, national or international. The universal character of the aspirations expressed by university students in almost every country in recent years is a hopeful force in the world. It justifies some belief that restrictive national frontiers are being crossed more freely and frequently by demands for excellence and for the creation of a community of the whole human race large enough to meet its joint problems by joint action. The modern revolution of communications, along with that of rising expectations, can both also be expected to result, sooner or later, in a broader and deeper attack on those powers and interests which are currently institutionalizing the balance of terror as a way of life.

In time the process of using assistance, military or other, to gain footholds of influence in the less developed world must yield to a more Olympian rivalry. The world would be better off if all help from all surplus-producing and compassionate nations were channeled through the United Nations. It would be still better off if that organization made all assistance contractually contingent on performance, on the accomplishment of definite steps to increase opportunity for those lacking it, to eliminate poverty, disease and illiteracy, and automatically shut it off as soon as the contract was broken by the nation requesting help.

Three important human goals, all necessary for the future of mankind, could be achieved by such an alteration in the character of the great power competition. The disparity between the industrial and non-industrial areas, which holds a threat to world peace, also the dichotomy between the very rich and the very poor within the disadvantaged areas, which holds the peril of internal strife in each area, and the menacing rivalry between the great powers for world influence, which contains the nuclear menace as its core, could all be lessened in this way. Other techniques could probably also be found to accomplish all three goals, once the peoples of all the nations had simultaneously made the enormous initial effort necessary to persuade their rulers that they preferred such a dynamic peace and fear-free future for mankind to the one which is now being offered to them by their governments. With that effort their future could well surpass their past.

We have now audaciously subjected the past to a second test, probing its usefulness to the third and fourth problem areas the United States will encounter. One dealt with the explosive areas of the world, the other with world peace. The test, it will be recalled, was whether understanding of these past failures of men to achieve their objectives had allowed us to plan and act more boldly and freely, as well as quickly enough, to avert new disasters. The usefulness of the study of the past may reasonably be considered to have met its second test sufficiently well if it has demonstrated that the worst human tragedies have been avertible up to some point in time, that better options were usually open than those used, that old concepts and procedures needed to be challenged more often and more vigorously, and that those options which were based on humane attitudes toward others might have been more successful than the courses taken. If, in addition, the recall of the past stimulates us to think about constructive ways to avert the hunger and poverty revolutions which threaten in much of the world, or to challenge effectively the continuance of great power rivalry in its present menacing form, the gain will be great. The past reminds us that ideals and goals which once seemed remote and impossible in due course became simple pragmatic requirements for unity and survival.

Wisdom obtained through the painful trial-and-error process of the past, like wisdom acquired in other ways, may not mean happiness to man or civilization, as Socrates thought it would. But it can help men avoid some grief, some frustration. It may even allow men to see the possibility of bypassing their old habit of first creating ruins and then trying to build up on their base. It may even encourage them to transfer the creative ingenuity which brought mastery of nature over to a mastery of the troubled relations between men and nations, while they still have time to do so.

Notes

CHAPTER 2

1. Stringfellow Barr, *The Will of Zeus* (Philadelphia: J. B. Lippincott, 1961), p. 320.
2. George Grote, *History of Greece* (Vol. VI; New York: Harper and Bros., 1853), p. 338.
3. M. I. Finley, *The Ancient Greeks* (New York: Viking Press, 1963), p. 113.
4. *Ibid.*, pp. 121–22.
5. Arnold J. Toynbee, *Hellenism: The History of a Civilization* (New York: Oxford University Press, 1959), pp. 141–42.

CHAPTER 3

1. Frank B. Marsh, A *History of the Roman World from 146 to 30* B.C. (London: Methuen, 1953), p. 31.
2. John H. Randall, *The Creative Centuries* (London: Longmans, Green, 1945), p. 67.
3. *Cambridge Ancient History* (Vol. IX; Cambridge: The University Press, 1932), p. 473.
4. Charles N. Cochrane, *Christianity and the Classical Culture* (New York: Oxford University Press, 1957), pp. 34, 35.
5. Theodore Mommsen, *The History of Rome* (New York: Meridian Books, 1958), p. 387.
6. *Ibid.*, p. 406 *seq.*
7. Guglielmo Ferrero, *The Greatness and Decline of Rome* (Vol. III; New York: G. P. Putnam's Sons, 1908), p. 615.

8. *Cambridge Ancient History* (Vol. X; Cambridge: The University Press, 1934), p. 706 *seq.*
9. Charles N. Cochrane, *op. cit.*, p. 307.
10. Chester G. Starr, *Civilization and the Caesars* (Ithaca, N.Y.: Cornell University Press, 1954), p. 274.

CHAPTER 4

1. Quoted by Charles N. Cochrane in *Christianity and the Classical Culture* (New York: Oxford University Press, 1957), p. 327.
2. Edward Gibbon, *The Decline and Fall of the Roman Empire* (New York: Modern Library, 1932), p. 866.
3. J. P. Whitney, *Cambridge Medieval History* (Vol. V; Cambridge: The University Press), pp. 12–13.

CHAPTER 5

1. H. M. Gwatkin, *The Reformation* (*Hastings' Encyclopedia of Religion and Ethics*, Vol. X; New York: Charles Scribner's Sons, 1952), p. 613.
2. J. A. Symonds, "The Renaissance" (*Encyclopaedia Britannica*, Vol. XIX; 1936), p. 129.
3. James Mackinnon, *The Origins of the Reformation* (New York: Longmans, Green, 1939), p. 220.
4. G. M. Trevelyan, *History of England* (New York: Longmans, Green, 1926), p. 245.
5. R. G. D. Laffan, *The Empire in the Fifteenth Century* (*Cambridge Medieval History*, Vol. VIII; Cambridge: The University Press, 1936), p. 139.

CHAPTER 6

1. Philip Schaff, *History of the Christian Church* (Vol. VI; New York: Charles Scribner's Sons, 1884), pp. 393–4.
2. John Erwin Fagg, *Latin America* (New York: Macmillan, 1963), p. 237.
3. Dwight Salmon, *Imperial Spain* (New York: Henry Holt, 1931), p. 137.

CHAPTER 7

1. Quoted by J. M. Thompson in *The French Revolution* (New York: Doubleday, 1955), p. 278.
2. Georges Lefebvre, *Études sur la Révolution* (Paris: Presses Universitaires, 1963), pp. 3–107.
3. Raymond Carr, *Spain 1808–1939* (Oxford: Clarendon Press, 1966), pp. 107–09.
4. David Thomson, *Europe Since Napoleon* (New York: Alfred Knopf, 1962), p. 85.

CHAPTER 8

1. J. G. Randall and David Donald, *The Divided Union* (Boston: Little, Brown, 1961), p. 132.
2. Harry V. Jaffa, *Crisis of the House Divided* (New York: Doubleday, 1959), pp. 73–74.
3. *Ibid.*, p. 60.
4. Quoted by Arthur M. Schlesinger in *Political and Social Growth of the United States, 1852–1933* (New York: Macmillan, 1935), p. 30.
5. F. E. Chadwick, *Causes of the Civil War* (New York: Harper and Bros., 1906), p. 117.
6. J. G. Randall and David Donald, *op. cit.*, p. 528.
7. George R. Bentley, A *History of the Freedmen's Bureau* (Philadelphia: University of Pennsylvania Press, 1955), p. 36.
8. William A. Dunning, *Reconstruction, Political and Economic, 1865–77* (New York: Harper and Bros., 1907), p. 111.
9. James Ford Rhodes, *History of the United States* (Vol. VI; New York: Macmillan, 1921), p. 323.
10. Quoted by Moorfield Storey in *Charles Sumner* (Boston: Houghton Mifflin, 1900), p. 313.
11. John P. Frank, *Cases and Materials on Constitutional Law* (Chicago: Callaghan, 1952), p. 735.
12. Eric L. McKitrick, *Andrew Johnson and Reconstruction* (Chicago: University of Chicago Press, 1964), p. 426.
13. James Ford Rhodes, *op. cit.*, p. 13.
14. *Ibid.*, p. 203.
15. *Ibid.*, p. 293.
16. Hampton M. Jarrell, *Wade Hampton and the Negro* (Columbia, S.C.: University of South Carolina Press, 1949), p. 31.
17. *U.S.* vs. *Cruikshank*, 92. U.S. 542.
18. William A. Dunning, *op. cit.*, p. 341.
19. C. Vann Woodward, *Reunion and Reaction* (Boston: Little, Brown, 1951), p. 12.
20. *U.S.* vs. *Reese* et al., 92. U.S. 214.
21. John E. E. Dalberg-Acton, *The History of Freedom and Other Essays*, (London: Macmillan and Co., 1909), pp. 77–78.

CHAPTER 9

1. Paul Miliukov with C. Seignobos and L. Eisenman, *Histoire de Russie* (*Bibliothèque du Monde Slave, Réformes, Réactions, Révolutions* (1855–1932), (Vol. III; Paris: Librairie Ernest Laroux, 1933), p. 1148.
2. Quoted by Gus Tyler, "The Illusions That Were and the Illusions That Are," *New Republic*, November 4, 1957.

3. George F. Kennan, *Russia and the West under Lenin and Stalin* (Boston: Little, Brown, 1960), p. 117.

CHAPTER 10

1. A. J. P. Taylor, *The Course of German History* (New York: Coward-McCann, 1946), p. 195.
2. John W. Wheeler-Bennett, *The Nemesis of Power* (*The German Army in Politics 1918–1945*) (New York: St. Martin's Press, 1954), p. 185.
3. Koppel S. Pinson, *Modern Germany, Its History and Civilization* (New York: Macmillan, 1954), pp. 446–49; Ralph Flenley, *Modern German History* (London: J. M. Dent and Sons, 1959 ed.), p. 359; D. W. Brogan, *France under the Republic* (New York: Harper and Bros., 1940), p. 578; Paul Einzig, *Appeasement Before, During and After the War* (London: Macmillan, 1942), p. 45.
4. Ruth Fischer, *Stalin and German Communism* (Cambridge, Mass.: Harvard University Press, 1948), p. 268.
5. Quoted by Koppel S. Pinson, *op. cit.*, p. 241.

CHAPTER 11

1. Quoted by G. M. Gawthorne-Hardy in *A Short History of International Affairs, 1920–1939* (London: Oxford University Press), p. 378.
2. A. J. P. Taylor, *From Napoleon to Hitler* (London: Hamish Hamilton, 1950), p. 127.
3. Quoted by John W. Wheeler-Bennett in *Munich, Prologue to Tragedy* (London: Macmillan, 1948), p. 32.
4. Quoted by G. M. Gawthorne-Hardy, *op. cit.*, p. 399.
5. G. Hilger and Alfred G. Meyer, *The Incompatible Allies* (New York: Macmillan, 1953), p. 277.
6. Bruno Gebhardi, *Handbuch der Deutschen Geschichte* (Vol. 4; Stuttgart: Union Verlag, 1959), p. 233; John W. Wheeler-Bennett, *op. cit.*, p. 389.
7. P. A. Reynolds, *British Foreign Policy in the Interwar Years* (London: Longmans, Green, 1954), p. 139.
8. John W. Wheeler-Bennett, *op. cit.*, p. 100.
9. *Ibid.*, p. 97.
10. *Ibid.*, p. 100.
11. P. A. Reynolds, *op. cit.*, p. 143.
12. Quoted in John W. Wheeler-Bennett, *op. cit.*, p. 155.
13. Charles Loch Mowat, *Britain Between the Wars, 1918–1940* (London: Methuen and Co., 1955), pp. 617–18.
14. Quoted in John W. Wheeler-Bennett, *op. cit.*, p. 314.
15. A. J. P. Taylor, *The Course of German History* (New York: Coward-McCann, 1946), p. 216.

16. William E. Hocking, *Experiment in Education* (Chicago: Henry Regnery, 1954), p. 36.
17. William L. Shirer, *Rise and Fall of the Third Reich* (New York: Simon and Schuster, 1960 ed.), pp. 952, 958.
18. *Ibid.*, pp. 938, 939.
19. Quoted by L. B. Namier in *Diplomatic Prelude, 1938–1939* (London: Macmillan, 1948), p. 140.
20. Arnold J. and Veronica M. Toynbee (editors), *The Eve of War, 1939* (London: Oxford University Press, 1958), p. 486.
21. G. Hilger and Alfred G. Meyer, *op. cit.*, p. 323. (Gebhardi, *op. cit.*, p. 267, gives July 31, 1940, as the date.)

Additional
References

CHAPTER 2

AGARD, WALTER RAYMOND. *The Greek Mind.* Anvil Series. Princeton: D. Van Nostrand, 1957.
BURY, J. B. *A History of Greece.* New York: Modern Library, 1937.
GOLTZ, GUSTAVE, with ROBERT COHEN. *Histoire Ancienne,* 2me Partie, *Histoire Grecque,* Vol. II. Paris: Les Presses Universitaires de France, 1931.
HAMMOND, N. G. L. *A History of Greece to 322 B.C.* Oxford: Clarendon Press, 1959.
JAEGER, WERNER. *Paideia: The Ideals of Greek Culture.* Translated from the German by Gilbert Highet. Vol. I: *The Mind of Athens.* New York: Oxford University Press, 1945.
LAISTNER, M. L. W. *A History of the Greek World, 479–323 B.C.* London: Methuen, 1957.
QUIGLEY, CARROLL. *The Evolution of Civilizations.* New York: Macmillan, 1961.
STARR, CHESTER G. *The Origins of Greek Civilization 1100–650 B.C.* New York: Alfred Knopf, 1961.
THUCYDIDES. *The Complete Writings.* New York: Modern Library, 1934.

CHAPTER 3

BOAK, E. R. *A History of Rome to 565 A.D.* New York: Macmillan, 1955.
Cambridge Ancient History. Vol. VII: *The Hellenistic Monarchies and the Rise of Rome.* Cambridge: The University Press, 1928.

DILL, SAMUEL. *Roman Society from Nero to Marcus Aurelius.* New York: Meridian Press, 1956.

HEITLAND, W. E. *The Roman Fate.* Cambridge: The University Press, 1922.

TURNER, RALPH E. *The Great Classical Traditions.* Vol. II: *The Classical Empires.* New York: McGraw-Hill, 1941.

CHAPTER 4

BURY, J. B. *History of the Later Roman Empire.* London: Macmillan, 1923.

BAYNES, N. H. Volume XII, Chapter 19, *Cambridge Ancient History.* Cambridge: The University Press, 1939.

ELLIOTT-BINNS, L. E. *The Beginnings of Western Christendom.* London: Lutterworth Press, 1948.

FOAKES-JACKSON, F. J. *An Introduction to the History of Christianity.* New York: Macmillan, 1921.

HEITLAND, W. E. *The Roman Republic.* Vol. III. Cambridge: The University Press, 1909.

LIETZMAN, HANS. *From Constantine to Julian.* Vol. III. London: Lutterworth Press, 1950.

MOORE, GEORGE FOOT. *History of Religions.* Vol. II. New York: Charles Scribner's Sons, 1919.

SCHAFF, PHILIP. *History of the Christian Church.* Vol. III: *Nicean and Post-Nicean Christianity.* New York: Charles Scribner's Sons, 1884.

THOMPSON, JAMES W. *Economic and Social History of the Middle Ages (300–1300).* New York: Frederick Ungar, 1959.

CHAPTER 5

BAINTON, ROLAND H. *The Travail of Religious Liberty.* Philadelphia: Westminster Press, 1951.

BURSCHE, EDMUND. *Die Reformarbeit des Basler Konzils.* Lodz: Z. Mantius, 1921.

ELLIOTT-BINNS, L. E. *The History of the Decline and Fall of the Medieval Papacy.* London: Methuen, 1920.

HEFELE, K. J. VON. *Conciliengeschichte.* Vol. VII. Freiburg im Breisgau: Herder'sche Verlag, 1869.

KITTS, EUSTACE J. *In the Days of the Councils.* London: Archibald Constable, 1918.

MACKINNON, JAMES. *The Origins of the Reformation.* New York: Longmans, Green, 1939.

PFENDER, CHARLES. *Bâle, Constance, Pisa,* Vol. V of *Grande Encyclopédie.* Paris: H. Lamivault, 1898.

TOYNBEE, ARNOLD J. *A Study of History.* Vol. IV. New York: Oxford University Press, 1940.

VALOIS, NOEL. *Le Pape et le Concile.* Vol. II. Paris: Alphonse Picard et fils, 1909.

WAUGH, W. T. *The Councils of Constance and Basle.* Vol. VIII of *The Cambridge Medieval History.* Cambridge: The University Press, 1936.

CHAPTER 6

CHAPMAN, CHARLES. *The History of Spain.* New York: Macmillan, 1931.

HAMILTON, E. J. *American Treasure and the Price Revolution in Spain.* Cambridge, Mass.: Harvard University Press, 1934.

HULME, MARTIN A. S. *Spain, Its Greatness and Decay.* Cambridge: The University Press, 1940.

LOTH, DAVID G. *Philip of Spain.* New York: Brentano's, 1932.

MADARIAGA, SALVADOR DE. *Spain.* New York: Creative Age Press, 1943.

NICHOLS, JAMES H. *Democracy and the Churches.* Philadelphia: Westminster Press, 1951.

ORTEGA Y GASSET, JOSÉ. *Invertebrate Spain.* New York: W. W. Norton, 1937.

RANDALL, J. H. *Making of the Modern Mind.* Boston: Houghton Mifflin, 1926.

Also: *Cambridge Medieval History,* Vol. VIII: *The Close of the Middle Ages. New Cambridge Modern History,* Vol. I: *The Renaissance,* Vol. II: *The Reformation.* Cambridge: The University Press, 1938, 1957, 1958.

CHAPTER 7

BOWEN, RALPH R. *Chapters in Western Civilization.* Vol. I, Chapter XIII. New York: Columbia University Press, 1954.

BROGAN, D. W. *The Price of Revolution.* London: Hamish Hamilton, 1951.

DALBERG-ACTON, JOHN E. *Lectures on the French Revolution.* London: Macmillan, 1910.

TOCQUEVILLE, ALEXIS DE. *The Old Regime and the French Revolution.* New York: Doubleday, 1955.

GERSHOY, LEO. *The French Revolution.* New York: Appleton-Century-Crofts, 1933.

GOTTSCHALK, LOUIS R. *The Era of the French Revolution.* Cambridge, Mass.: Riverside Press, 1929.

PALMER, R. R. *The Age of the Democratic Revolution.* Princeton: Princeton University Press, 1959.

SALVEMINI, GAETANO. *The French Revolution, 1789–1792.* London: Jonathan Cape, 1954.

SOREL, ALBERT. *L'Europe et la Révolution Française.* Vols. VII, VIII. Paris: Plon, 1904.

TAINE, HIPPOLYTE A. *The Origins of Contemporary France.* Vols. I, II. Translated by John Durand. New York: Peter Smith, 1931.

CHAPTER 8

BEALE, HOWARD K. *The Critical Year.* New York: Harcourt, Brace, 1930.

BUCK, PAUL. *The Road to Reunion.* Boston: Little, Brown, 1947.

COLE, ARTHUR C. *The Irrepressible Conflict, 1850–1865.* New York: Macmillan, 1934.

COULTER, E. MERTON. *The South During Reconstruction.* Baton Rouge, La.: Louisiana State University Press, 1947.

CRAVEN, AVERY. *The Coming of the Civil War.* Chicago: University of Chicago Press, 1957.

FLEMING, WALTER. *The Sequel of Appomattox.* New Haven, Conn.: Yale University Press, 1919.

McPHERSON, EDWARD (EDITOR). *The Political History of the United States During the Period of Reconstruction.* Washington, D.C.: Solomons and Chapman, 1875.

NEVINS, ALLAN. *Ordeal of the Union,* Vols. I, II. New York: Charles Scribner's Sons, 1947.

RANDALL, J. G. *The Civil War and Reconstruction.* Boston: D. C. Heath, 1937, 1953.

WHITRIDGE, ARNOLD. *No Compromise!* New York: Farrar, Straus, 1960.

CHAPTER 9

CARR, EDWARD H. *A History of Soviet Russia.* Part I: *The Bolshevik Revolution,* Vols. I, II. London: Methuen, 1950. Part II: *The Interregnum 1923–1924.* New York: Macmillan, 1954.

MAYNARD, SIR JOHN. *Russia in Ferment.* New York: Macmillan, 1948.

PARES, SIR BERNARD. *A History of Russia.* New York: Alfred Knopf, 1953.

PIPES, RICHARD. *The Formation of the Soviet Union.* Cambridge, Mass.: Harvard University Press, 1954.

SCHUMAN, FREDERICK L. *Russia Since 1917.* New York: Alfred Knopf, 1957.

SETON-WATSON, SIR HUGH. *The Decline of Imperial Russia 1855–1914.* London: Methuen, 1952.

VERNADSKY, GEORGE. *A History of Russia.* New Haven, Conn.: Yale University Press, 1948.

WOLFE, BERTRAM. *Three Who Made a Revolution.* New York: Dial Press, 1948.

WOYTINSKY, WALDIMIR. *Stormy Passage.* New York: Vanguard Press, 1961.

CHAPTERS 10 AND 11

ARON, RAYMOND. *The Century of Total War.* New York: Doubleday, 1954.

BIRDSALL, PAUL. *Versailles, Twenty Years After.* New York: Reynal and Hitchcock, 1941.

BRECHT, ARNOLD. *Prelude to Silence*. New York: Oxford University Press, 1944.

CARR, EDWARD H. *The Twenty-Year Crisis, 1919–1939*. London: Methuen, 1939.

————. *German-Soviet Relations Between the Two World Wars, 1919–1939*. Baltimore: Johns Hopkins Press, 1951

KEYNES, JOHN MAYNARD. *The Economic Consequences of the Peace*. London: Macmillan, 1919.

QUIGLEY, CARROLL. *Tragedy and Hope*, Chapters IX–XIII. New York: Macmillan, 1966.

RAUSHENBUSH, STEPHEN. *The March of Fascism*. New Haven, Conn.: Yale University Press, 1939.

ROSENBERG, ARTHUR. *A History of the German Republic*. London: Methuen, 1936.

STAMPFER, FRIEDERICH. *Die Vierzehn Jahre der Ersten Deutschen Republik*. Karlsbad, 1936.

Index

DATE DUE

GAYLORD			PRINTED IN U.S.A.